VAMPIRE KNIGHT

Story & Art by
Matsuri Hino

Vol. 6

D0448547

VAMPIRE KNIGHT

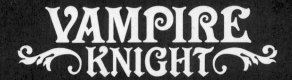

Contents

SURPRISE!

You may be reading the wrong way!

It's true: In keeping with the original Japanese comic format, this book reads from right to left—so action, sound effects, and word balloons are completely reversed. This preserves the orientation of the original artwork—plus, it's fun! Check out the diagram shown here to get the hang of things, and then turn to the other side of the book to get started!

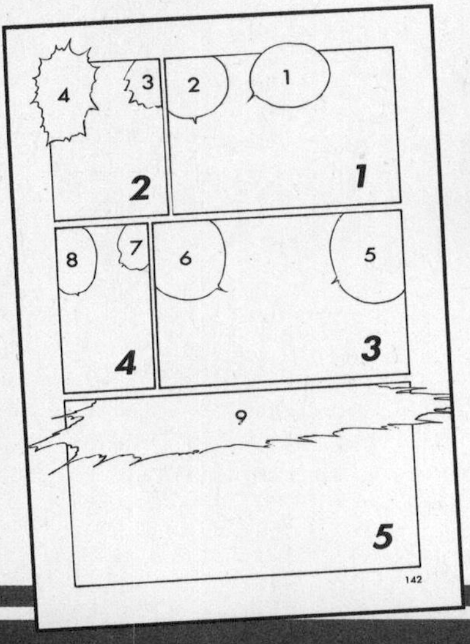

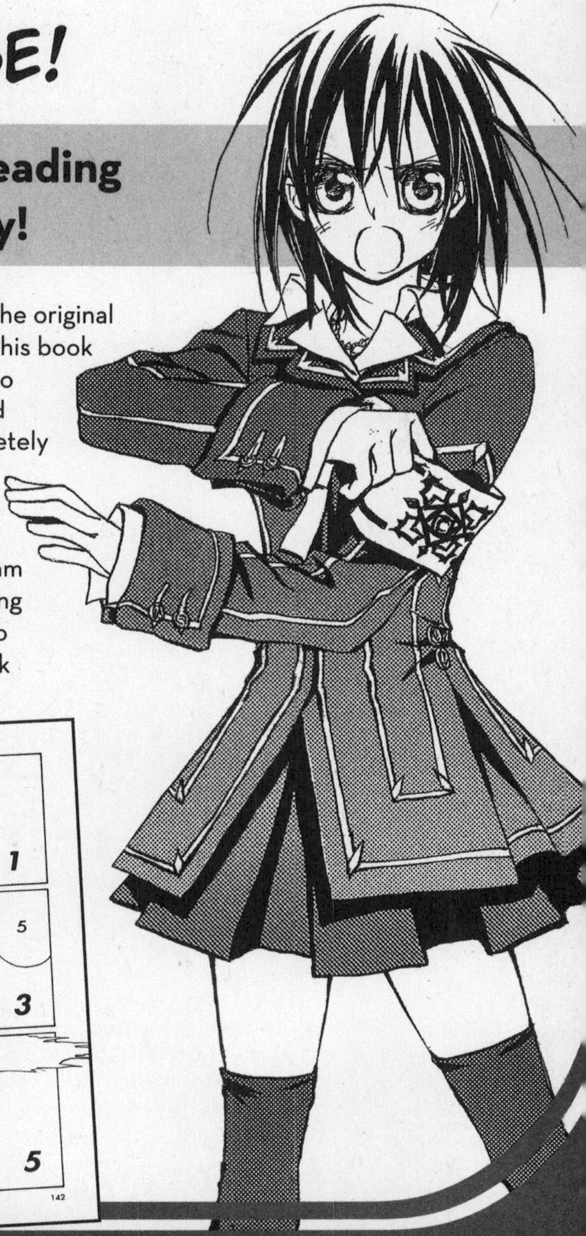

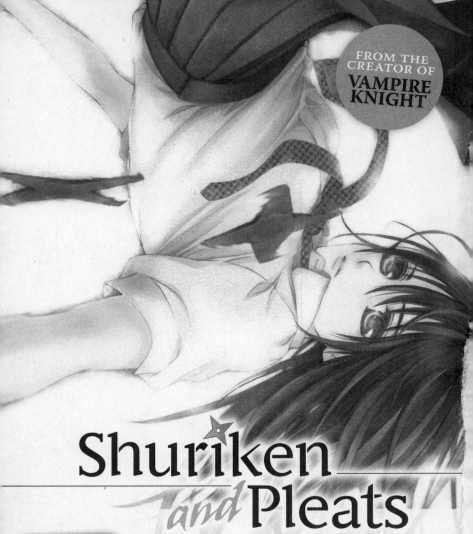

FROM THE
CREATOR OF
**VAMPIRE
KNIGHT**

Shuriken
and Pleats

When the master she has sworn to protect is killed, Mikage Kirio, a skilled ninja, travels to Japan to start a new, peaceful life for herself. But as soon as she arrives, she finds herself fighting to protect the life of Mahito Wakashimatsu, a man who is under attack by a band of ninja. From that time on, Mikage is drawn deeper into the machinations of his powerful family.

www.viz.com

ratings.viz.com

Shuriken to Pleats © Matsuri Hino 2015/HAKUSENSHA, Inc.

Natsume's
BOOK of FRIENDS

STORY and ART by
Yuki Midorikawa

Make Some Unusual New Friends

The power to see hidden spirits has always felt like a curse to troubled high schooler Takashi Natsume. But he's about to discover he inherited a lot more than just the Sight from his mysterious grandmother!

Available at your local bookstore or comic store.

www.shojobeat.com

Natsume Yujincho © Yuki Midorikawa 2005/HAKUSENSHA, Inc.

RATED
T
FOR
TEEN
ratings.viz.com

VIZ
media
www.viz.com

VAMPIRE KNIGHT
Vol. 6
Shojo Beat Edition

This manga contains material that was originally published in English in
Shojo Beat magazine, July–November 2008 issues. Artwork in the magazine
may have been slightly altered from that presented here.

STORY AND ART BY
MATSURI HINO

Translation & English Adaptation/Tomo Kimura
Touch-up Art & Lettering/George Caltsoudas
Graphic Design/Nozomi Akashi
Editor/Nancy Thistlethwaite

Vampire Knight by Matsuri Hino © Matsuri Hino 2007. All rights reserved.
First published in Japan in 2007 by HAKUSENSHA, Inc., Tokyo. English
language translation rights arranged with HAKUSENSHA, Inc., Tokyo.

The stories, characters and incidents mentioned in this publication are
entirely fictional.

No portion of this book may be reproduced or transmitted in any form or by
any means without written permission from the copyright holders.

Printed in the U.S.A.

Published by VIZ Media, LLC
P.O. Box 77010
San Francisco, CA 94107

10 9 8 7 6 5
First printing, March 2009
Fifth printing, April 2015

www.viz.com

www.shojobeat.com

PARENTAL ADVISORY
VAMPIRE KNIGHT is rated T+ for Older Teen and is
recommended for ages 16 and up. This volume
contains sexual themes and violence.
ratings.viz.com

The Story of VAMPIRE KNIGHT

1 Cross Academy, a private boarding school, is where the Day Class and the Night Class coexist. The Night Class—a group of beautiful elite students—are all vampires!

2 Four years ago, the pureblood Shizuka bit Zero and turned him into a vampire. Yuki has vowed to protect him. Shizuka's blood is necessary to save Zero from madness. Yuki tries to offer herself to Shizuka to save him, but Kaname secretly kills Shizuka.

3 Zero is accused of killing Shizuka. Kaname defends Zero and uses the occasion to warn the Vampire Senate not to interfere with Cross Academy. Zero wanted revenge against Shizuka, but he starts to change as Yuki's tenderness touches him. But with Shizuka dead, Zero cannot escape his fate from falling to Level E!!

NIGHT CLASS
DAY CLASS
She adores him.
He saved her 10 years ago.
Childhood friends
CLASSMATE
FOSTER FATHER
KANAME KURAN
Night Class President and pureblood vampire. Yuki adores him.
YUKI CROSS
The heroine.
The adopted daughter of the Headmaster, and a Guardian who protects Cross Academy.
ZERO KIRYU
Yuki's childhood friend, and a Guardian. Shizuka turned him into a vampire. He will eventually lose his sanity, falling to Level E.
HEADMASTER CROSS
NIGHT CLASS STUDENTS
COUSINS
HANABUSA AIDO
Nickname: Idol
AKATSUKI KAIN
Nickname: Wild
ICHIRU
Zero's younger twin brother. He betrayed his family and served Shizuka.
SHIZUKA HIO
The pureblood who robbed Zero of his family. Kaname killed her.
※Purebloods are vampires who do not have a single drop of human blood in their lineage. They are very powerful, and they can turn humans into vampires by drinking their blood.

SORRY.

I want Yuki to smile... Zero becomes aware of his sinful feelings!

IT'S NOTHING.

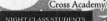

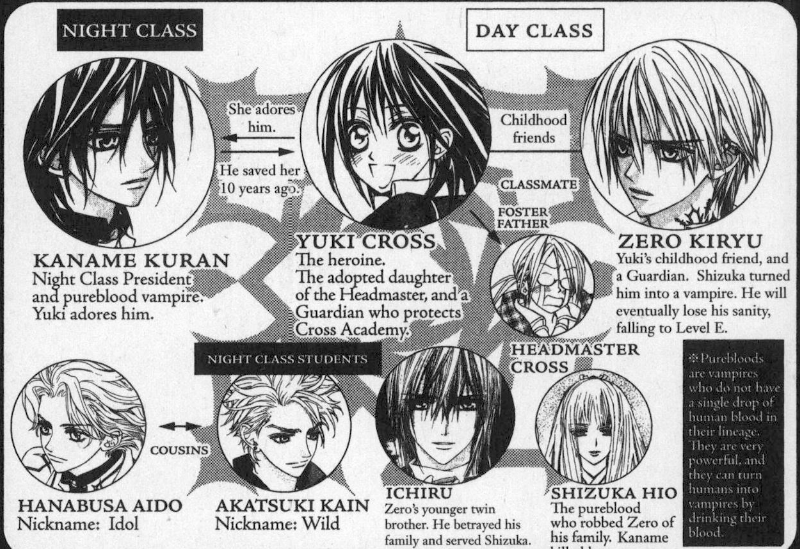

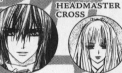

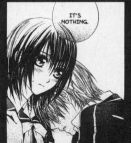

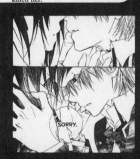

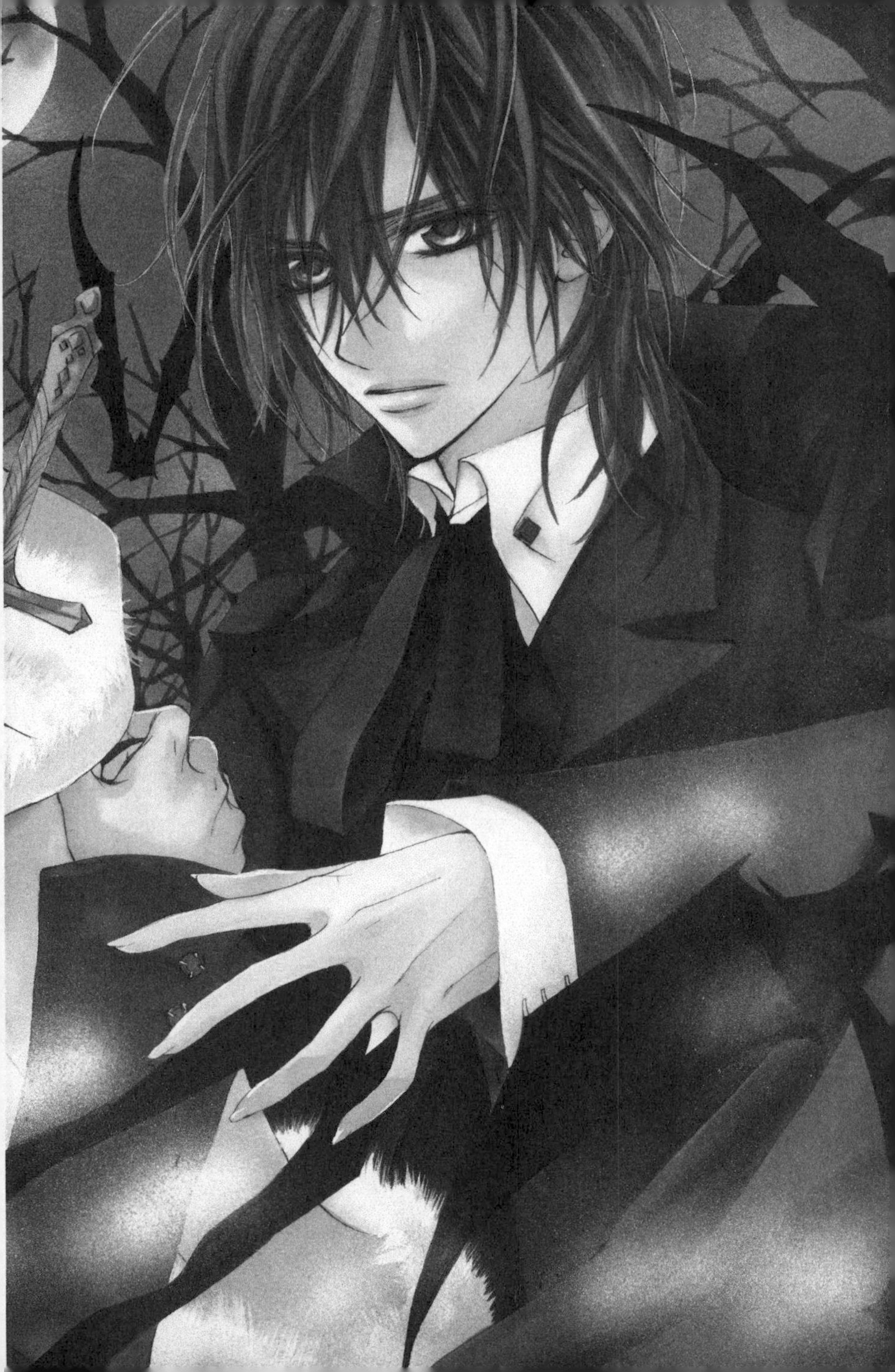

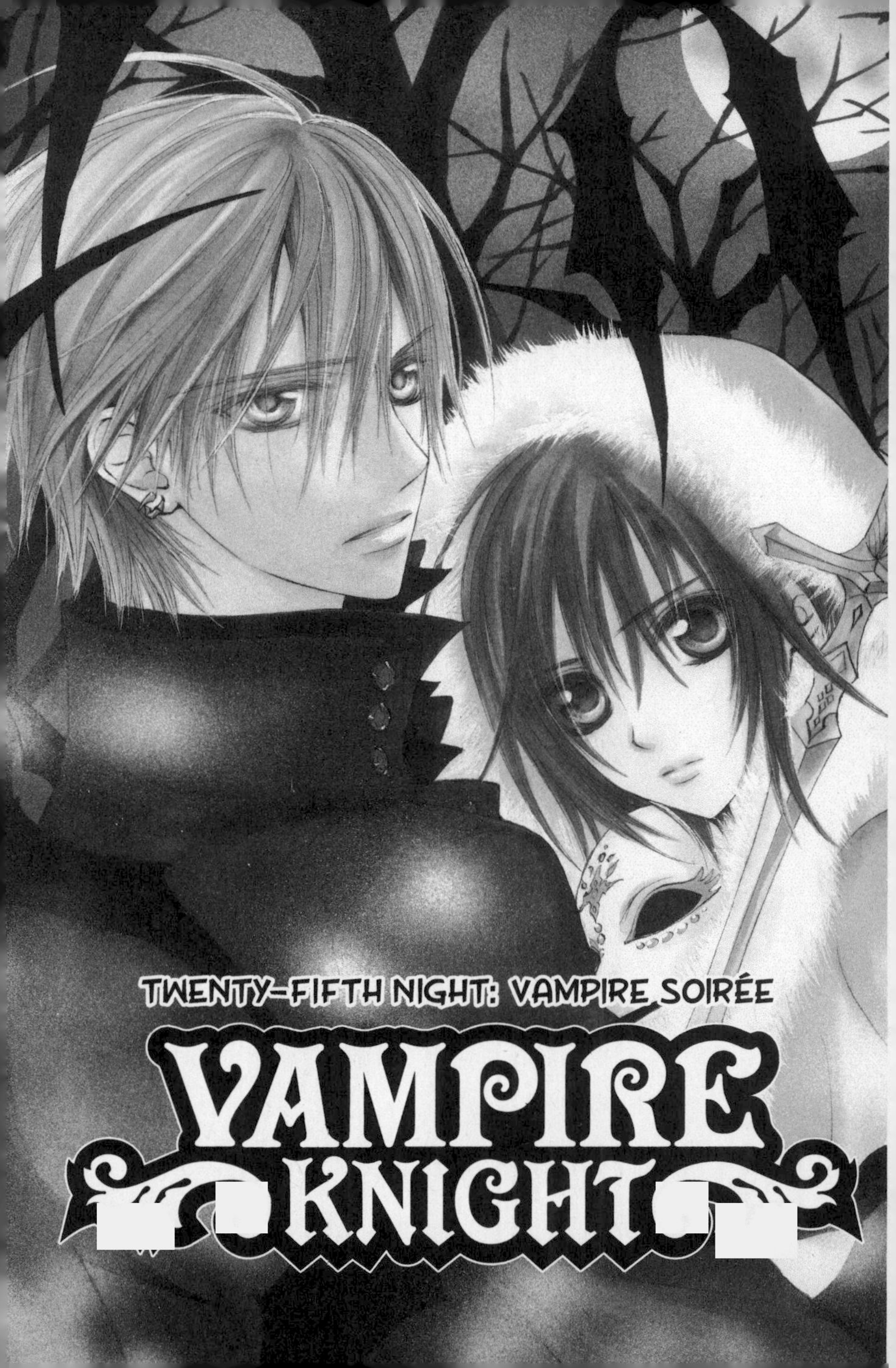
TWENTY-FIFTH NIGHT: VAMPIRE SOIRÉE
VAMPIRE
KNIGHT

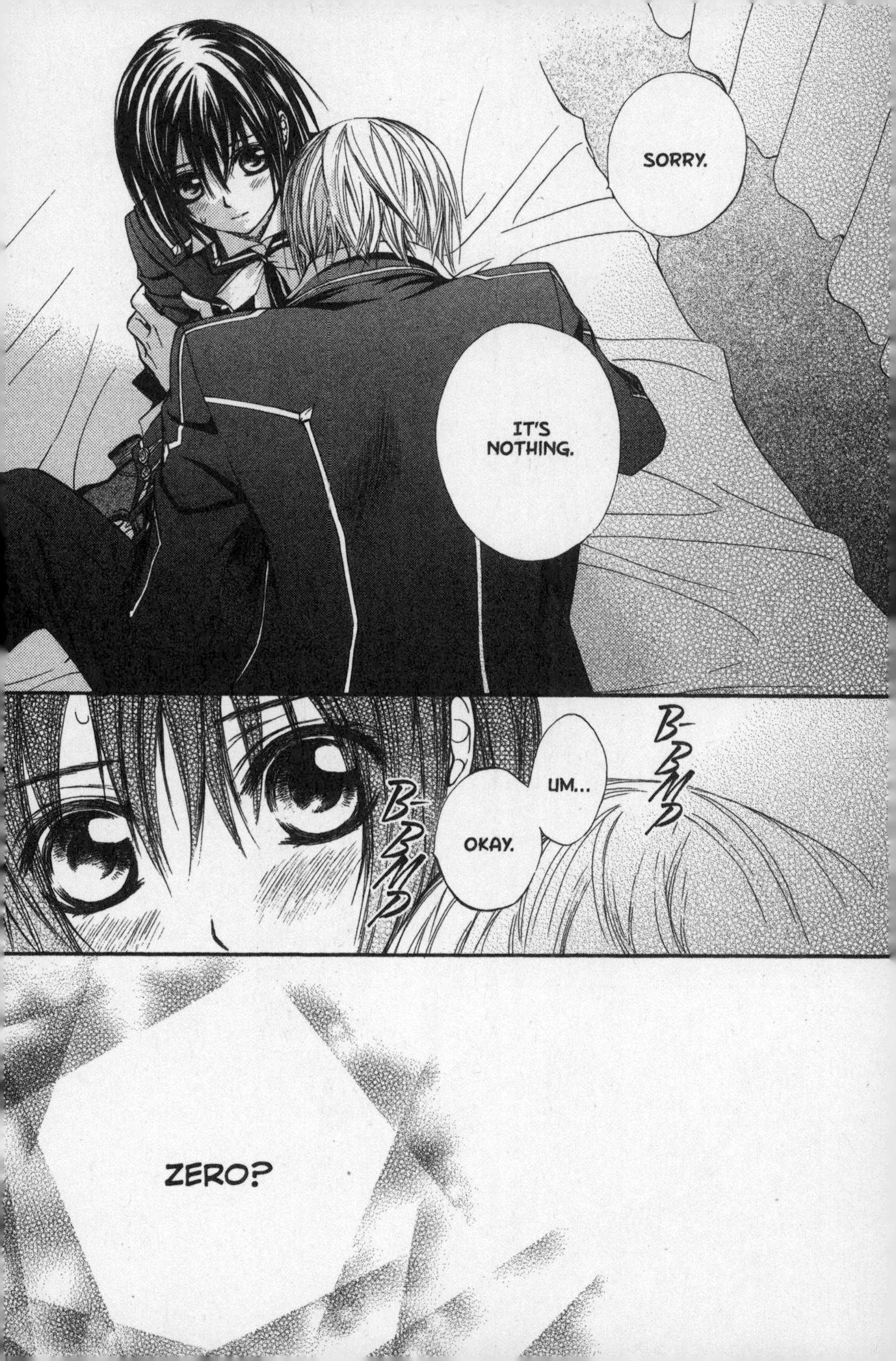
SORRY.
IT'S NOTHING.
B-BMP
UM...
OKAY.
B-BMP
ZERO?

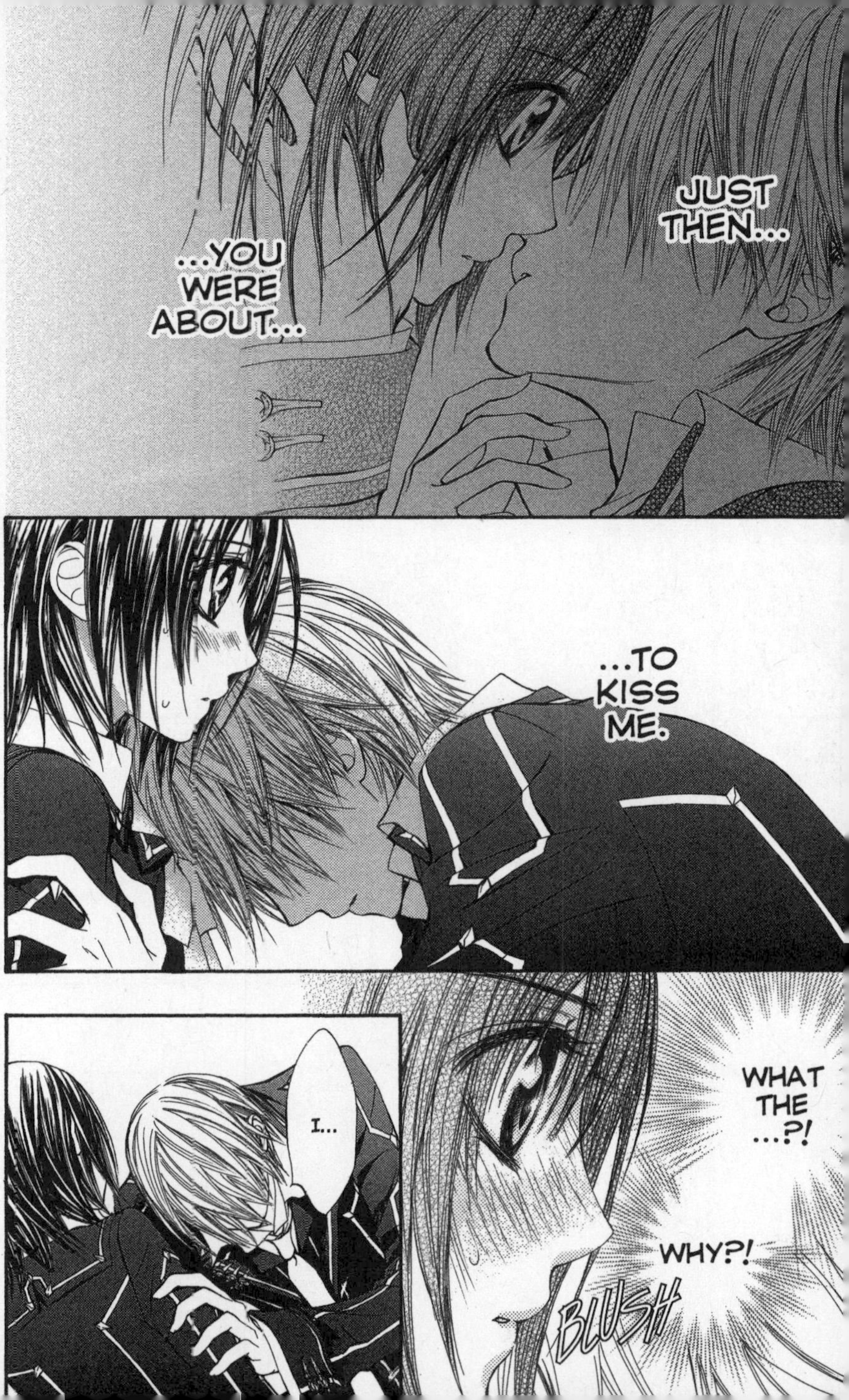
JUST THEN...
...YOU WERE ABOUT...
...TO KISS ME.
WHAT THE ...?!
WHY?!
BLUSH
I...

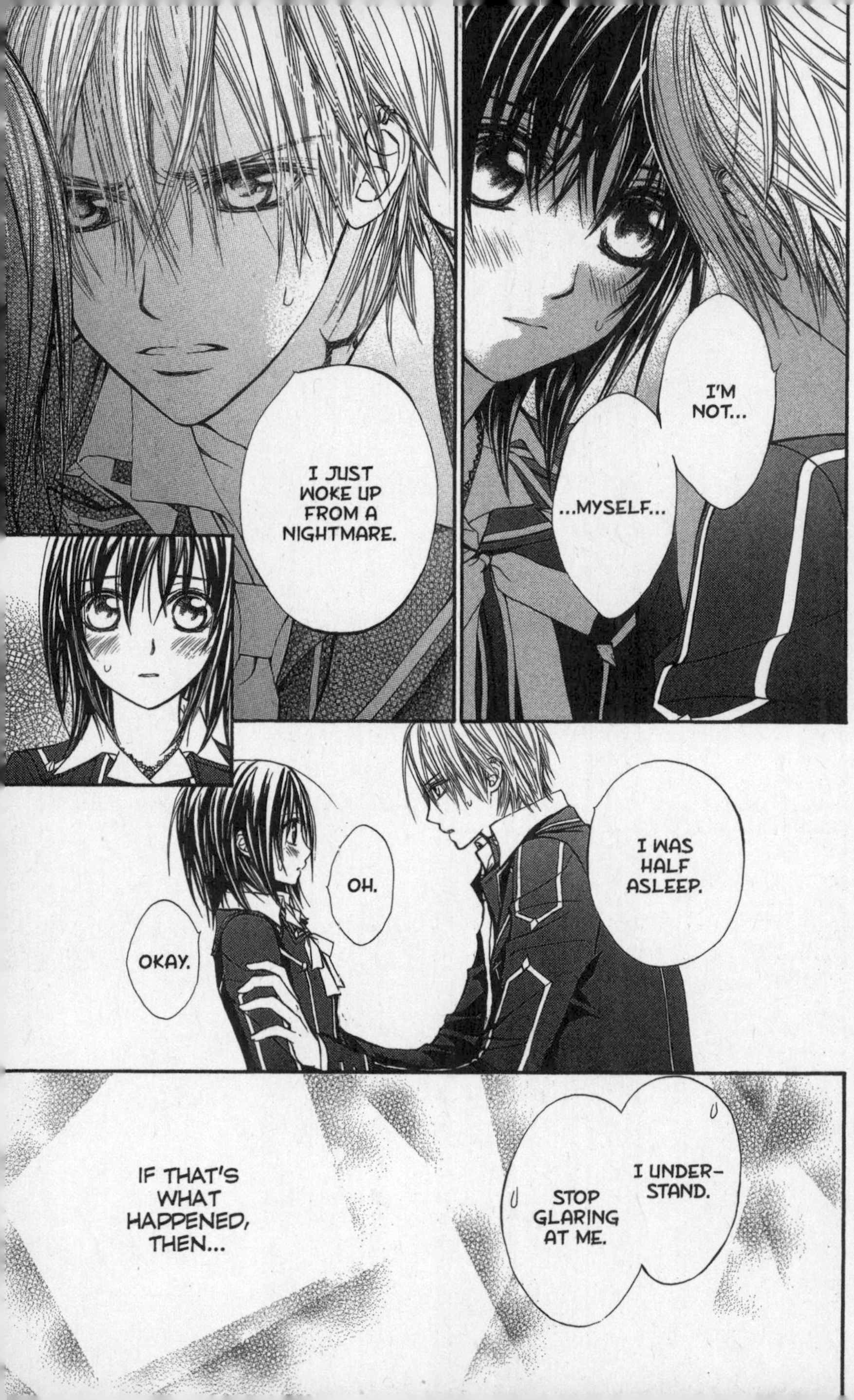
I'M NOT...
...MYSELF...
I JUST WOKE UP FROM A NIGHTMARE.
I WAS HALF ASLEEP.
OH.
OKAY.
I UNDER-STAND.
STOP GLARING AT ME.
IF THAT'S WHAT HAPPENED, THEN...

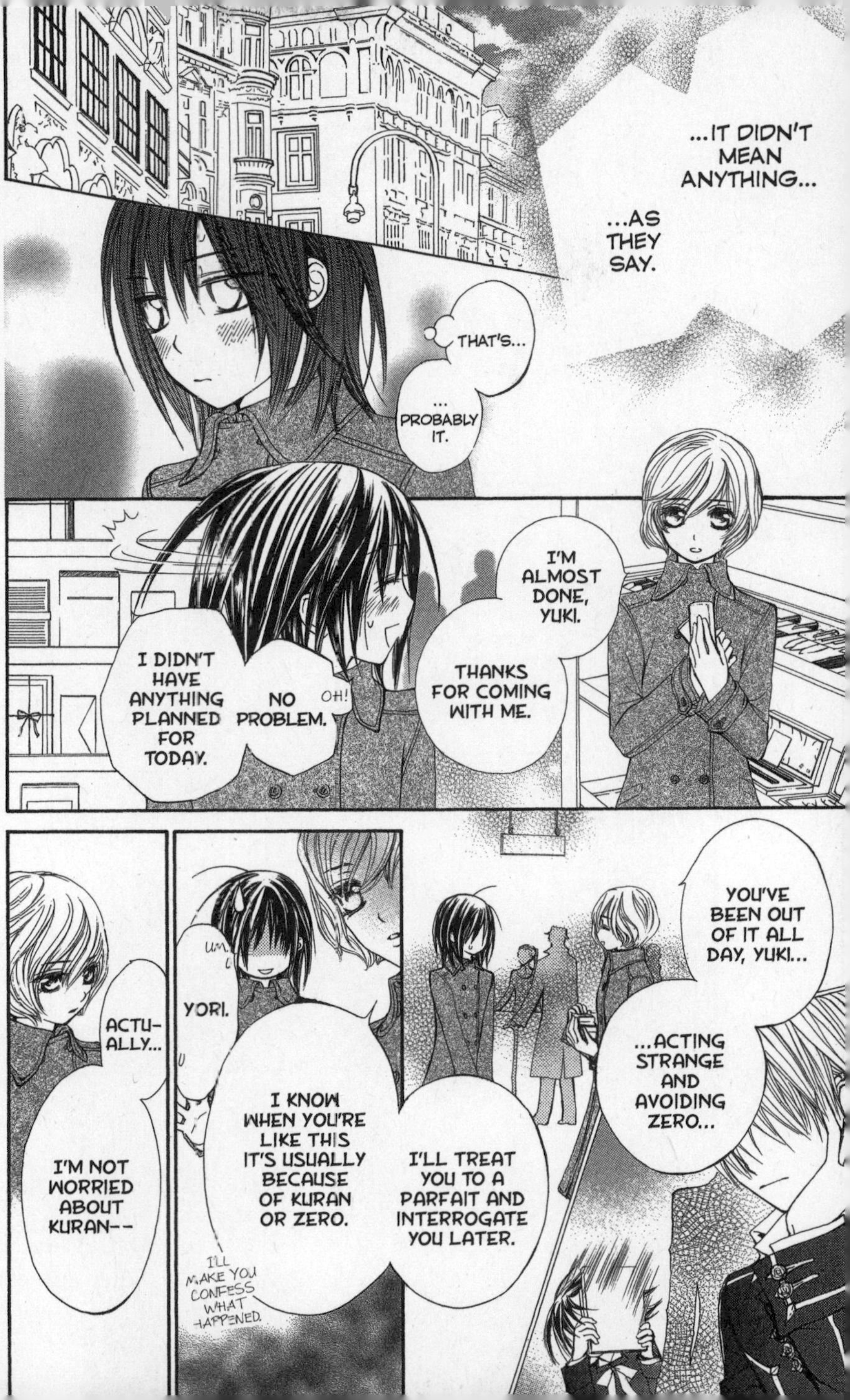
...IT DIDN'T MEAN ANYTHING...
...AS THEY SAY.
THAT'S...
...PROBABLY IT.
I'M ALMOST DONE, YUKI.
THANKS FOR COMING WITH ME.
OH!
NO PROBLEM.
I DIDN'T HAVE ANYTHING PLANNED FOR TODAY.
YOU'VE BEEN OUT OF IT ALL DAY, YUKI...
...ACTING STRANGE AND AVOIDING ZERO...
I'LL TREAT YOU TO A PARFAIT AND INTERROGATE YOU LATER.
I KNOW WHEN YOU'RE LIKE THIS IT'S USUALLY BECAUSE OF KURAN OR ZERO.
I'LL MAKE YOU CONFESS WHAT HAPPENED.
UM.
YORI.
ACTU-ALLY...
I'M NOT WORRIED ABOUT KURAN--

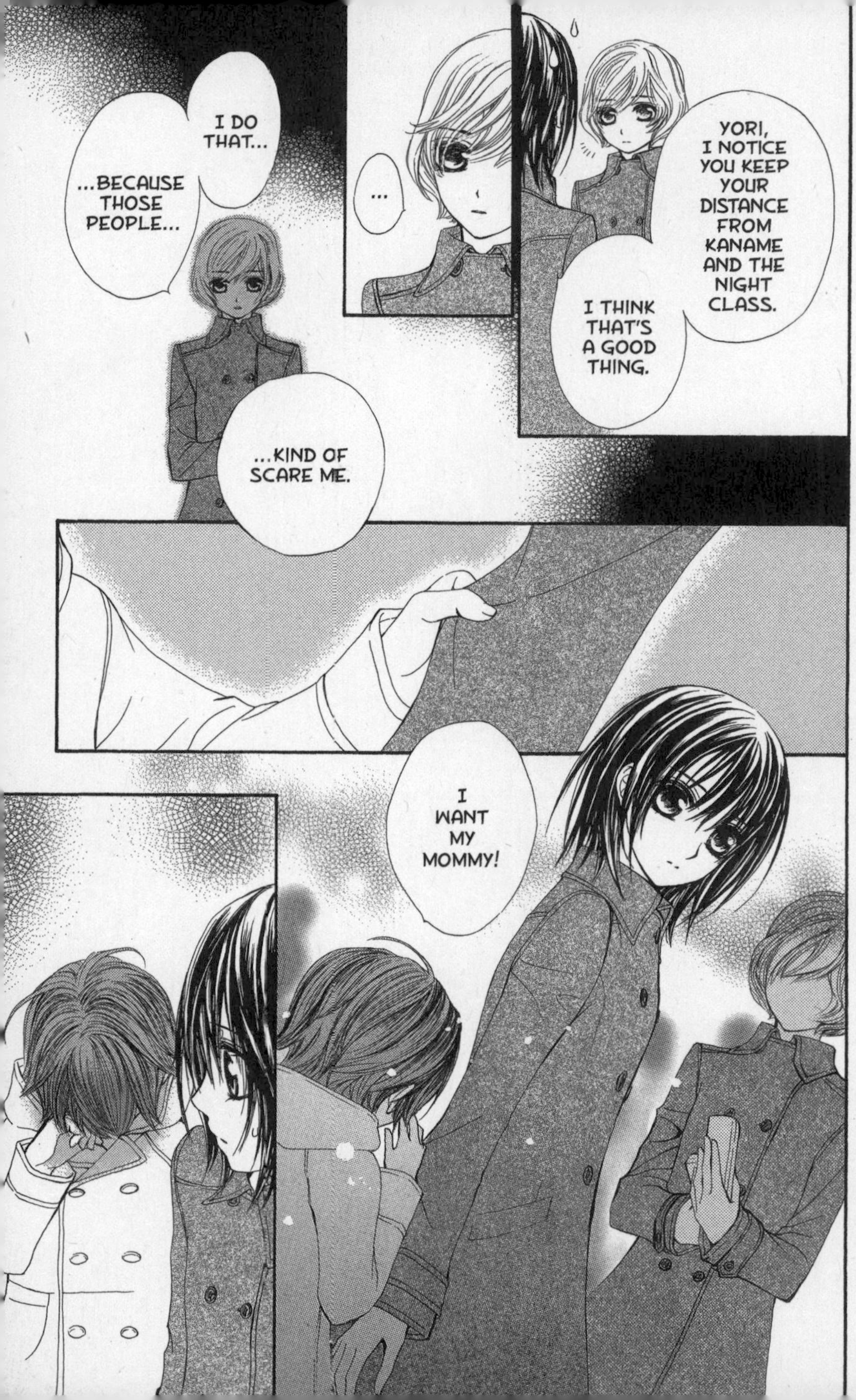
YORI, I NOTICE YOU KEEP YOUR DISTANCE FROM KANAME AND THE NIGHT CLASS.
I THINK THAT'S A GOOD THING.
...
I DO THAT...
...BECAUSE THOSE PEOPLE...
...KIND OF SCARE ME.
I WANT MY MOMMY!

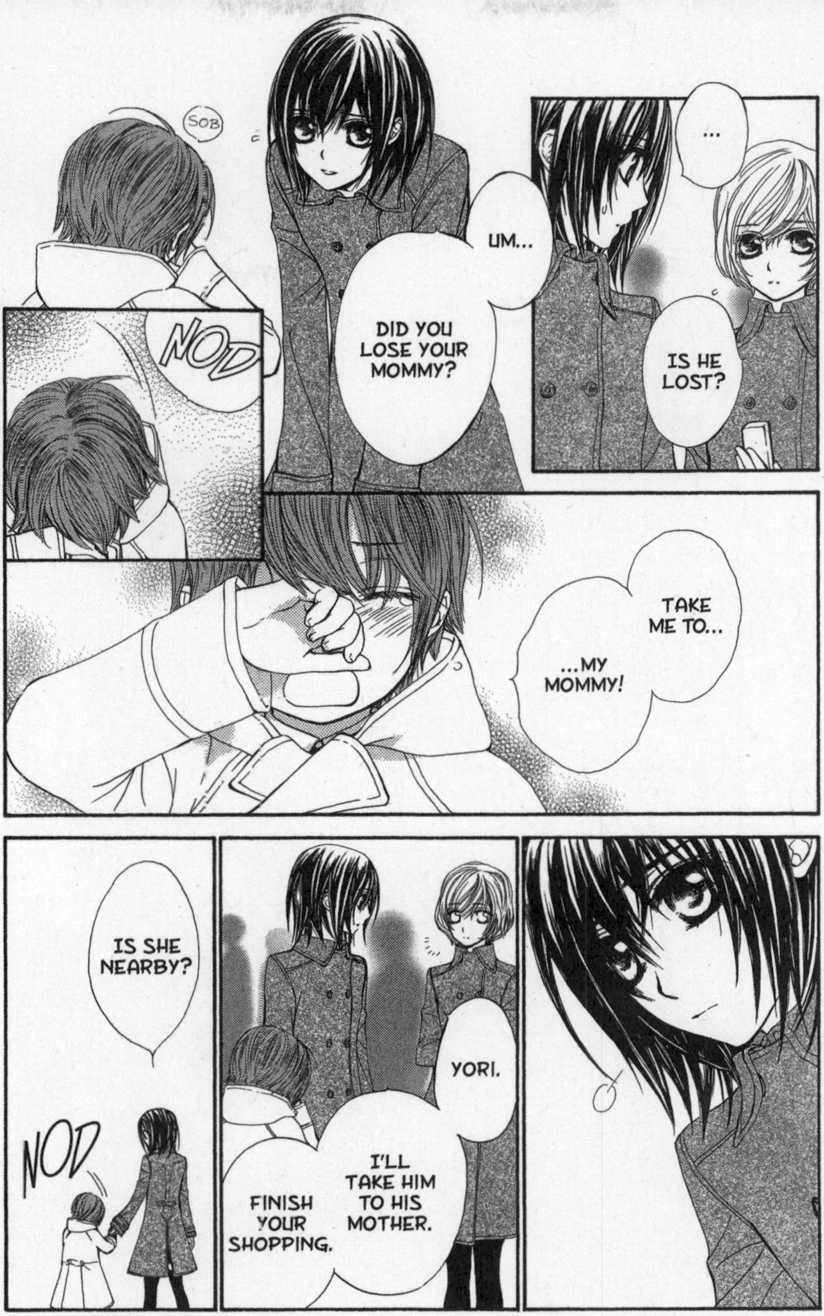
...
IS HE LOST?
SOB
UM...
DID YOU LOSE YOUR MOMMY?
NOD
TAKE ME TO...
...MY MOMMY!
YORI.
I'LL TAKE HIM TO HIS MOTHER.
FINISH YOUR SHOPPING.
IS SHE NEARBY?
NOD

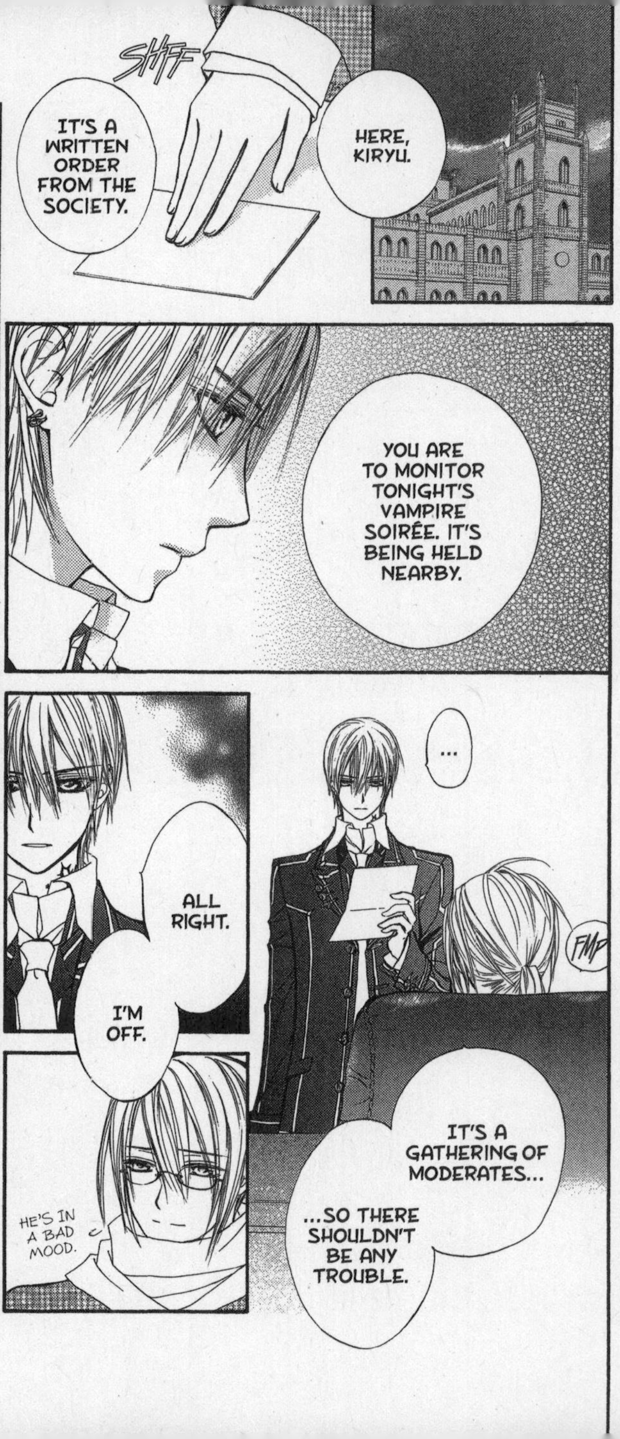
HERE, KIRYU.
SHFF
IT'S A WRITTEN ORDER FROM THE SOCIETY.
YOU ARE TO MONITOR TONIGHT'S VAMPIRE SOIRÉE. IT'S BEING HELD NEARBY.
...
FMP
IT'S A GATHERING OF MODERATES...
...SO THERE SHOULDN'T BE ANY TROUBLE.
ALL RIGHT.
I'M OFF.
HE'S IN A BAD MOOD.

Hello everyone!

5 volumes total... 4 volumes total... Now... For the first time, one of my series has gone on longer than five volumes. It makes me feel sentimental. I really feel that this is all thanks to my readers. Thank you for reading volume 6 too!

Hmm... But now that I'm on my 16th book, I've finally run out of things to write in the sidebars. Maybe there are things I could write about... But right now, my brain is filled to capacity with what will happen in the story from now on. (Because I've got no brains.)

If people have been looking forward to reading the sidebars, I'm sorry! But I did my best with drawing new material for this volume!! I'll think of something to do in the sidebars in volume 7.

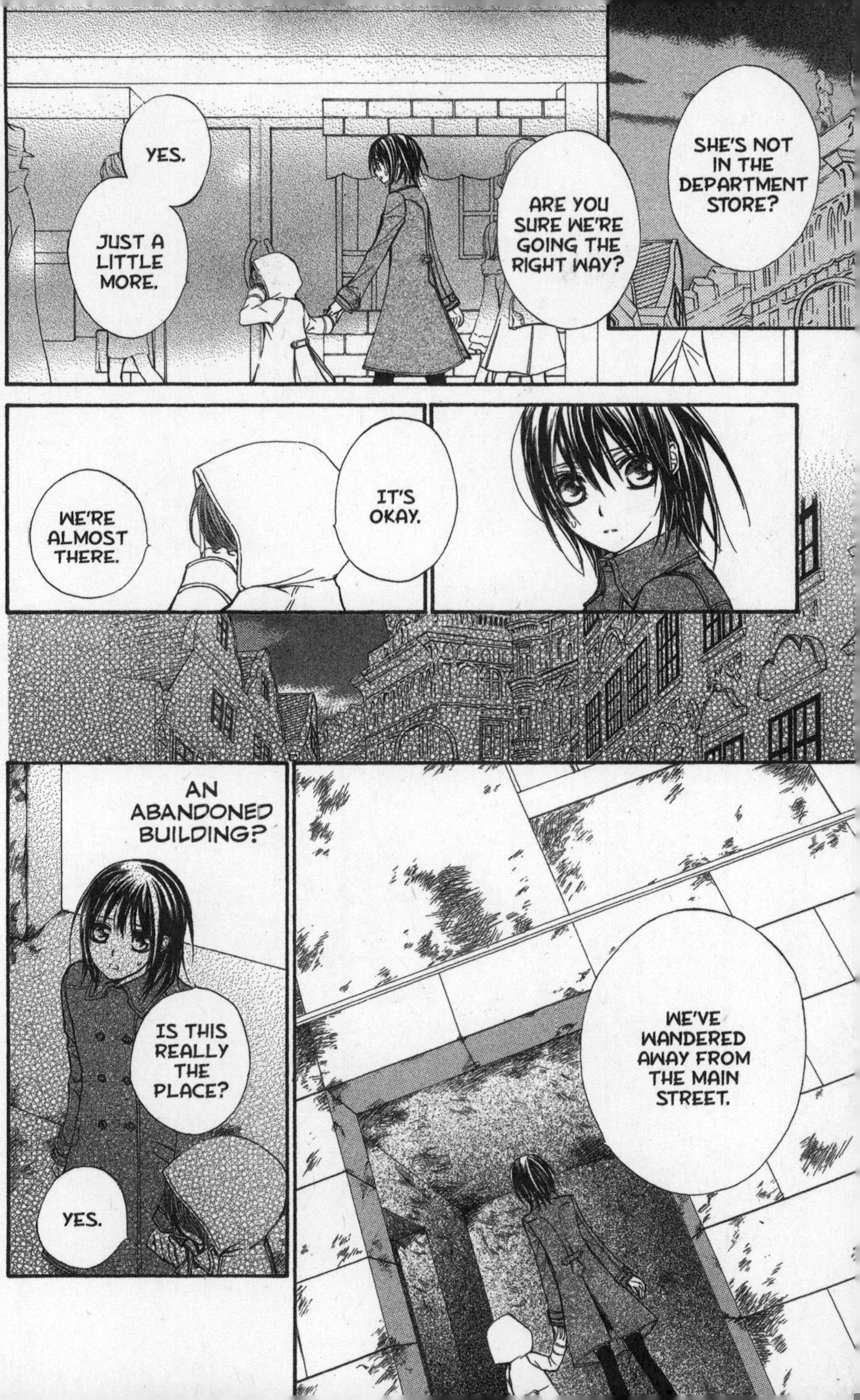
SHE'S NOT IN THE DEPARTMENT STORE?
ARE YOU SURE WE'RE GOING THE RIGHT WAY?
YES.
JUST A LITTLE MORE.
IT'S OKAY.
WE'RE ALMOST THERE.
WE'VE WANDERED AWAY FROM THE MAIN STREET.
AN ABANDONED BUILDING?
IS THIS REALLY THE PLACE?
YES.

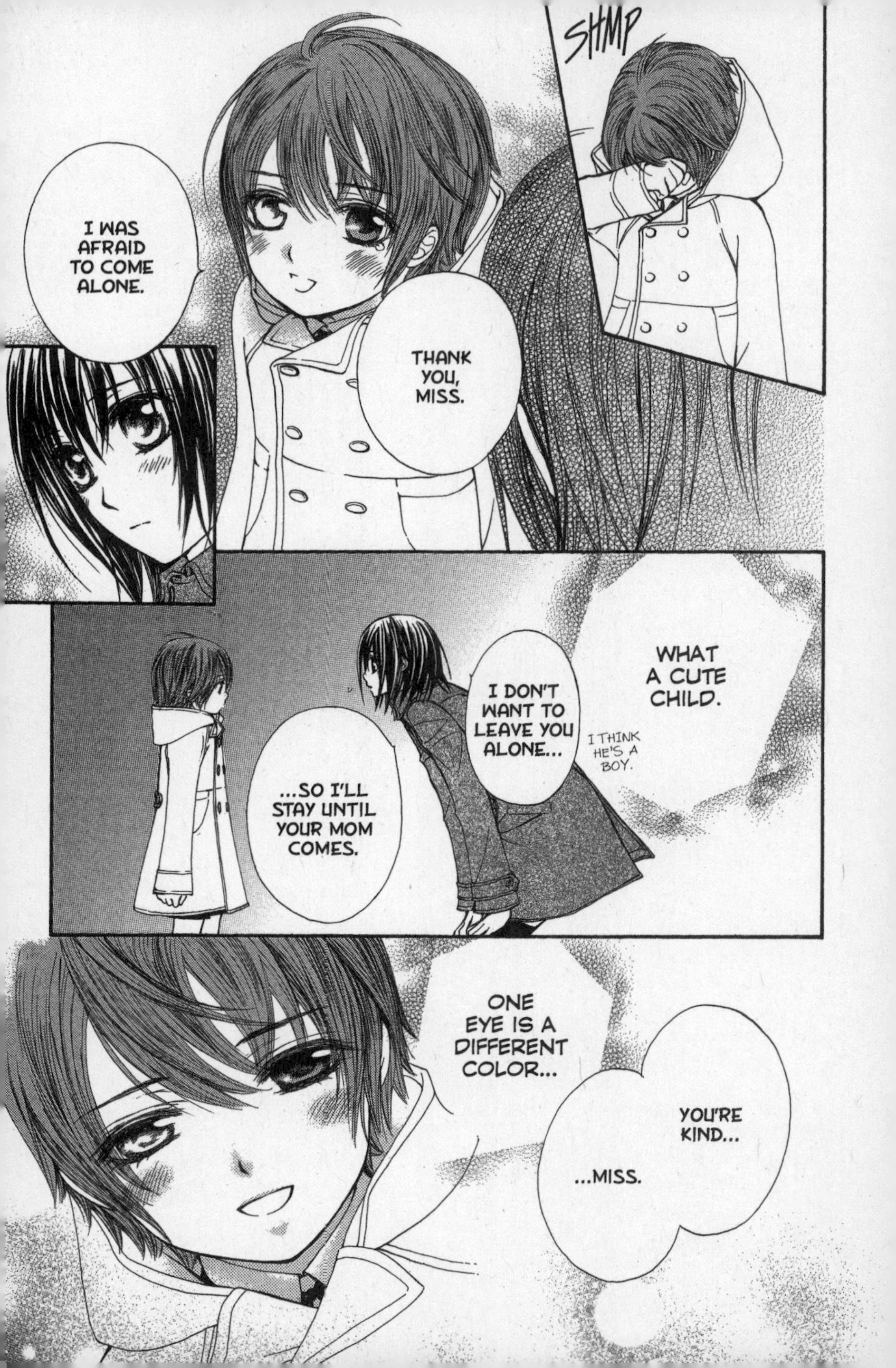
SHMP
THANK YOU, MISS.
I WAS AFRAID TO COME ALONE.
WHAT A CUTE CHILD.
I THINK HE'S A BOY.
I DON'T WANT TO LEAVE YOU ALONE...
...SO I'LL STAY UNTIL YOUR MOM COMES.
ONE EYE IS A DIFFERENT COLOR...
YOU'RE KIND...
...MISS.

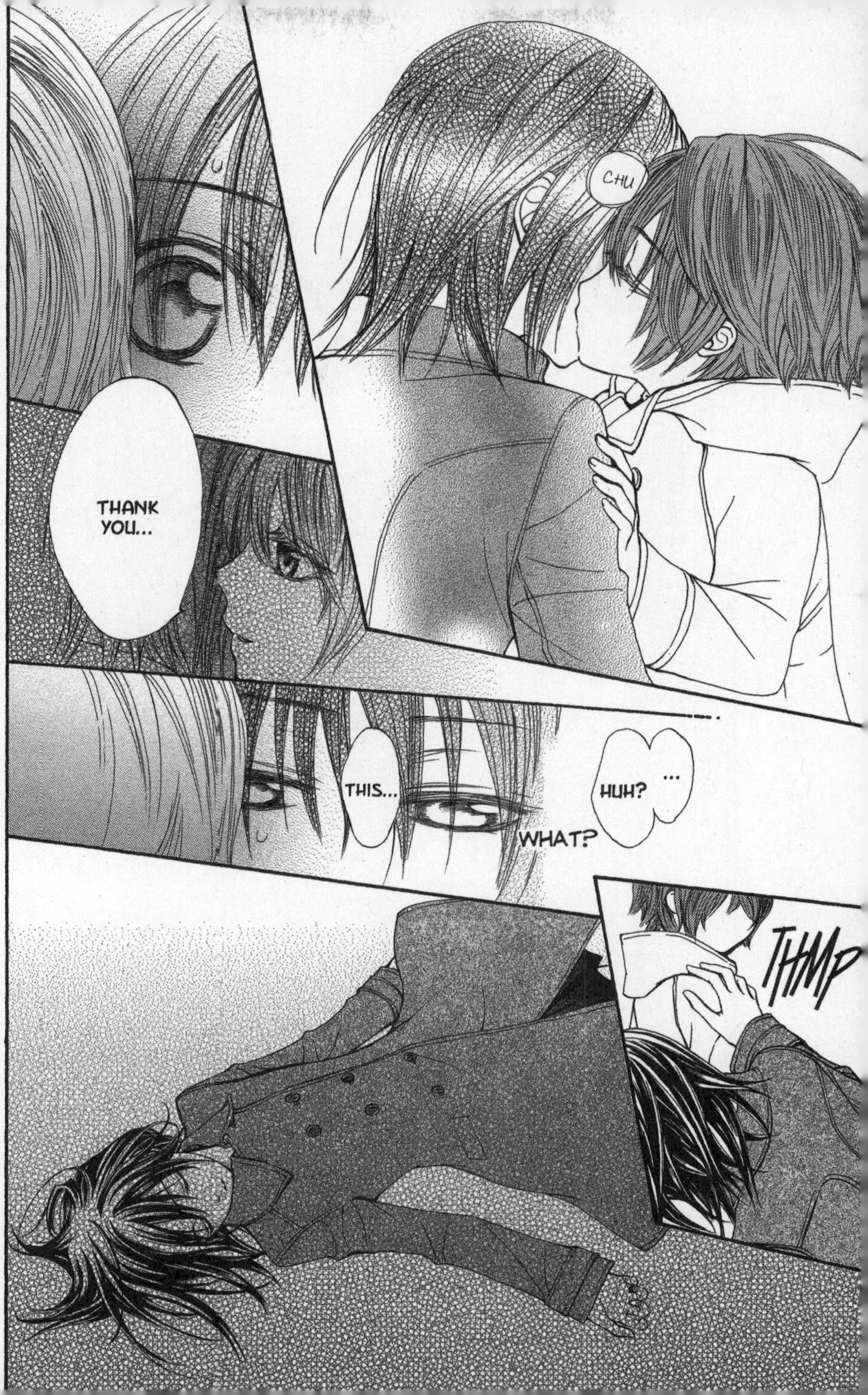
CHU
THANK YOU...
...
HUH?
WHAT?
THIS...
THMP

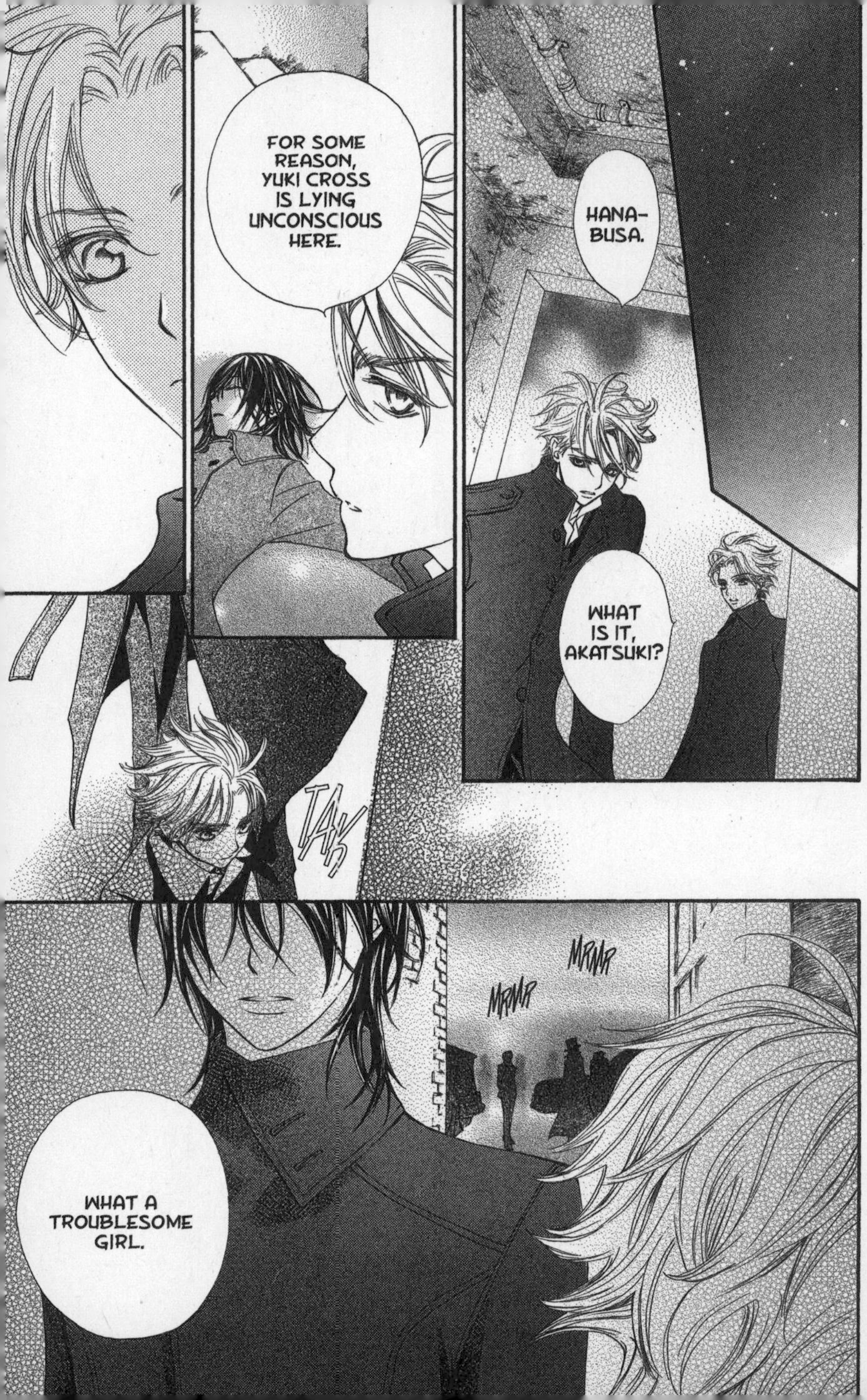
HANA-BUSA.
WHAT IS IT, AKATSUKI?
FOR SOME REASON, YUKI CROSS IS LYING UNCONSCIOUS HERE.
TAK
MRMR
MRMR
WHAT A TROUBLESOME GIRL.

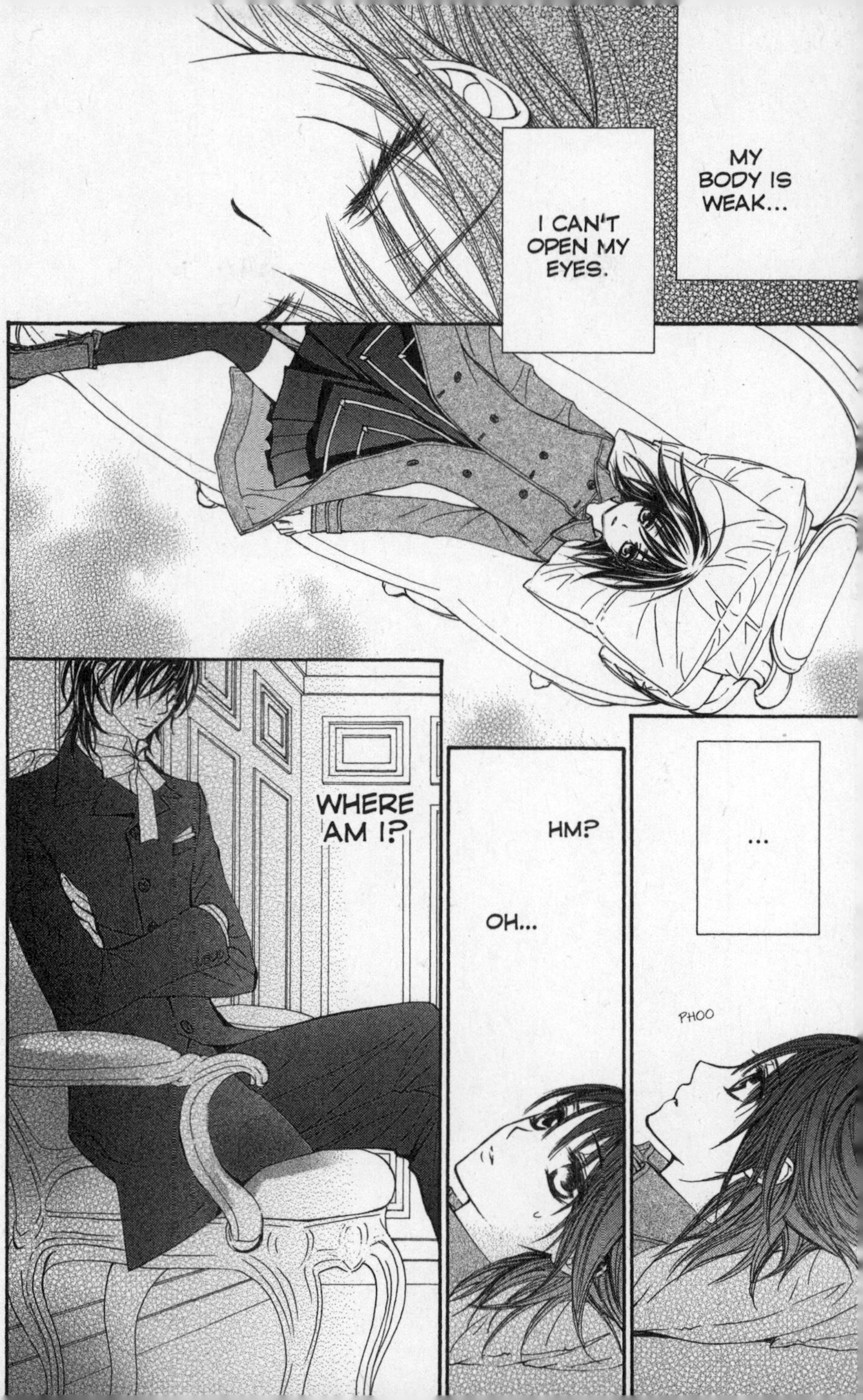
MY BODY IS WEAK...
I CAN'T OPEN MY EYES.
...
PHOO
HM?
OH...
WHERE AM I?

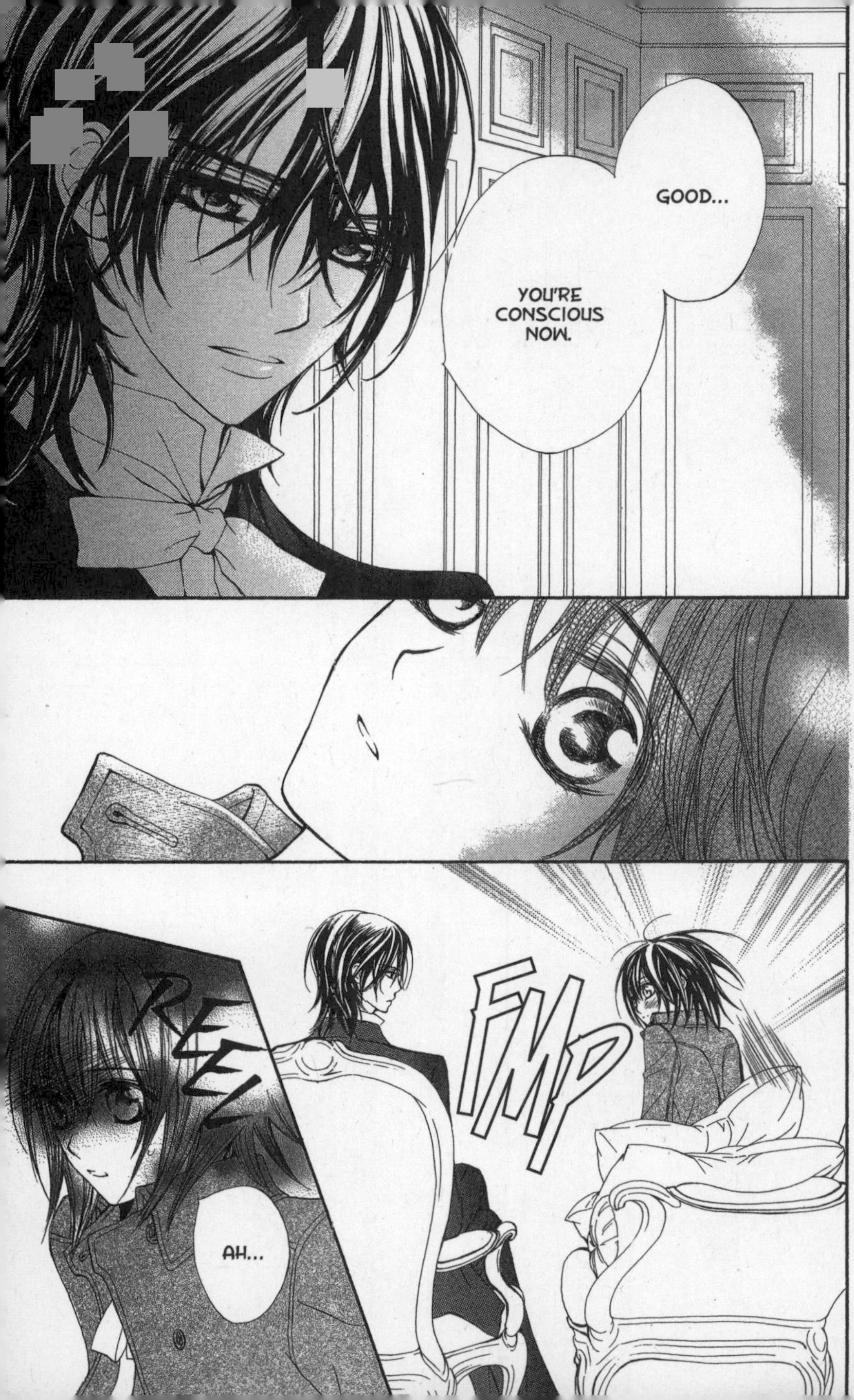
GOOD...
YOU'RE CONSCIOUS NOW.
FMP
REEL
AH...

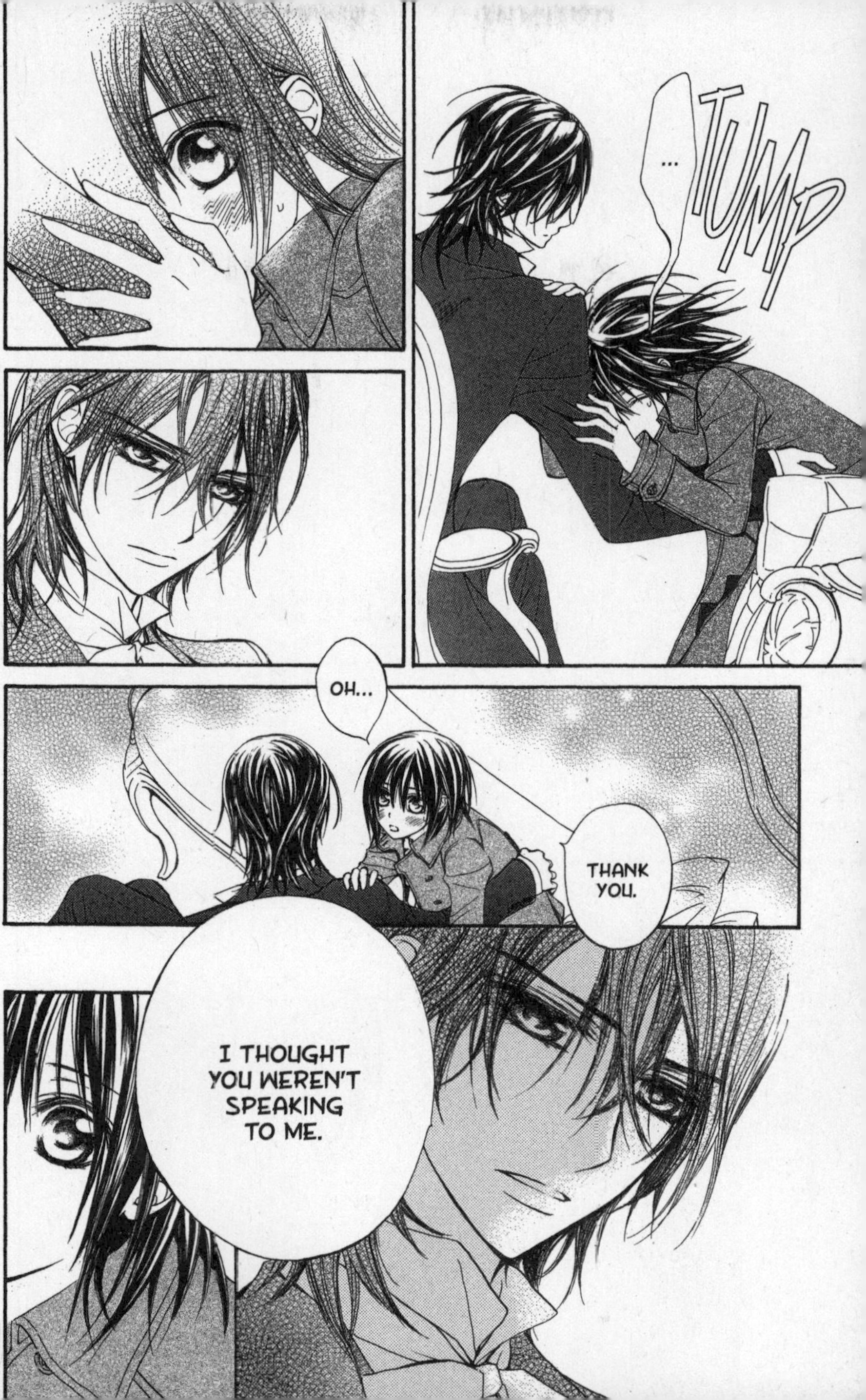
TUMP
...
OH...
THANK YOU.
I THOUGHT YOU WEREN'T SPEAKING TO ME.

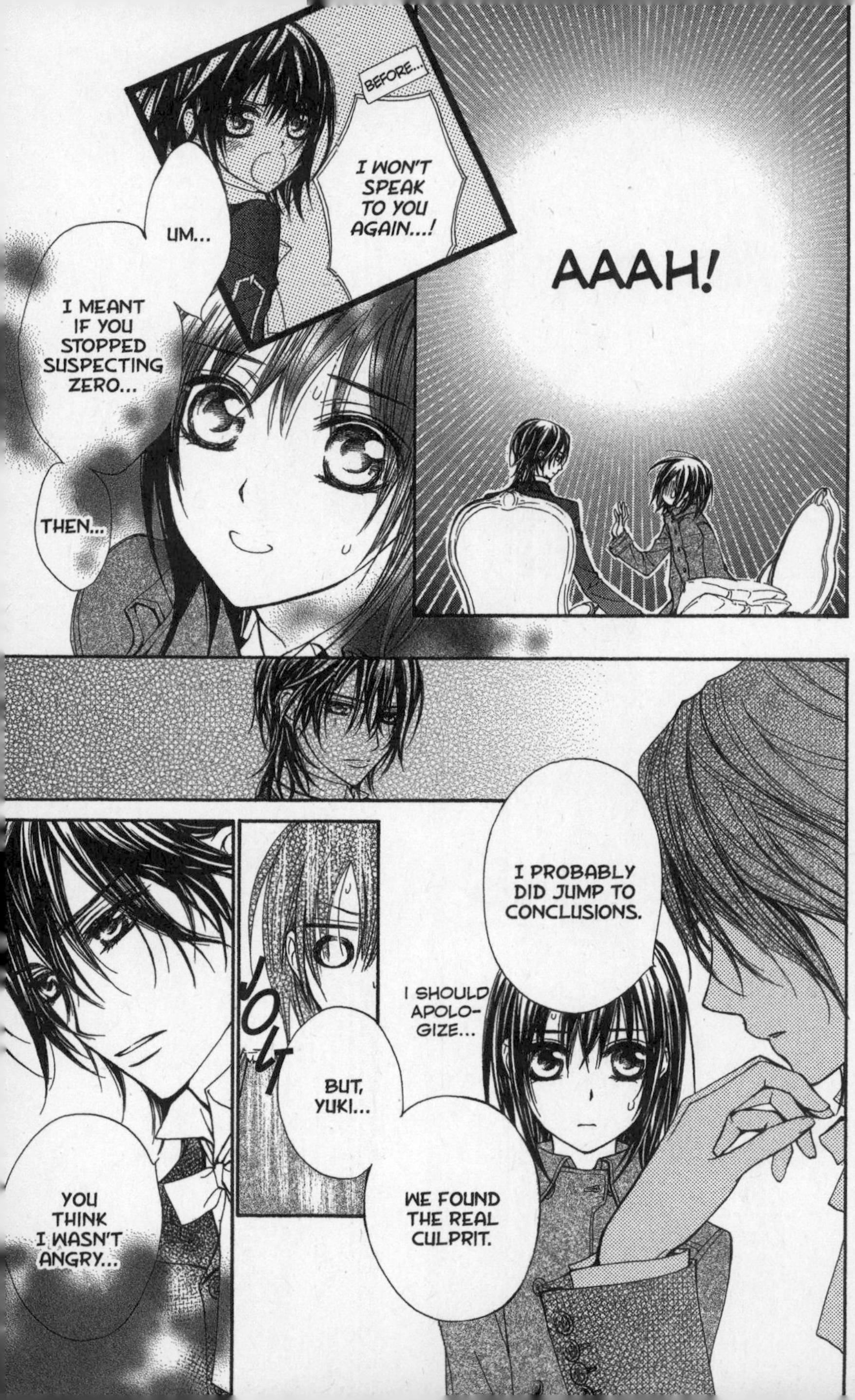
AAAH!
BEFORE...
I WON'T SPEAK TO YOU AGAIN...!
UM...
I MEANT IF YOU STOPPED SUSPECTING ZERO...
THEN...
I PROBABLY DID JUMP TO CONCLUSIONS.
I SHOULD APOLOGIZE...
WE FOUND THE REAL CULPRIT.
JOLT
BUT, YUKI...
YOU THINK I WASN'T ANGRY...

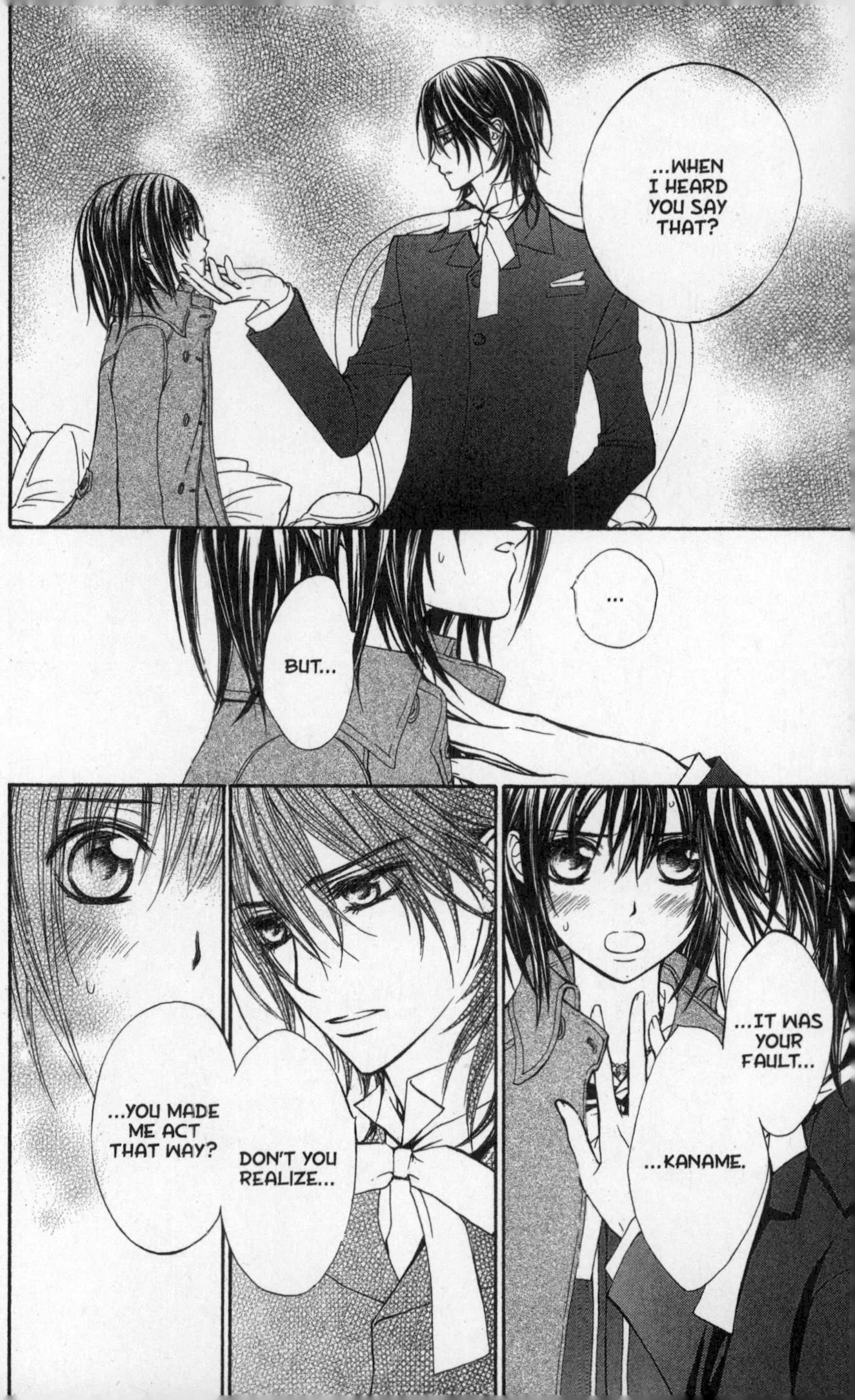
...WHEN I HEARD YOU SAY THAT?
...
BUT...
...IT WAS YOUR FAULT...
...KANAME.
DON'T YOU REALIZE...
...YOU MADE ME ACT THAT WAY?

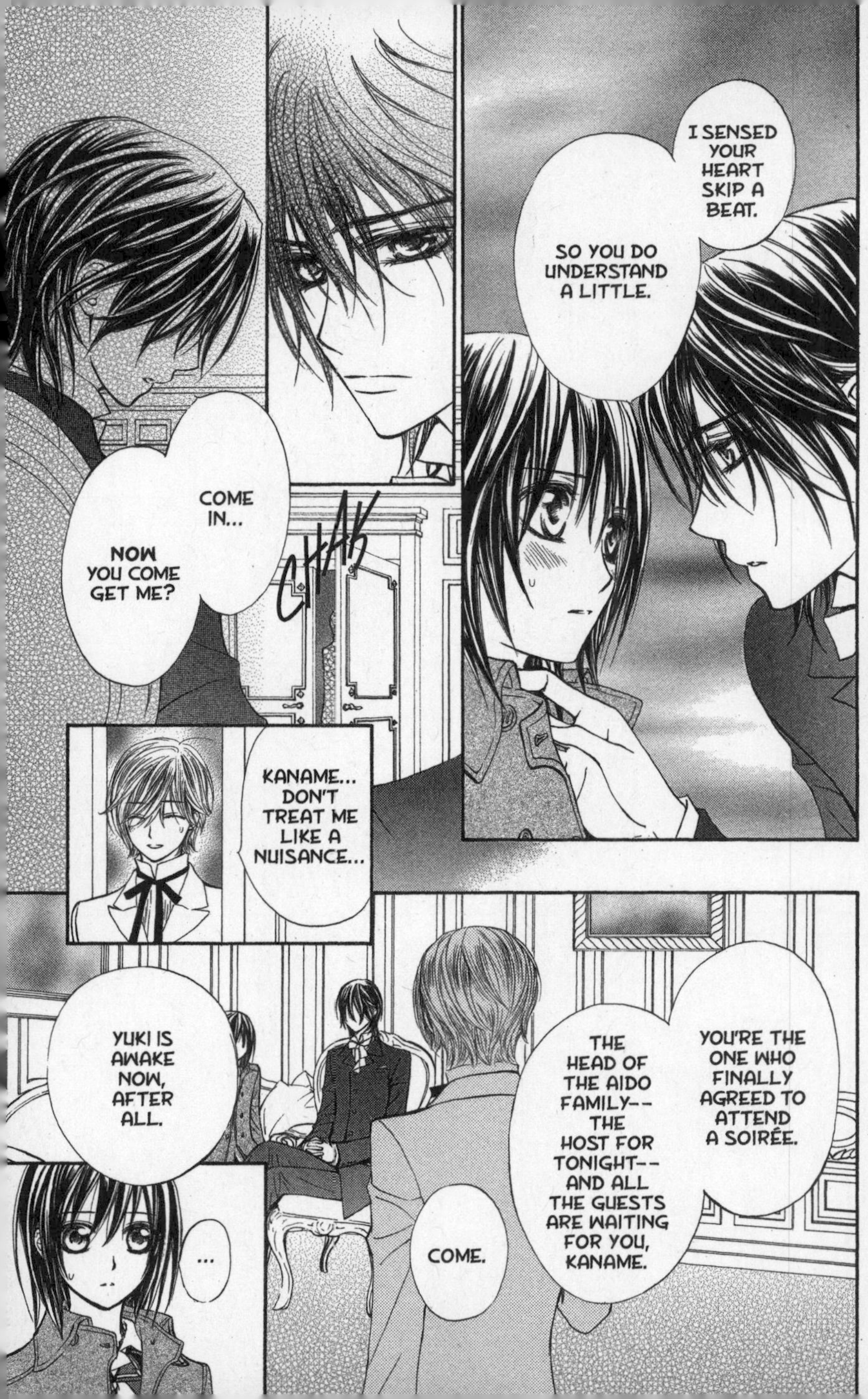

I SENSED YOUR HEART SKIP A BEAT.
SO YOU DO UNDERSTAND A LITTLE.
COME IN...
NOW YOU COME GET ME?
CHAK
KANAME... DON'T TREAT ME LIKE A NUISANCE...
YOU'RE THE ONE WHO FINALLY AGREED TO ATTEND A SOIRÉE.
THE HEAD OF THE AIDO FAMILY--THE HOST FOR TONIGHT--AND ALL THE GUESTS ARE WAITING FOR YOU, KANAME.
COME.
YUKI IS AWAKE NOW, AFTER ALL.
...

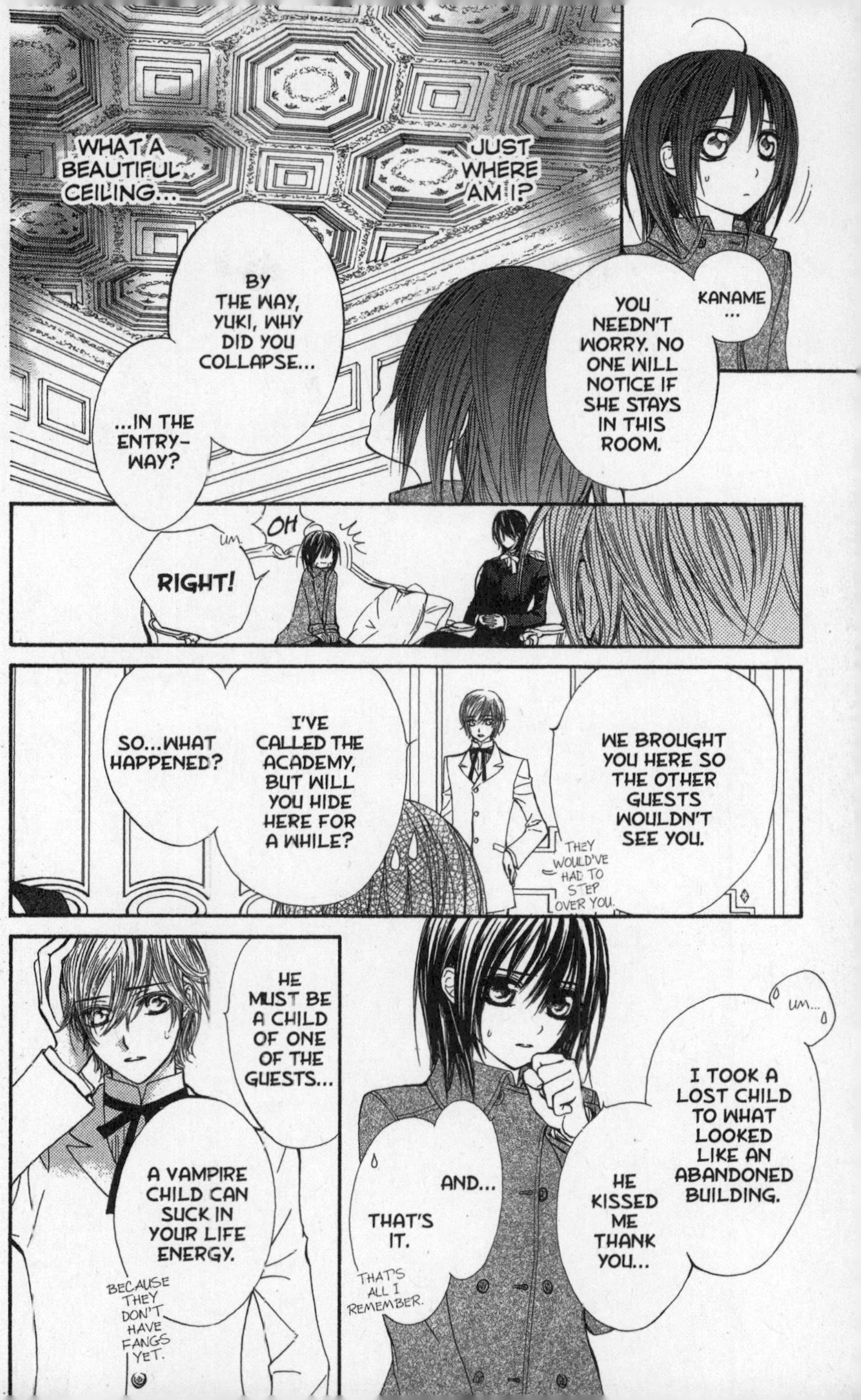
KANAME ...
JUST WHERE AM I?
WHAT A BEAUTIFUL CEILING...
YOU NEEDN'T WORRY. NO ONE WILL NOTICE IF SHE STAYS IN THIS ROOM.
BY THE WAY, YUKI, WHY DID YOU COLLAPSE...
...IN THE ENTRY-WAY?
OH
UM.
RIGHT!
WE BROUGHT YOU HERE SO THE OTHER GUESTS WOULDN'T SEE YOU.
THEY WOULD'VE HAD TO STEP OVER YOU.
I'VE CALLED THE ACADEMY, BUT WILL YOU HIDE HERE FOR A WHILE?
SO...WHAT HAPPENED?
UM...
I TOOK A LOST CHILD TO WHAT LOOKED LIKE AN ABANDONED BUILDING.
HE KISSED ME THANK YOU...
AND...
THAT'S IT.
THAT'S ALL I REMEMBER.
HE MUST BE A CHILD OF ONE OF THE GUESTS...
A VAMPIRE CHILD CAN SUCK IN YOUR LIFE ENERGY.
BECAUSE THEY DON'T HAVE FANGS YET.

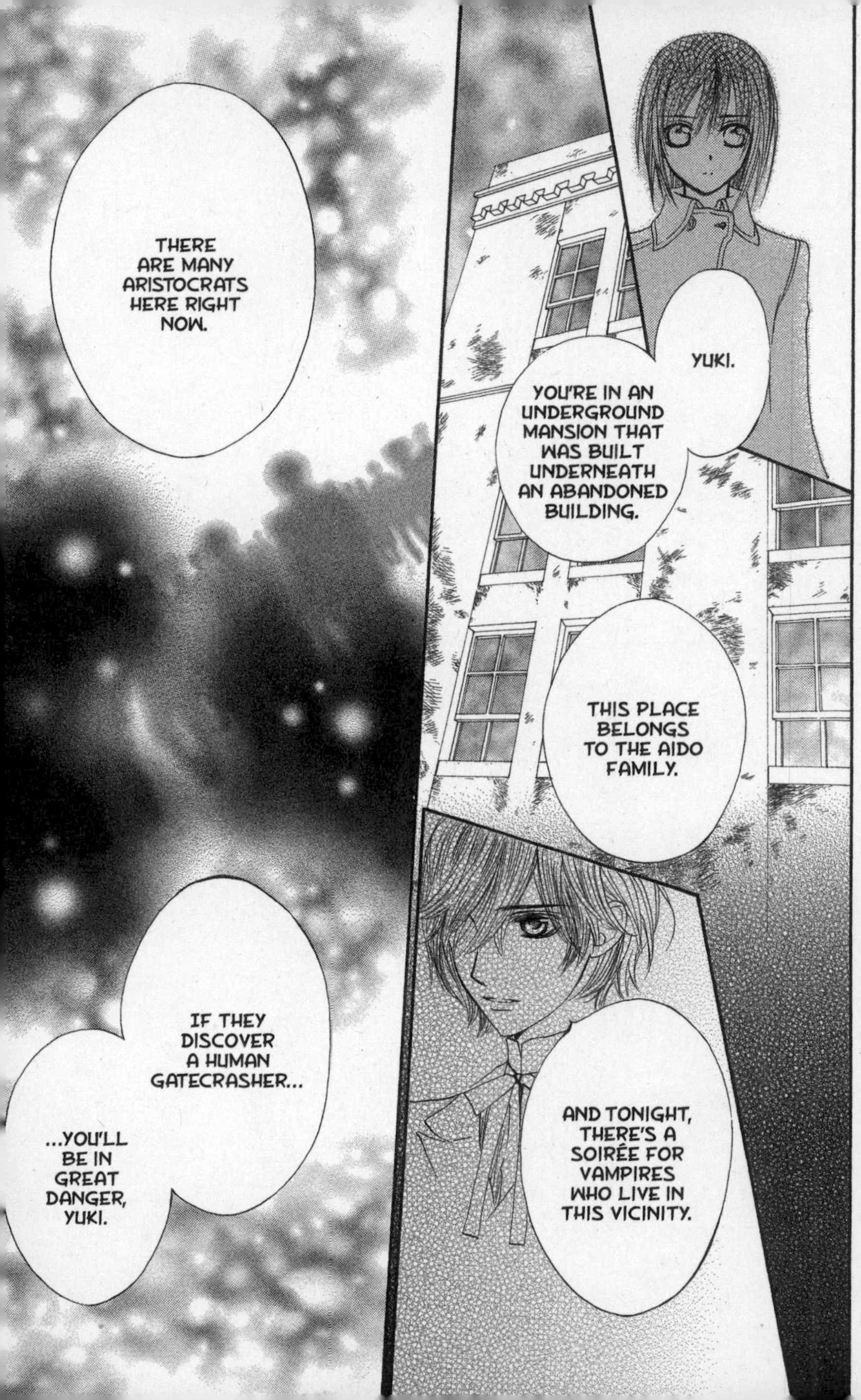
YUKI.
YOU'RE IN AN UNDERGROUND MANSION THAT WAS BUILT UNDERNEATH AN ABANDONED BUILDING.
THIS PLACE BELONGS TO THE AIDO FAMILY.
AND TONIGHT, THERE'S A SOIRÉE FOR VAMPIRES WHO LIVE IN THIS VICINITY.
THERE ARE MANY ARISTOCRATS HERE RIGHT NOW.
IF THEY DISCOVER A HUMAN GATECRASHER...
...YOU'LL BE IN GREAT DANGER, YUKI.

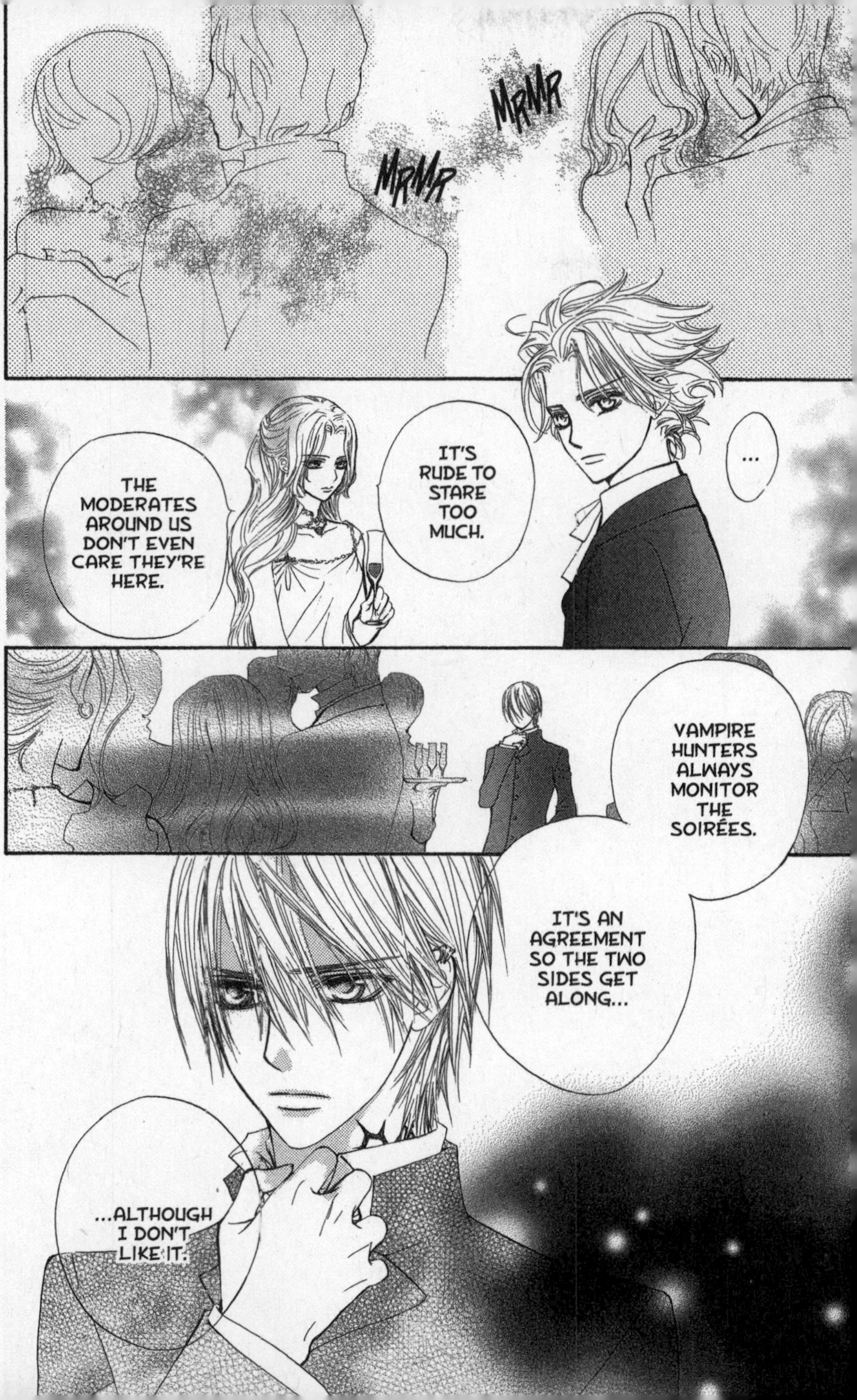
MRMR
MRMR
...
IT'S RUDE TO STARE TOO MUCH.
THE MODERATES AROUND US DON'T EVEN CARE THEY'RE HERE.
VAMPIRE HUNTERS ALWAYS MONITOR THE SOIRÉES.
IT'S AN AGREEMENT SO THE TWO SIDES GET ALONG...
...ALTHOUGH I DON'T LIKE IT.

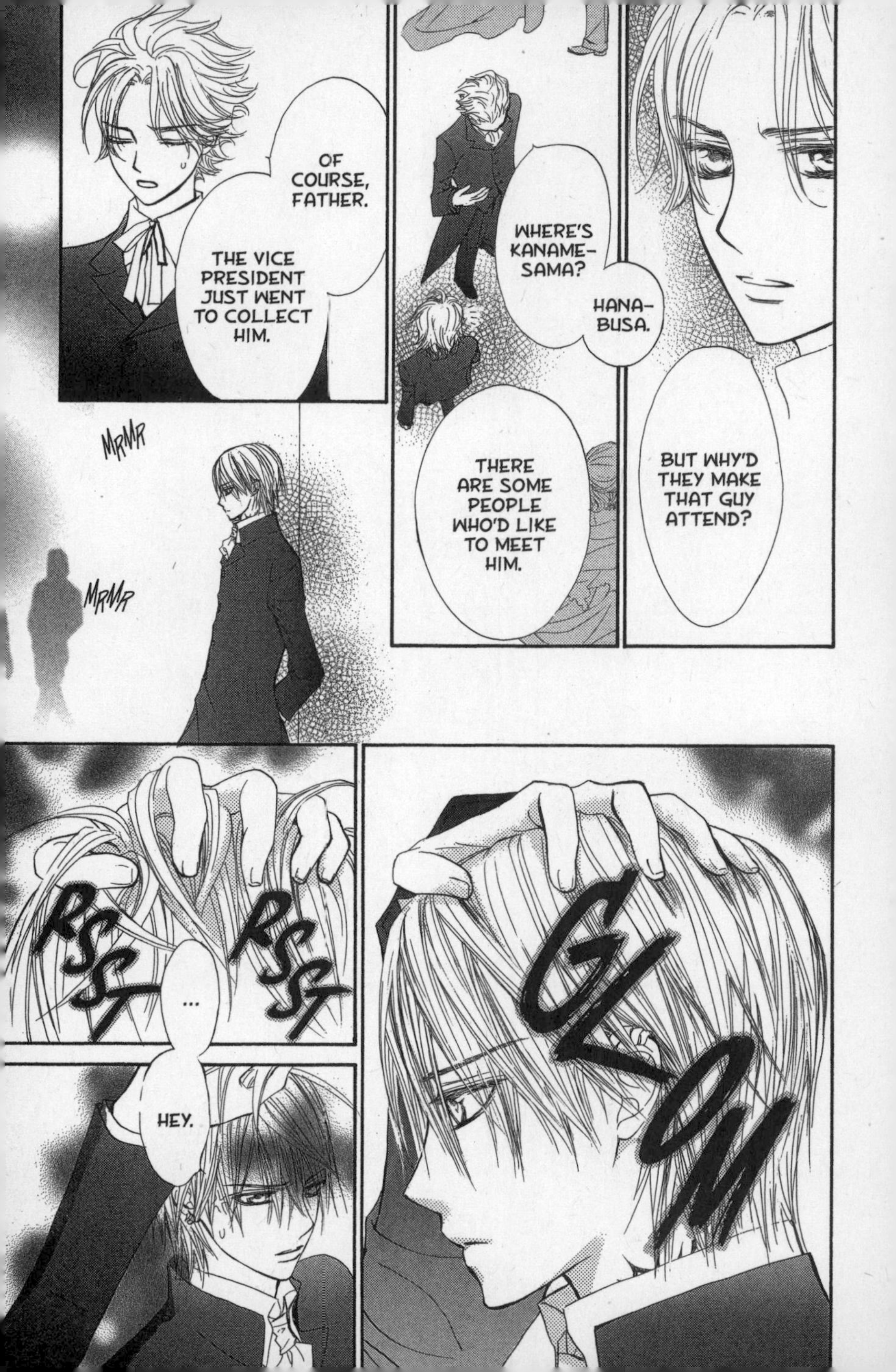
BUT WHY'D THEY MAKE THAT GUY ATTEND?
WHERE'S KANAME-SAMA?
HANA-BUSA.
THERE ARE SOME PEOPLE WHO'D LIKE TO MEET HIM.
OF COURSE, FATHER.
THE VICE PRESIDENT JUST WENT TO COLLECT HIM.
MRMR
MRMR
GLOM
RSST
RSST
...
HEY.

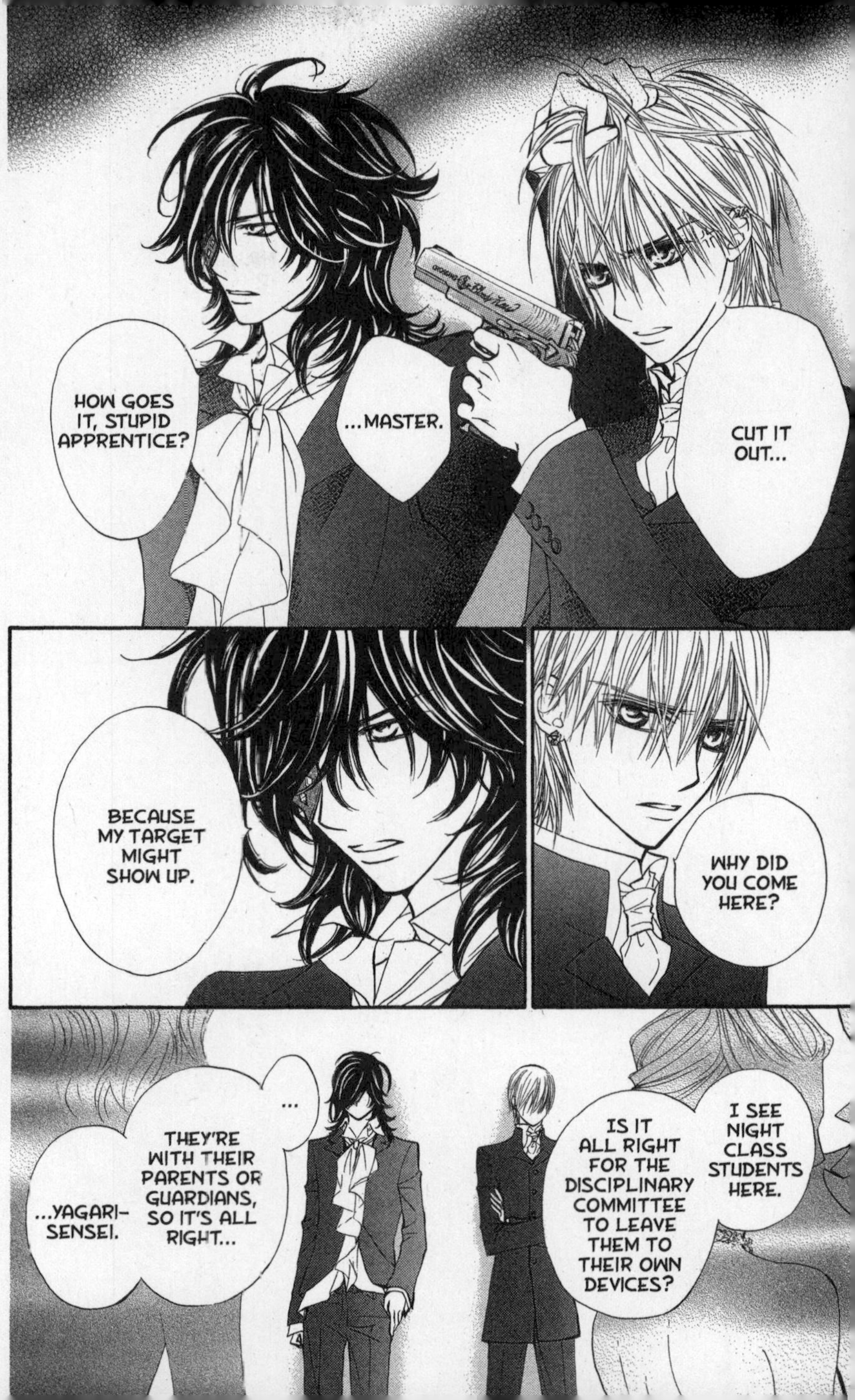
CUT IT OUT...
...MASTER.
HOW GOES IT, STUPID APPRENTICE?
WHY DID YOU COME HERE?
BECAUSE MY TARGET MIGHT SHOW UP.
I SEE NIGHT CLASS STUDENTS HERE.
IS IT ALL RIGHT FOR THE DISCIPLINARY COMMITTEE TO LEAVE THEM TO THEIR OWN DEVICES?
...
THEY'RE WITH THEIR PARENTS OR GUARDIANS, SO IT'S ALL RIGHT...
...YAGARI-SENSEI.

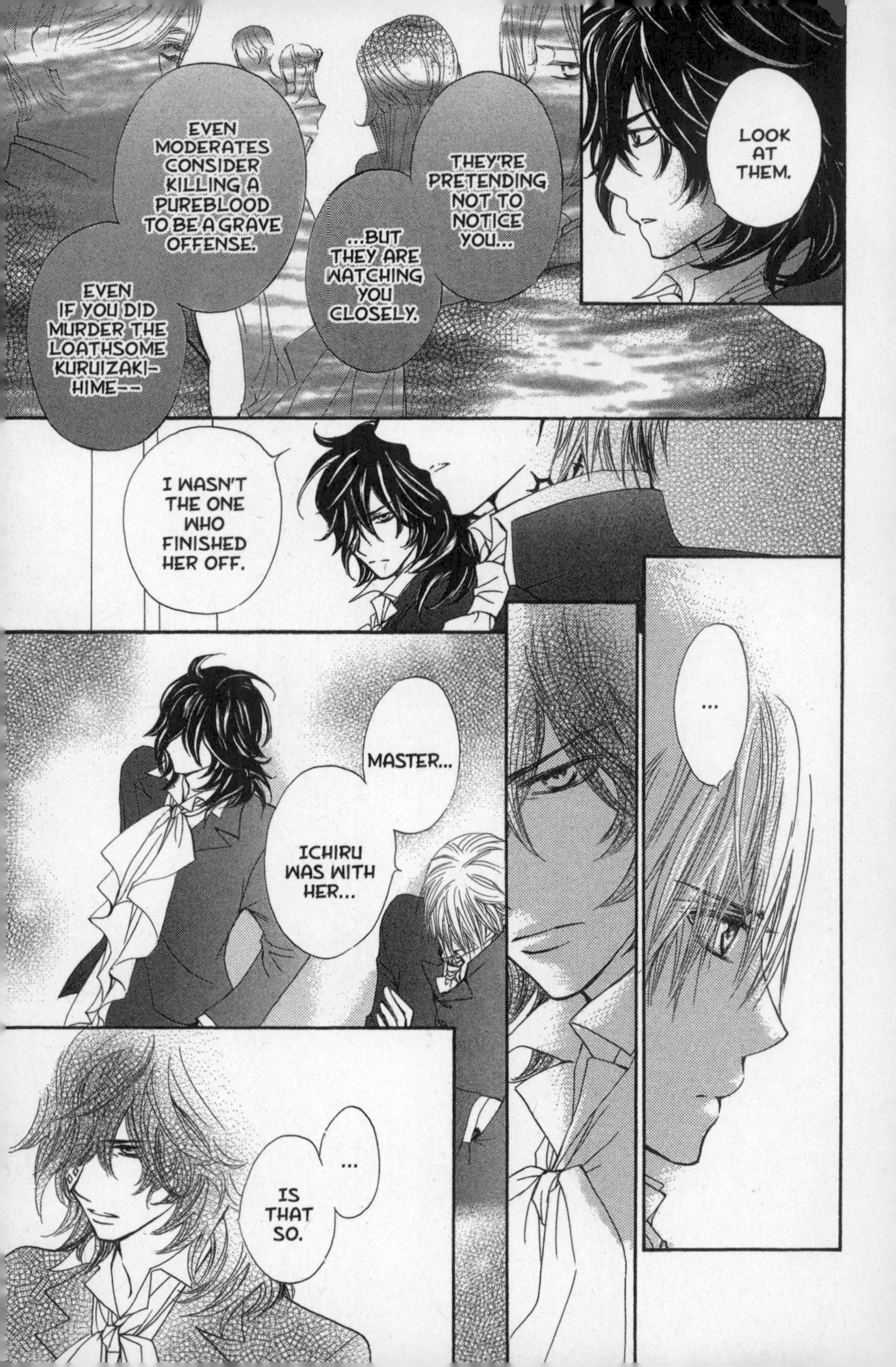
LOOK AT THEM.
THEY'RE PRETENDING NOT TO NOTICE YOU...
...BUT THEY ARE WATCHING YOU CLOSELY.
EVEN MODERATES CONSIDER KILLING A PUREBLOOD TO BE A GRAVE OFFENSE.
EVEN IF YOU DID MURDER THE LOATHSOME KURUIZAKI-HIME--
I WASN'T THE ONE WHO FINISHED HER OFF.
...
MASTER...
ICHIRU WAS WITH HER...
... IS THAT SO.

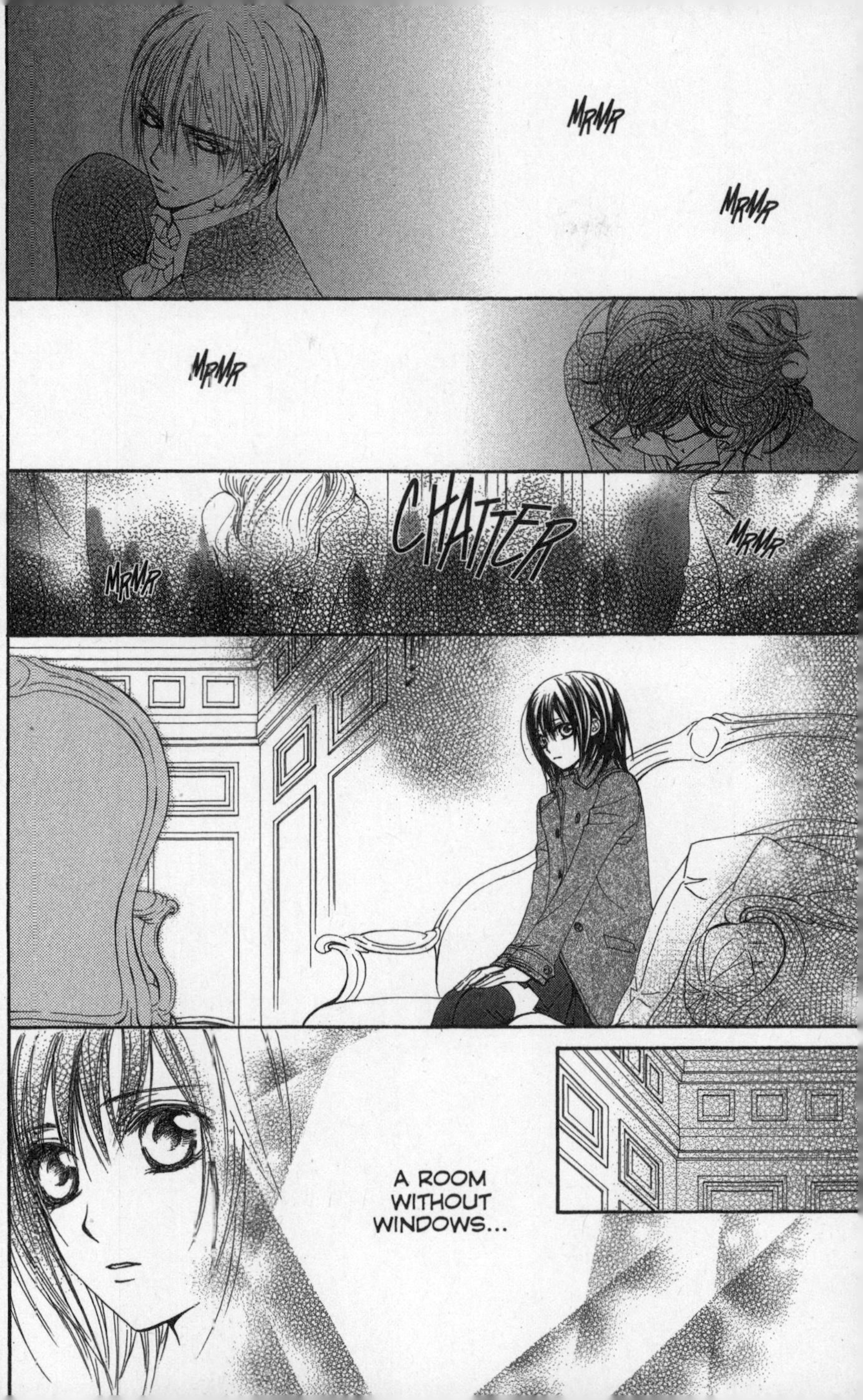
MRMR
MRMR
MRMR
CHATTER
MRMR
MRMR
A ROOM WITHOUT WINDOWS...

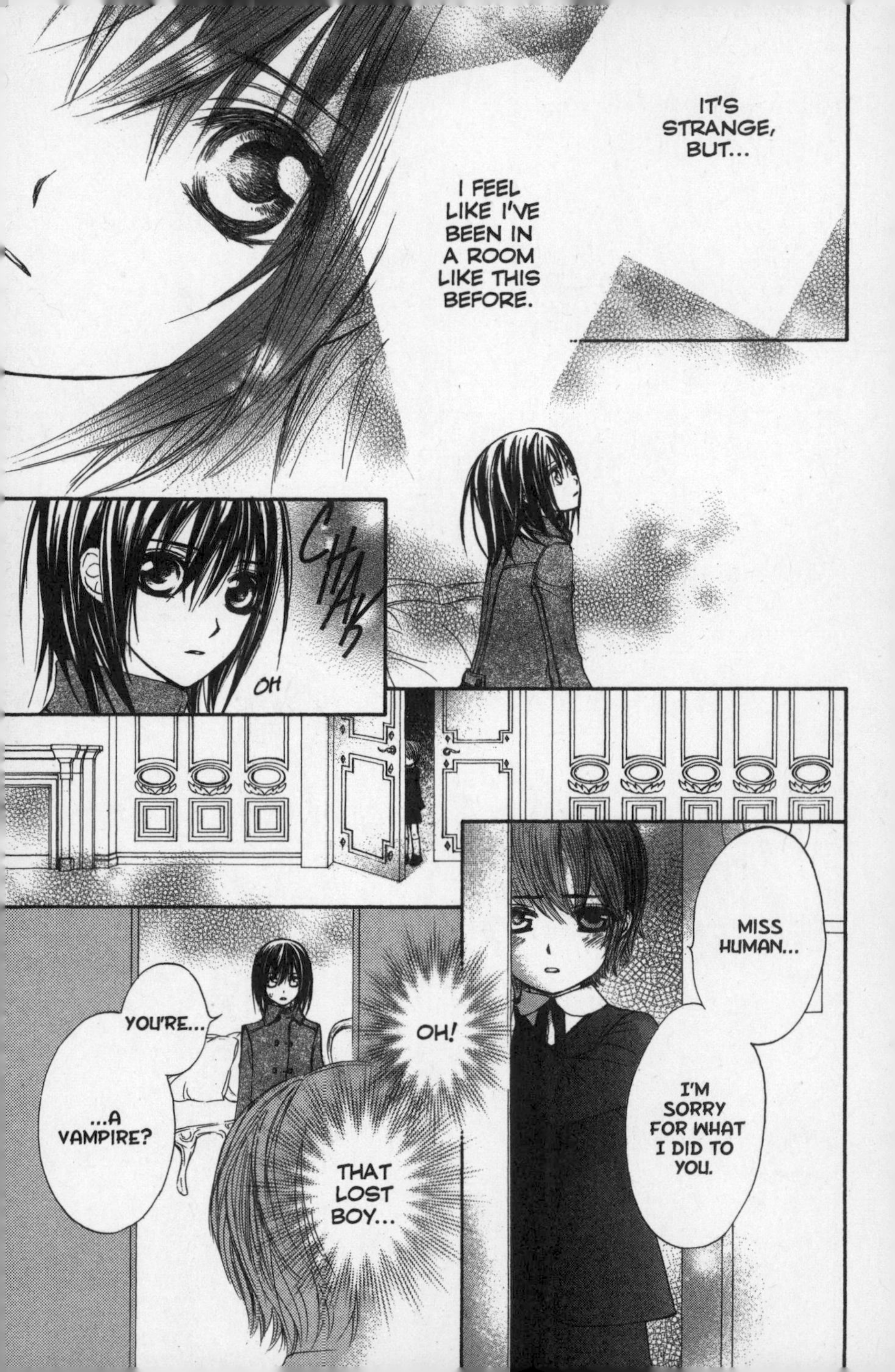
IT'S STRANGE, BUT...
I FEEL LIKE I'VE BEEN IN A ROOM LIKE THIS BEFORE.
CHAK
OH
MISS HUMAN...
I'M SORRY FOR WHAT I DID TO YOU.
OH!
THAT LOST BOY...
YOU'RE...
...A VAMPIRE?

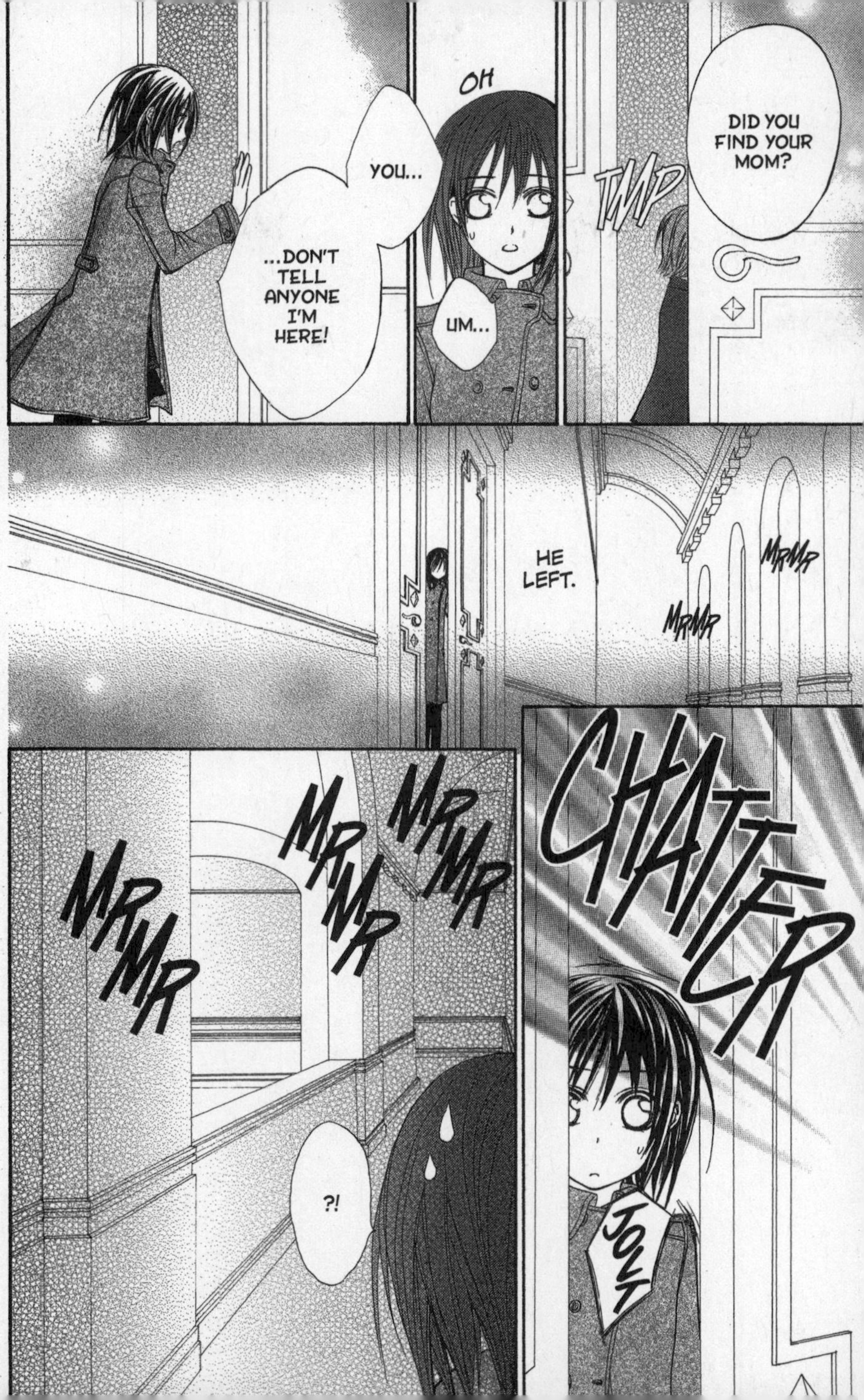
DID YOU FIND YOUR MOM?
TMP
OH
UM...
YOU...
...DON'T TELL ANYONE I'M HERE!
MRMR
MRMR
HE LEFT.
CHATTER
JOLT
MRMR
MRMR
MRMR
?!

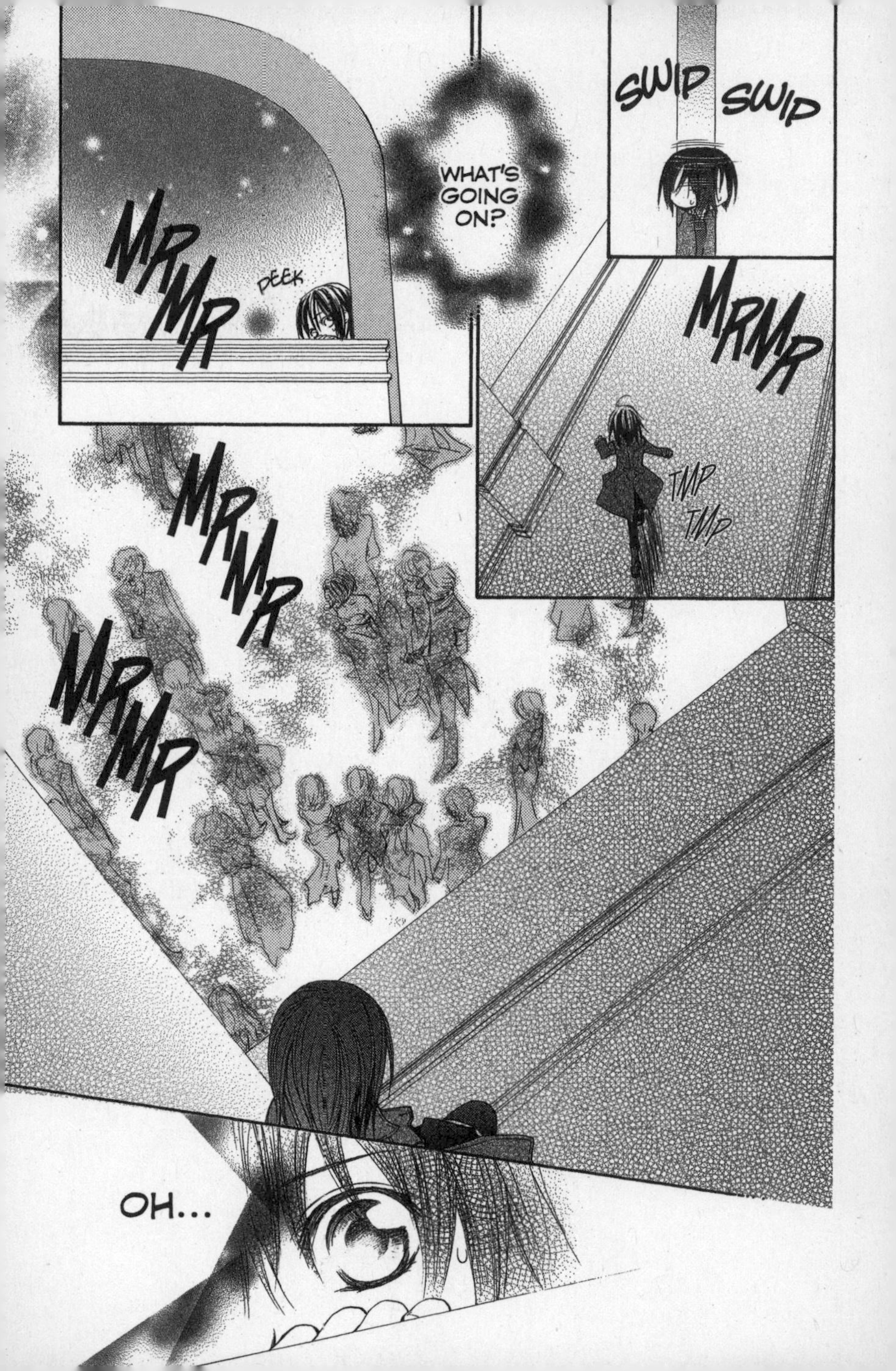
SWIP SWIP
MRMR
PEEK
WHAT'S GOING ON?
MRMR
TMP TMP
MRMR
MRMR
OH...

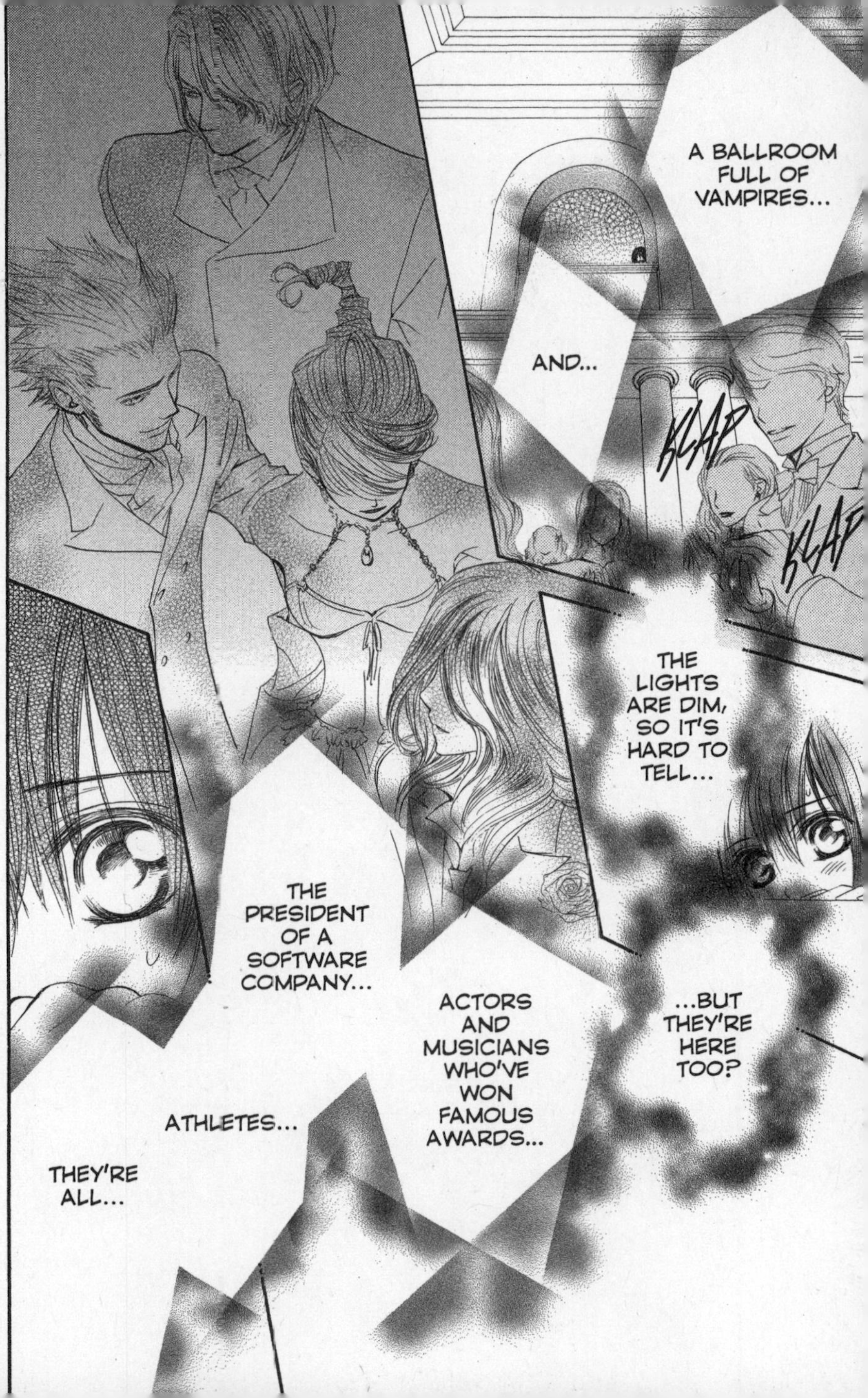
A BALLROOM FULL OF VAMPIRES...
AND...
KLAP
KLAP
THE LIGHTS ARE DIM, SO IT'S HARD TO TELL...
THE PRESIDENT OF A SOFTWARE COMPANY...
...BUT THEY'RE HERE TOO?
ACTORS AND MUSICIANS WHO'VE WON FAMOUS AWARDS...
ATHLETES...
THEY'RE ALL...

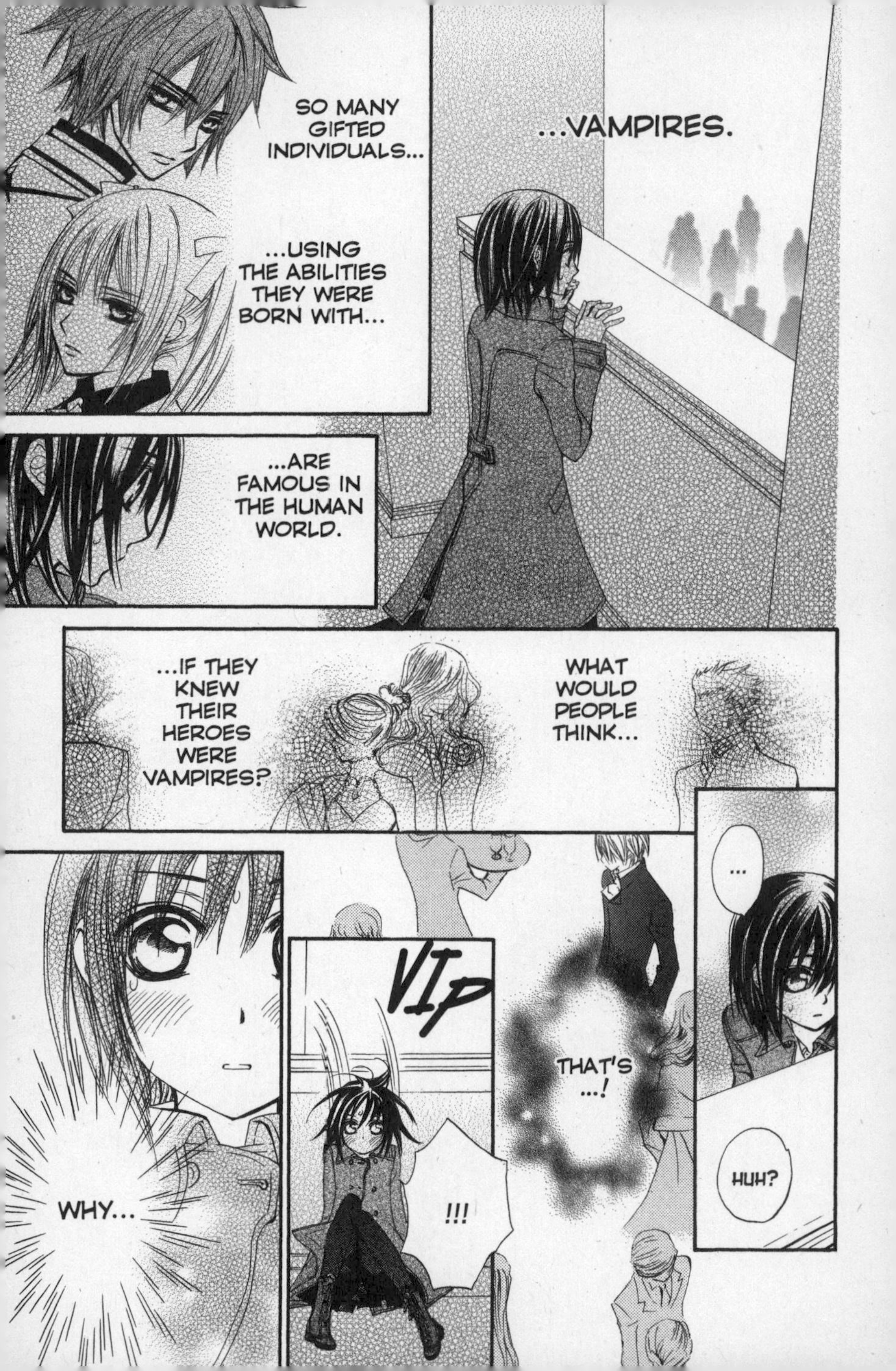
...VAMPIRES.
SO MANY GIFTED INDIVIDUALS...
...USING THE ABILITIES THEY WERE BORN WITH...
...ARE FAMOUS IN THE HUMAN WORLD.
WHAT WOULD PEOPLE THINK...
...IF THEY KNEW THEIR HEROES WERE VAMPIRES?
...
HUH?
THAT'S ...!
VIP
!!!
WHY...

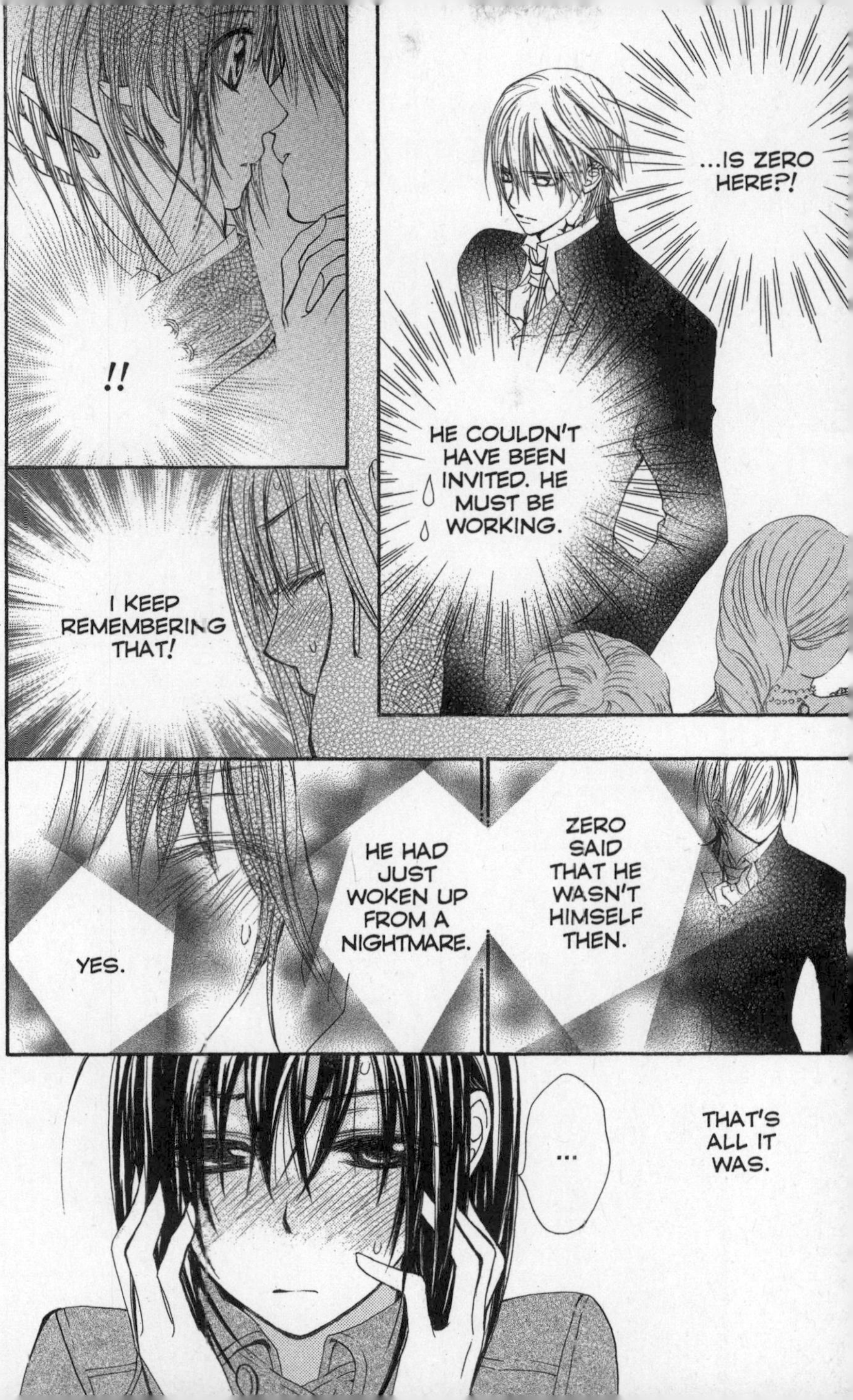
...IS ZERO HERE?!
HE COULDN'T HAVE BEEN INVITED. HE MUST BE WORKING.
!!
I KEEP REMEMBERING THAT!
ZERO SAID THAT HE WASN'T HIMSELF THEN.
HE HAD JUST WOKEN UP FROM A NIGHTMARE.
YES.
THAT'S ALL IT WAS.
...

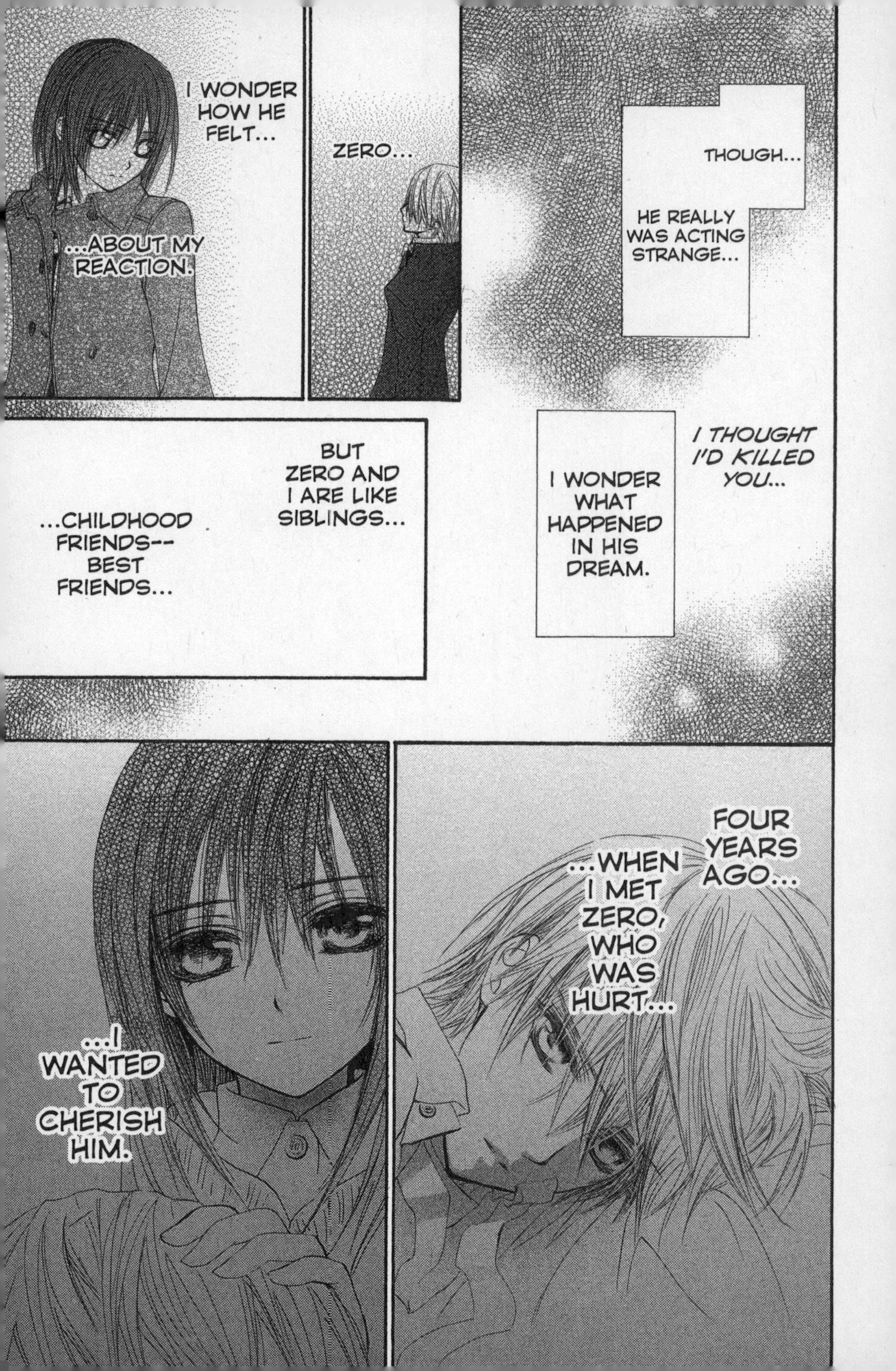
THOUGH...
HE REALLY WAS ACTING STRANGE...
I THOUGHT I'D KILLED YOU...
I WONDER WHAT HAPPENED IN HIS DREAM.
ZERO...
I WONDER HOW HE FELT...
...ABOUT MY REACTION.
BUT ZERO AND I ARE LIKE SIBLINGS...
...CHILDHOOD FRIENDS--BEST FRIENDS...
FOUR YEARS AGO...
...WHEN I MET ZERO, WHO WAS HURT...
...I WANTED TO CHERISH HIM.

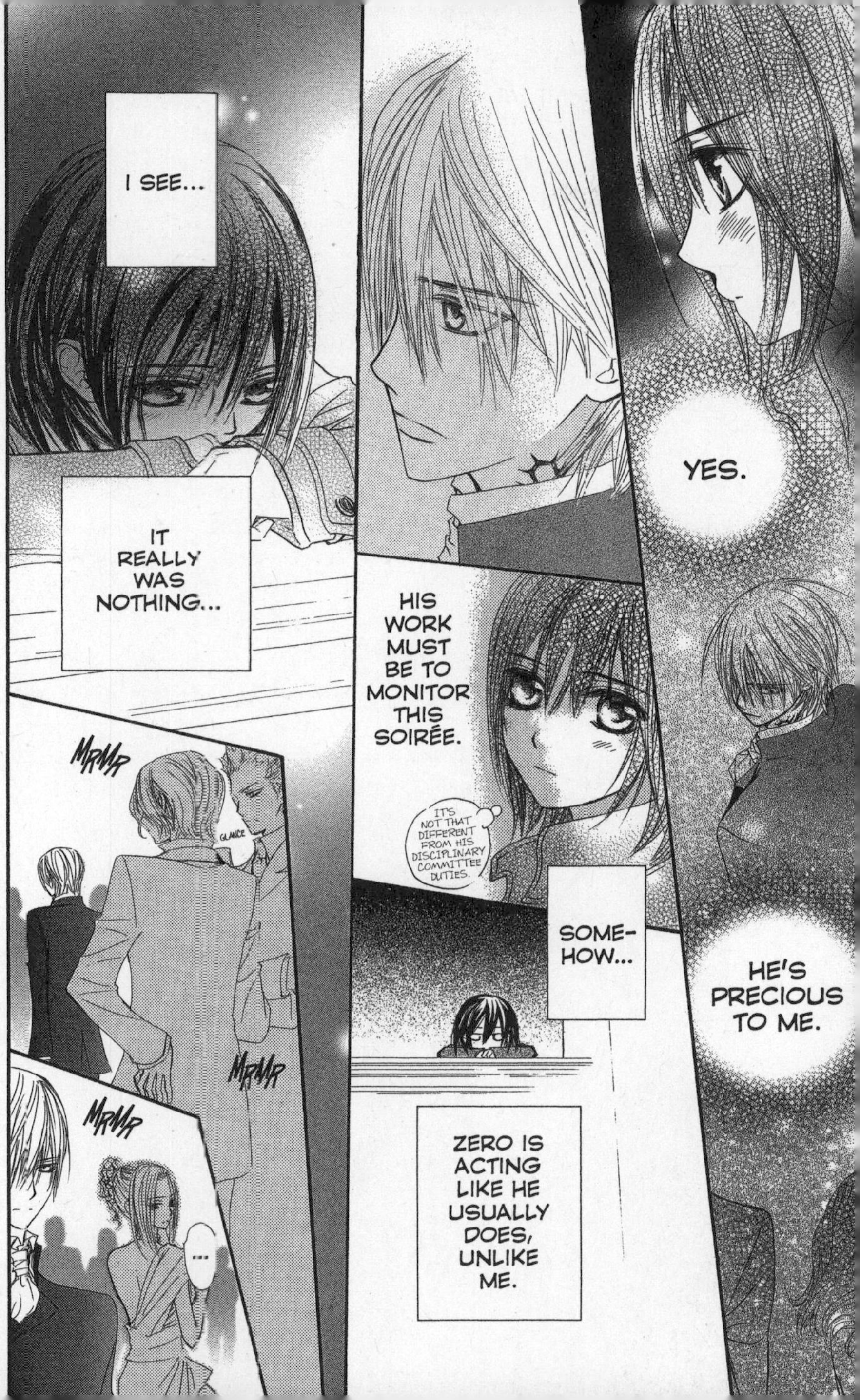
YES.
HE'S PRECIOUS TO ME.
HIS WORK MUST BE TO MONITOR THIS SOIRÉE.
IT'S NOT THAT DIFFERENT FROM HIS DISCIPLINARY COMMITTEE DUTIES.
SOME-HOW...
ZERO IS ACTING LIKE HE USUALLY DOES, UNLIKE ME.
I SEE...
IT REALLY WAS NOTHING...
MRMR
GLANCE
MRMR
MRMR
...

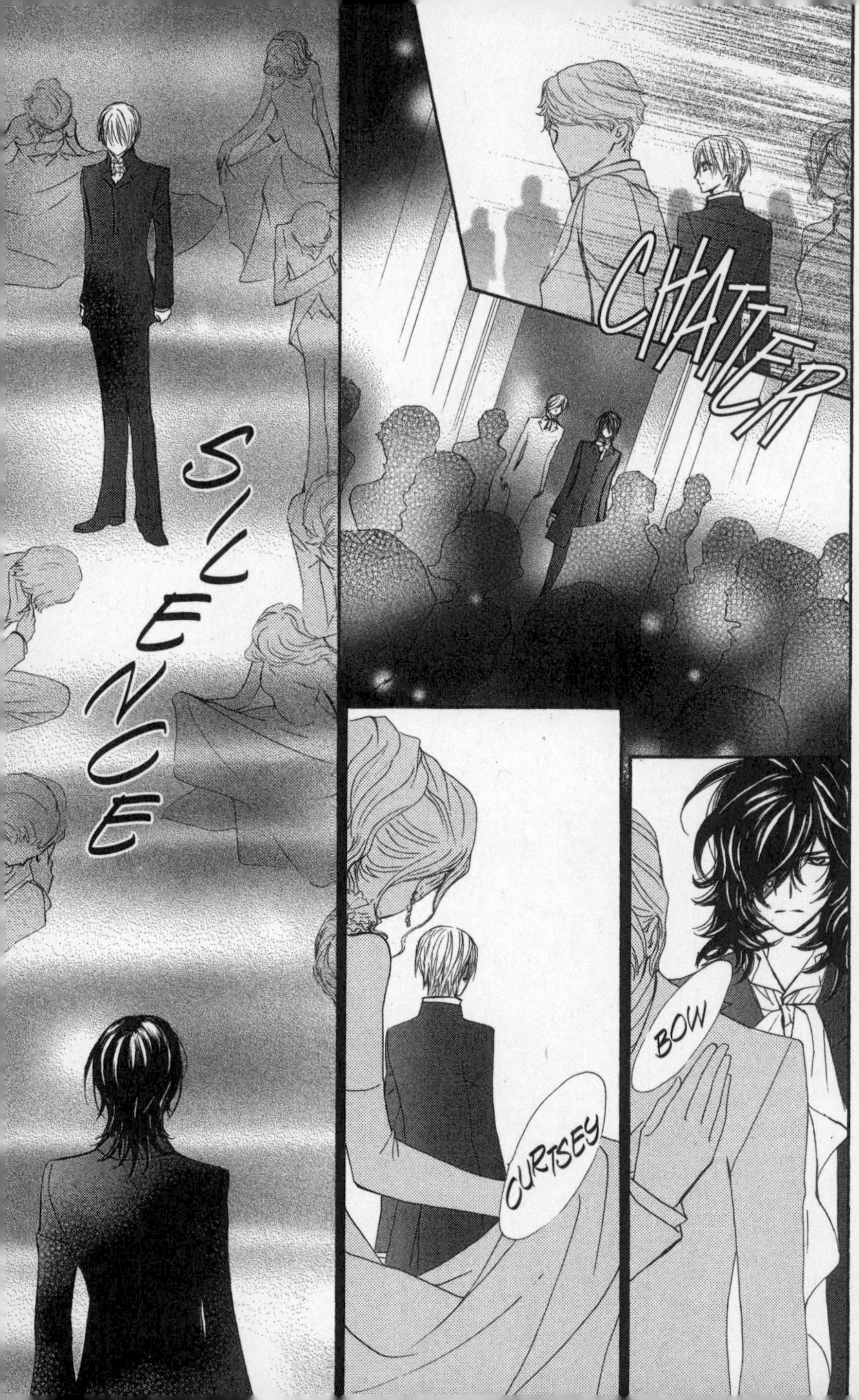
CHATTER
BOW
CURTSEY
SILENCE

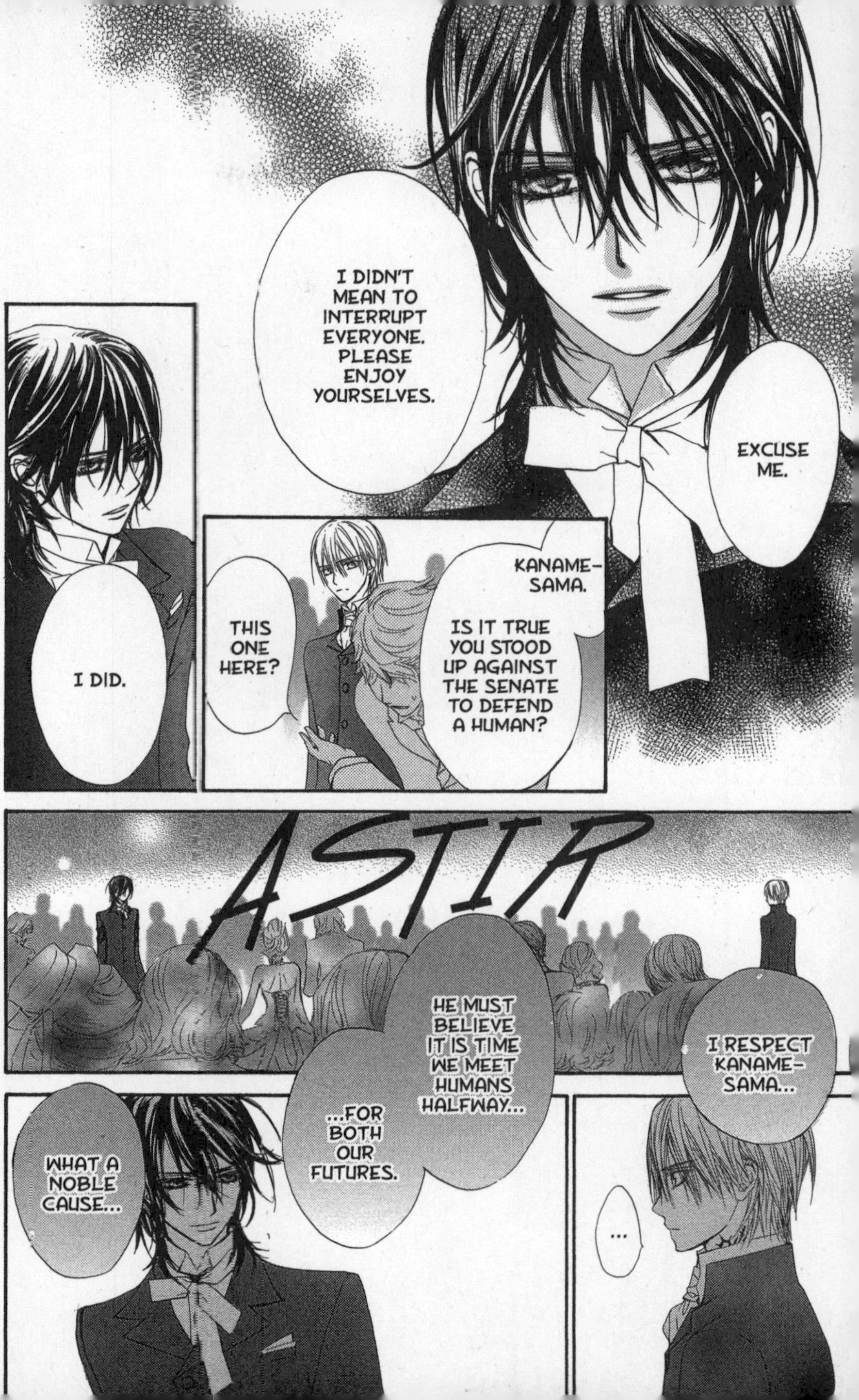
EXCUSE ME.
I DIDN'T MEAN TO INTERRUPT EVERYONE. PLEASE ENJOY YOURSELVES.
KANAME-SAMA.
IS IT TRUE YOU STOOD UP AGAINST THE SENATE TO DEFEND A HUMAN?
THIS ONE HERE?
I DID.
ASTIR
I RESPECT KANAME-SAMA...
HE MUST BELIEVE IT IS TIME WE MEET HUMANS HALFWAY...
...FOR BOTH OUR FUTURES.
...
WHAT A NOBLE CAUSE...

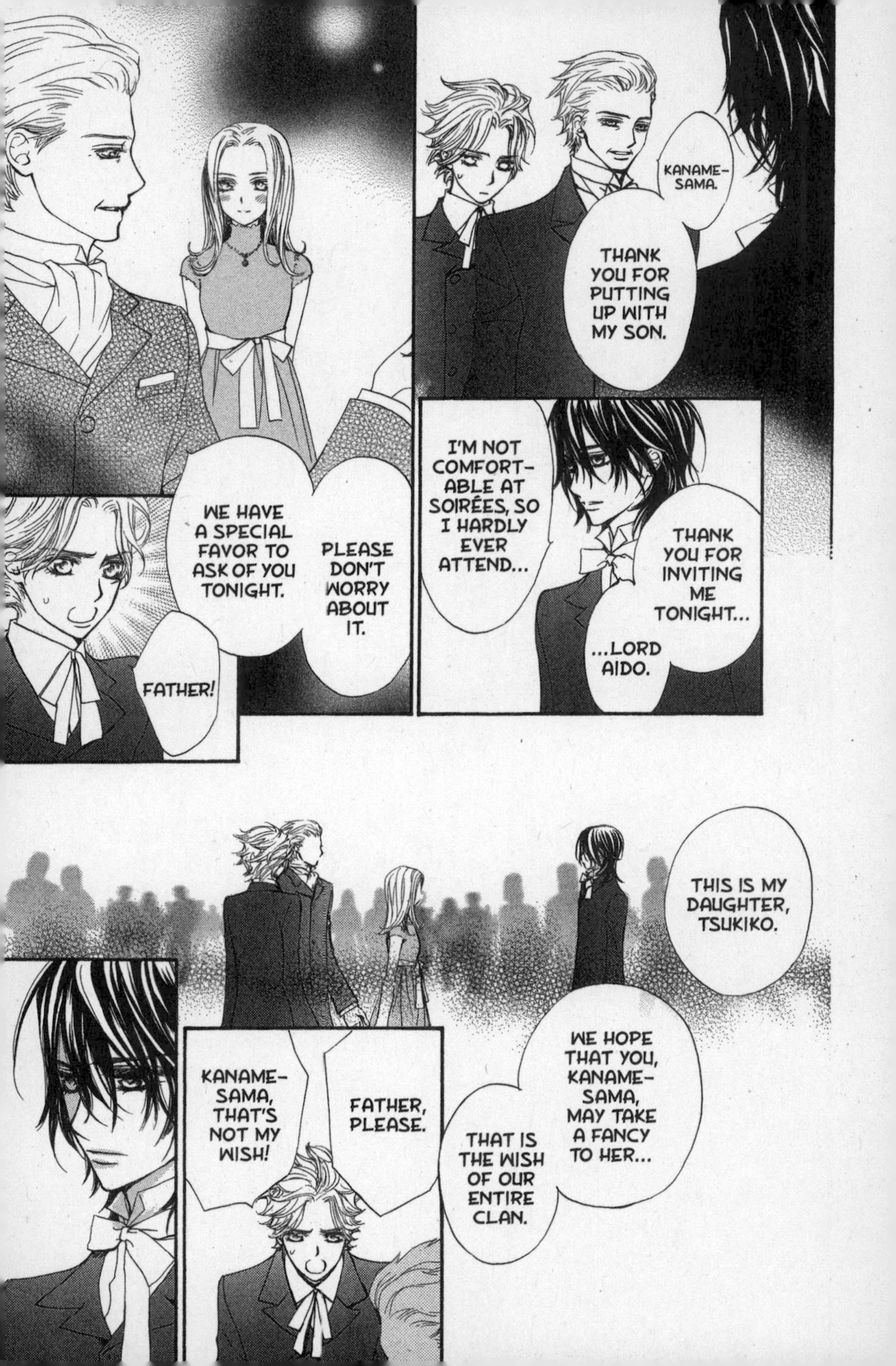
KANAME-SAMA.
THANK YOU FOR PUTTING UP WITH MY SON.
I'M NOT COMFORTABLE AT SOIRÉES, SO I HARDLY EVER ATTEND...
THANK YOU FOR INVITING ME TONIGHT...
...LORD AIDO.
PLEASE DON'T WORRY ABOUT IT.
WE HAVE A SPECIAL FAVOR TO ASK OF YOU TONIGHT.
FATHER!
THIS IS MY DAUGHTER, TSUKIKO.
WE HOPE THAT YOU, KANAME-SAMA, MAY TAKE A FANCY TO HER...
THAT IS THE WISH OF OUR ENTIRE CLAN.
FATHER, PLEASE.
KANAME-SAMA, THAT'S NOT MY WISH!

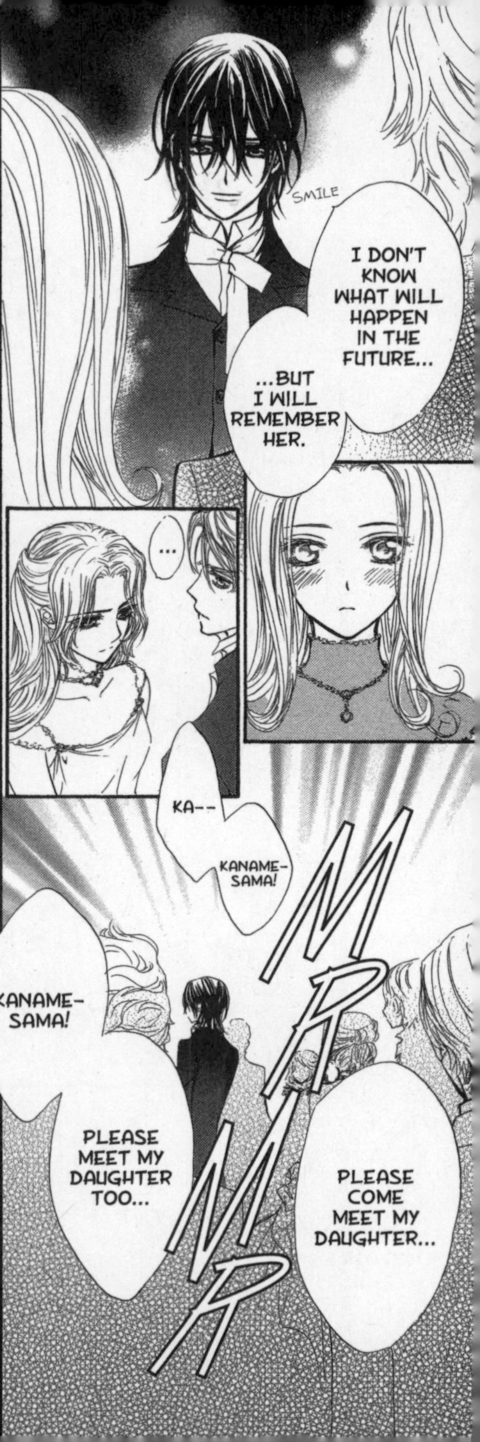
SMILE
I DON'T KNOW WHAT WILL HAPPEN IN THE FUTURE...
...BUT I WILL REMEMBER HER.
...
KA--
KANAME-SAMA!
MRMR
PLEASE COME MEET MY DAUGHTER...
KANAME-SAMA!
PLEASE MEET MY DAUGHTER TOO...
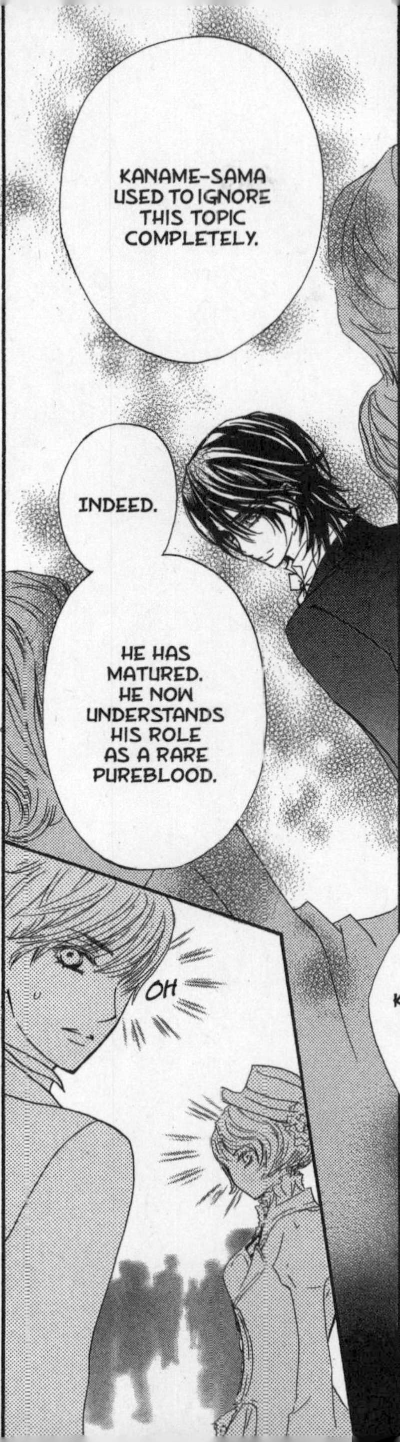
KANAME-SAMA USED TO IGNORE THIS TOPIC COMPLETELY.
INDEED.
HE HAS MATURED. HE NOW UNDERSTANDS HIS ROLE AS A RARE PUREBLOOD.
OH

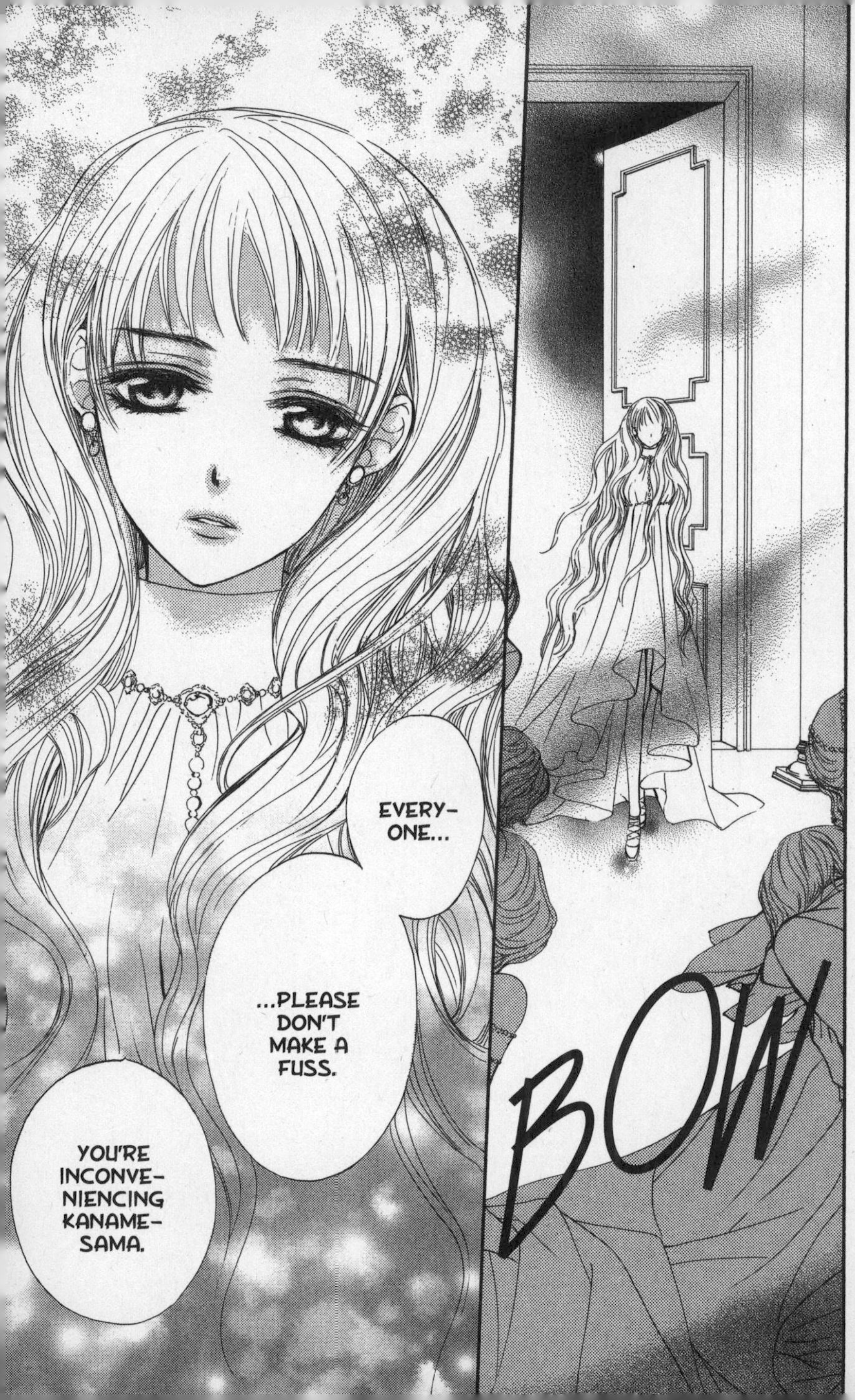
BOW
EVERYONE...
...PLEASE DON'T MAKE A FUSS.
YOU'RE INCONVENIENCING KANAME-SAMA.

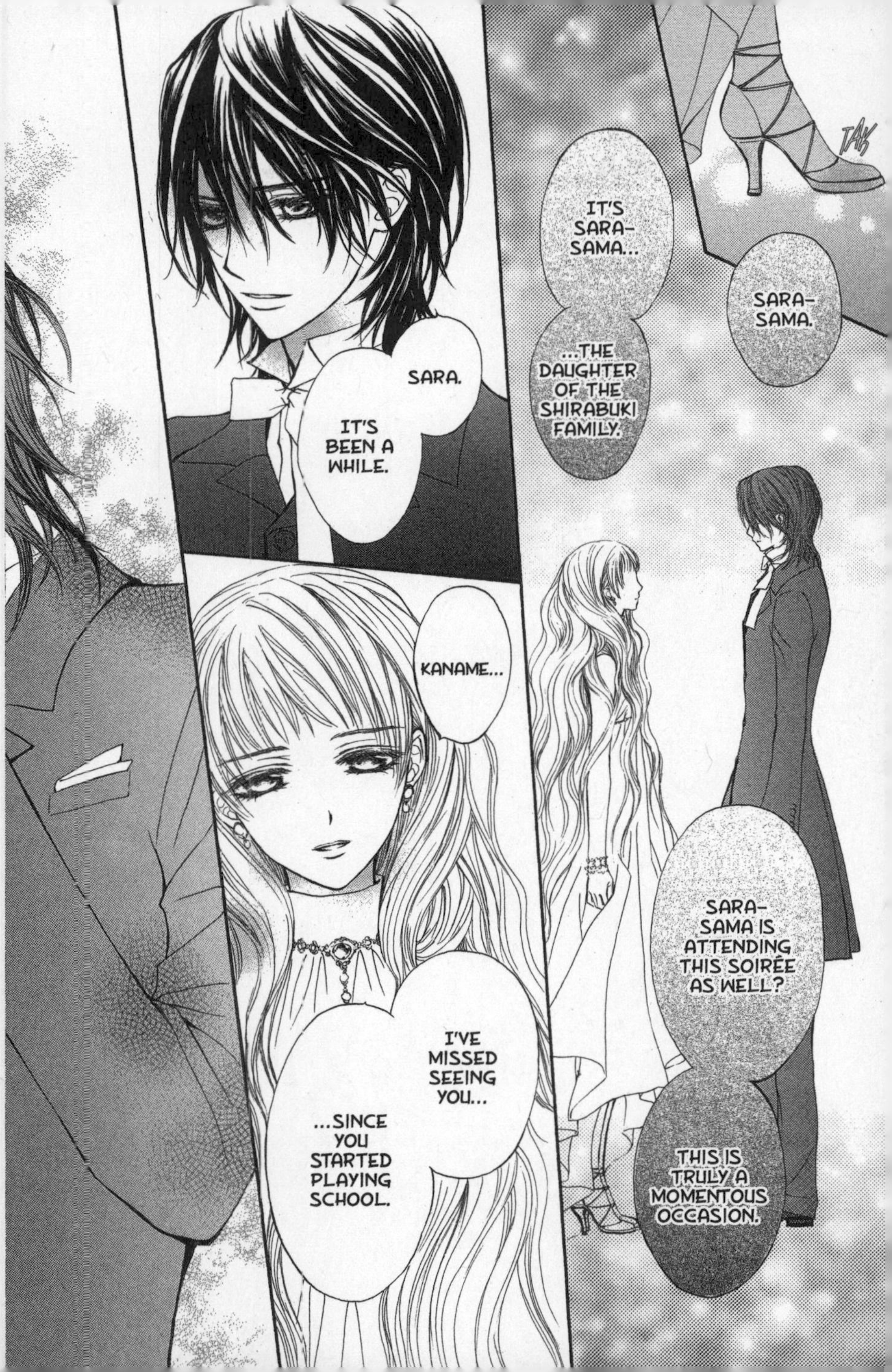
TAK
SARA-SAMA.
IT'S SARA-SAMA...
...THE DAUGHTER OF THE SHIRABUKI FAMILY.
SARA-SAMA IS ATTENDING THIS SOIRÉE AS WELL?
THIS IS TRULY A MOMENTOUS OCCASION.
SARA.
IT'S BEEN A WHILE.
KANAME...
I'VE MISSED SEEING YOU...
...SINCE YOU STARTED PLAYING SCHOOL.

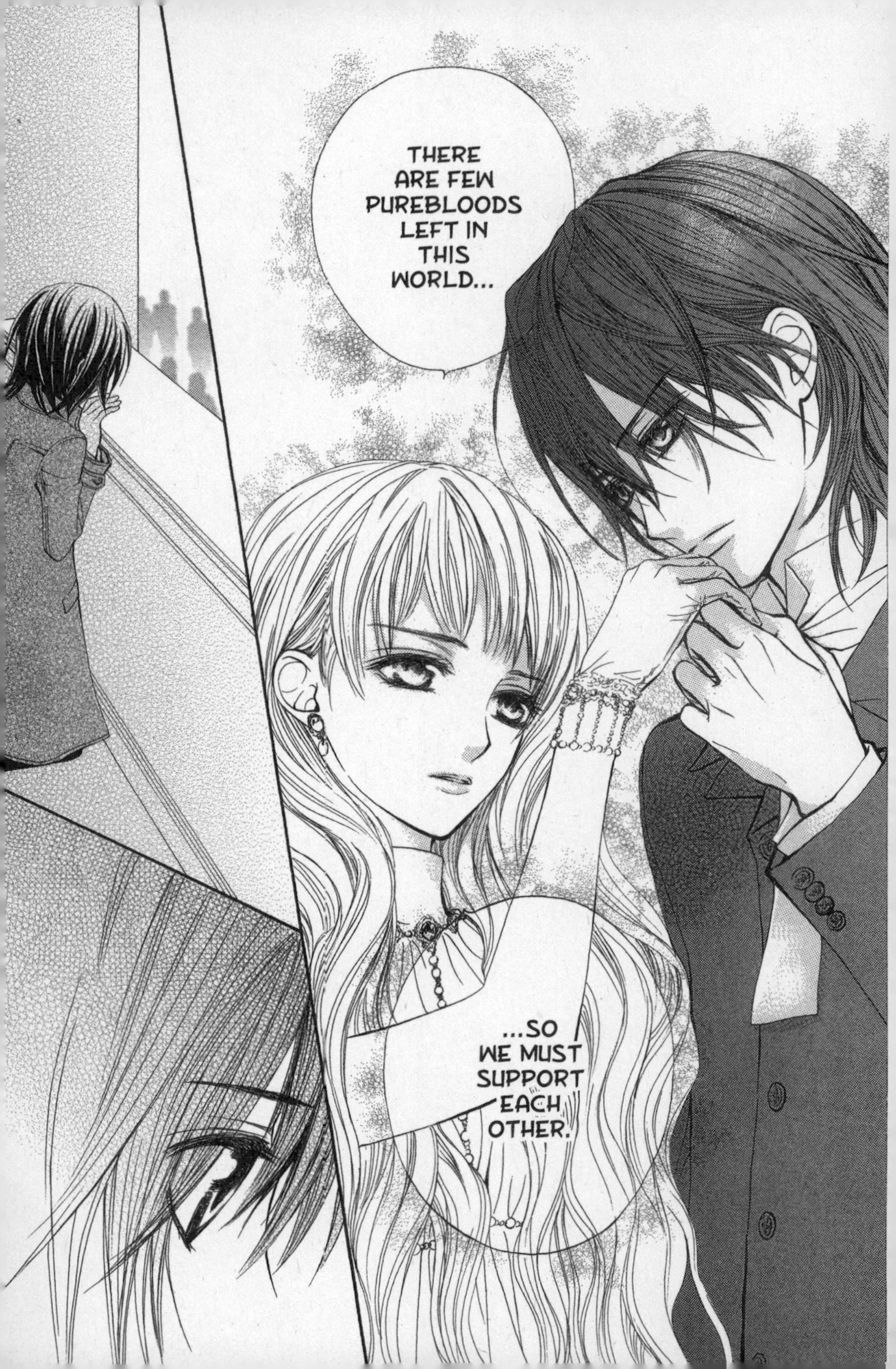
THERE ARE FEW PUREBLOODS LEFT IN THIS WORLD...
...SO WE MUST SUPPORT EACH OTHER.

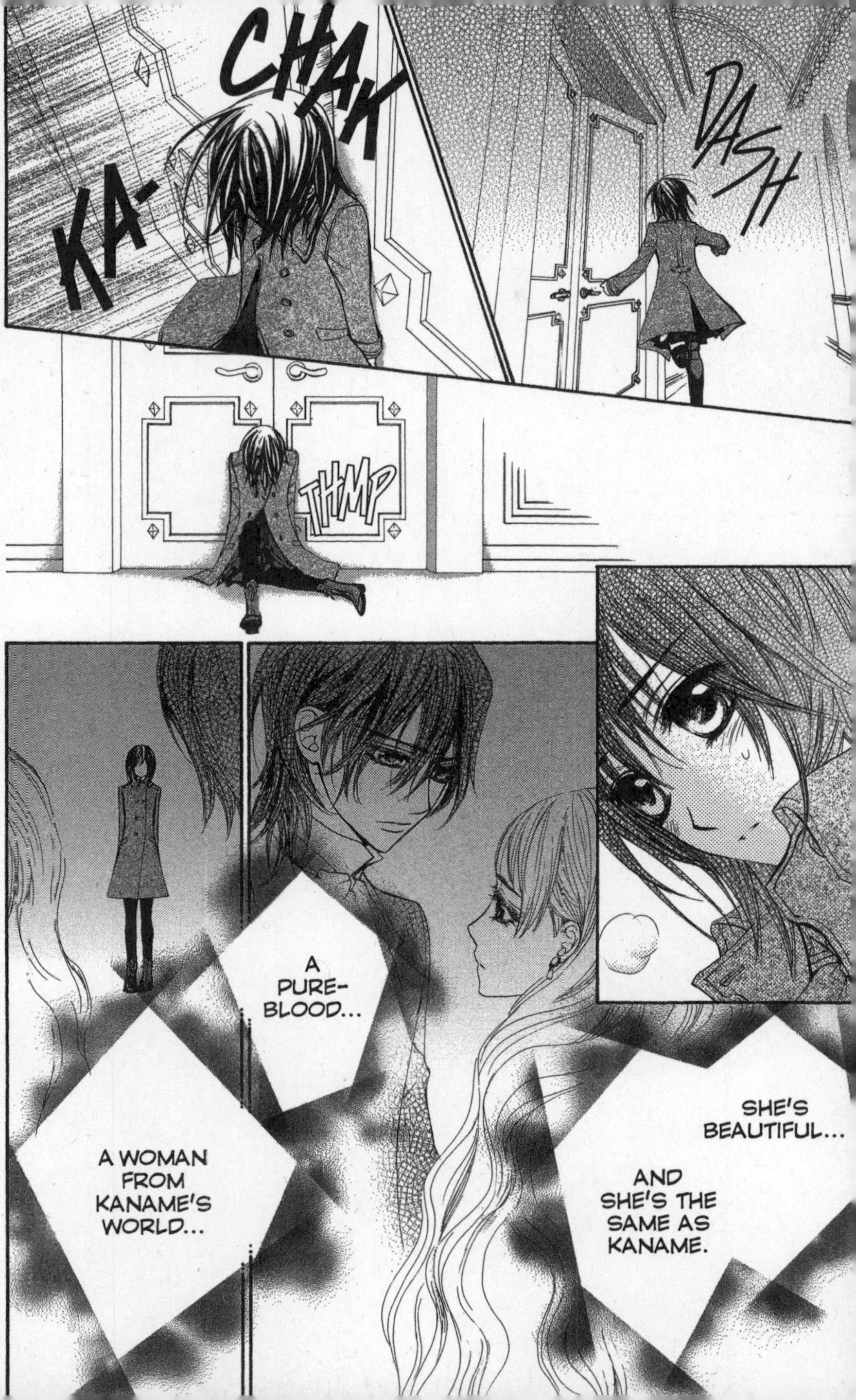
DASH
KA-CHAK
THMP
A PURE-BLOOD...
SHE'S BEAUTIFUL...
AND SHE'S THE SAME AS KANAME.
A WOMAN FROM KANAME'S WORLD...

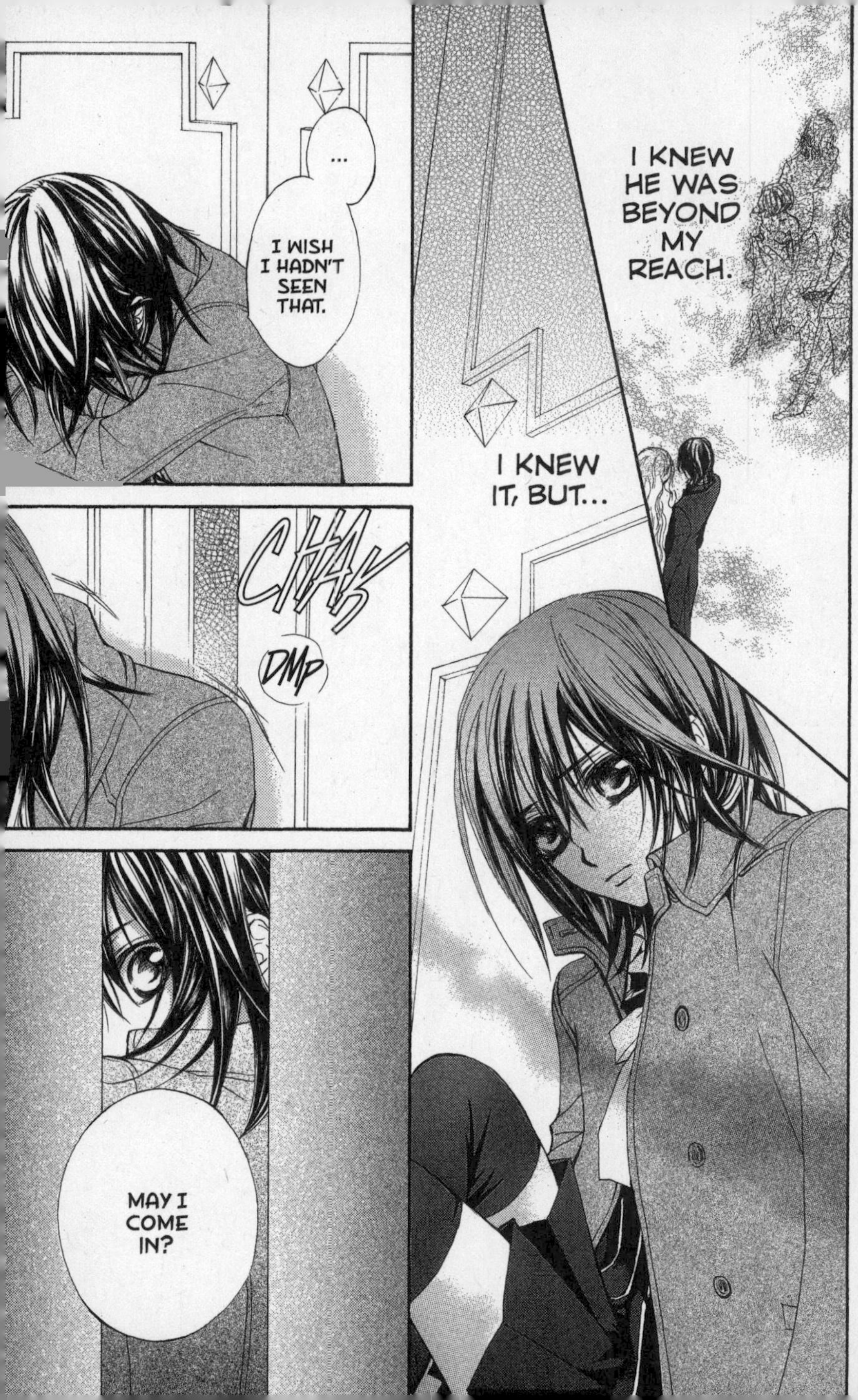
I KNEW HE WAS BEYOND MY REACH.
I KNEW IT, BUT...
...
I WISH I HADN'T SEEN THAT.
CHAK
DMP
MAY I COME IN?

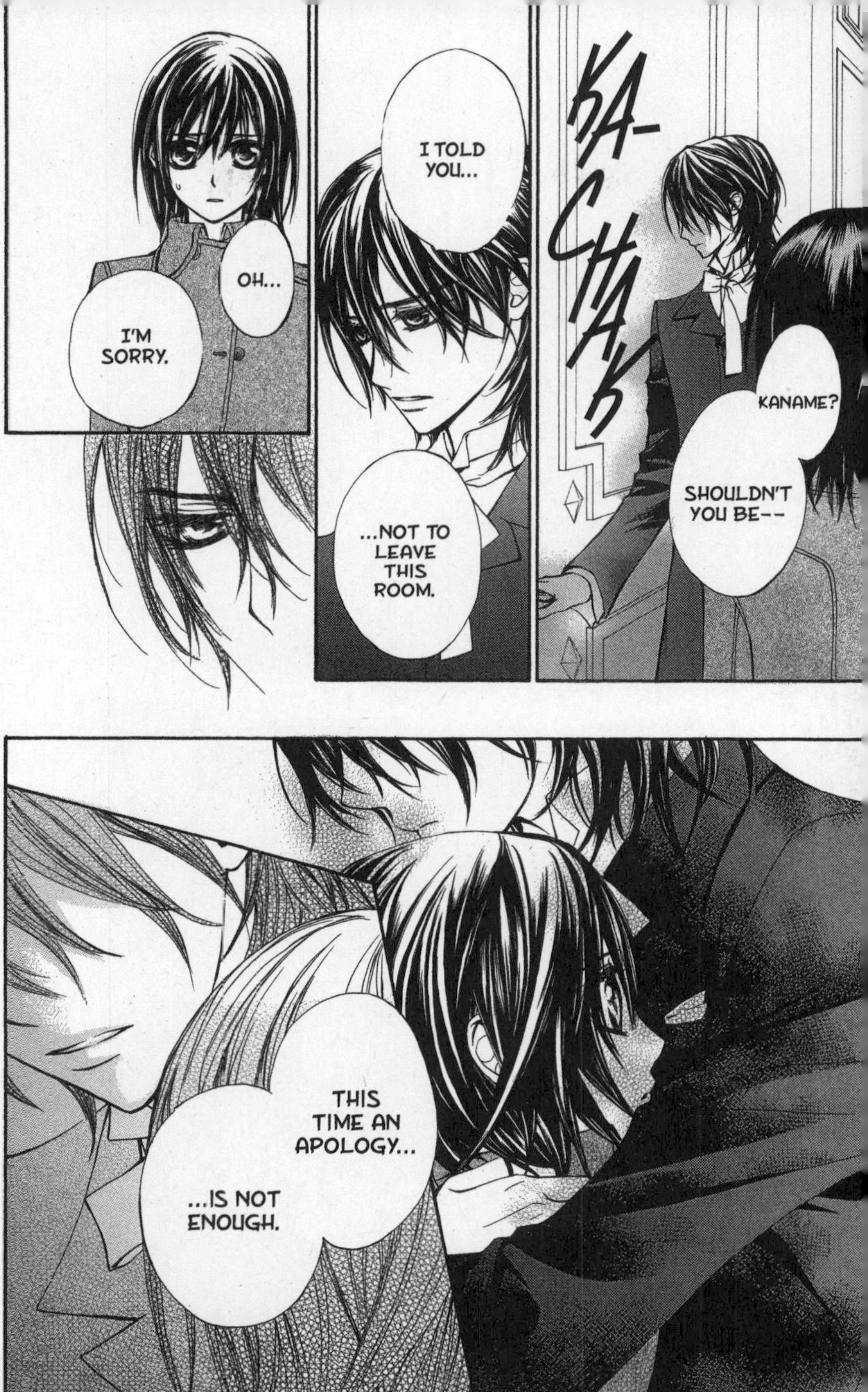
KA-CHAK
KANAME?
SHOULDN'T YOU BE--
I TOLD YOU...
...NOT TO LEAVE THIS ROOM.
OH...
I'M SORRY.
THIS TIME AN APOLOGY...
...IS NOT ENOUGH.

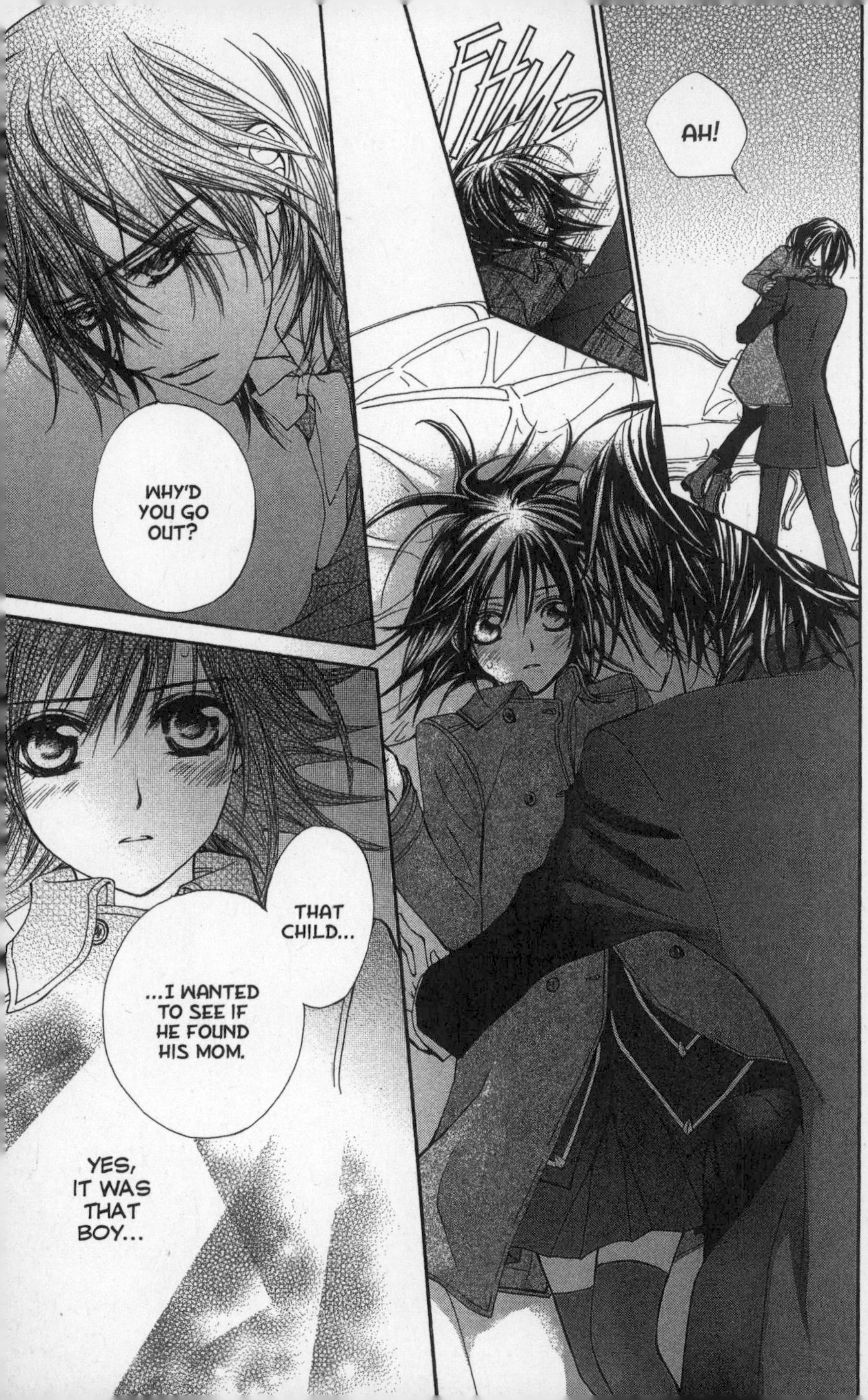
AH!
FHWD
WHY'D YOU GO OUT?
THAT CHILD...
...I WANTED TO SEE IF HE FOUND HIS MOM.
YES, IT WAS THAT BOY...

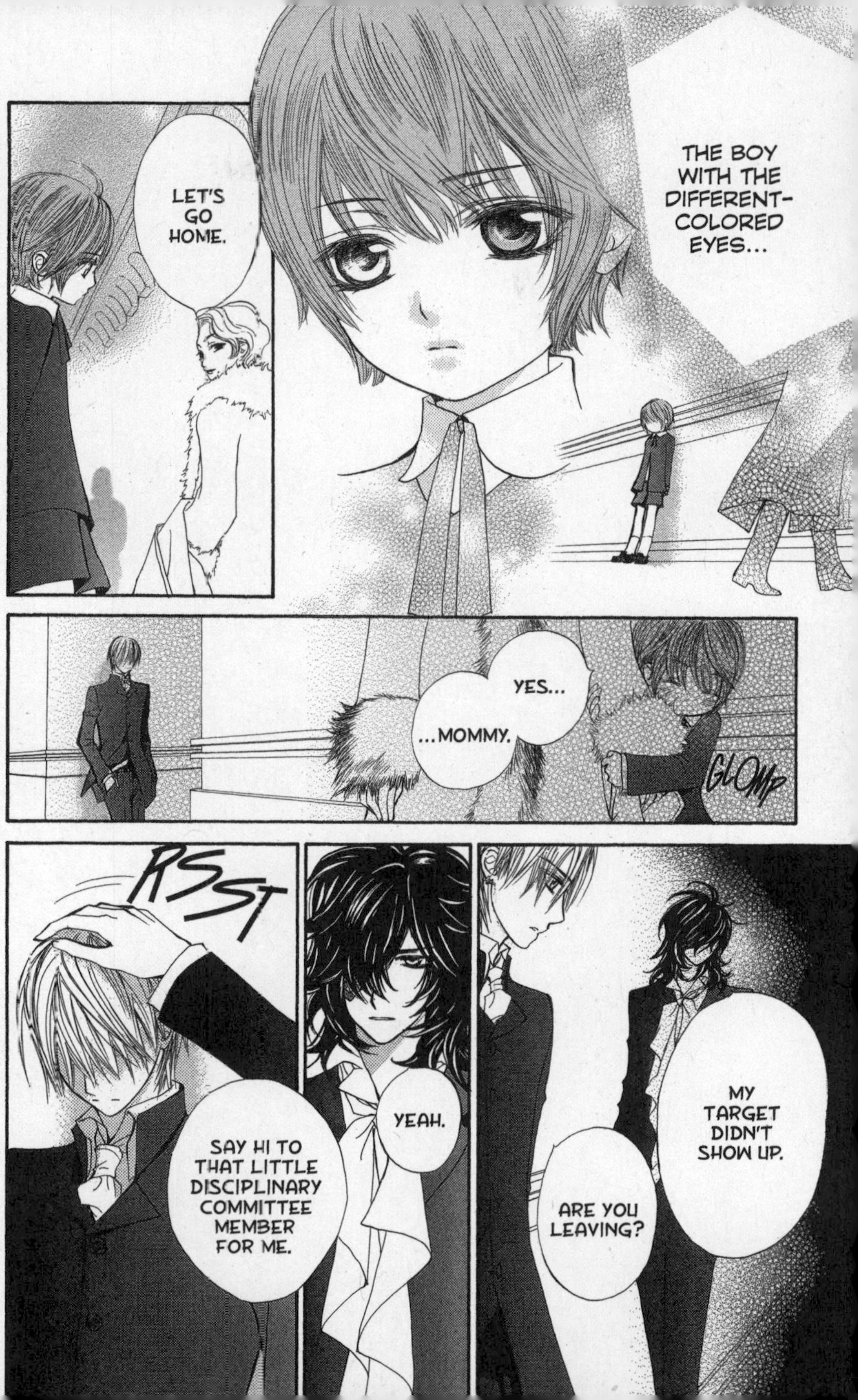
THE BOY WITH THE DIFFERENT-COLORED EYES...
LET'S GO HOME.
YES...
...MOMMY.
GLOMP
MY TARGET DIDN'T SHOW UP.
ARE YOU LEAVING?
YEAH.
RSST
SAY HI TO THAT LITTLE DISCIPLINARY COMMITTEE MEMBER FOR ME.

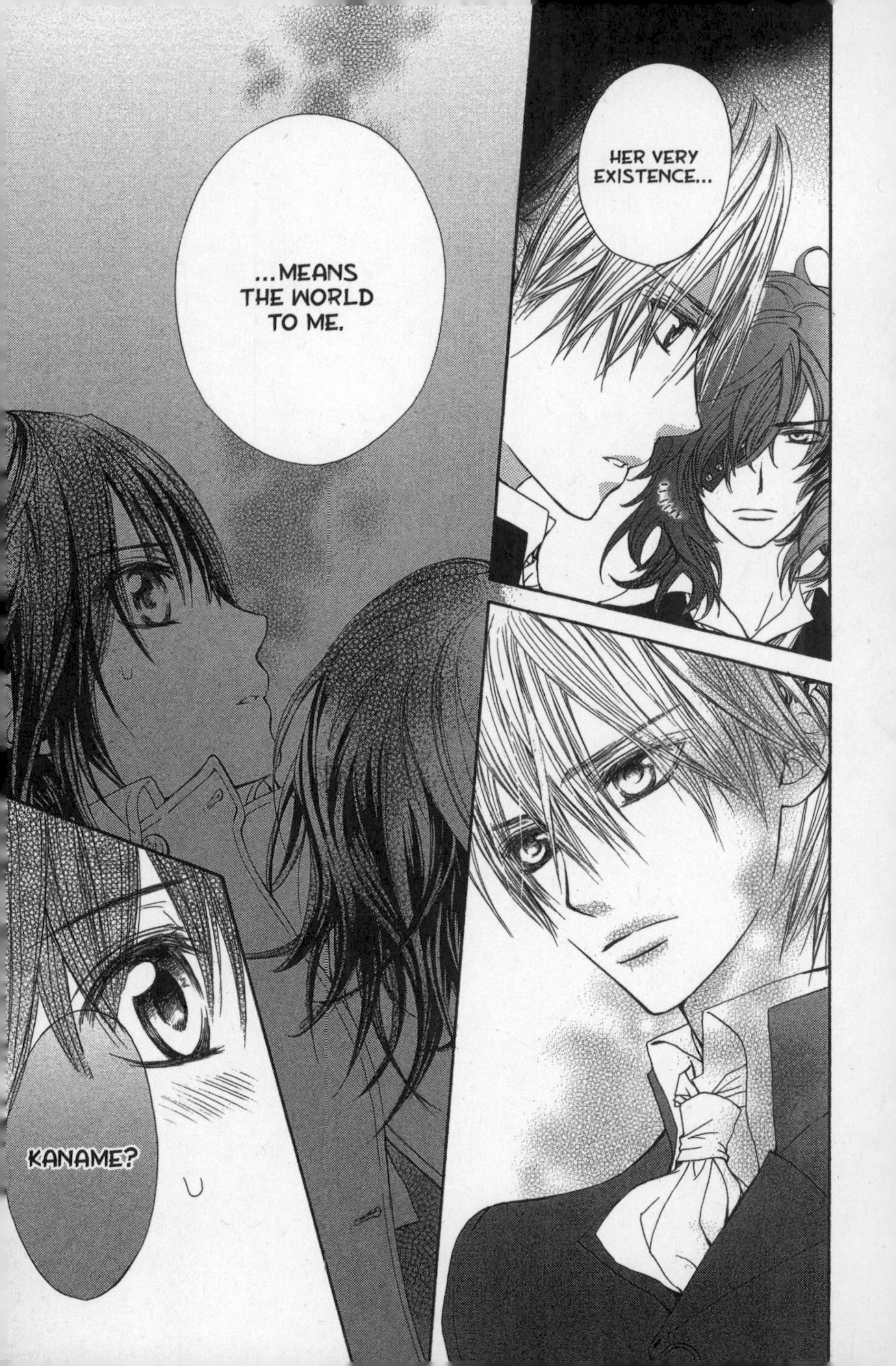
HER VERY EXISTENCE...
...MEANS THE WORLD TO ME.
KANAME?

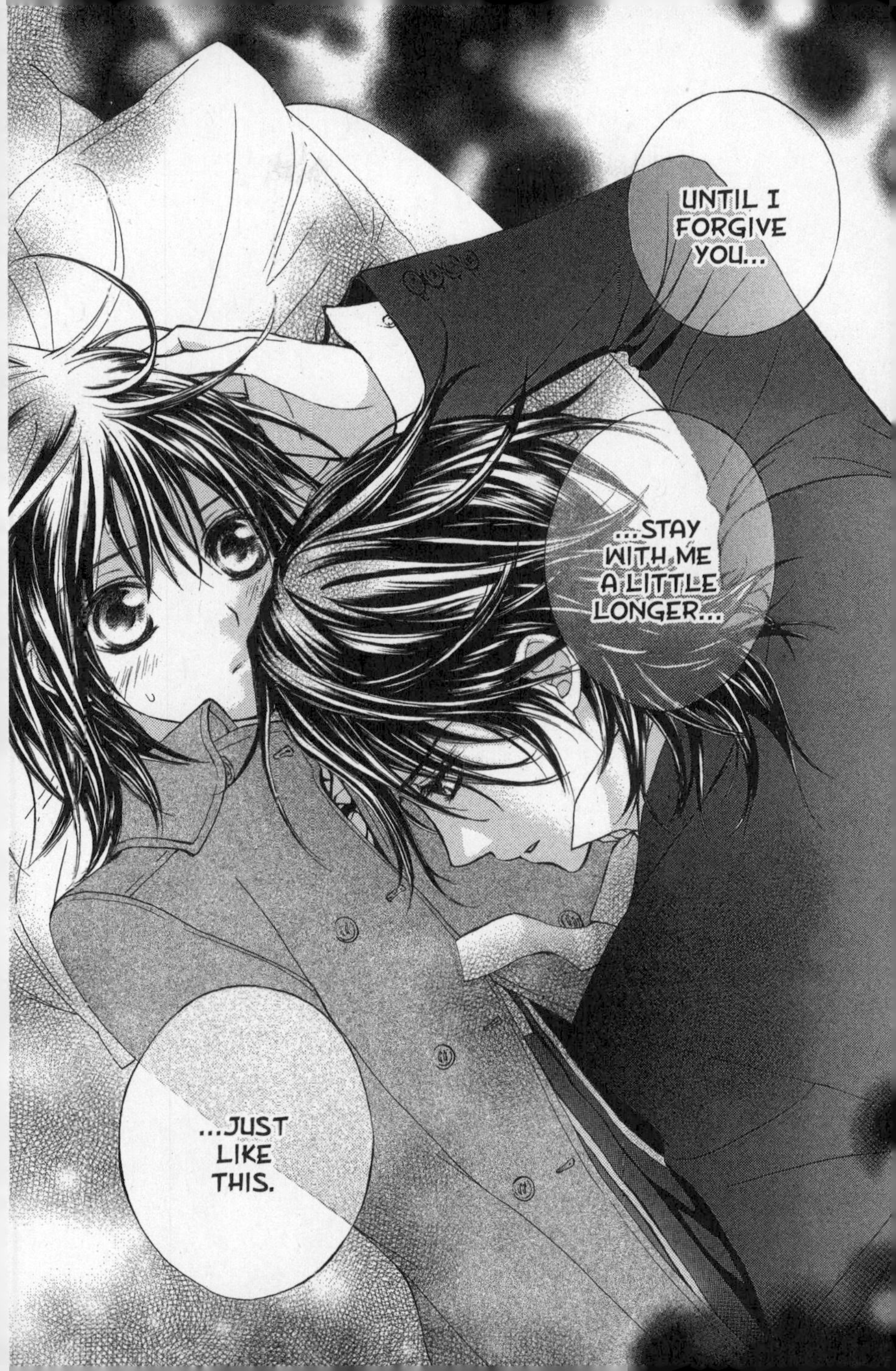
UNTIL I FORGIVE YOU...
...STAY WITH ME A LITTLE LONGER...
...JUST LIKE THIS.

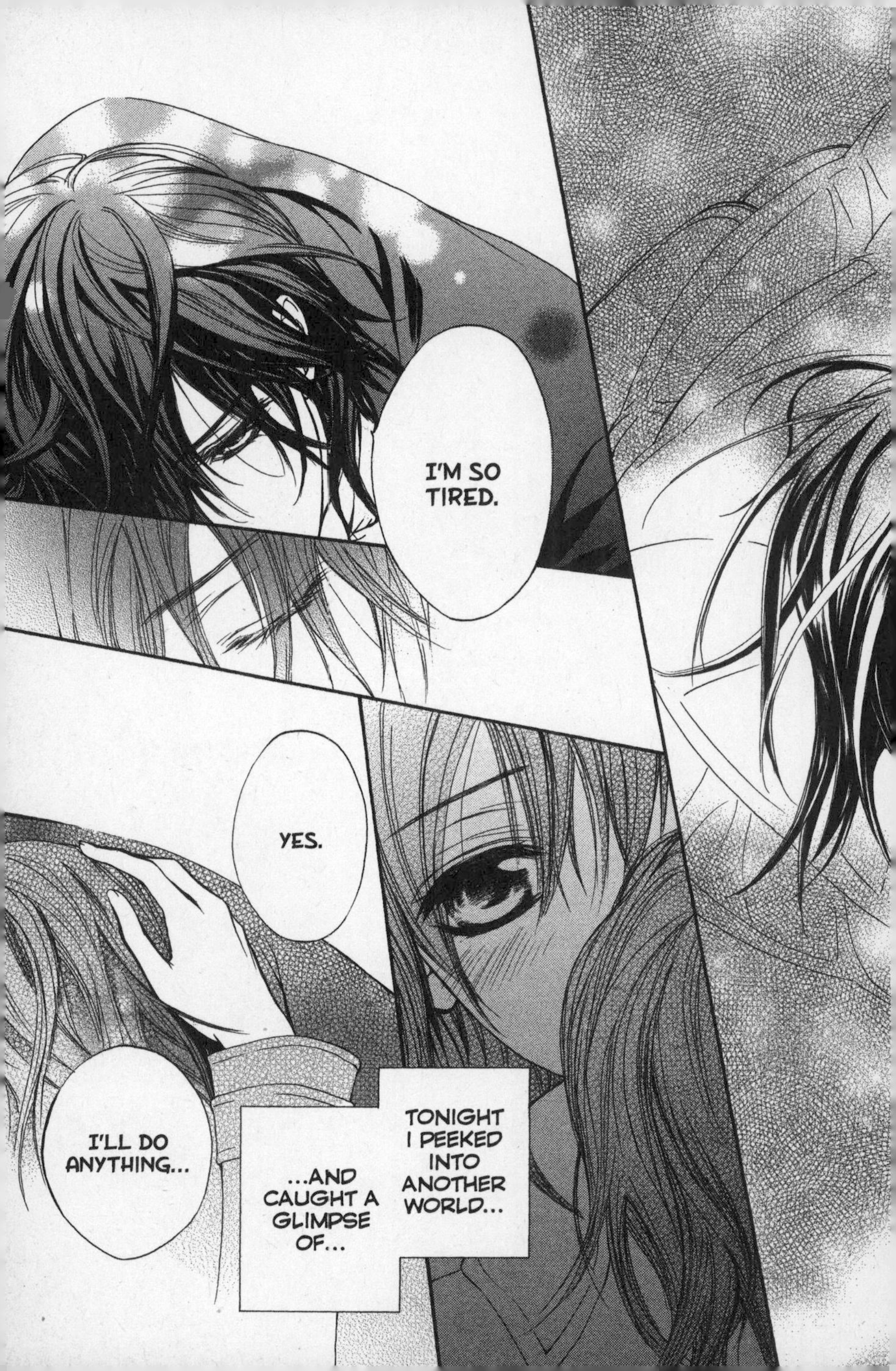
I'M SO TIRED.
YES.
TONIGHT I PEEKED INTO ANOTHER WORLD...
...AND CAUGHT A GLIMPSE OF...
I'LL DO ANYTHING...

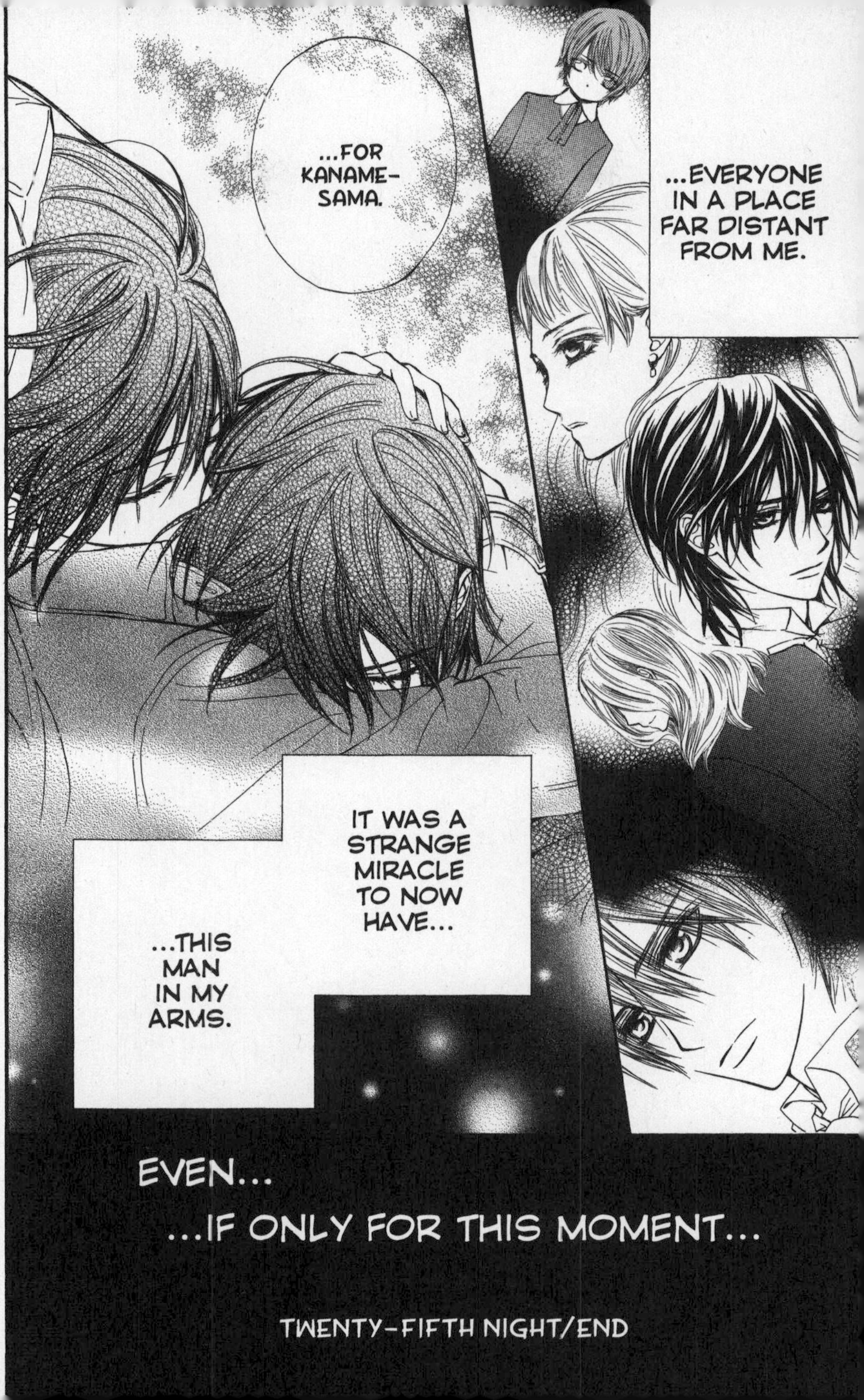
...EVERYONE IN A PLACE FAR DISTANT FROM ME.
...FOR KANAME-SAMA.
IT WAS A STRANGE MIRACLE TO NOW HAVE...
...THIS MAN IN MY ARMS.
EVEN...
...IF ONLY FOR THIS MOMENT...
TWENTY-FIFTH NIGHT/END

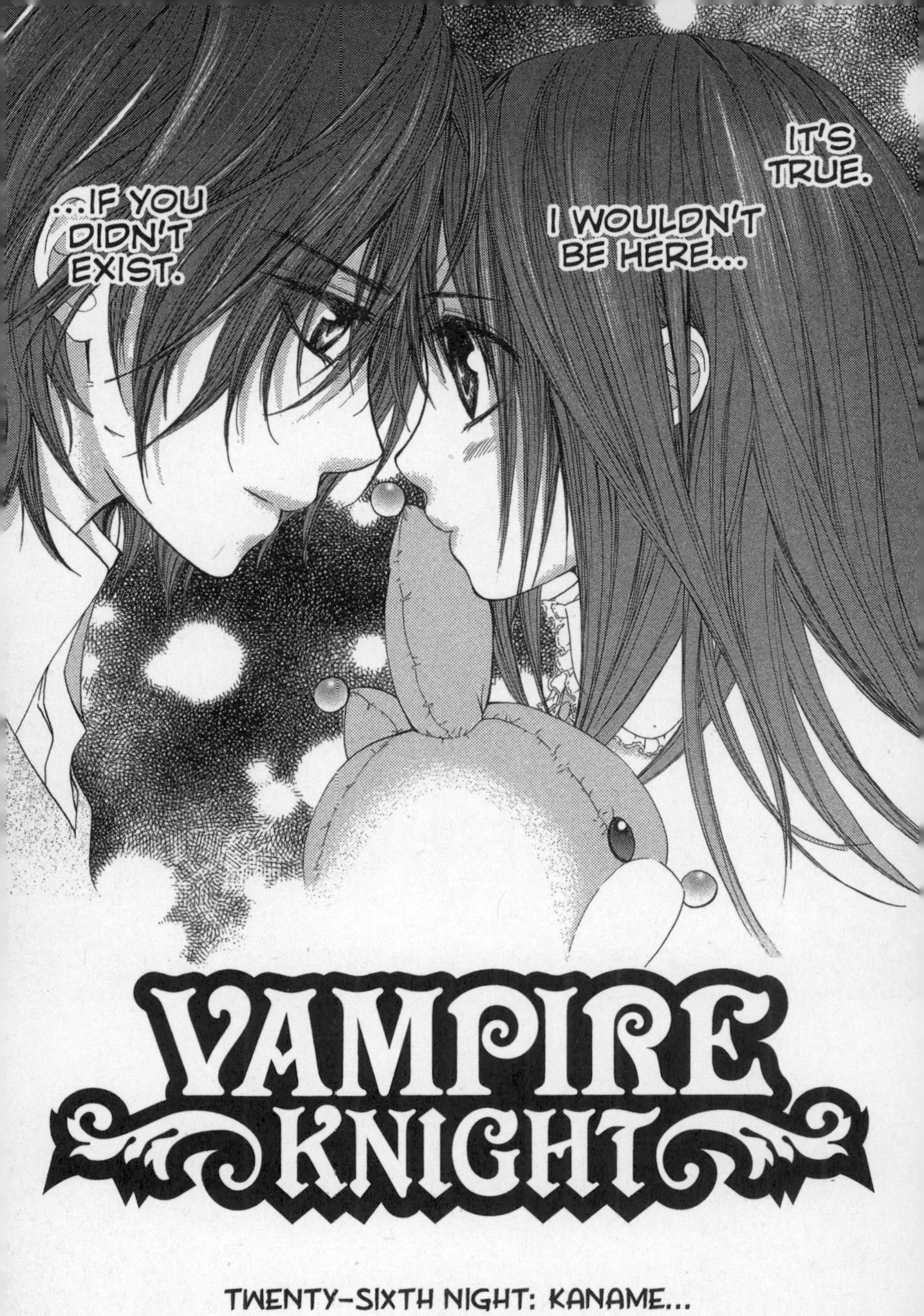
IT'S TRUE.
I WOULDN'T BE HERE...
...IF YOU DIDN'T EXIST.

VAMPIRE KNIGHT

TWENTY-SIXTH NIGHT: KANAME...

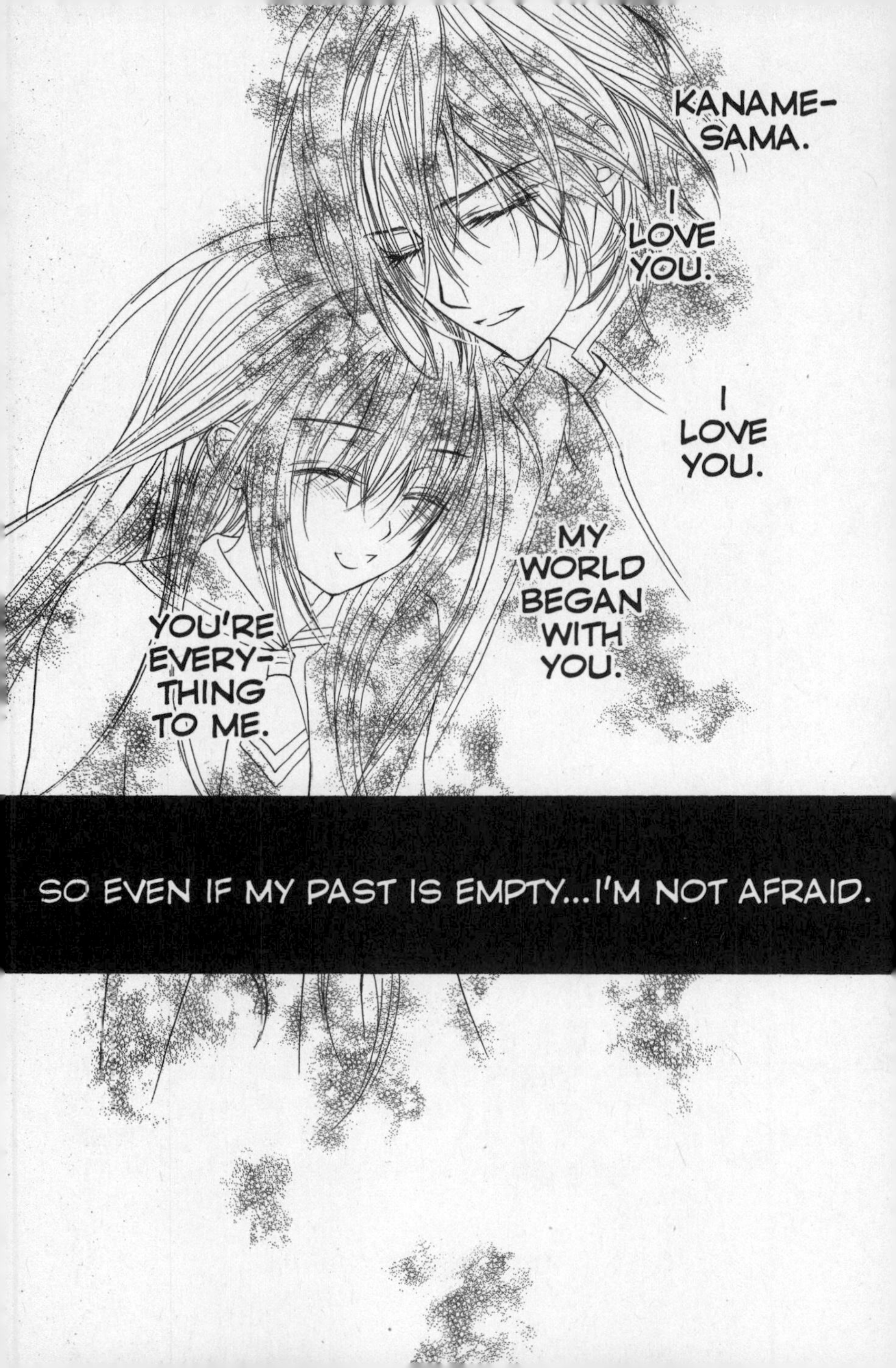
KANAME-SAMA.
I LOVE YOU.
I LOVE YOU.
MY WORLD BEGAN WITH YOU.
YOU'RE EVERYTHING TO ME.
SO EVEN IF MY PAST IS EMPTY...I'M NOT AFRAID.

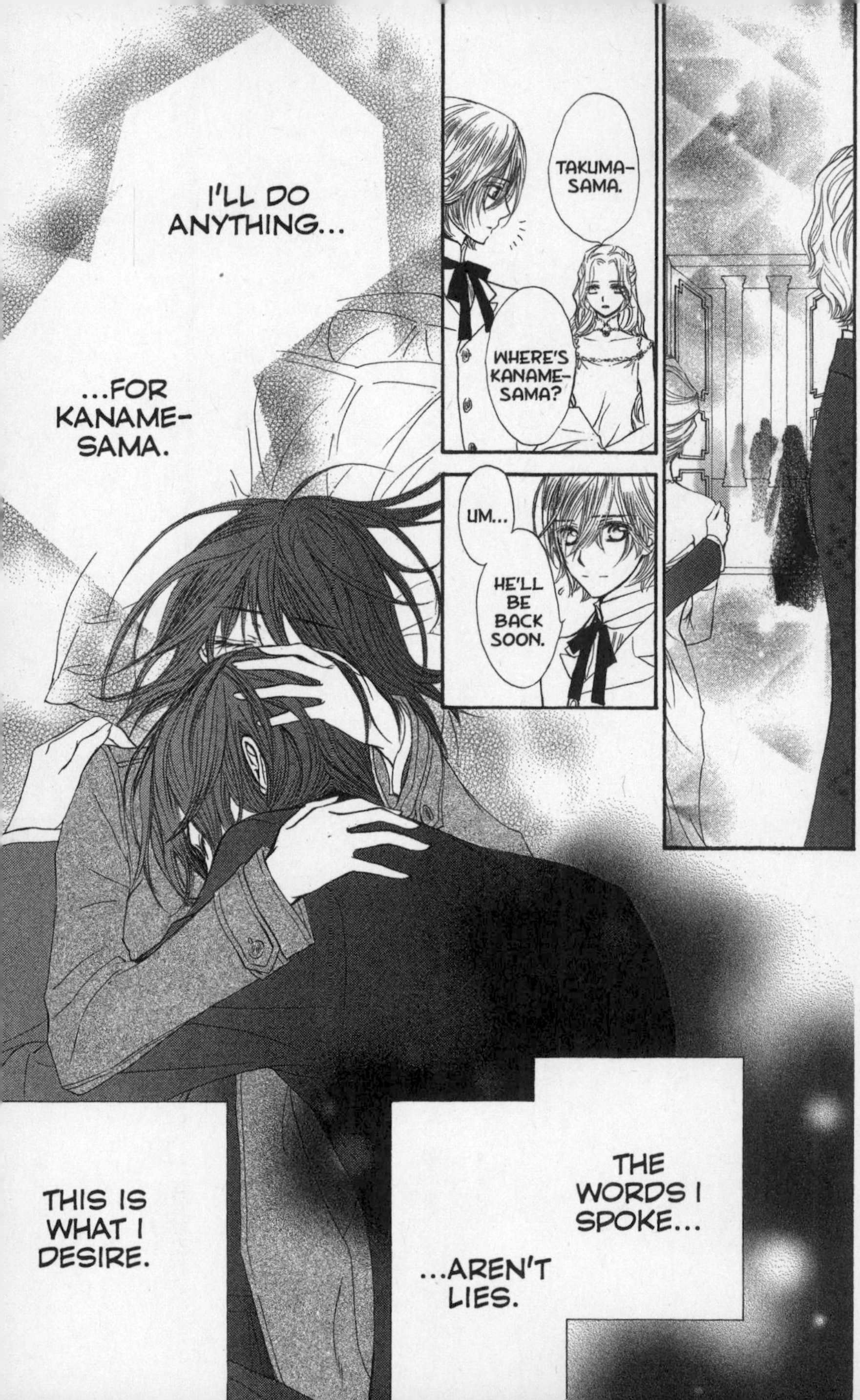
TAKUMA-SAMA.
WHERE'S KANAME-SAMA?
UM...
HE'LL BE BACK SOON.
I'LL DO ANYTHING...
...FOR KANAME-SAMA.
THE WORDS I SPOKE...
...AREN'T LIES.
THIS IS WHAT I DESIRE.

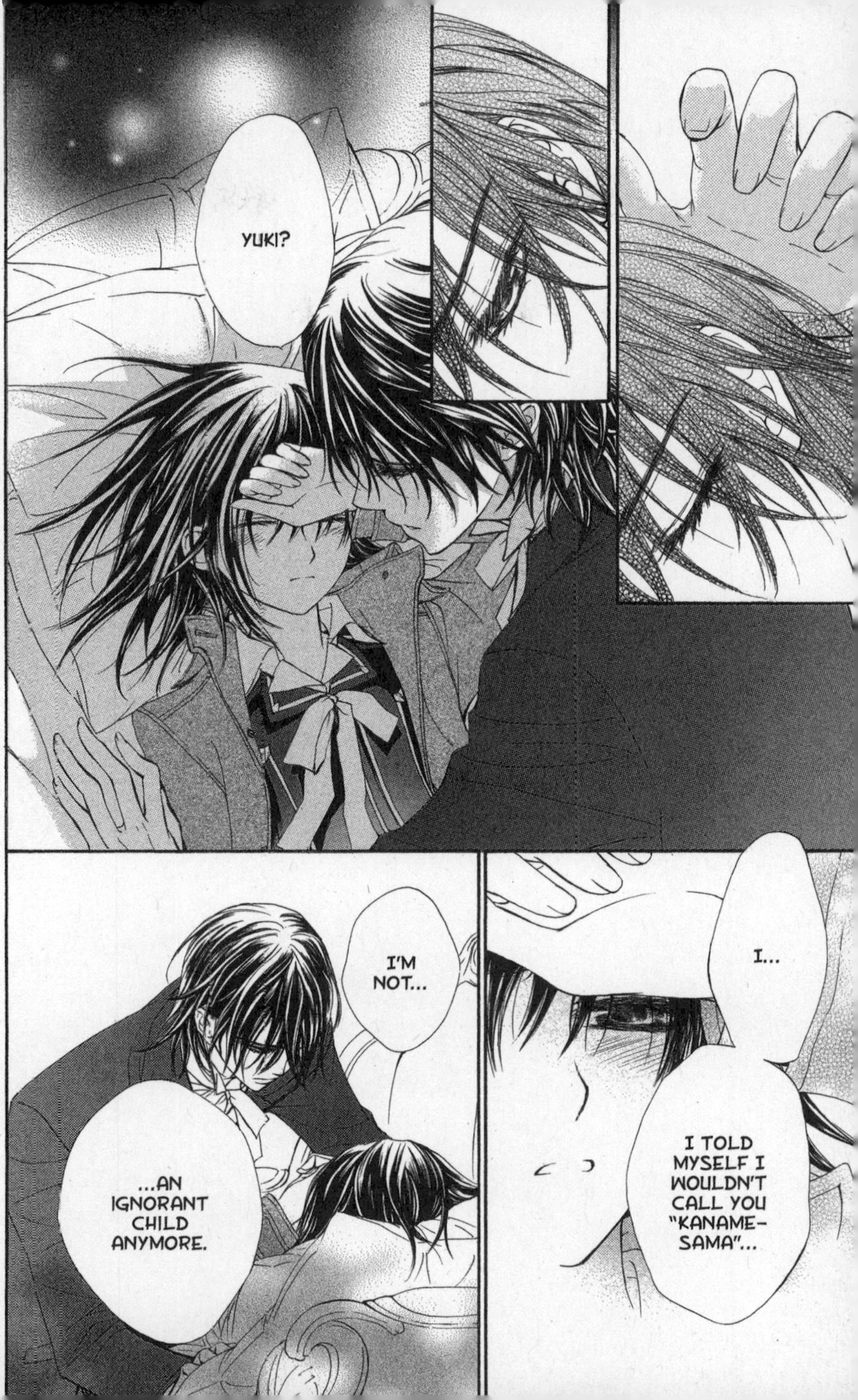
YUKI?
I...
I TOLD MYSELF I WOULDN'T CALL YOU "KANAME-SAMA"...
I'M NOT...
...AN IGNORANT CHILD ANYMORE.

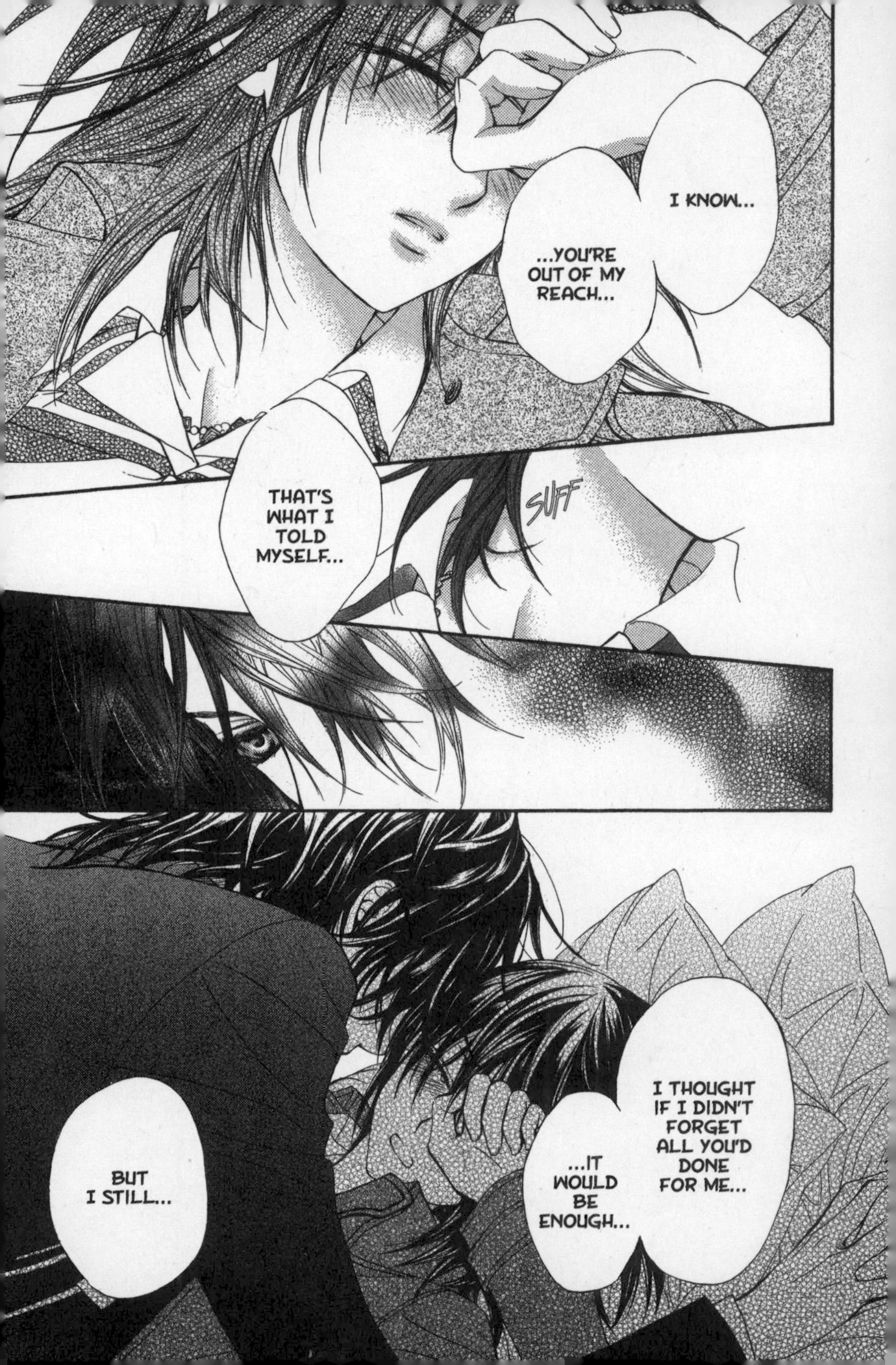
I KNOW...
...YOU'RE OUT OF MY REACH...
THAT'S WHAT I TOLD MYSELF...
SUFF
I THOUGHT IF I DIDN'T FORGET ALL YOU'D DONE FOR ME...
...IT WOULD BE ENOUGH...
BUT I STILL...

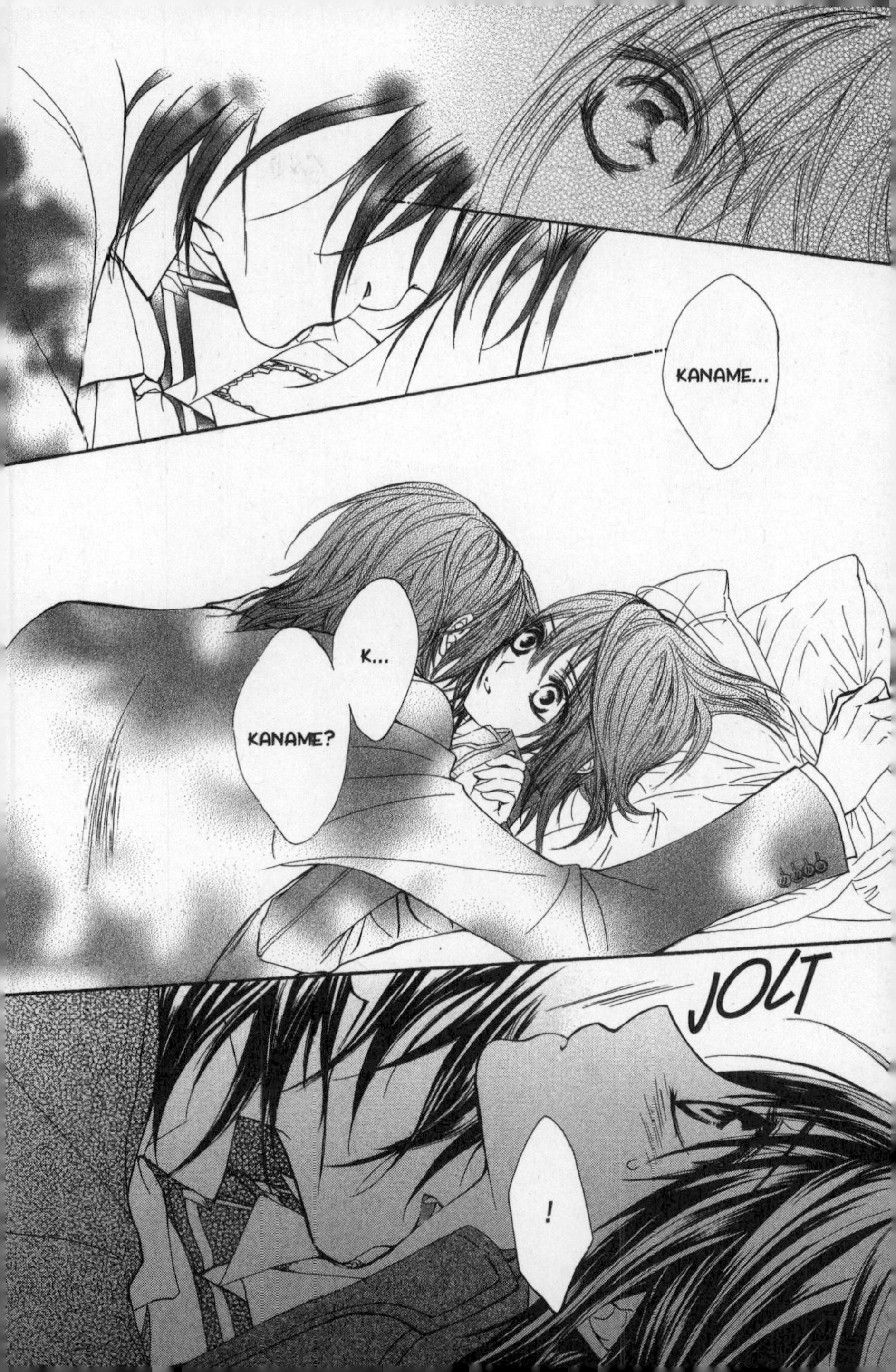
KANAME...
K...
KANAME?
JOLT
!

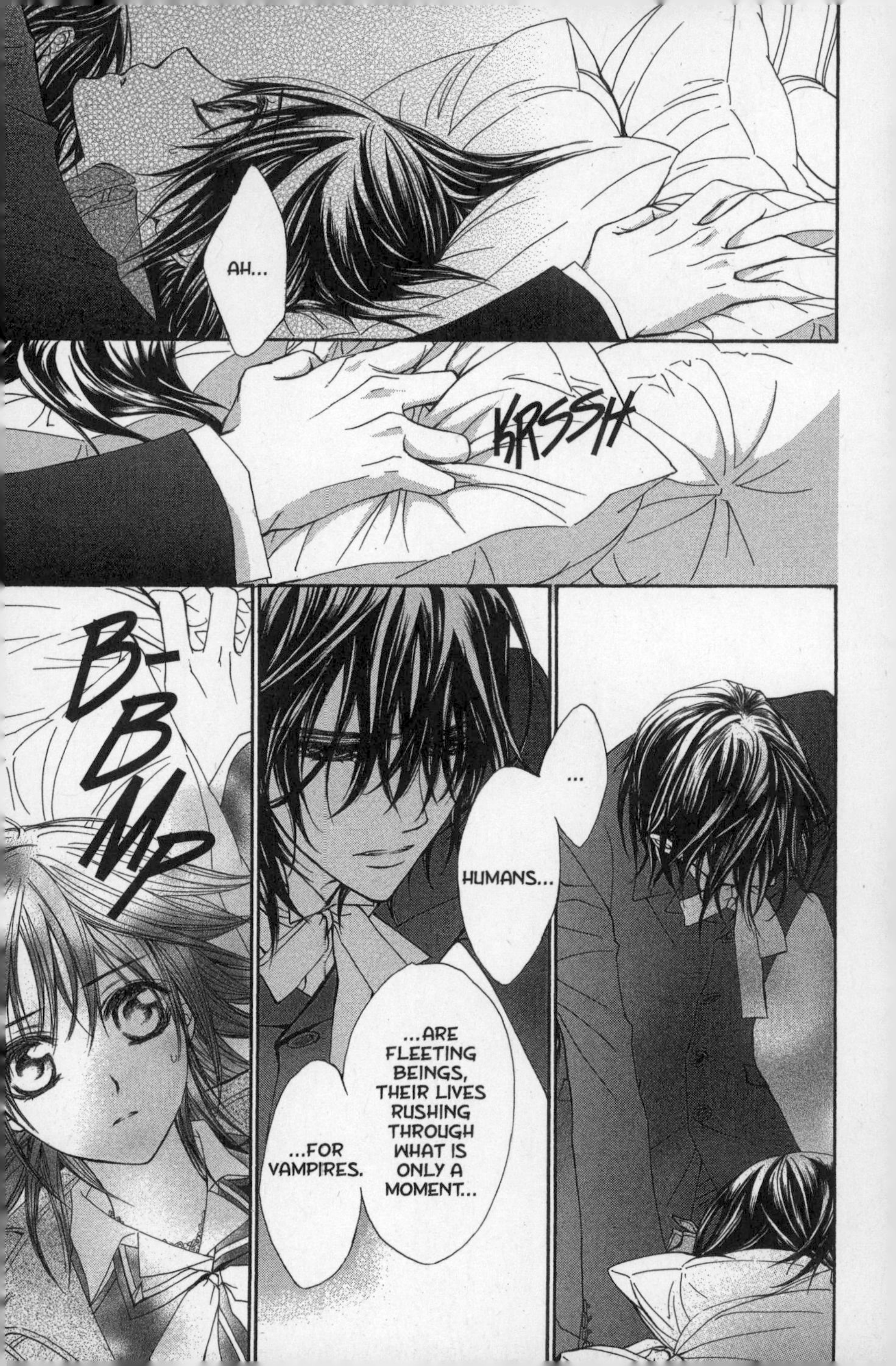
AH...
KRSSH
...
HUMANS...
...ARE FLEETING BEINGS, THEIR LIVES RUSHING THROUGH WHAT IS ONLY A MOMENT...
...FOR VAMPIRES.
B-BMP

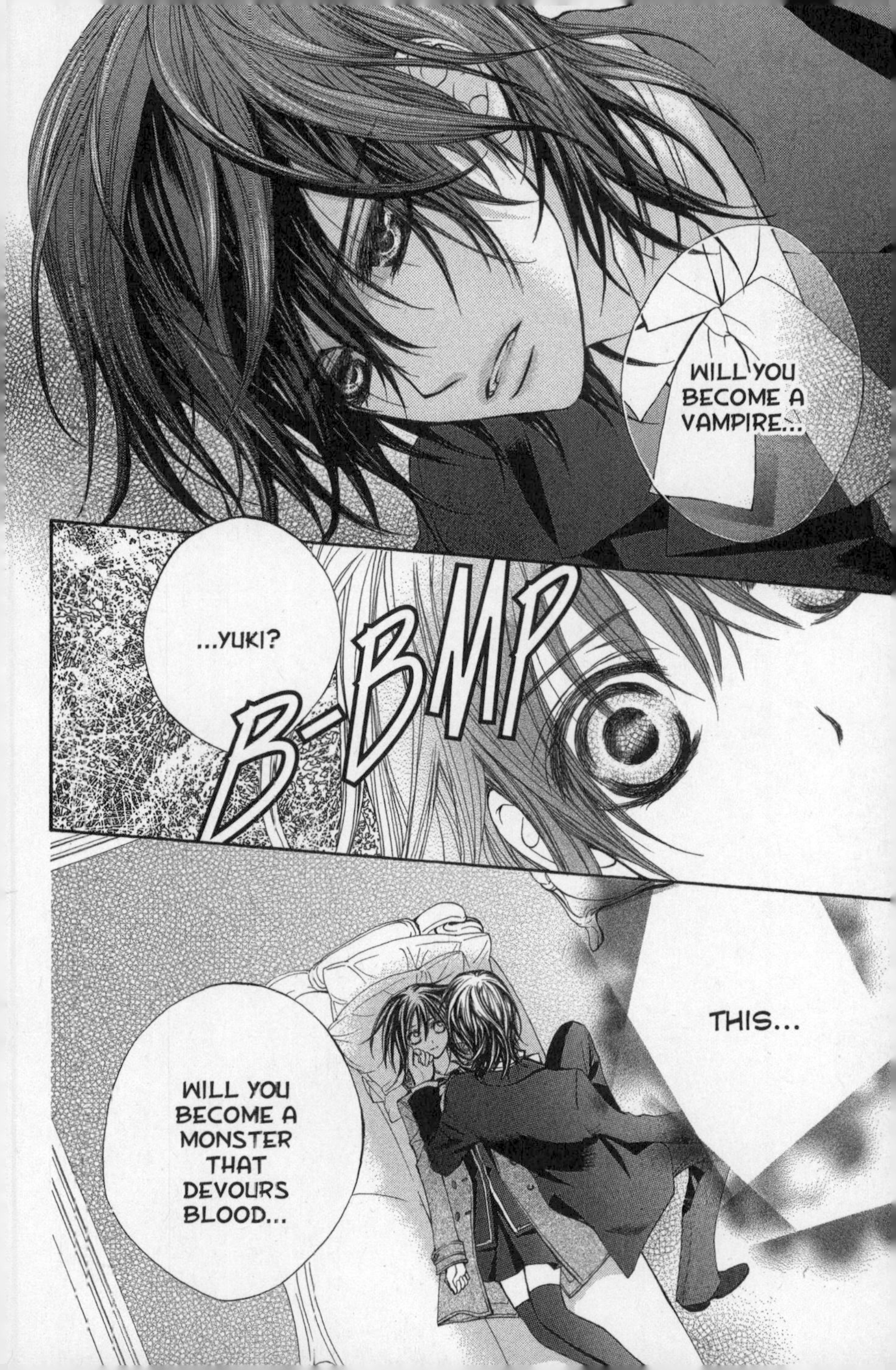
WILL YOU BECOME A VAMPIRE...
B-BMP
...YUKI?
THIS...
WILL YOU BECOME A MONSTER THAT DEVOURS BLOOD...

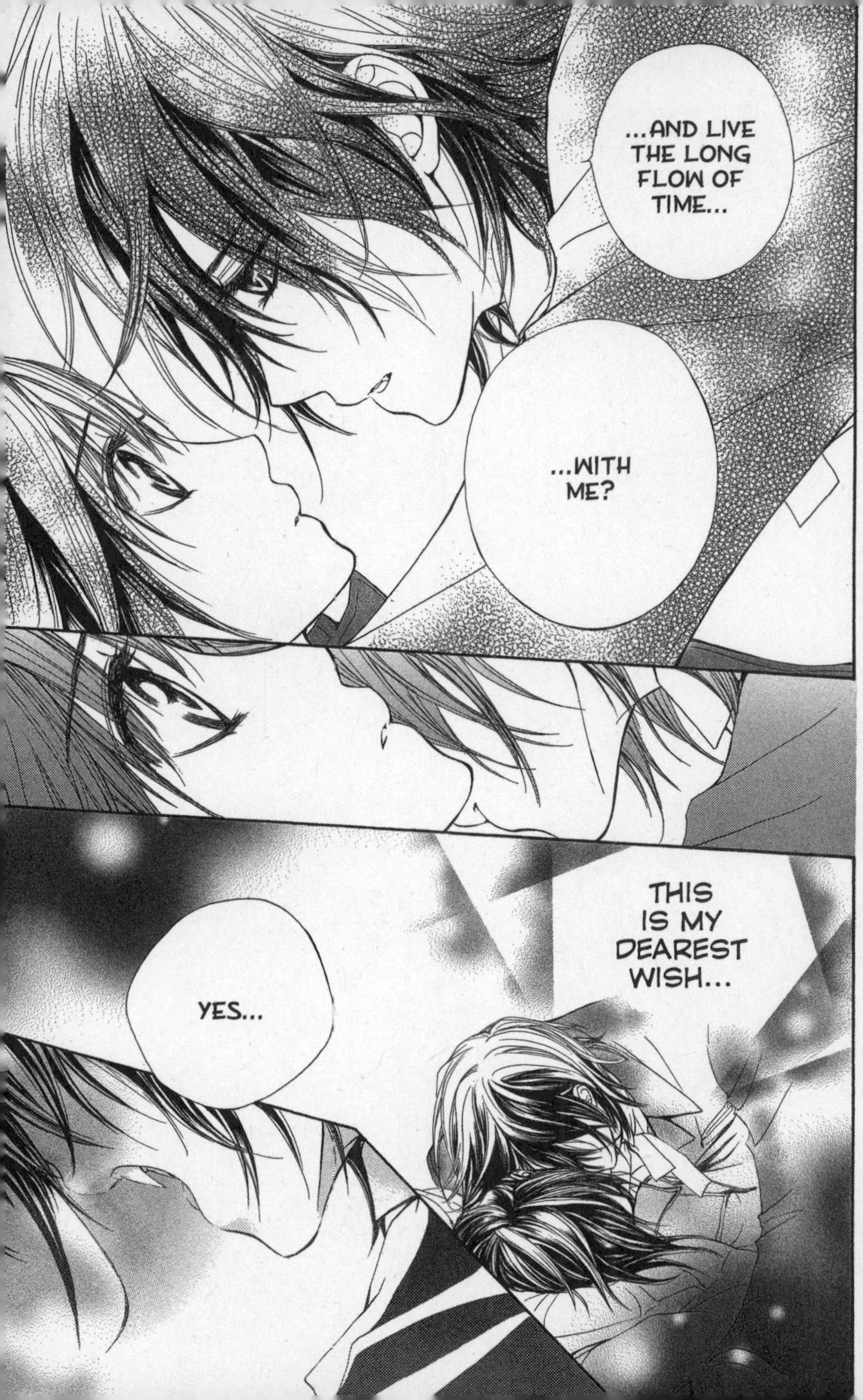
...AND LIVE THE LONG FLOW OF TIME...
...WITH ME?
THIS IS MY DEAREST WISH...
YES...

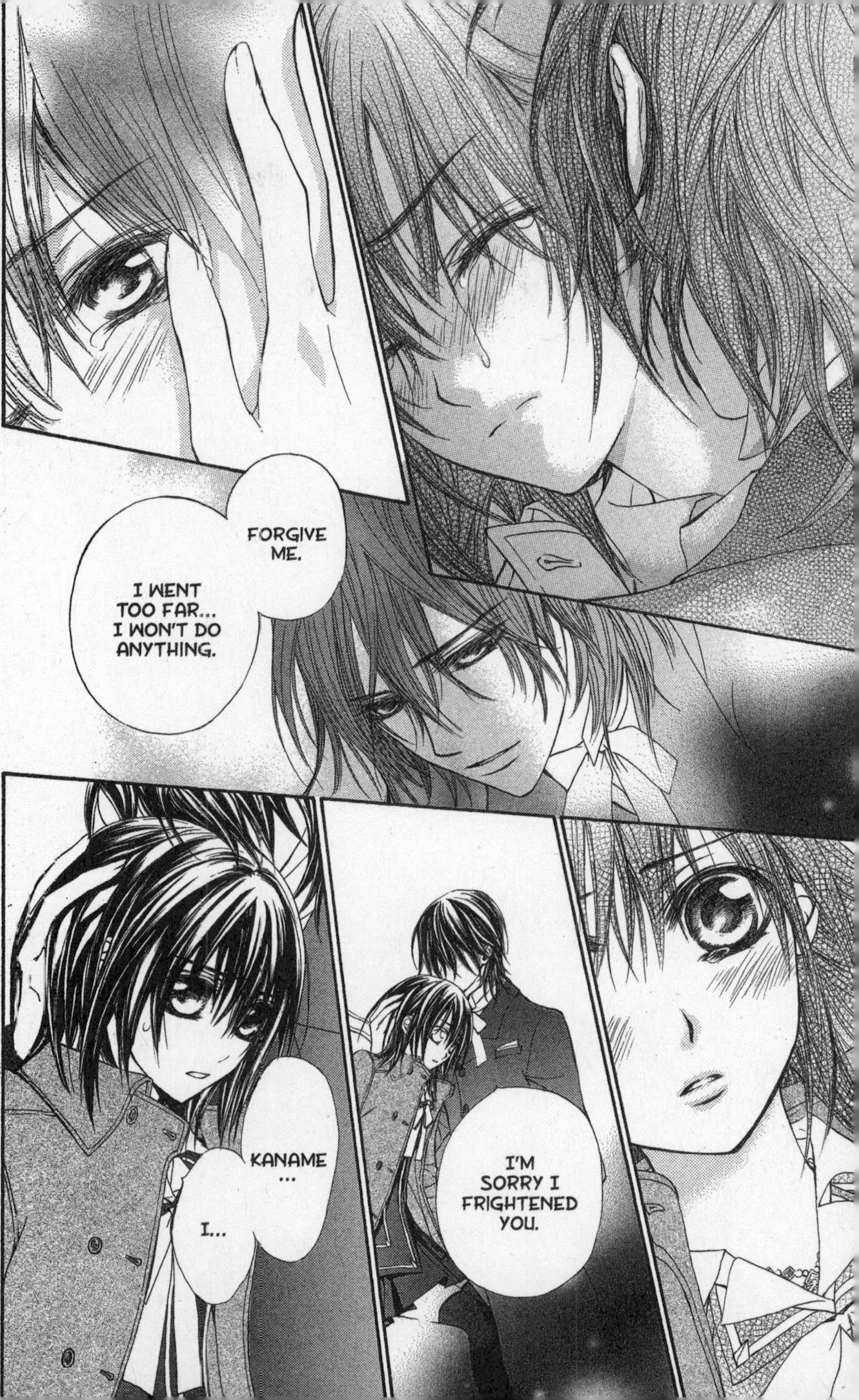
FORGIVE ME.
I WENT TOO FAR... I WON'T DO ANYTHING.
I'M SORRY I FRIGHTENED YOU.
KANAME ...
I...

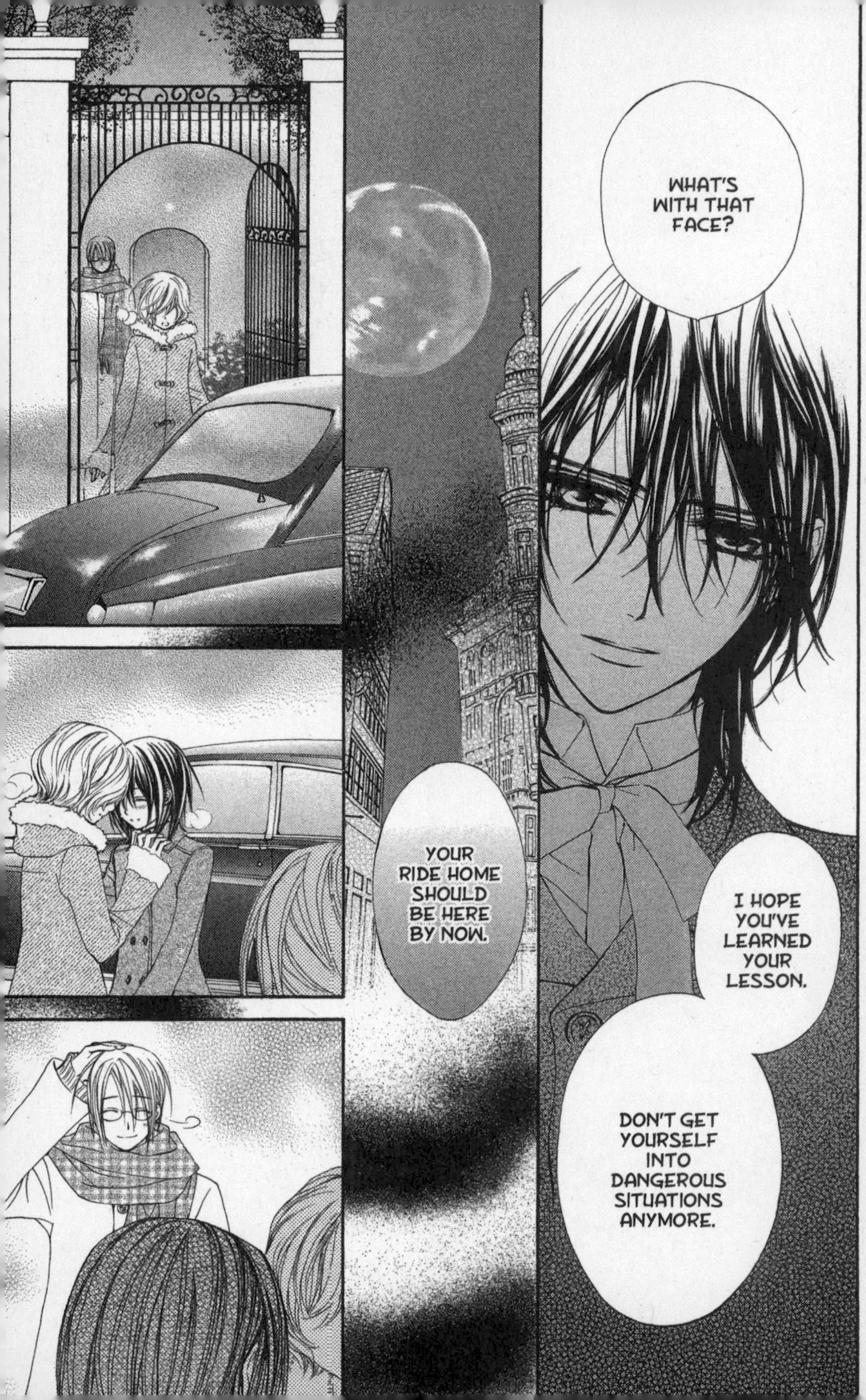
WHAT'S WITH THAT FACE?
I HOPE YOU'VE LEARNED YOUR LESSON.
DON'T GET YOURSELF INTO DANGEROUS SITUATIONS ANYMORE.
YOUR RIDE HOME SHOULD BE HERE BY NOW.

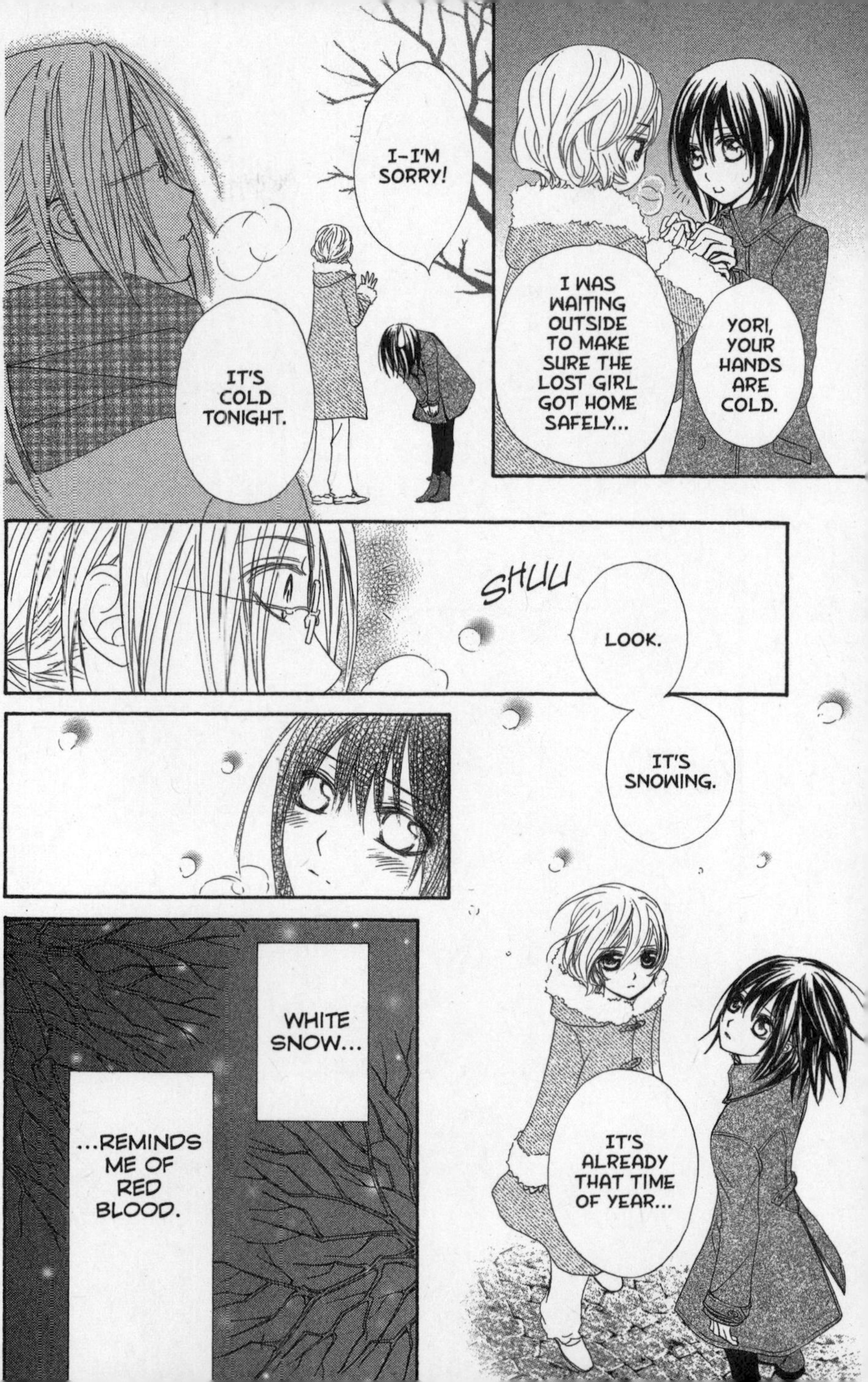
YORI, YOUR HANDS ARE COLD.
I WAS WAITING OUTSIDE TO MAKE SURE THE LOST GIRL GOT HOME SAFELY...
I-I'M SORRY!
IT'S COLD TONIGHT.
SHUU
LOOK.
IT'S SNOWING.
IT'S ALREADY THAT TIME OF YEAR...
WHITE SNOW...
...REMINDS ME OF RED BLOOD.

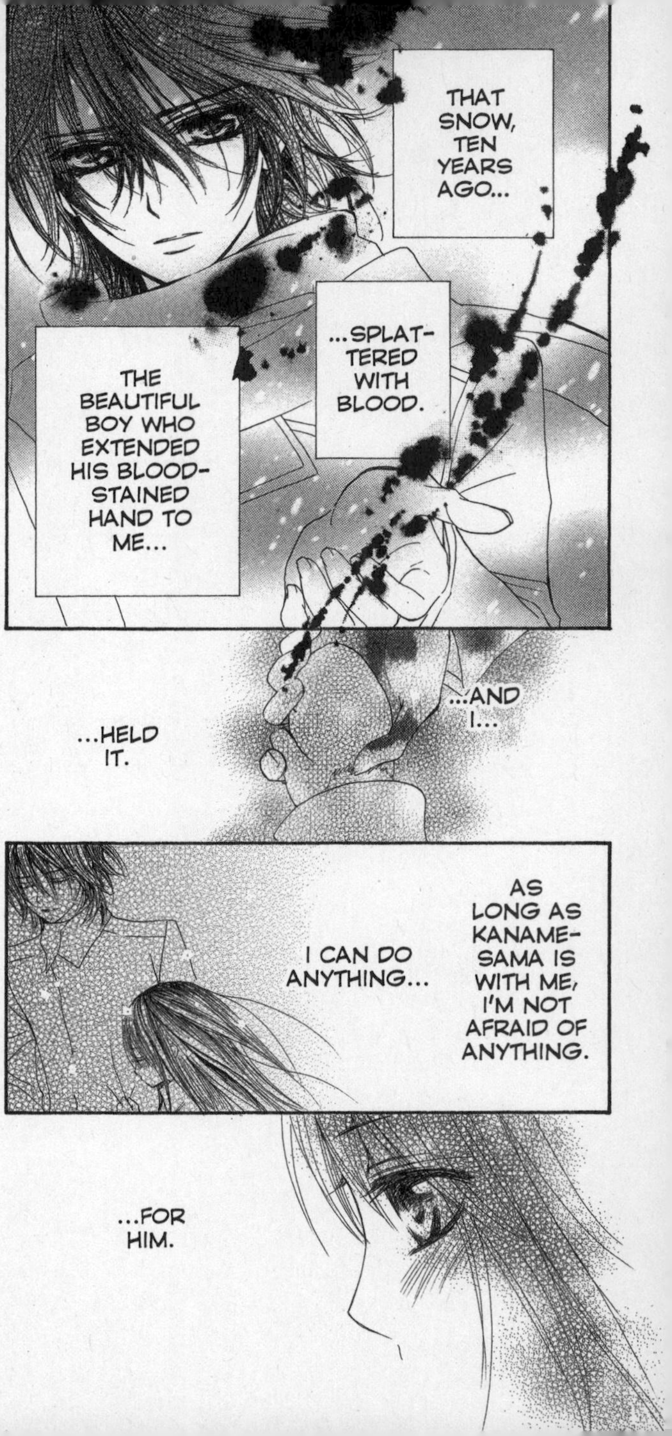
THAT SNOW, TEN YEARS AGO...
...SPLAT-TERED WITH BLOOD.
THE BEAUTIFUL BOY WHO EXTENDED HIS BLOOD-STAINED HAND TO ME...
...AND I...
...HELD IT.
AS LONG AS KANAME-SAMA IS WITH ME, I'M NOT AFRAID OF ANYTHING.
I CAN DO ANYTHING...
...FOR HIM.

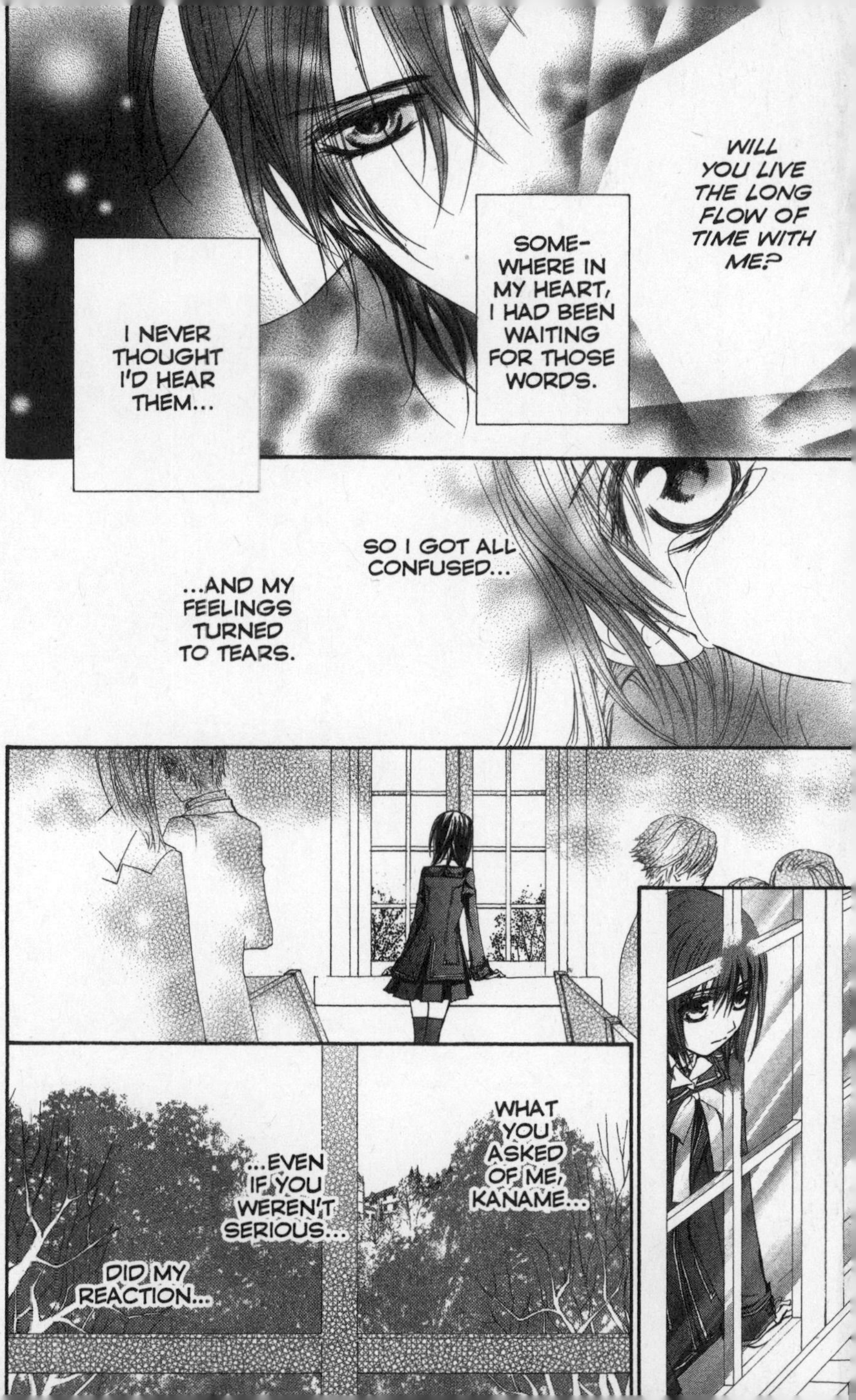
WILL YOU LIVE THE LONG FLOW OF TIME WITH ME?
SOME-WHERE IN MY HEART, I HAD BEEN WAITING FOR THOSE WORDS.
I NEVER THOUGHT I'D HEAR THEM...
SO I GOT ALL CONFUSED...
...AND MY FEELINGS TURNED TO TEARS.
WHAT YOU ASKED OF ME, KANAME...
...EVEN IF YOU WEREN'T SERIOUS...
DID MY REACTION...

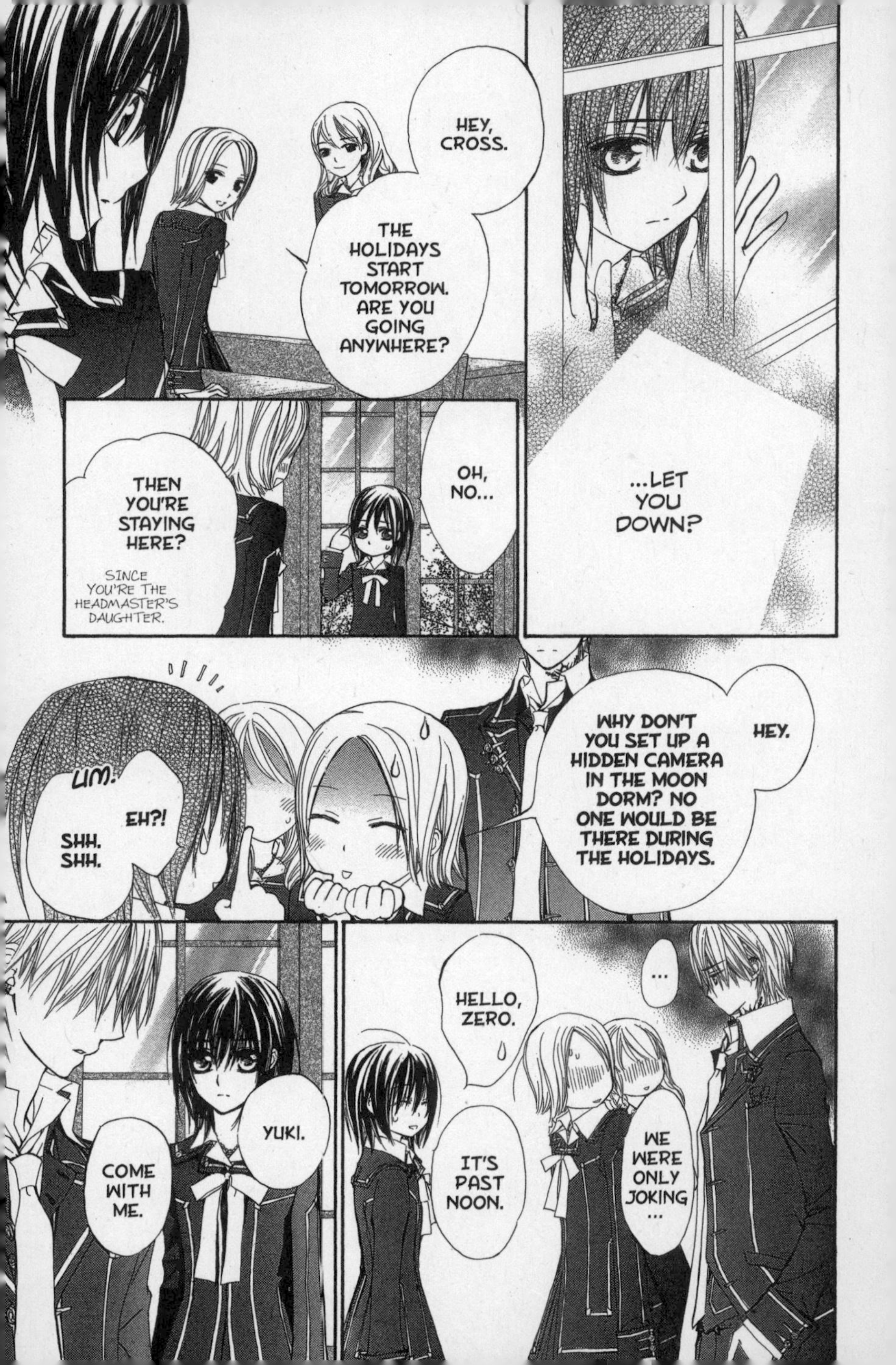
...LET YOU DOWN?
HEY, CROSS.
THE HOLIDAYS START TOMORROW. ARE YOU GOING ANYWHERE?
OH, NO...
THEN YOU'RE STAYING HERE?
SINCE YOU'RE THE HEADMASTER'S DAUGHTER.
HEY.
WHY DON'T YOU SET UP A HIDDEN CAMERA IN THE MOON DORM? NO ONE WOULD BE THERE DURING THE HOLIDAYS.
EH?!
UM.
SHH. SHH.
...
HELLO, ZERO.
WE WERE ONLY JOKING...
IT'S PAST NOON.
YUKI.
COME WITH ME.

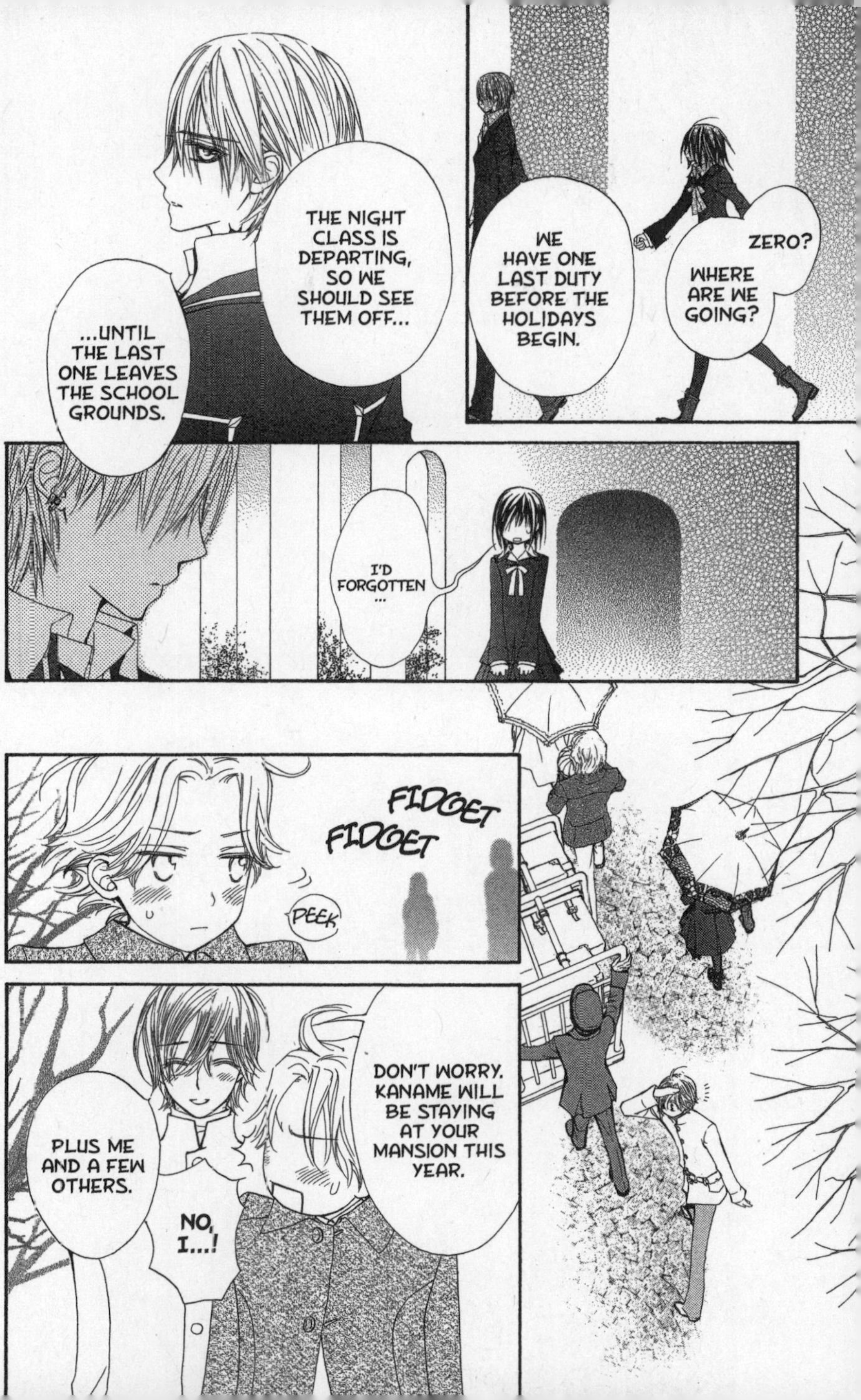
ZERO? WHERE ARE WE GOING?
WE HAVE ONE LAST DUTY BEFORE THE HOLIDAYS BEGIN.
THE NIGHT CLASS IS DEPARTING, SO WE SHOULD SEE THEM OFF...
...UNTIL THE LAST ONE LEAVES THE SCHOOL GROUNDS.
I'D FORGOTTEN ...
FIDGET
FIDGET
PEEK
DON'T WORRY. KANAME WILL BE STAYING AT YOUR MANSION THIS YEAR.
PLUS ME AND A FEW OTHERS.
NO, I...!

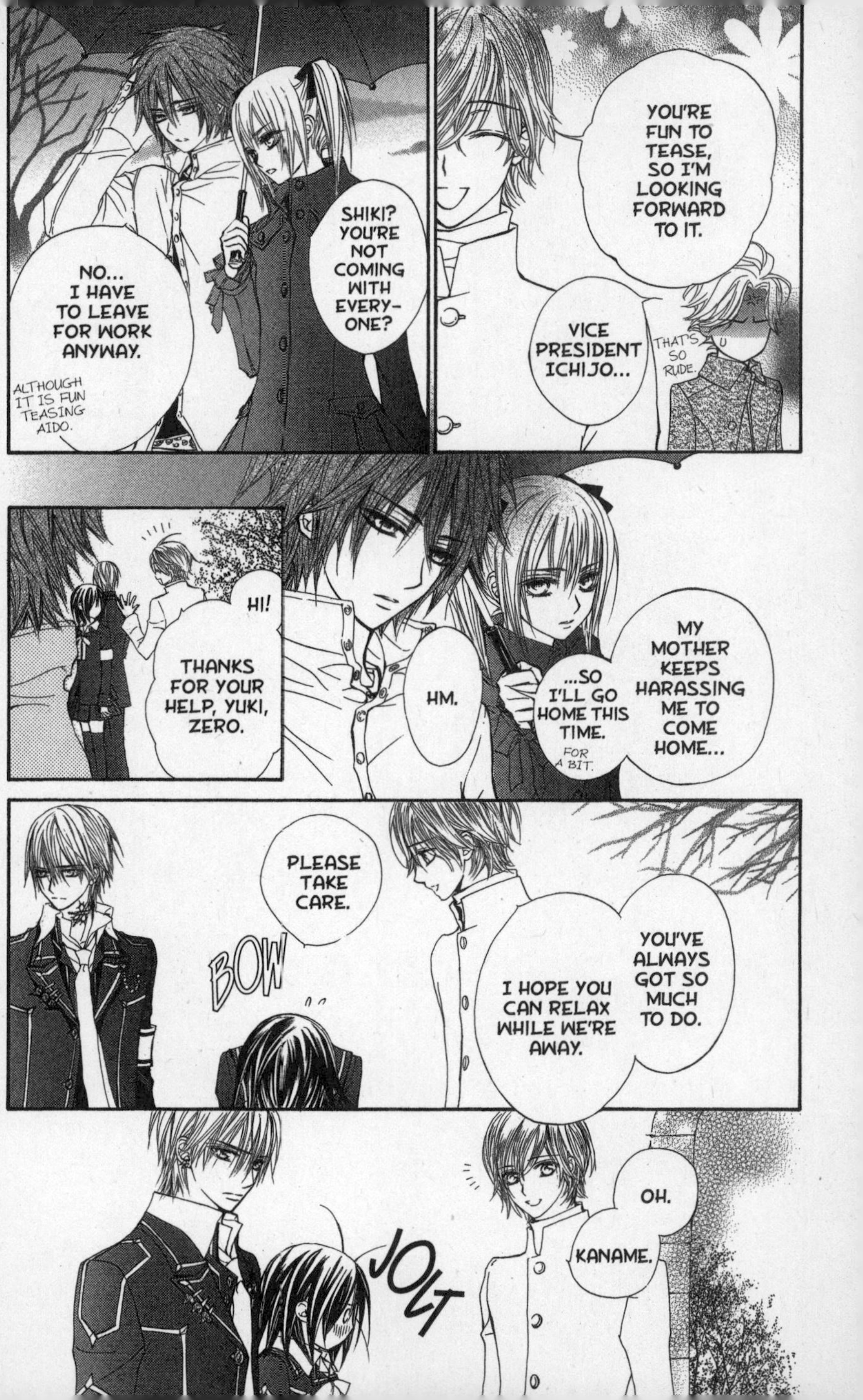
YOU'RE FUN TO TEASE, SO I'M LOOKING FORWARD TO IT.
VICE PRESIDENT ICHIJO...
THAT'S SO RUDE.
SHIKI? YOU'RE NOT COMING WITH EVERY-ONE?
NO... I HAVE TO LEAVE FOR WORK ANYWAY.
ALTHOUGH IT IS FUN TEASING AIDO.
MY MOTHER KEEPS HARASSING ME TO COME HOME...
...SO I'LL GO HOME THIS TIME.
FOR A BIT.
HM.
HI!
THANKS FOR YOUR HELP, YUKI, ZERO.
YOU'VE ALWAYS GOT SO MUCH TO DO.
I HOPE YOU CAN RELAX WHILE WE'RE AWAY.
PLEASE TAKE CARE.
BOW
OH.
KANAME.
JOLT

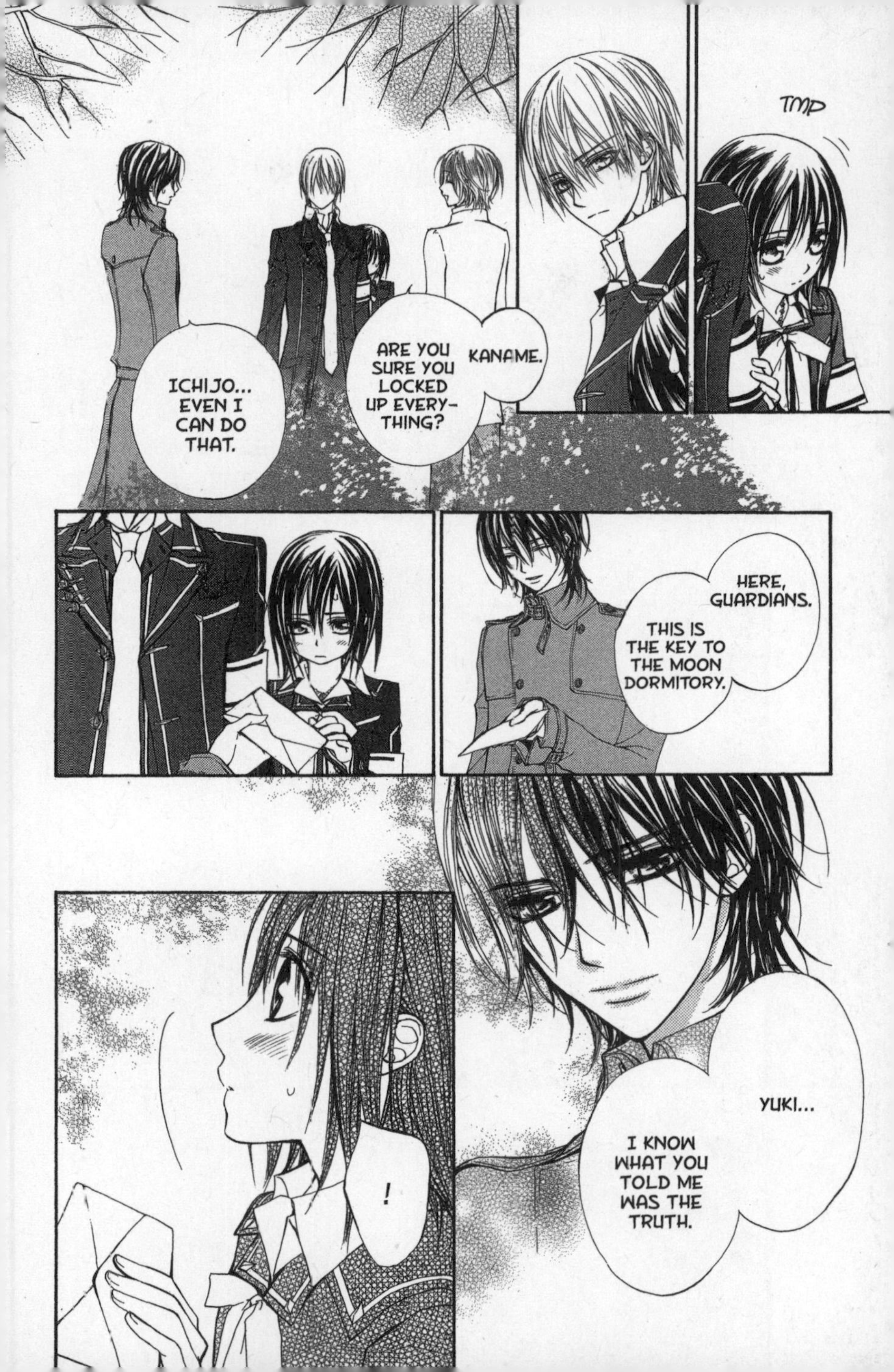
TMP
KANAME.
ARE YOU SURE YOU LOCKED UP EVERY-THING?
ICHIJO... EVEN I CAN DO THAT.
HERE, GUARDIANS.
THIS IS THE KEY TO THE MOON DORMITORY.
YUKI...
I KNOW WHAT YOU TOLD ME WAS THE TRUTH.
!

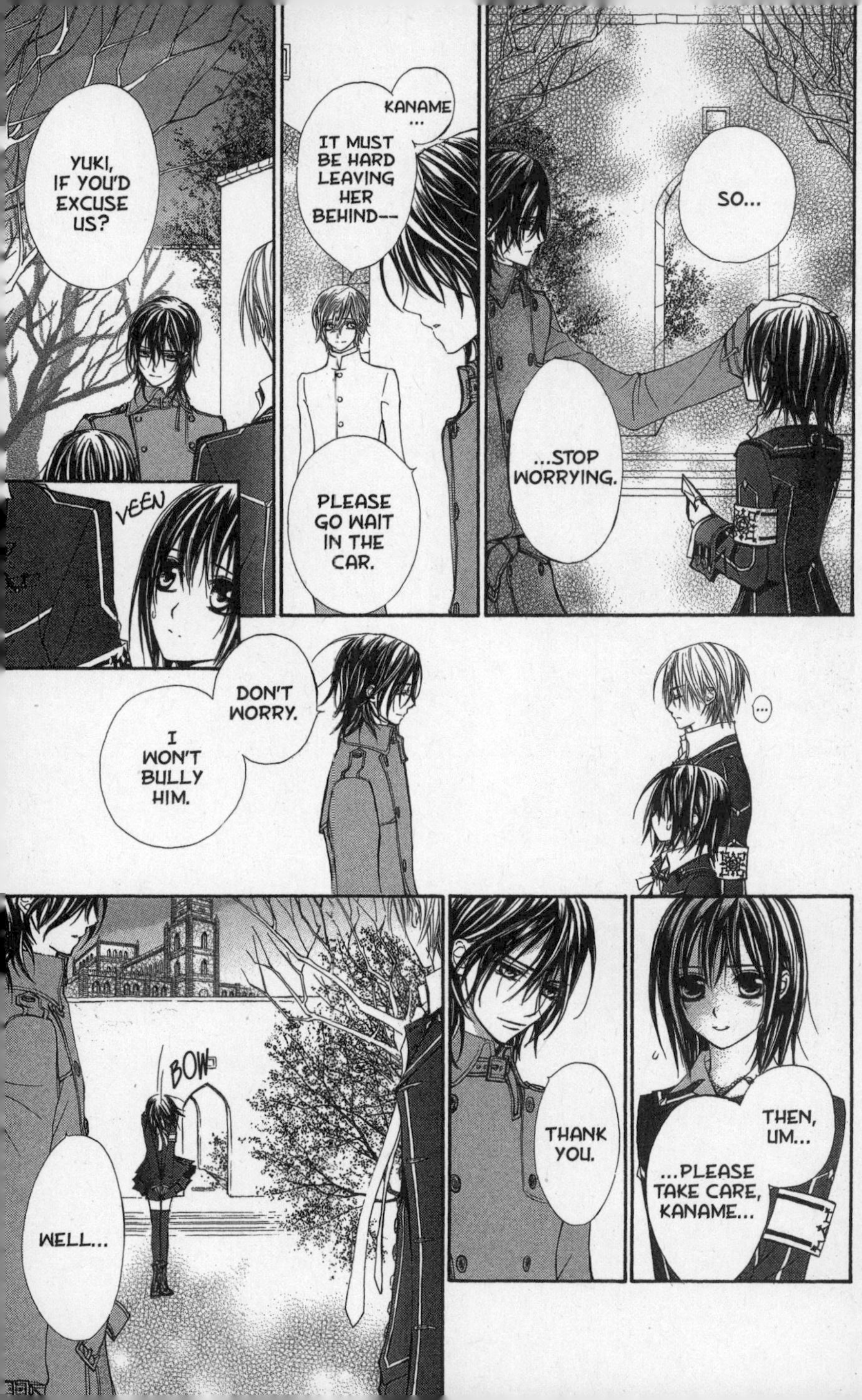
SO...
...STOP WORRYING.
KANAME...
IT MUST BE HARD LEAVING HER BEHIND--
PLEASE GO WAIT IN THE CAR.
YUKI, IF YOU'D EXCUSE US?
VEEN
...
DON'T WORRY.
I WON'T BULLY HIM.
THEN, UM...
...PLEASE TAKE CARE, KANAME...
THANK YOU.
BOW
WELL...

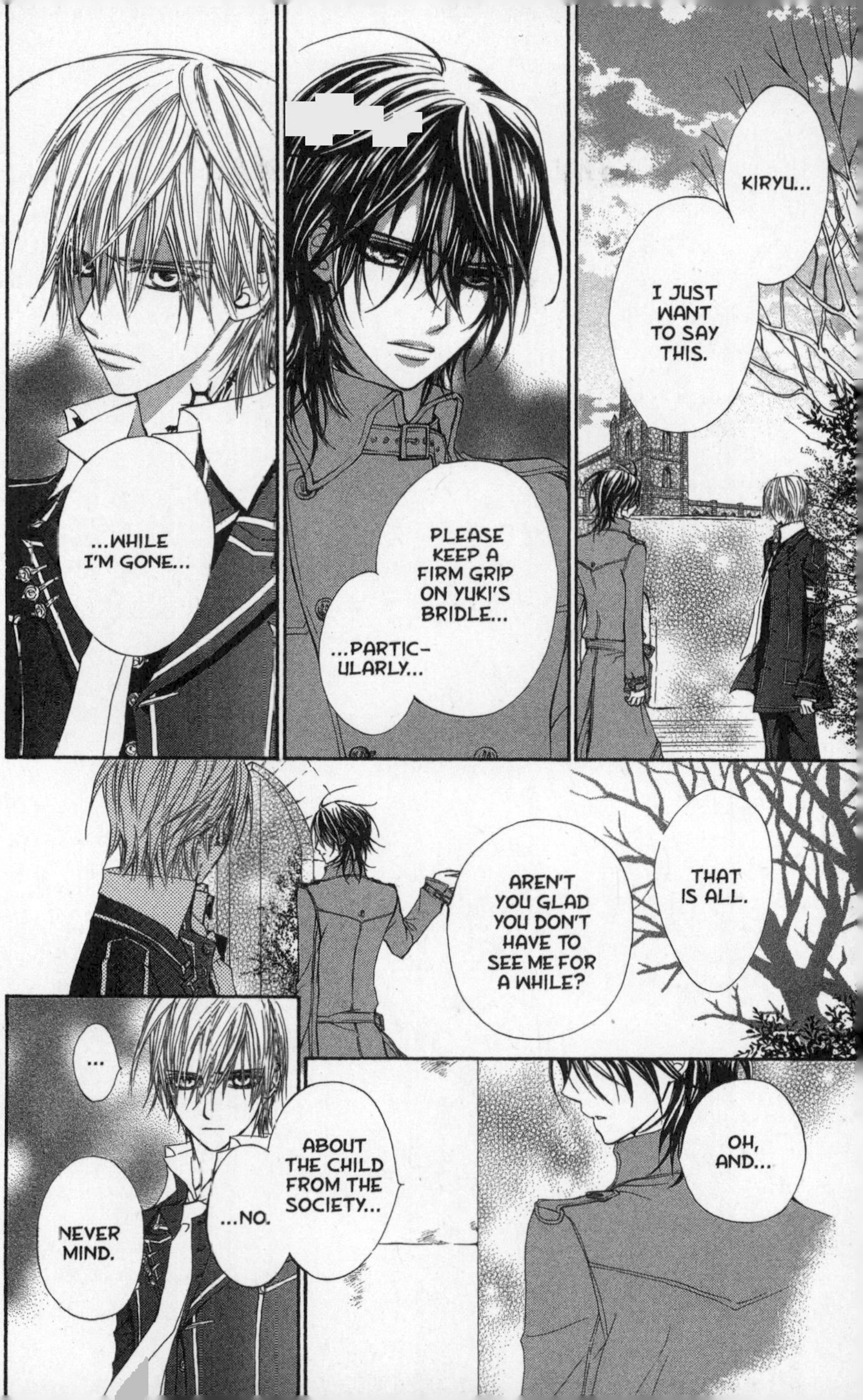
KIRYU...
I JUST WANT TO SAY THIS.
PLEASE KEEP A FIRM GRIP ON YUKI'S BRIDLE...
...PARTIC-ULARLY...
...WHILE I'M GONE...
THAT IS ALL.
AREN'T YOU GLAD YOU DON'T HAVE TO SEE ME FOR A WHILE?
OH, AND...
ABOUT THE CHILD FROM THE SOCIETY...
...
...NO.
NEVER MIND.

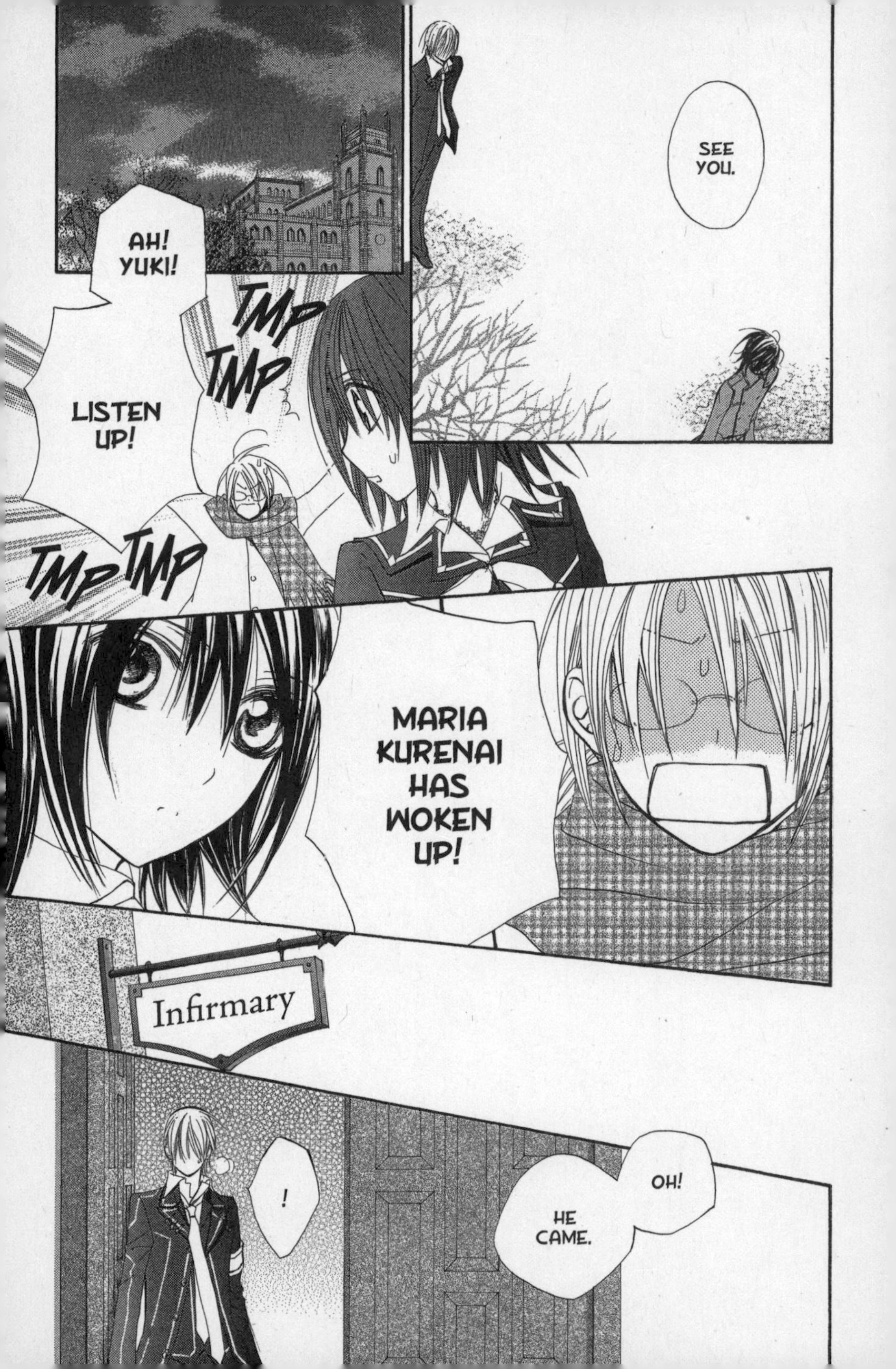

SEE YOU.
AH! YUKI!
TMP TMP
LISTEN UP!
TMP TMP
MARIA KURENAI HAS WOKEN UP!
Infirmary
OH!
HE CAME.
!

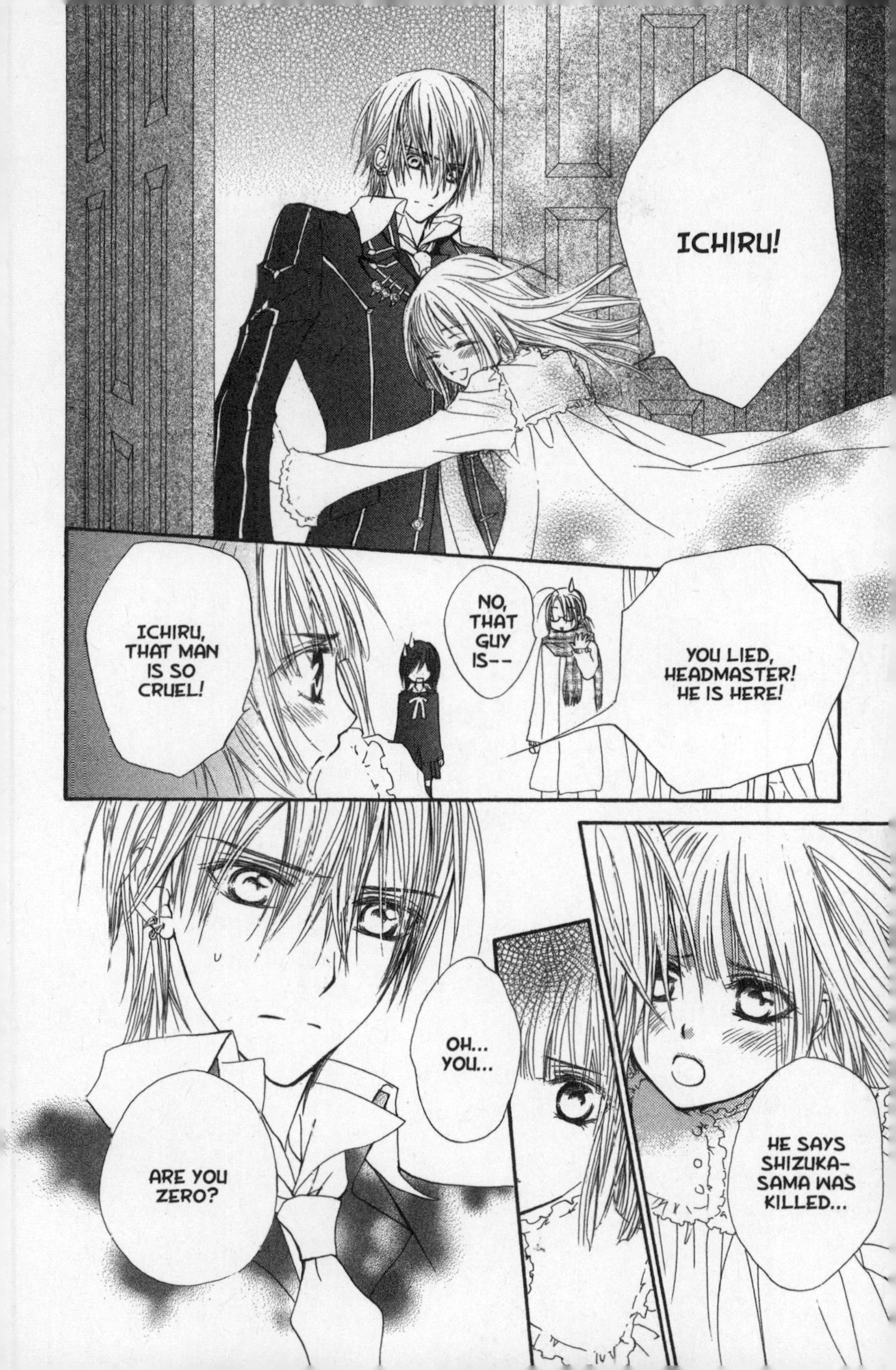
ICHIRU!
YOU LIED, HEADMASTER! HE IS HERE!
NO, THAT GUY IS--
ICHIRU, THAT MAN IS SO CRUEL!
HE SAYS SHIZUKA-SAMA WAS KILLED...
OH... YOU...
ARE YOU ZERO?

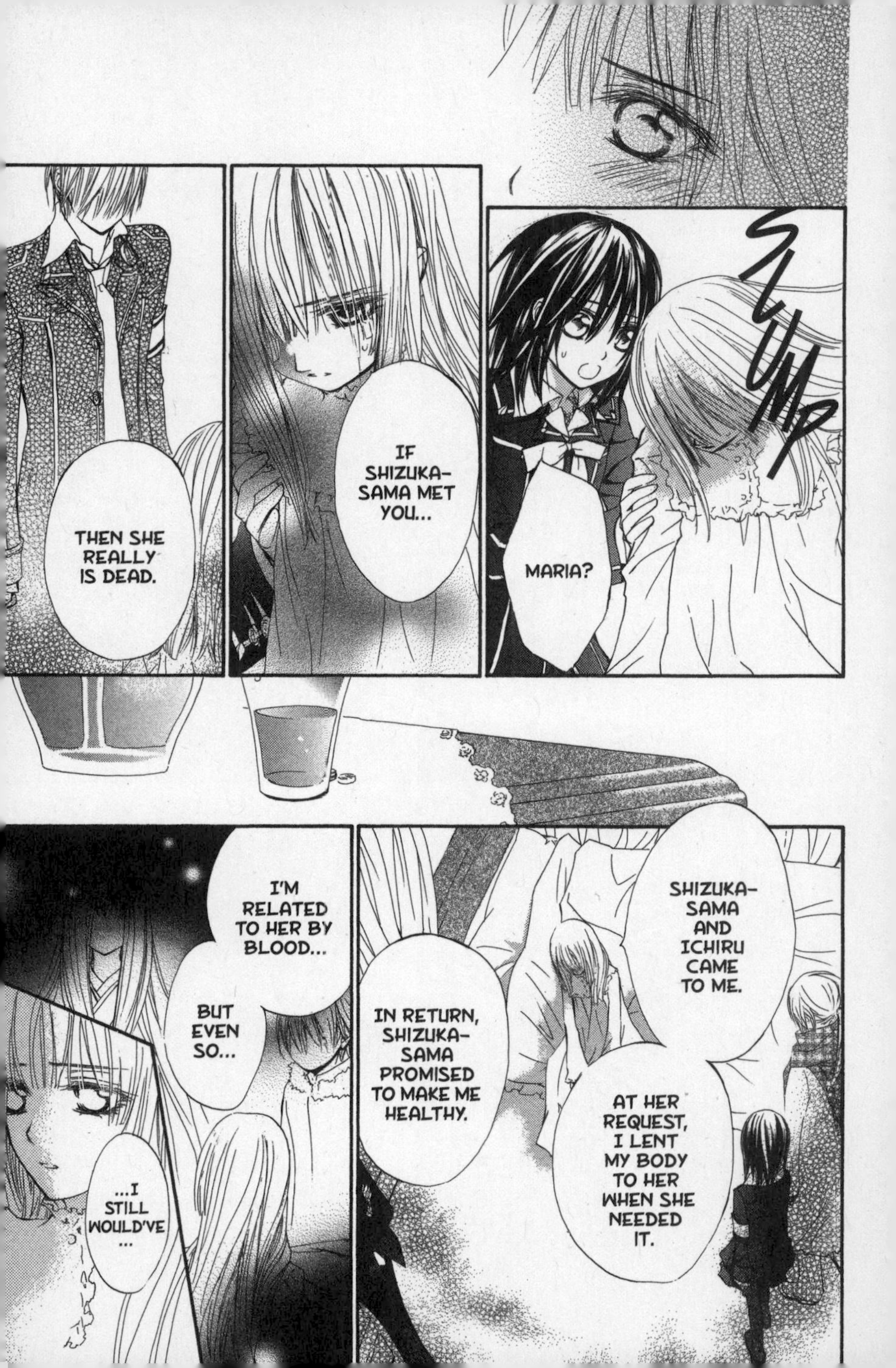
SLUMP
MARIA?
IF SHIZUKA-SAMA MET YOU...
THEN SHE REALLY IS DEAD.
SHIZUKA-SAMA AND ICHIRU CAME TO ME.
AT HER REQUEST, I LENT MY BODY TO HER WHEN SHE NEEDED IT.
IN RETURN, SHIZUKA-SAMA PROMISED TO MAKE ME HEALTHY.
I'M RELATED TO HER BY BLOOD...
BUT EVEN SO...
...I STILL WOULD'VE ...

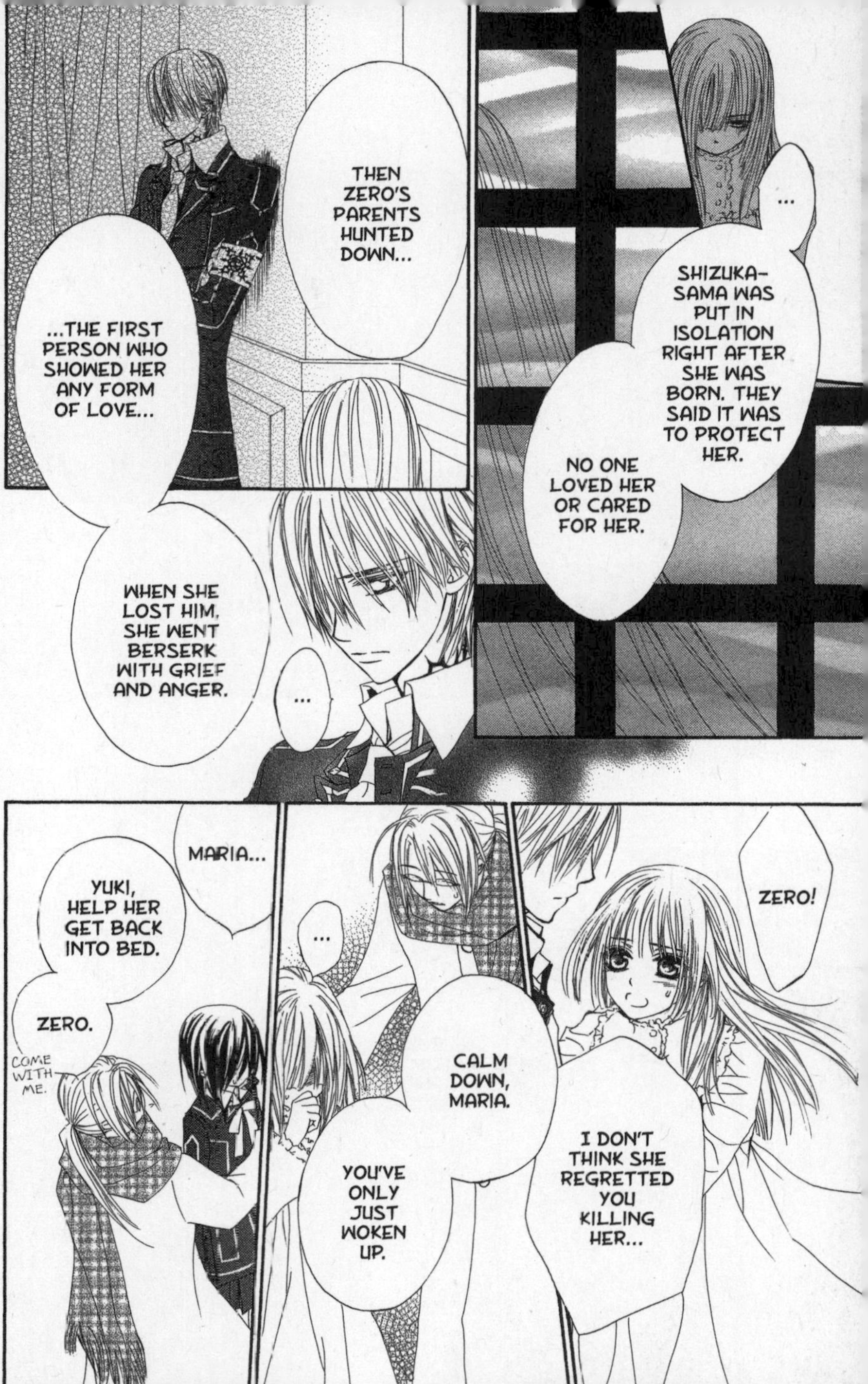
...
SHIZUKA-SAMA WAS PUT IN ISOLATION RIGHT AFTER SHE WAS BORN. THEY SAID IT WAS TO PROTECT HER.
NO ONE LOVED HER OR CARED FOR HER.
THEN ZERO'S PARENTS HUNTED DOWN...
...THE FIRST PERSON WHO SHOWED HER ANY FORM OF LOVE...
WHEN SHE LOST HIM, SHE WENT BERSERK WITH GRIEF AND ANGER.
...
ZERO!
I DON'T THINK SHE REGRETTED YOU KILLING HER...
CALM DOWN, MARIA.
YOU'VE ONLY JUST WOKEN UP.
...
MARIA...
YUKI, HELP HER GET BACK INTO BED.
ZERO.
COME WITH ME.

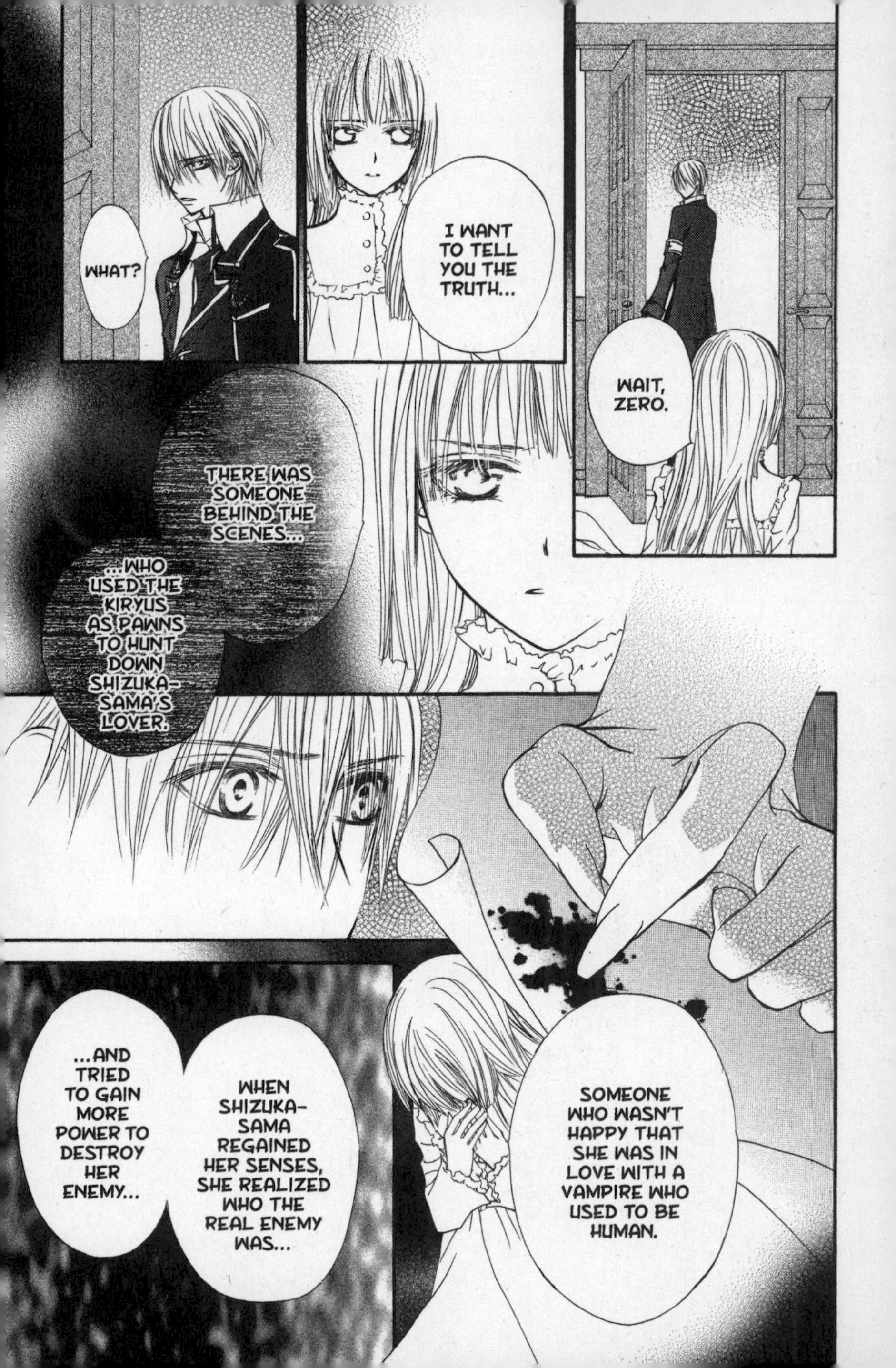
WAIT, ZERO.
I WANT TO TELL YOU THE TRUTH...
WHAT?
THERE WAS SOMEONE BEHIND THE SCENES...
...WHO USED THE KIRYUS AS PAWNS TO HUNT DOWN SHIZUKA-SAMA'S LOVER.
SOMEONE WHO WASN'T HAPPY THAT SHE WAS IN LOVE WITH A VAMPIRE WHO USED TO BE HUMAN.
WHEN SHIZUKA-SAMA REGAINED HER SENSES, SHE REALIZED WHO THE REAL ENEMY WAS...
...AND TRIED TO GAIN MORE POWER TO DESTROY HER ENEMY...

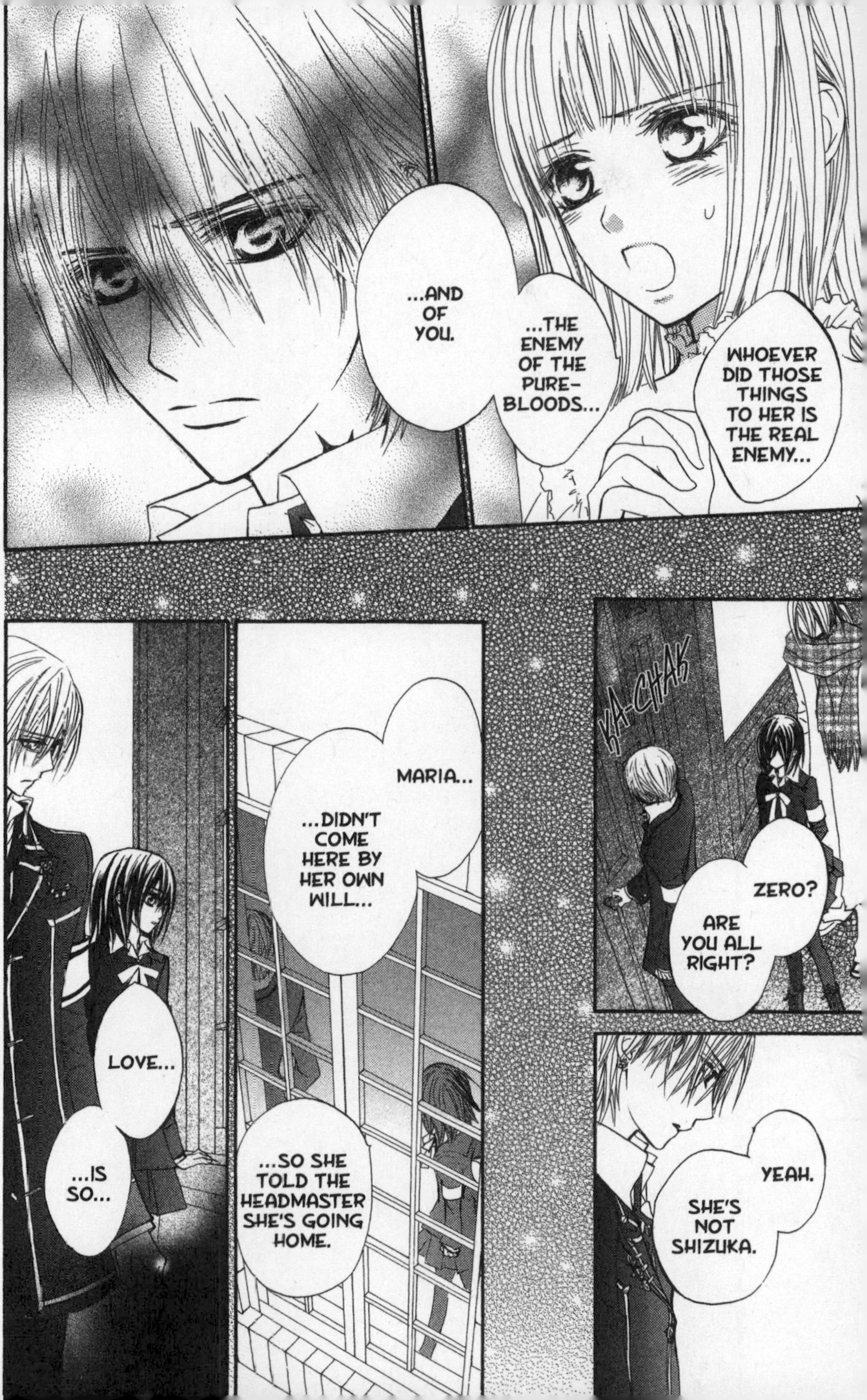
WHOEVER DID THOSE THINGS TO HER IS THE REAL ENEMY...
...THE ENEMY OF THE PURE-BLOODS...
...AND OF YOU.
KA-CHAK
ZERO?
ARE YOU ALL RIGHT?
YEAH.
SHE'S NOT SHIZUKA.
MARIA...
...DIDN'T COME HERE BY HER OWN WILL...
...SO SHE TOLD THE HEADMASTER SHE'S GOING HOME.
LOVE...
...IS SO...

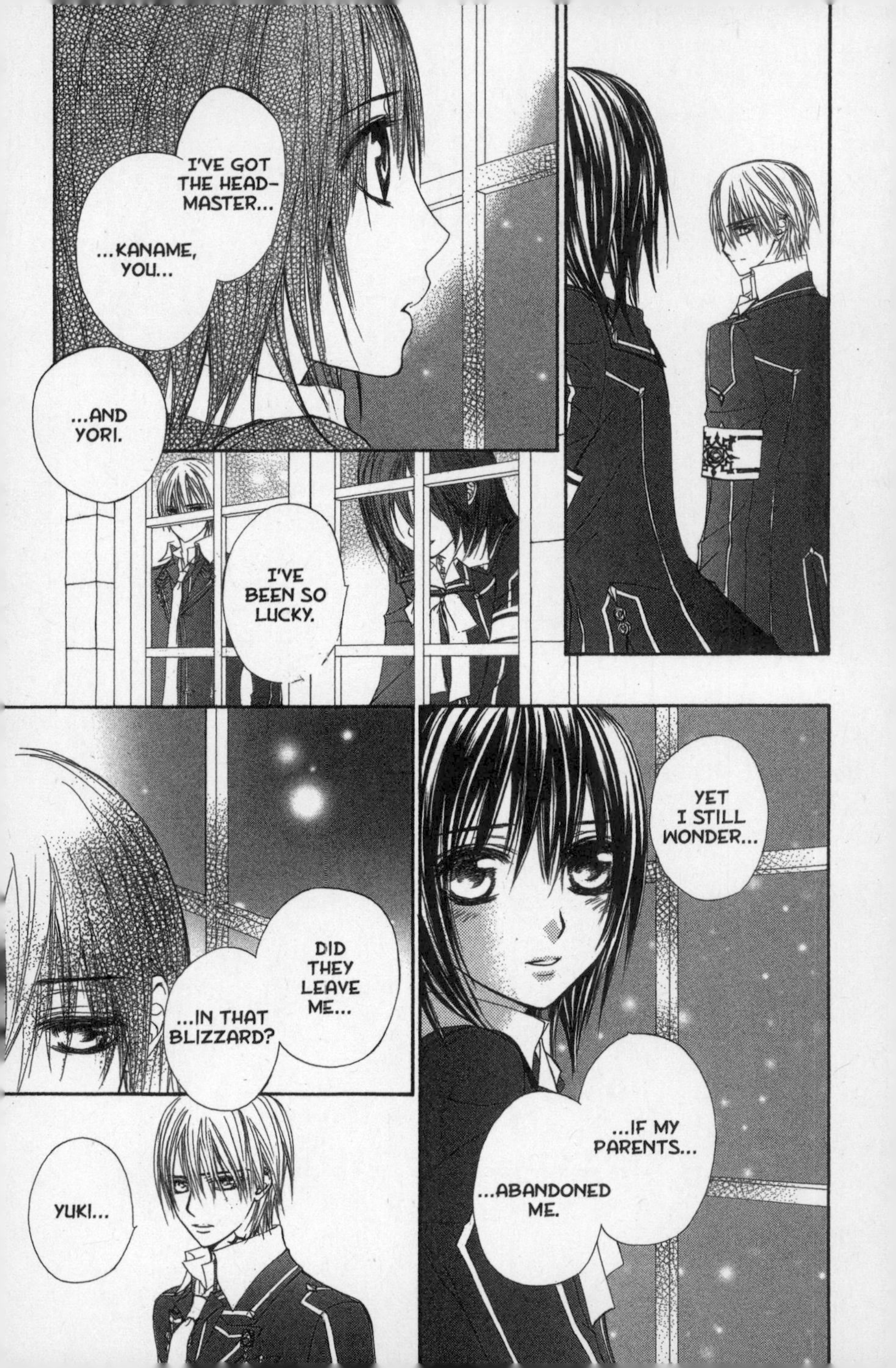
I'VE GOT THE HEAD-MASTER...
...KANAME, YOU...
...AND YORI.
I'VE BEEN SO LUCKY.
YET I STILL WONDER...
...IF MY PARENTS...
...ABANDONED ME.
DID THEY LEAVE ME...
...IN THAT BLIZZARD?
YUKI...

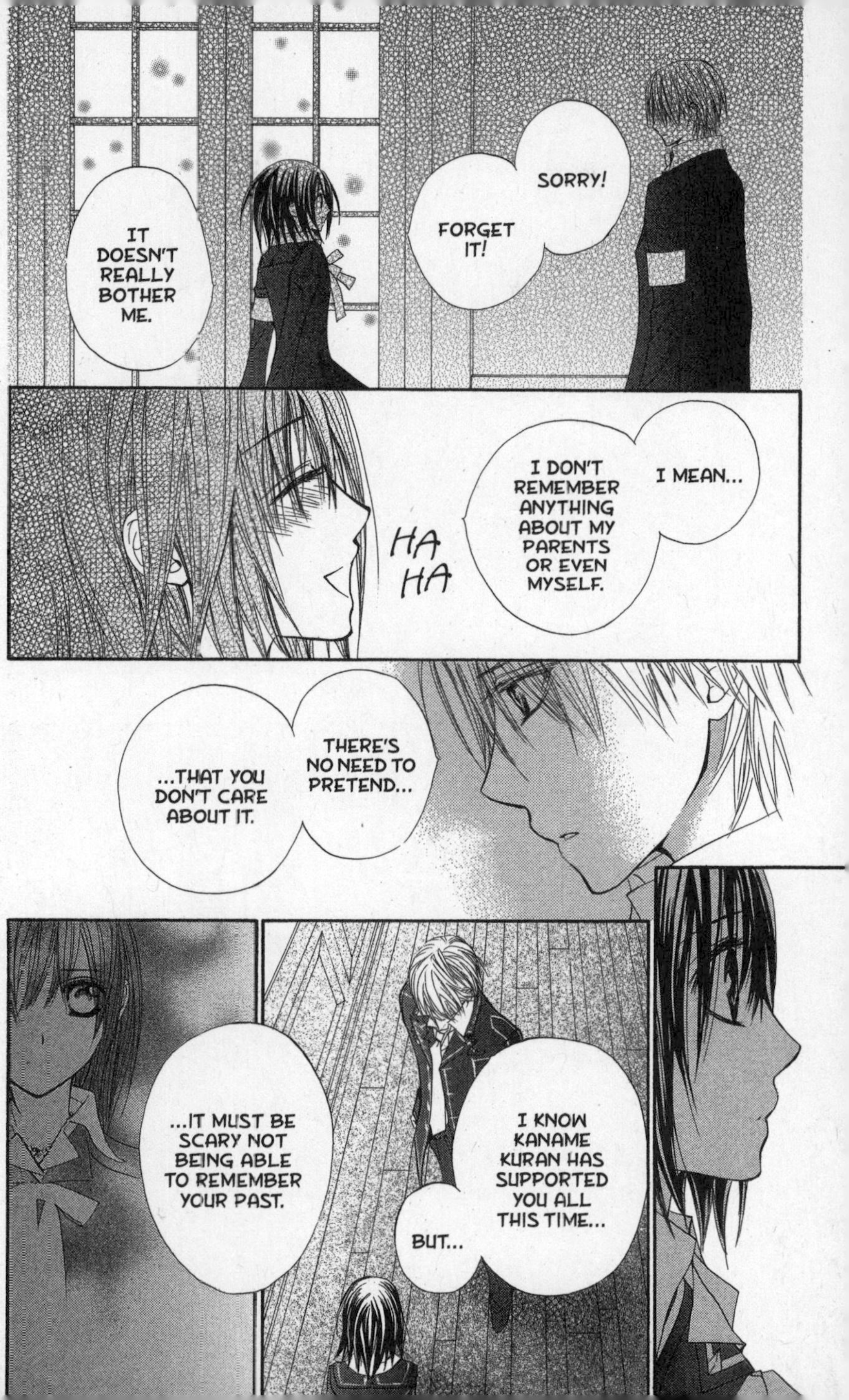
SORRY!
FORGET IT!
IT DOESN'T REALLY BOTHER ME.
I MEAN...
I DON'T REMEMBER ANYTHING ABOUT MY PARENTS OR EVEN MYSELF.
HA HA
THERE'S NO NEED TO PRETEND...
...THAT YOU DON'T CARE ABOUT IT.
I KNOW KANAME KURAN HAS SUPPORTED YOU ALL THIS TIME...
BUT...
...IT MUST BE SCARY NOT BEING ABLE TO REMEMBER YOUR PAST.

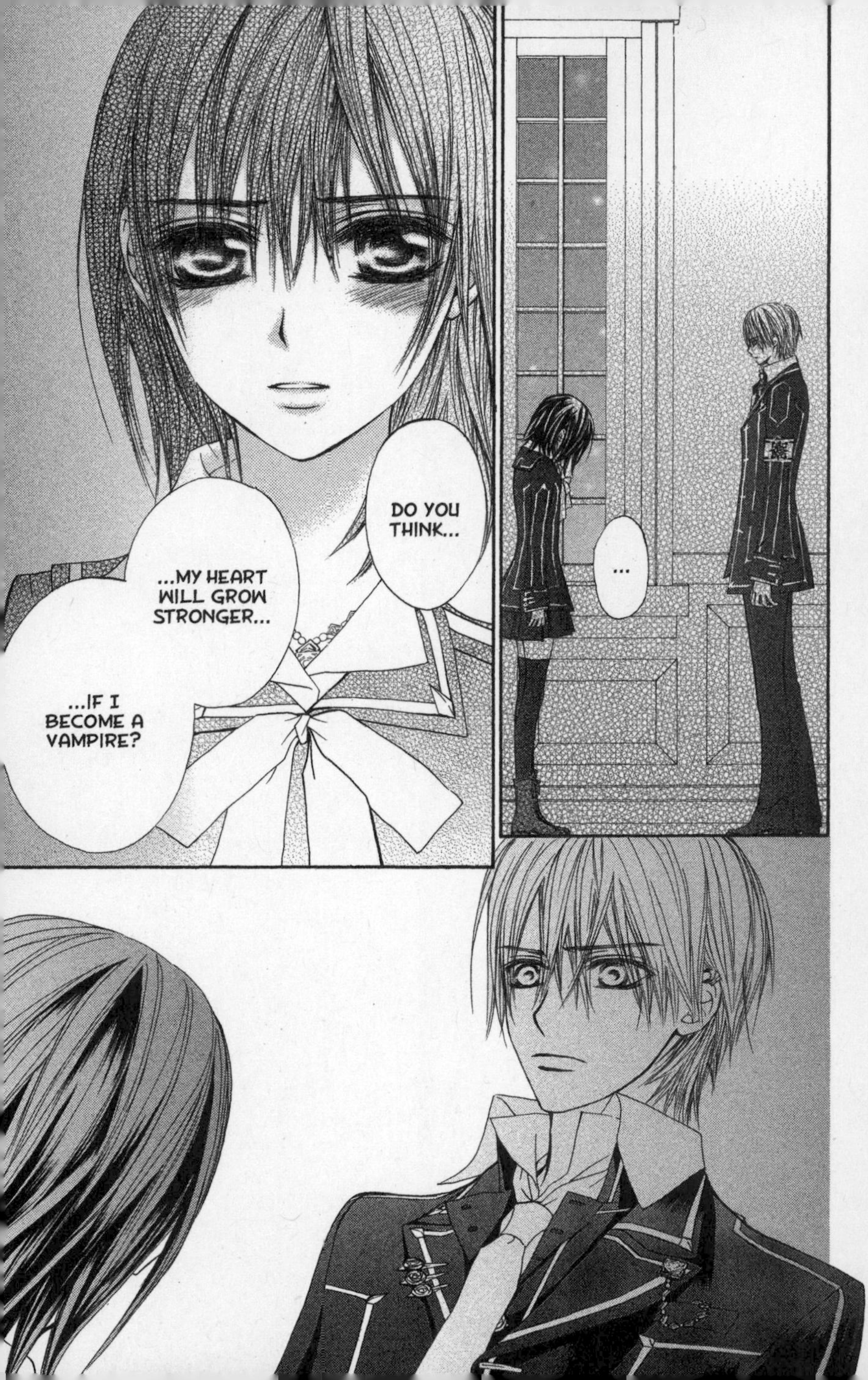
...
DO YOU THINK...
...MY HEART WILL GROW STRONGER...
...IF I BECOME A VAMPIRE?

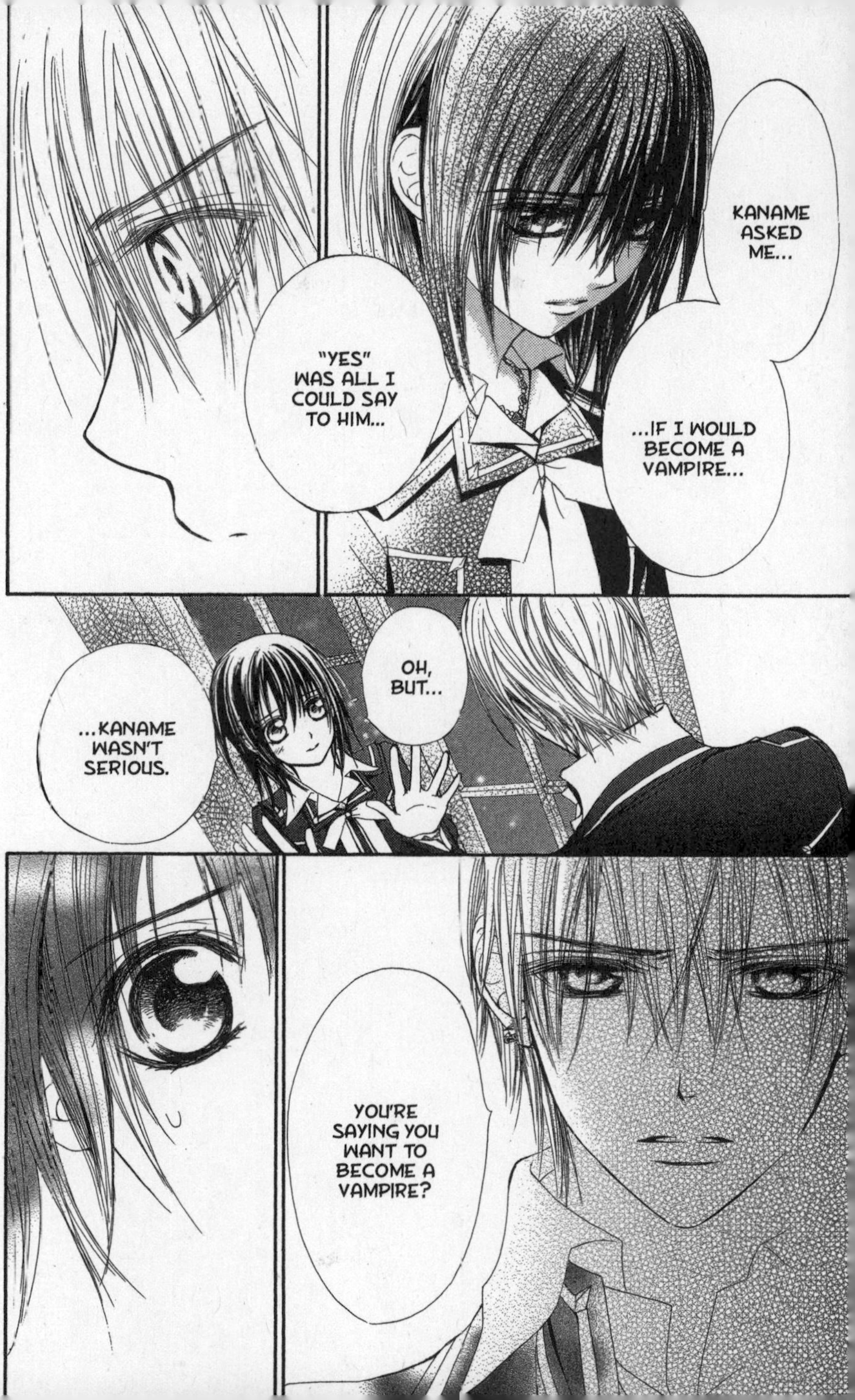
KANAME ASKED ME...
...IF I WOULD BECOME A VAMPIRE...
"YES" WAS ALL I COULD SAY TO HIM...
OH, BUT...
...KANAME WASN'T SERIOUS.
YOU'RE SAYING YOU WANT TO BECOME A VAMPIRE?

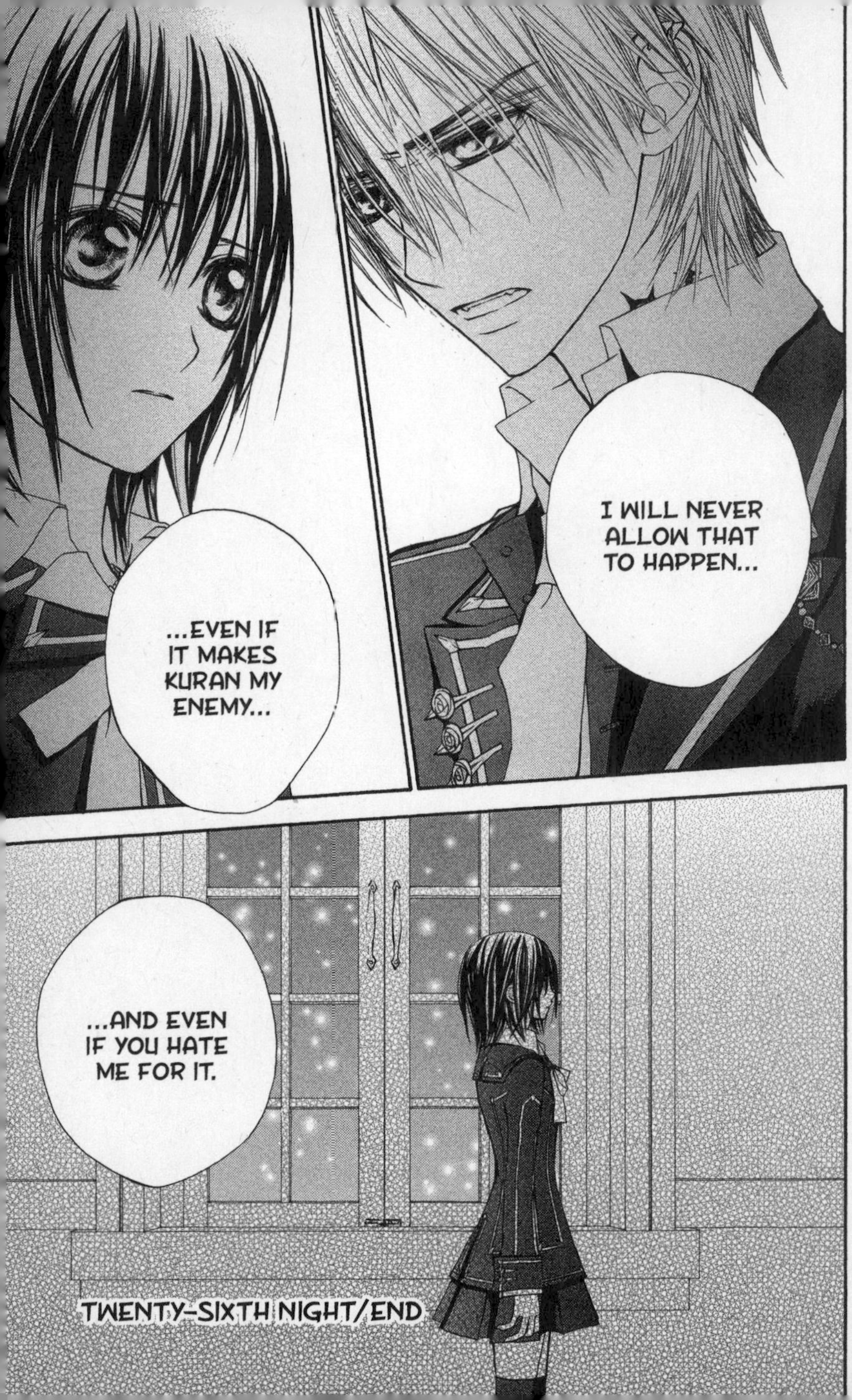
I WILL NEVER ALLOW THAT TO HAPPEN...
...EVEN IF IT MAKES KURAN MY ENEMY...
...AND EVEN IF YOU HATE ME FOR IT.
TWENTY-SIXTH NIGHT/END

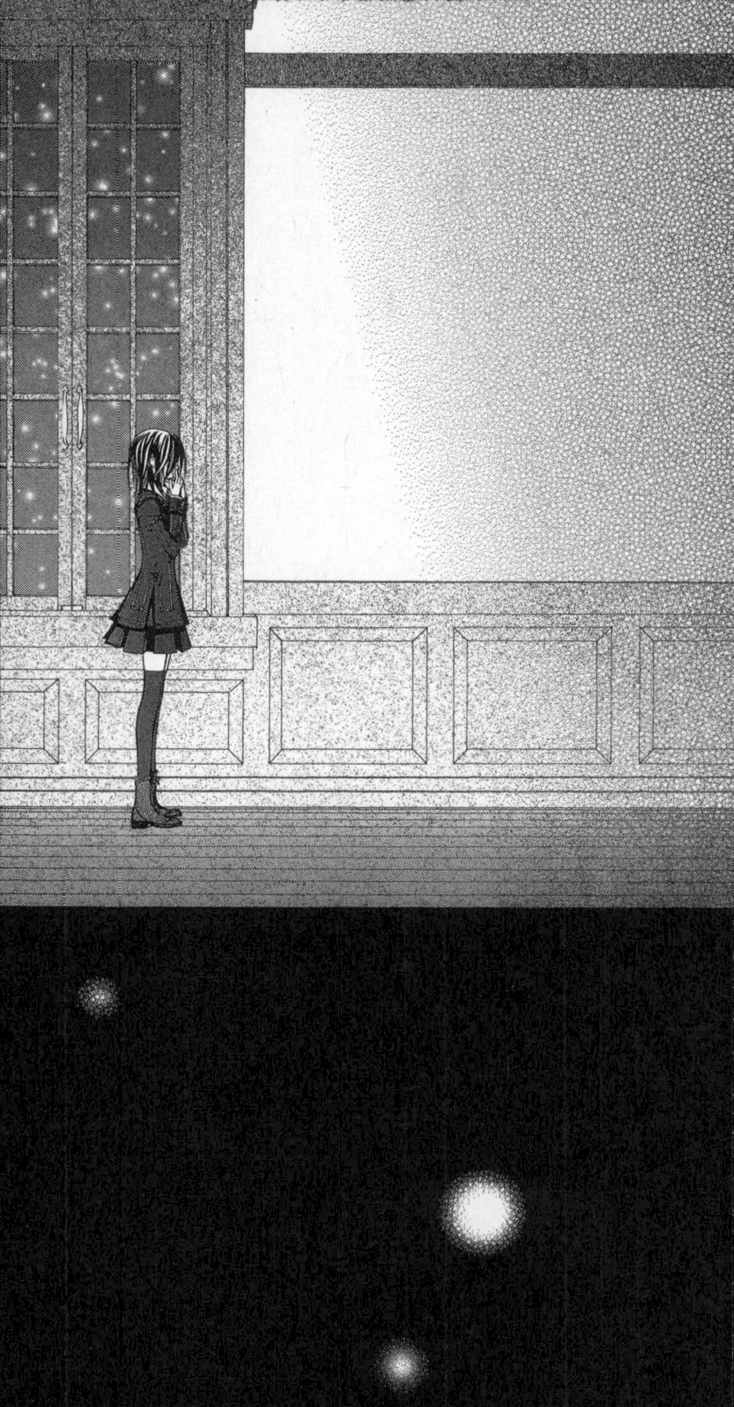

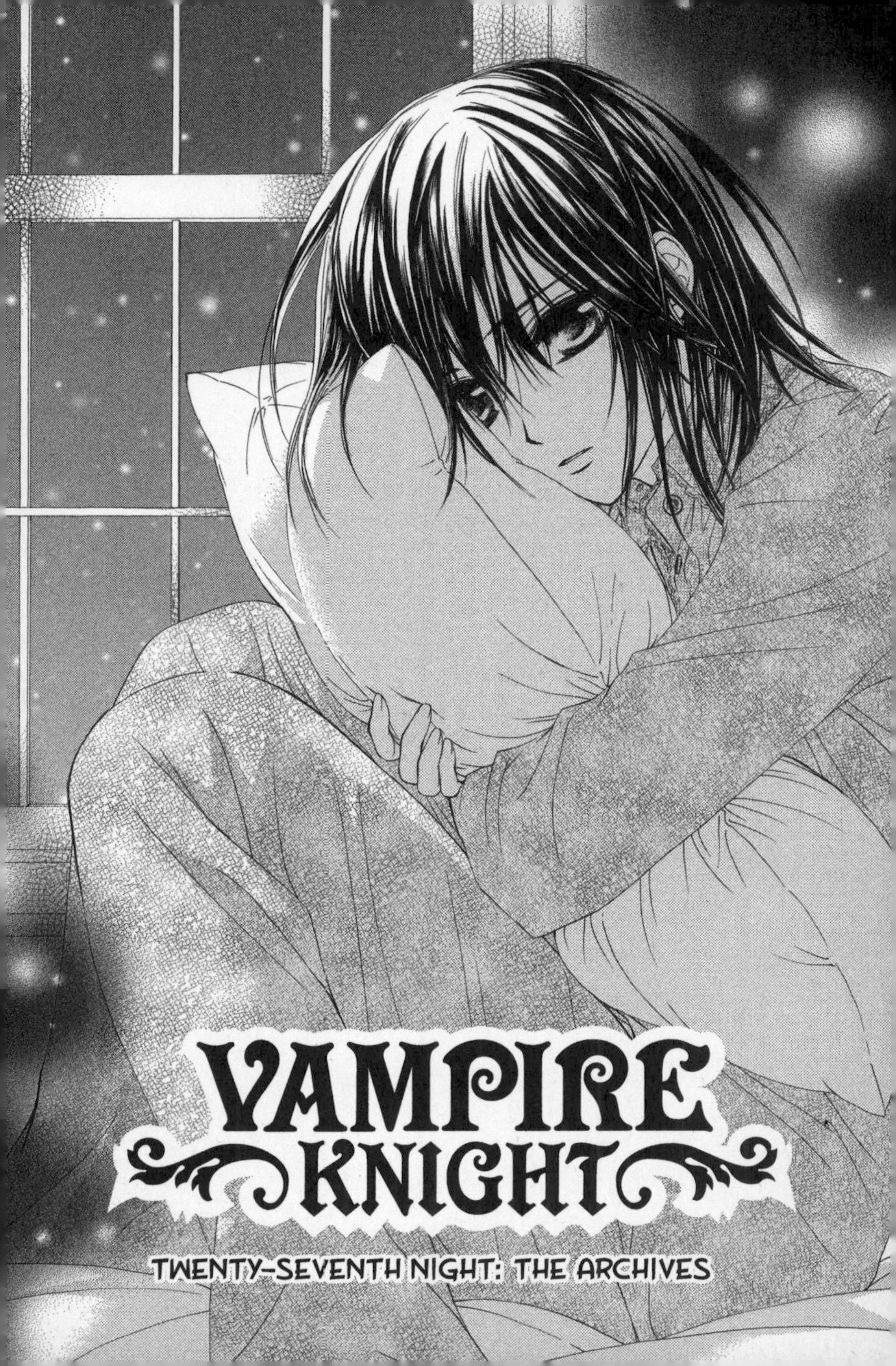
VAMPIRE KNIGHT
TWENTY-SEVENTH NIGHT: THE ARCHIVES

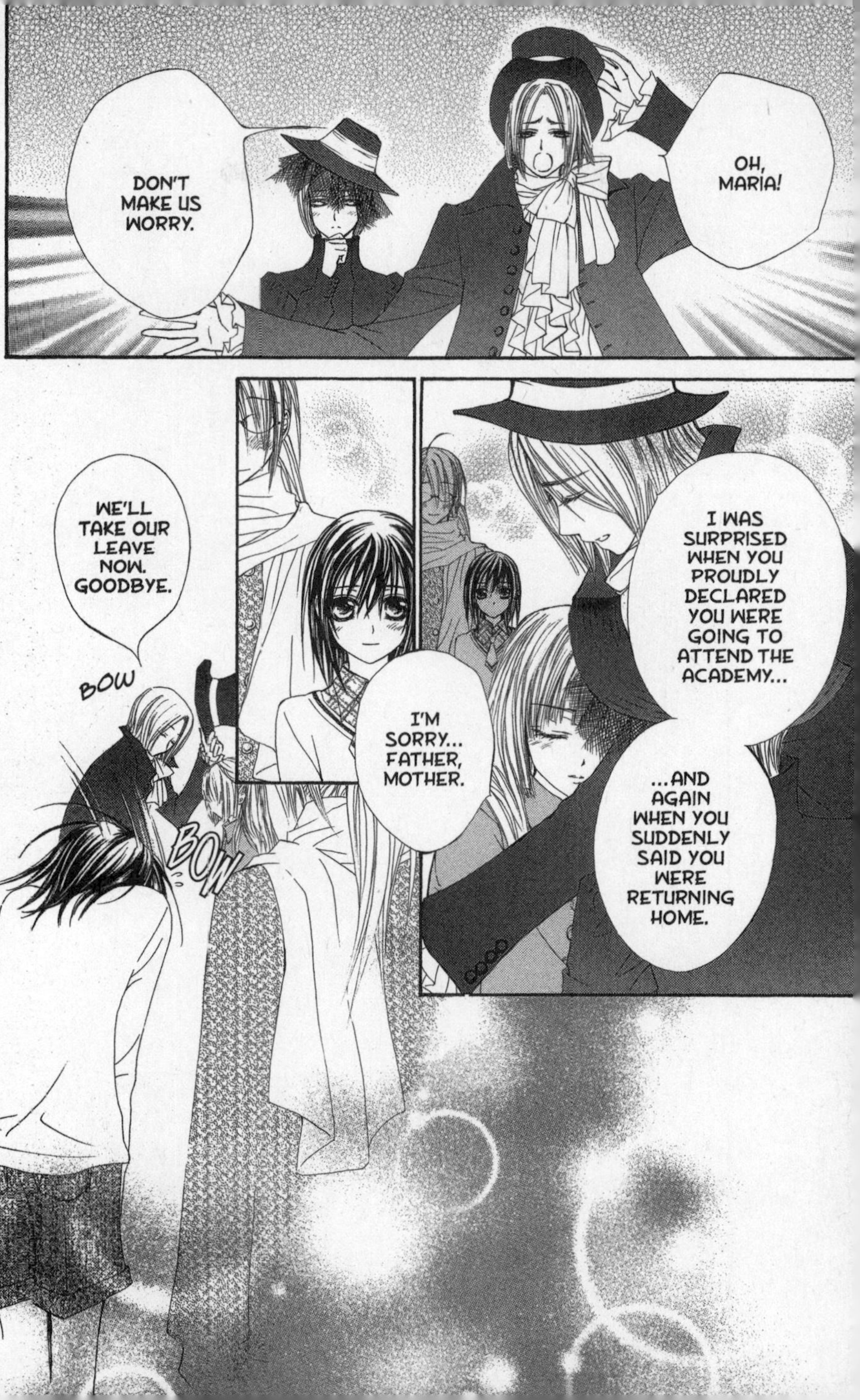
OH, MARIA!
DON'T MAKE US WORRY.
I WAS SURPRISED WHEN YOU PROUDLY DECLARED YOU WERE GOING TO ATTEND THE ACADEMY...
...AND AGAIN WHEN YOU SUDDENLY SAID YOU WERE RETURNING HOME.
I'M SORRY... FATHER, MOTHER.
WE'LL TAKE OUR LEAVE NOW. GOODBYE.
BOW
BOW

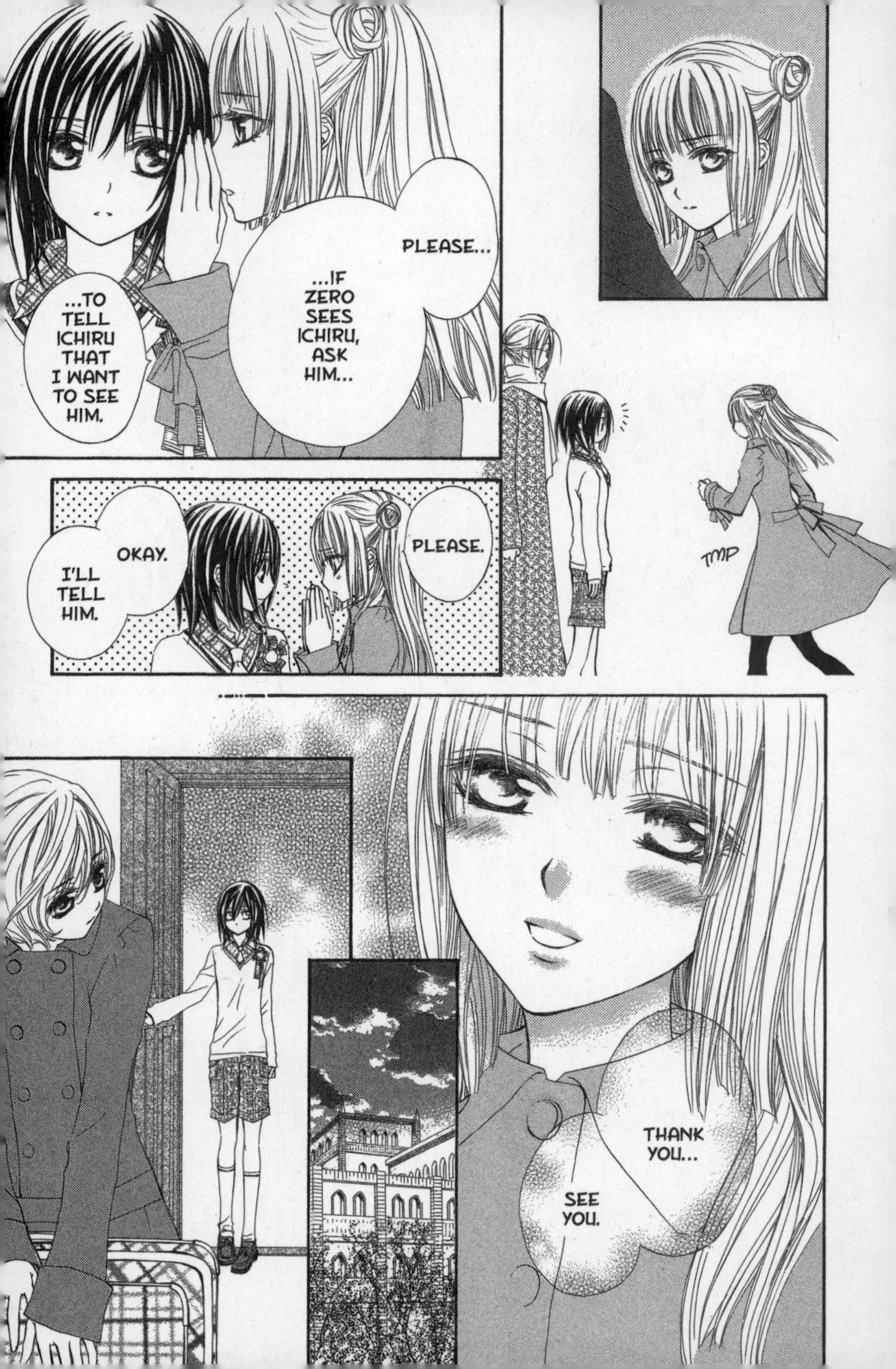
PLEASE...
...IF ZERO SEES ICHIRU, ASK HIM...
...TO TELL ICHIRU THAT I WANT TO SEE HIM.
PLEASE.
OKAY. I'LL TELL HIM.
TMP
THANK YOU...
SEE YOU.

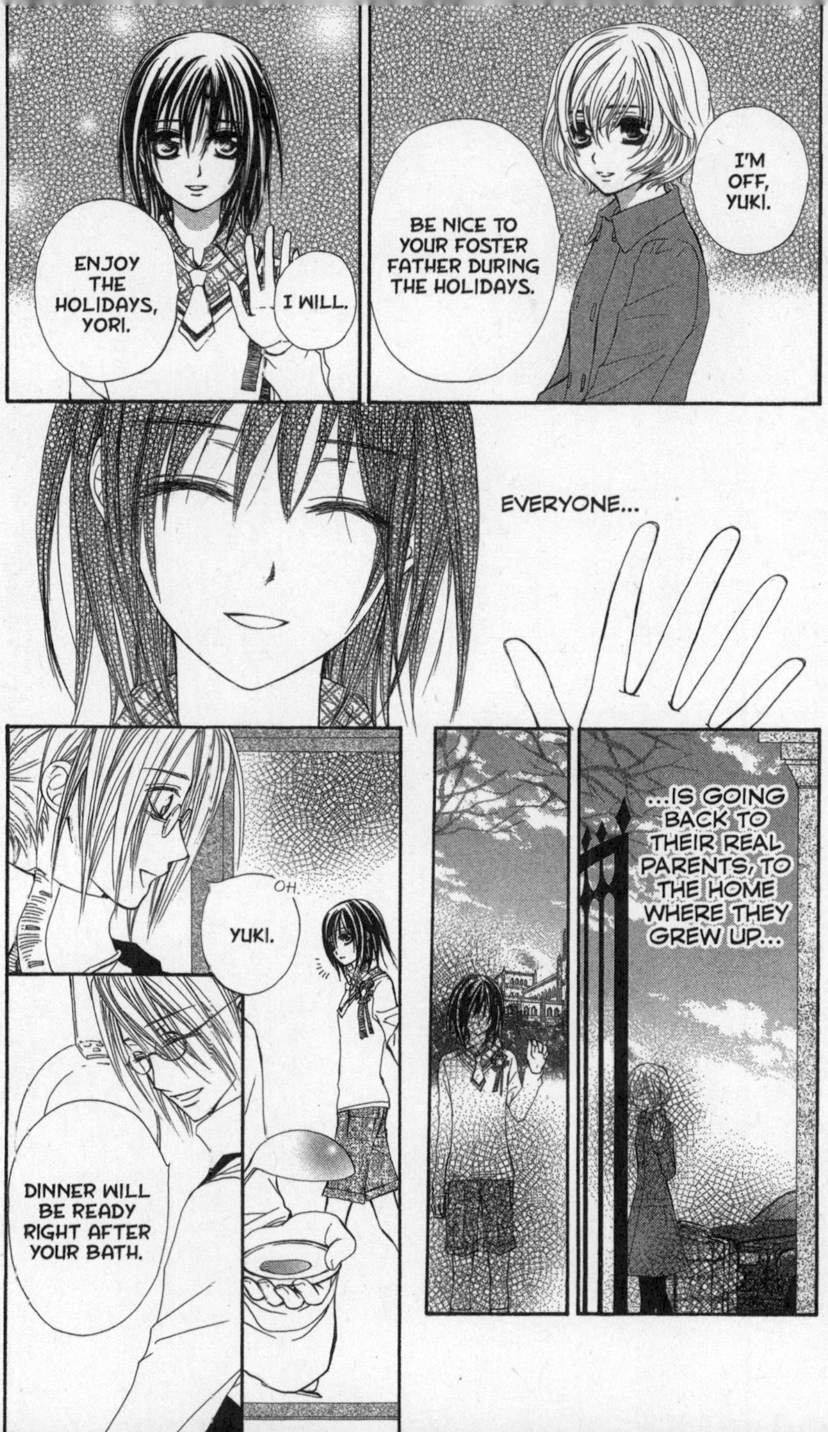
I'M OFF, YUKI.
BE NICE TO YOUR FOSTER FATHER DURING THE HOLIDAYS.
I WILL.
ENJOY THE HOLIDAYS, YORI.
EVERYONE...
...IS GOING BACK TO THEIR REAL PARENTS, TO THE HOME WHERE THEY GREW UP...
OH.
YUKI.
DINNER WILL BE READY RIGHT AFTER YOUR BATH.

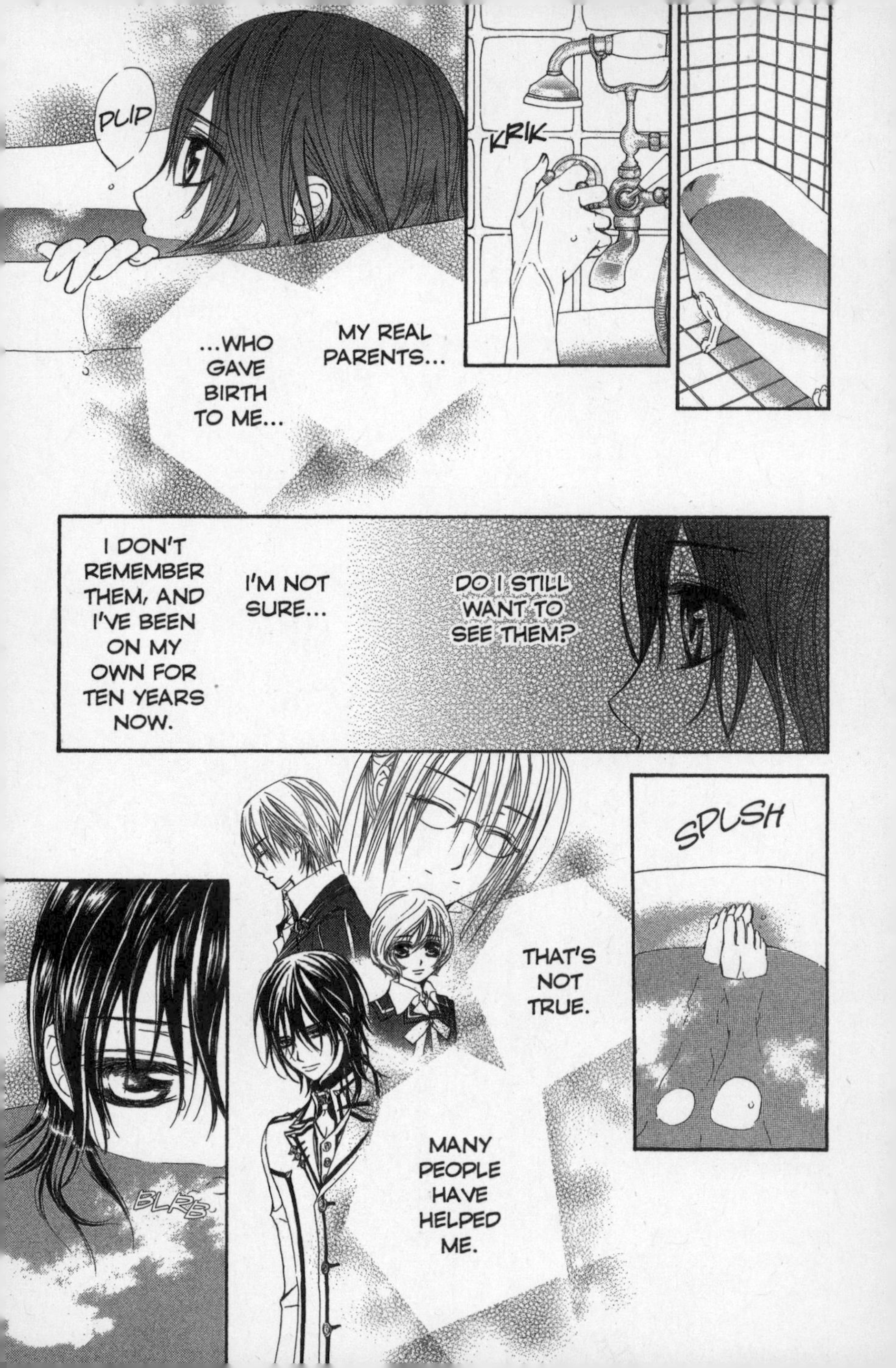
KRIK
PLUP
MY REAL PARENTS...
...WHO GAVE BIRTH TO ME...
DO I STILL WANT TO SEE THEM?
I'M NOT SURE...
I DON'T REMEMBER THEM, AND I'VE BEEN ON MY OWN FOR TEN YEARS NOW.
SPLSH
THAT'S NOT TRUE.
MANY PEOPLE HAVE HELPED ME.
BLRB

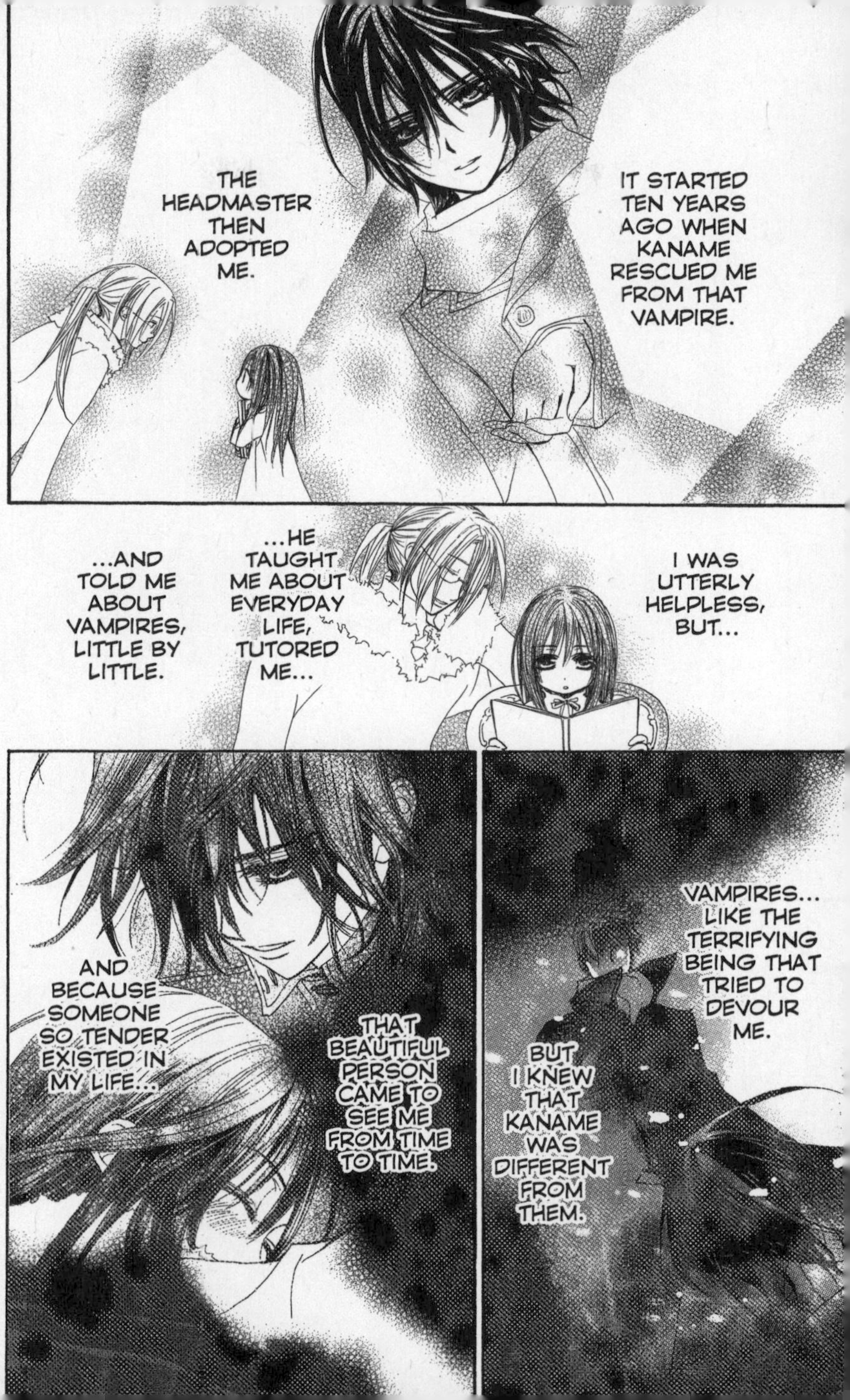
IT STARTED TEN YEARS AGO WHEN KANAME RESCUED ME FROM THAT VAMPIRE.
THE HEADMASTER THEN ADOPTED ME.
I WAS UTTERLY HELPLESS, BUT...
...HE TAUGHT ME ABOUT EVERYDAY LIFE, TUTORED ME...
...AND TOLD ME ABOUT VAMPIRES, LITTLE BY LITTLE.
VAMPIRES... LIKE THE TERRIFYING BEING THAT TRIED TO DEVOUR ME.
BUT I KNEW THAT KANAME WAS DIFFERENT FROM THEM.
THAT BEAUTIFUL PERSON CAME TO SEE ME FROM TIME TO TIME.
AND BECAUSE SOMEONE SO TENDER EXISTED IN MY LIFE...

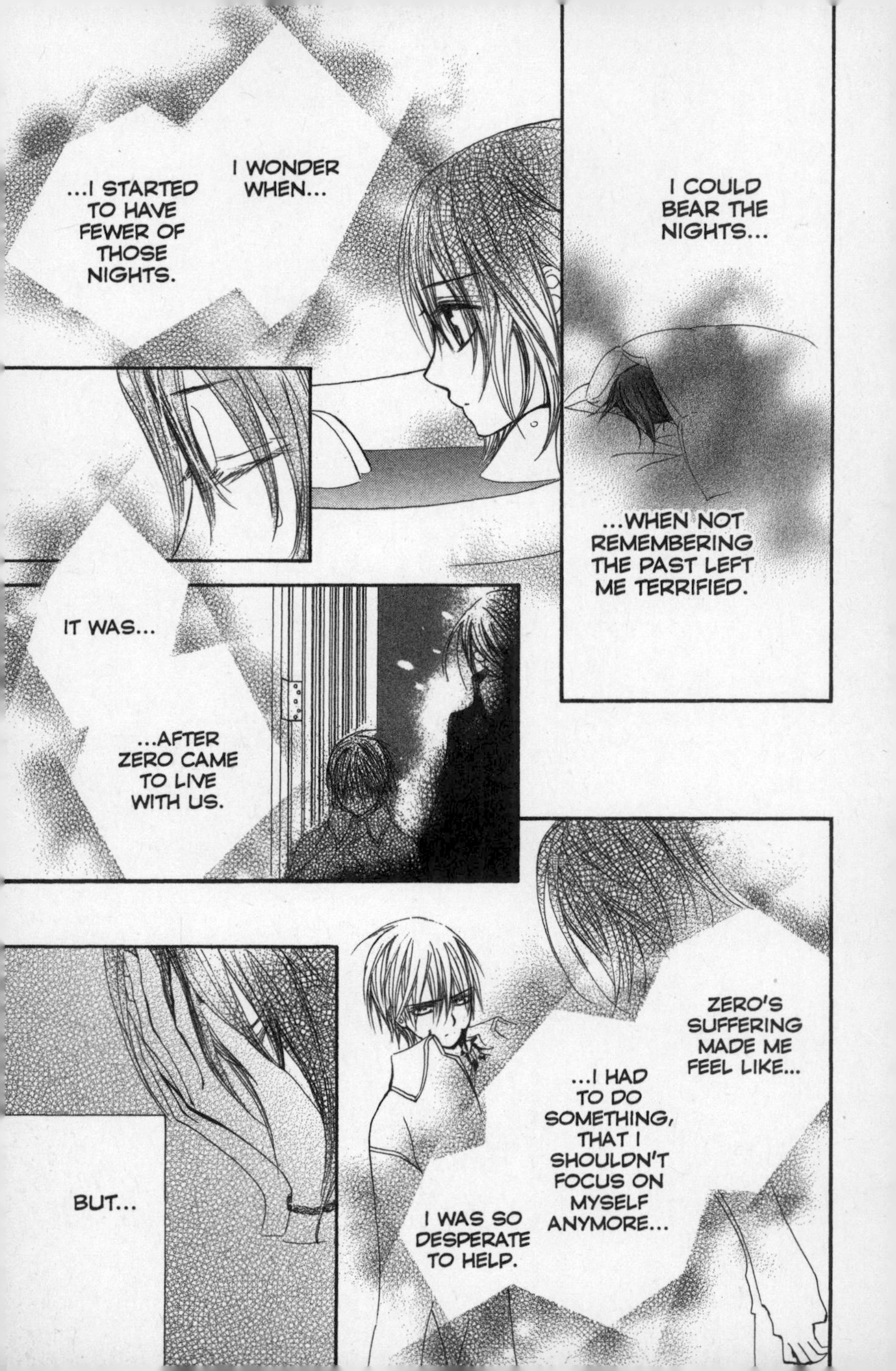
I COULD BEAR THE NIGHTS...
...WHEN NOT REMEMBERING THE PAST LEFT ME TERRIFIED.
I WONDER WHEN...
...I STARTED TO HAVE FEWER OF THOSE NIGHTS.
IT WAS...
...AFTER ZERO CAME TO LIVE WITH US.
ZERO'S SUFFERING MADE ME FEEL LIKE...
...I HAD TO DO SOMETHING, THAT I SHOULDN'T FOCUS ON MYSELF ANYMORE...
I WAS SO DESPERATE TO HELP.
BUT...

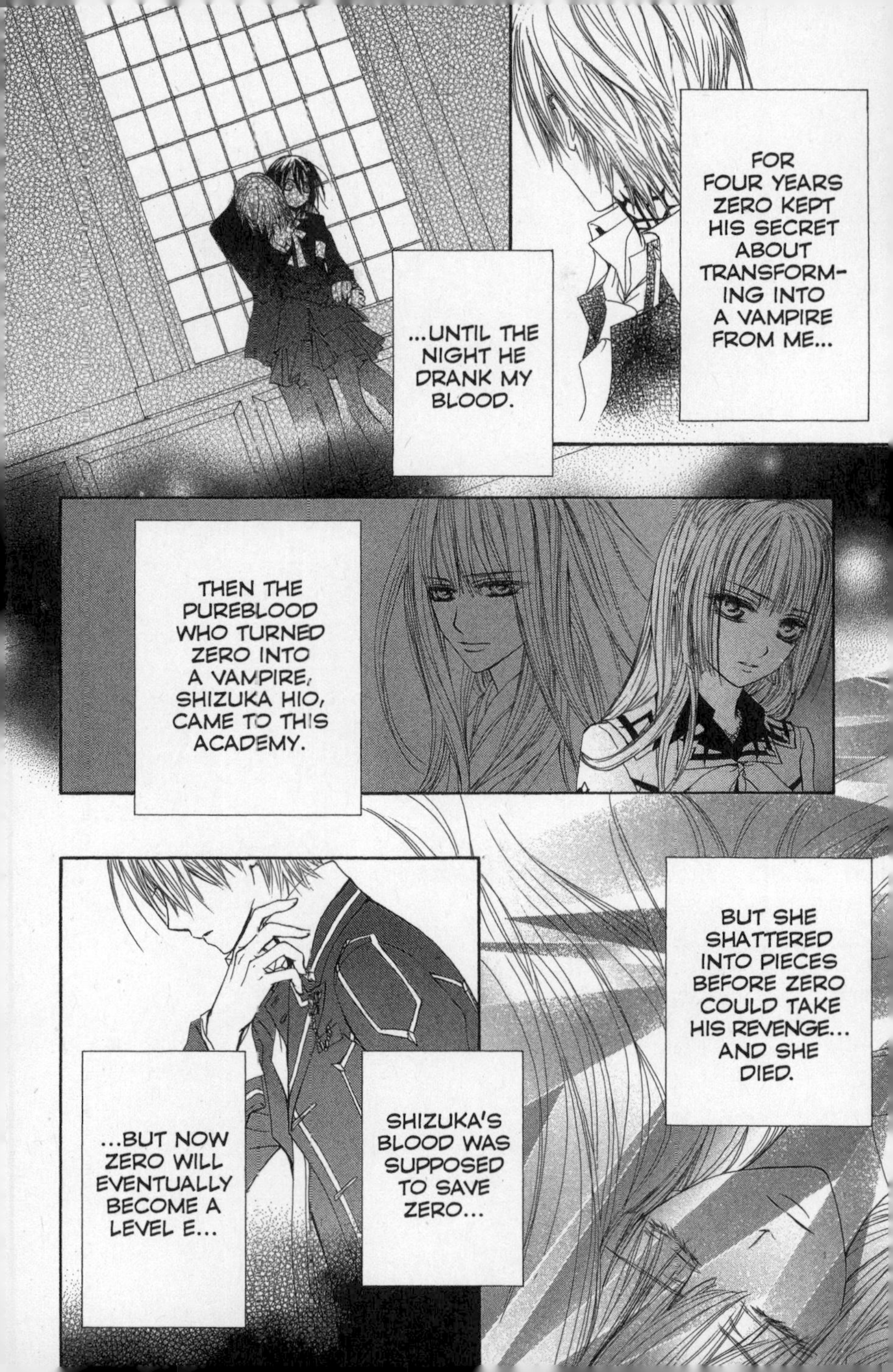
FOR FOUR YEARS ZERO KEPT HIS SECRET ABOUT TRANSFORMING INTO A VAMPIRE FROM ME...
...UNTIL THE NIGHT HE DRANK MY BLOOD.
THEN THE PUREBLOOD WHO TURNED ZERO INTO A VAMPIRE, SHIZUKA HIO, CAME TO THIS ACADEMY.
BUT SHE SHATTERED INTO PIECES BEFORE ZERO COULD TAKE HIS REVENGE... AND SHE DIED.
SHIZUKA'S BLOOD WAS SUPPOSED TO SAVE ZERO...
...BUT NOW ZERO WILL EVENTUALLY BECOME A LEVEL E...

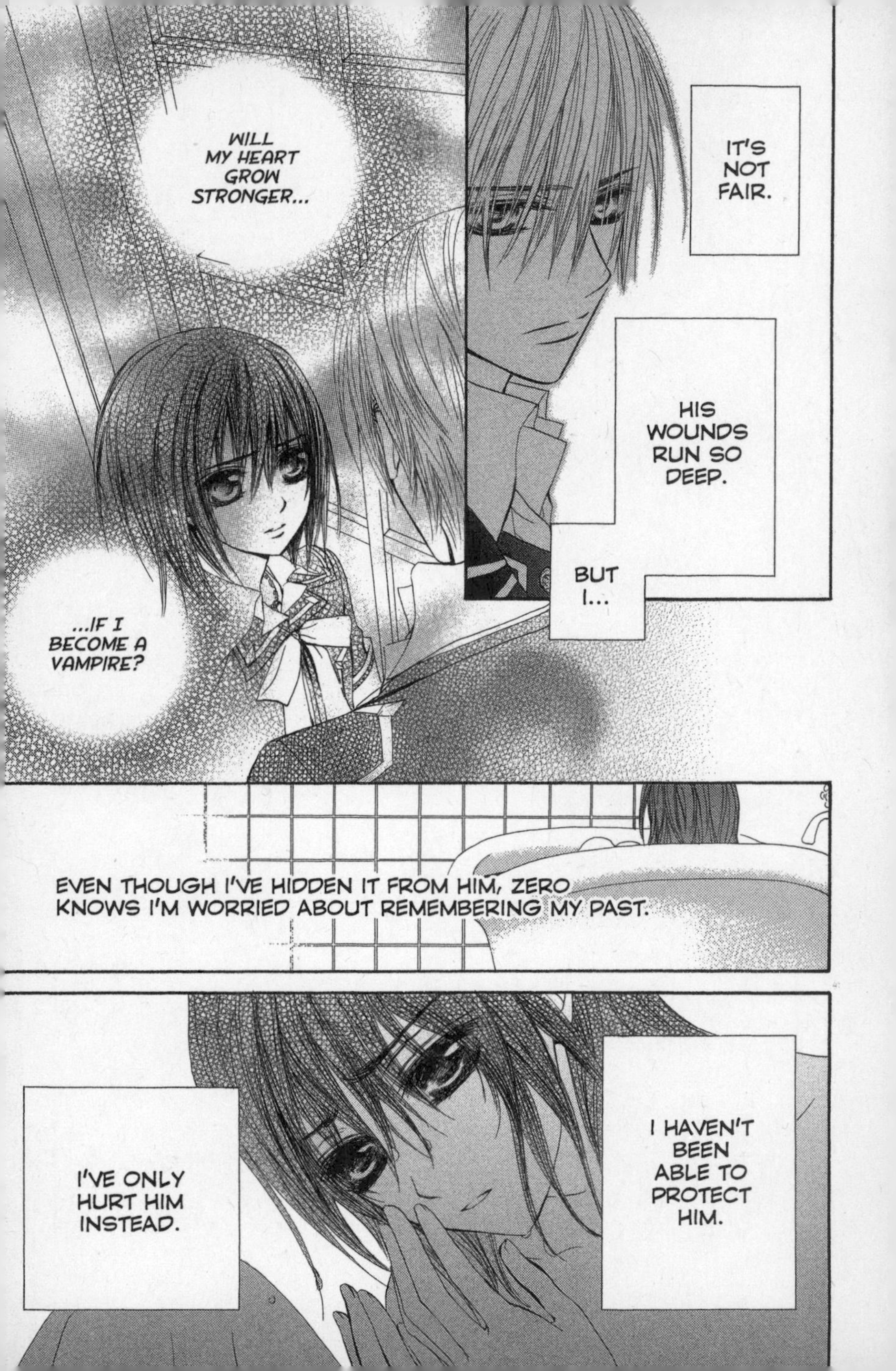
IT'S NOT FAIR.
HIS WOUNDS RUN SO DEEP.
BUT I...
WILL MY HEART GROW STRONGER...
...IF I BECOME A VAMPIRE?
EVEN THOUGH I'VE HIDDEN IT FROM HIM, ZERO KNOWS I'M WORRIED ABOUT REMEMBERING MY PAST.
I HAVEN'T BEEN ABLE TO PROTECT HIM.
I'VE ONLY HURT HIM INSTEAD.

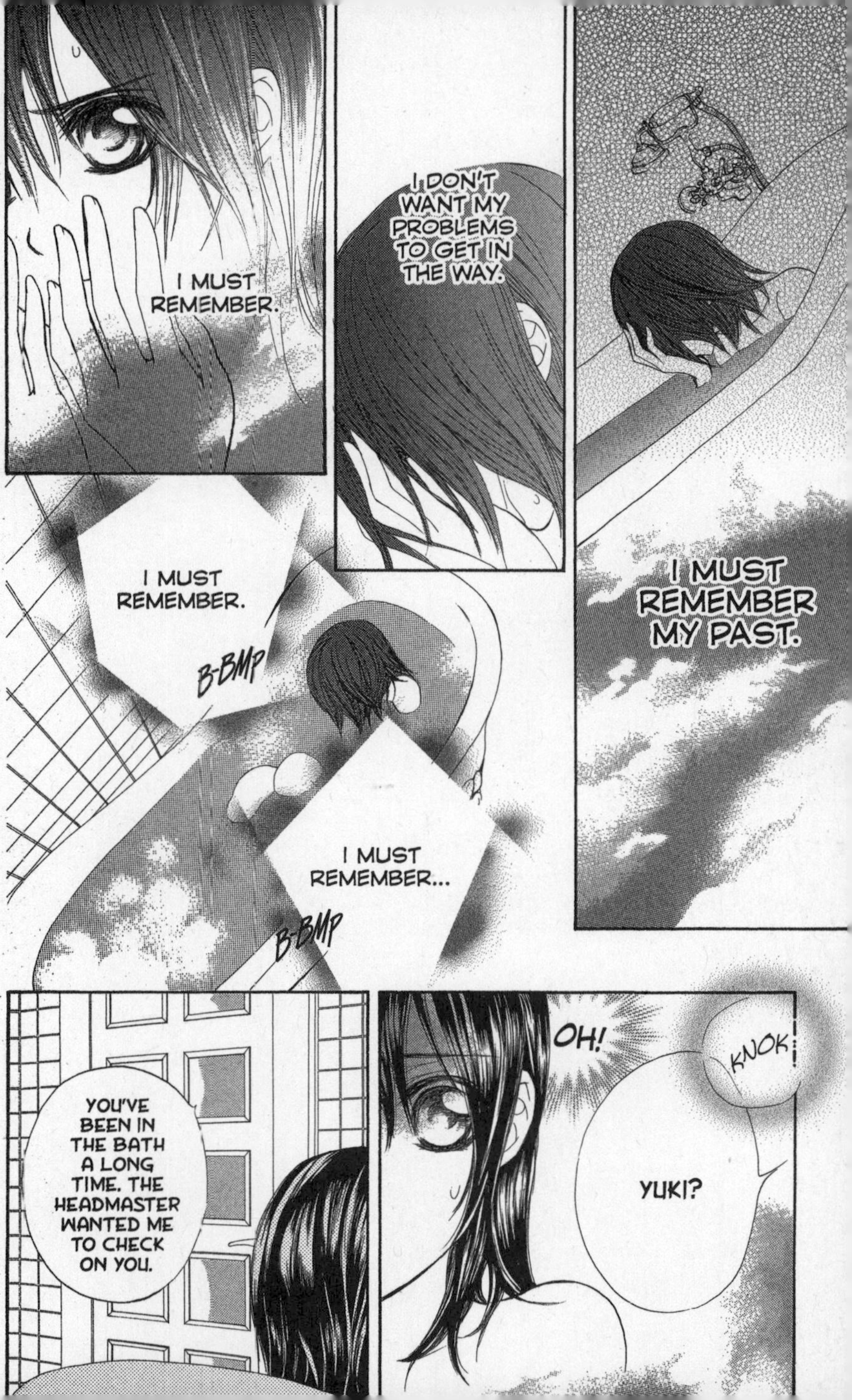
I MUST REMEMBER MY PAST.
I DON'T WANT MY PROBLEMS TO GET IN THE WAY.
I MUST REMEMBER.
I MUST REMEMBER.
B-BMP
I MUST REMEMBER...
B-BMP
KNOK
OH!
YUKI?
YOU'VE BEEN IN THE BATH A LONG TIME. THE HEADMASTER WANTED ME TO CHECK ON YOU.

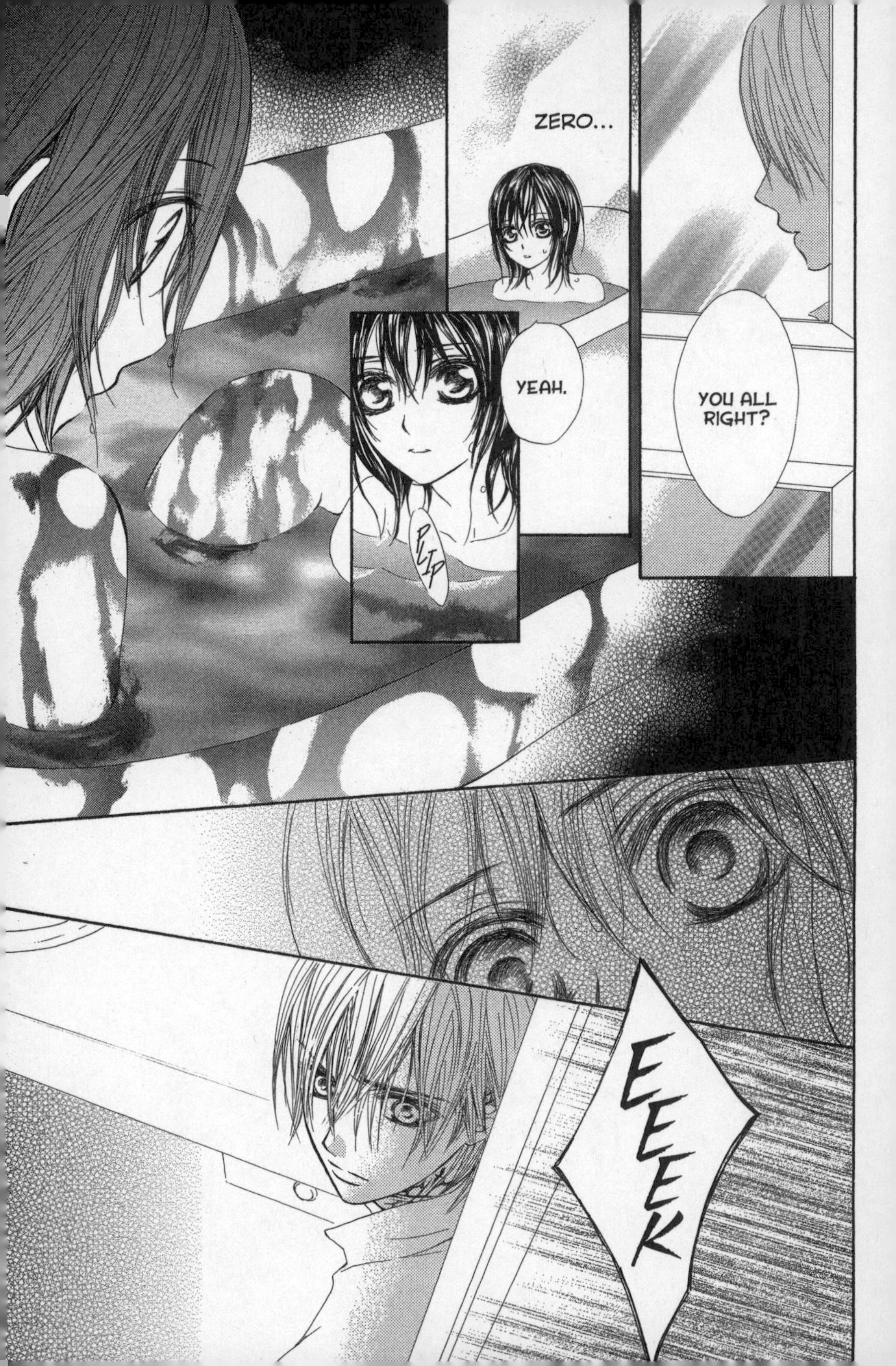
YOU ALL RIGHT?
ZERO...
YEAH.
PLIP
EEEK

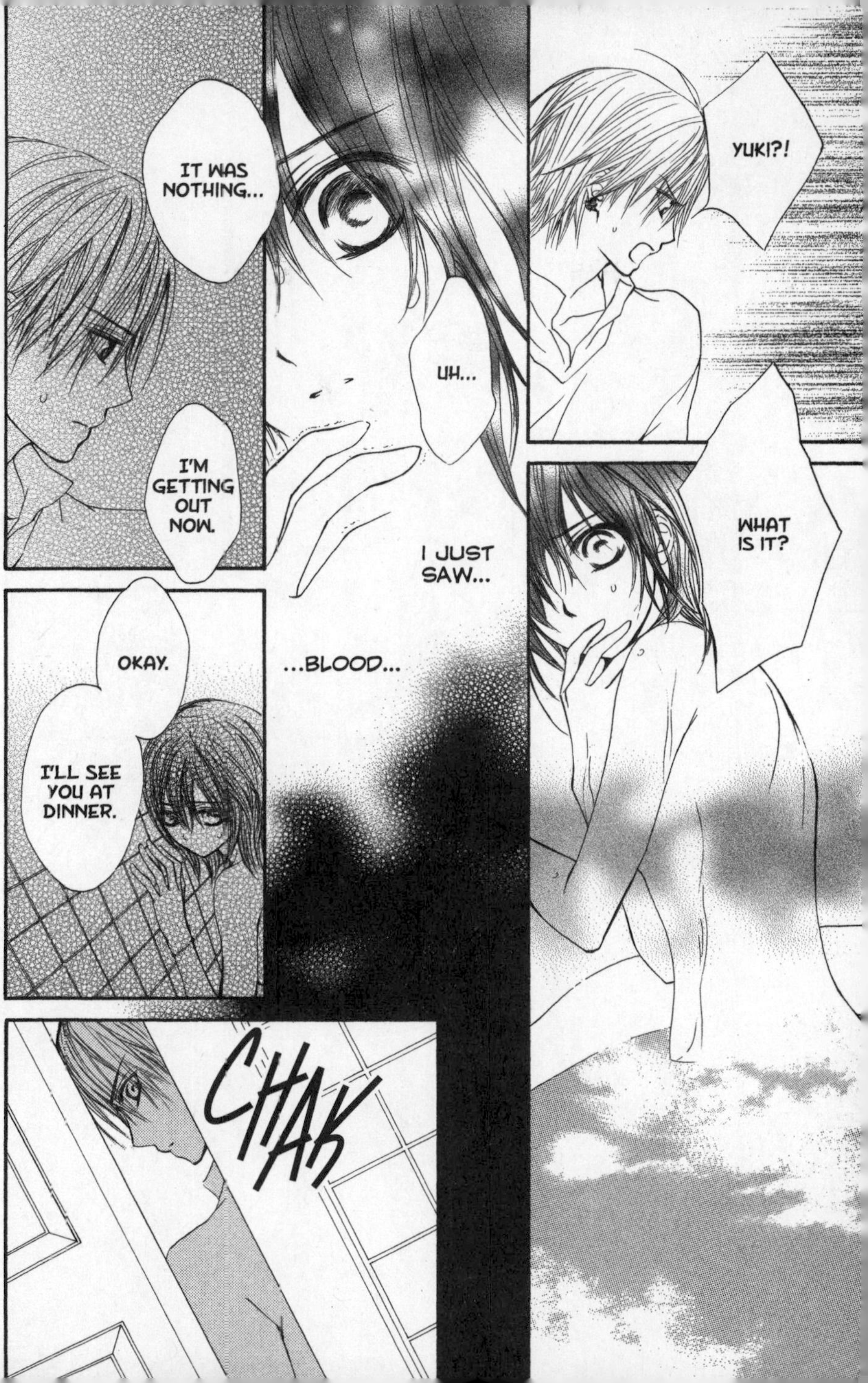
YUKI?!
WHAT IS IT?
UH...
I JUST SAW...
...BLOOD...
IT WAS NOTHING...
I'M GETTING OUT NOW.
OKAY.
I'LL SEE YOU AT DINNER.
CHAK

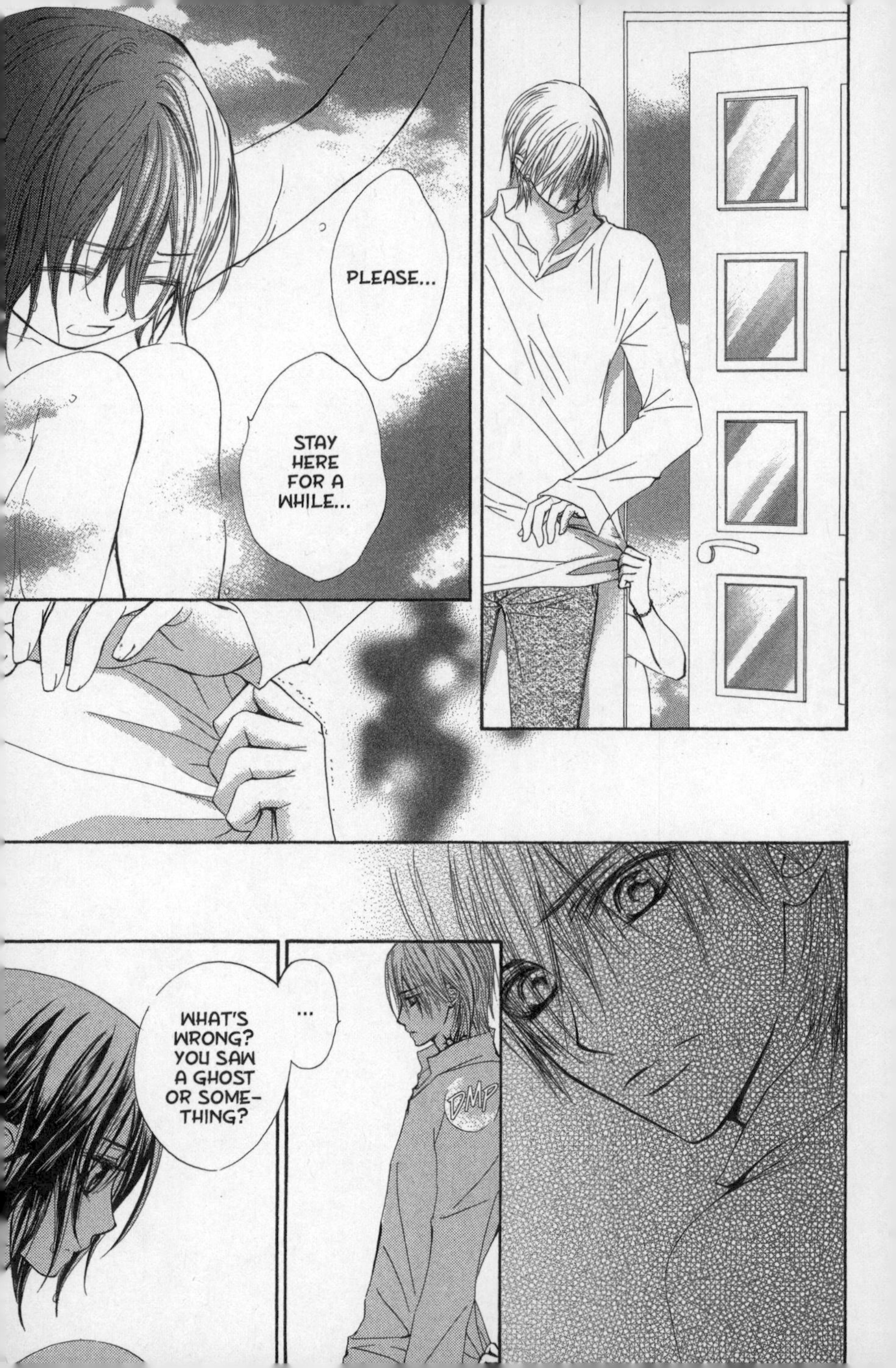
PLEASE...
STAY HERE FOR A WHILE...
...
WHAT'S WRONG? YOU SAW A GHOST OR SOME-THING?

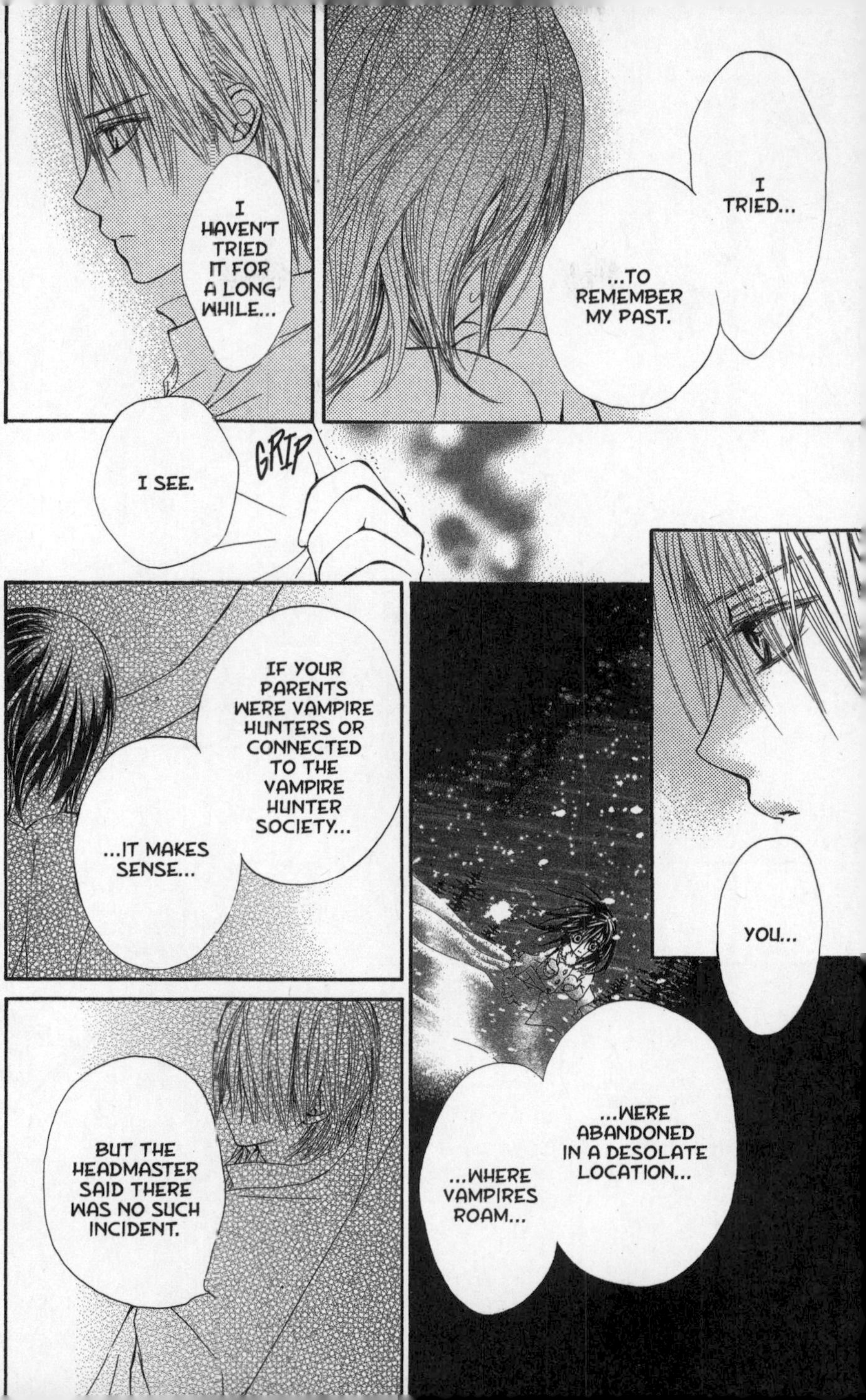
I TRIED...
...TO REMEMBER MY PAST.
I HAVEN'T TRIED IT FOR A LONG WHILE...
GRIP
I SEE.
YOU...
...WERE ABANDONED IN A DESOLATE LOCATION...
...WHERE VAMPIRES ROAM...
IF YOUR PARENTS WERE VAMPIRE HUNTERS OR CONNECTED TO THE VAMPIRE HUNTER SOCIETY...
...IT MAKES SENSE...
BUT THE HEADMASTER SAID THERE WAS NO SUCH INCIDENT.

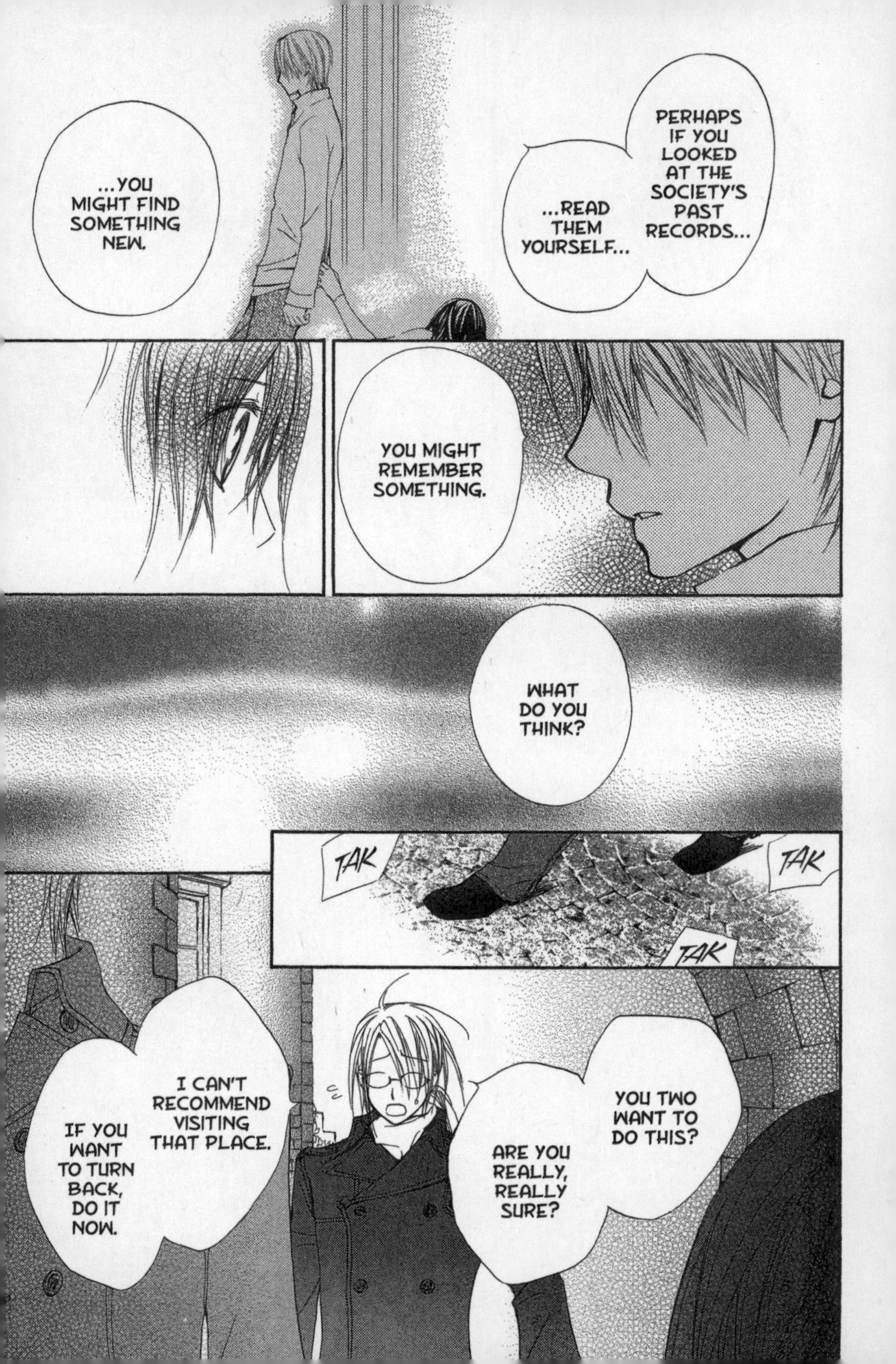
PERHAPS IF YOU LOOKED AT THE SOCIETY'S PAST RECORDS...
...READ THEM YOURSELF...
...YOU MIGHT FIND SOMETHING NEW.
YOU MIGHT REMEMBER SOMETHING.
WHAT DO YOU THINK?
TAK
TAK
TAK
YOU TWO WANT TO DO THIS?
ARE YOU REALLY, REALLY SURE?
I CAN'T RECOMMEND VISITING THAT PLACE.
IF YOU WANT TO TURN BACK, DO IT NOW.

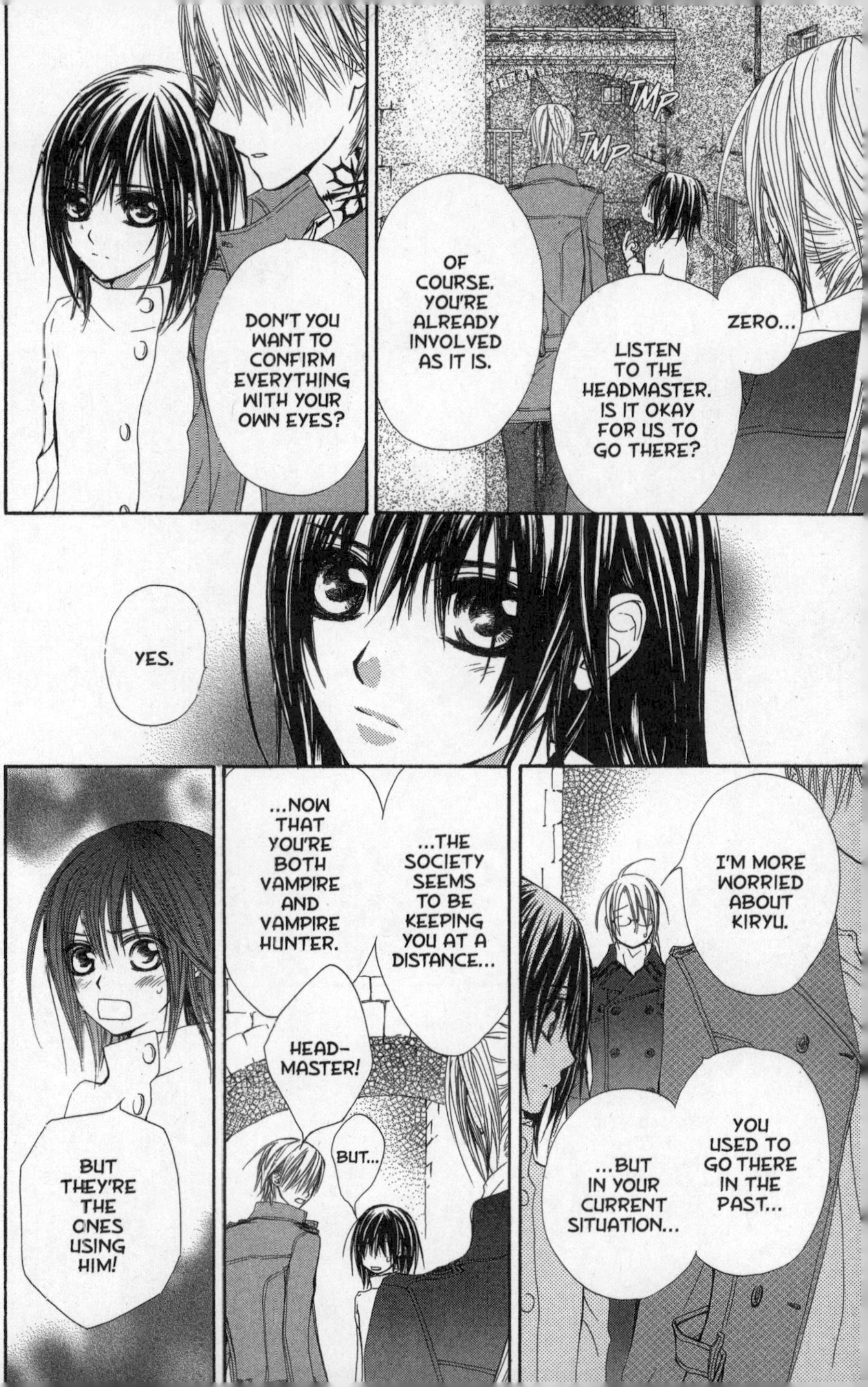
TMP
TMP
ZERO...
LISTEN TO THE HEADMASTER. IS IT OKAY FOR US TO GO THERE?
OF COURSE. YOU'RE ALREADY INVOLVED AS IT IS.
DON'T YOU WANT TO CONFIRM EVERYTHING WITH YOUR OWN EYES?
YES.
I'M MORE WORRIED ABOUT KIRYU.
YOU USED TO GO THERE IN THE PAST...
...BUT IN YOUR CURRENT SITUATION...
...THE SOCIETY SEEMS TO BE KEEPING YOU AT A DISTANCE...
...NOW THAT YOU'RE BOTH VAMPIRE AND VAMPIRE HUNTER.
HEAD-MASTER!
BUT...
BUT THEY'RE THE ONES USING HIM!

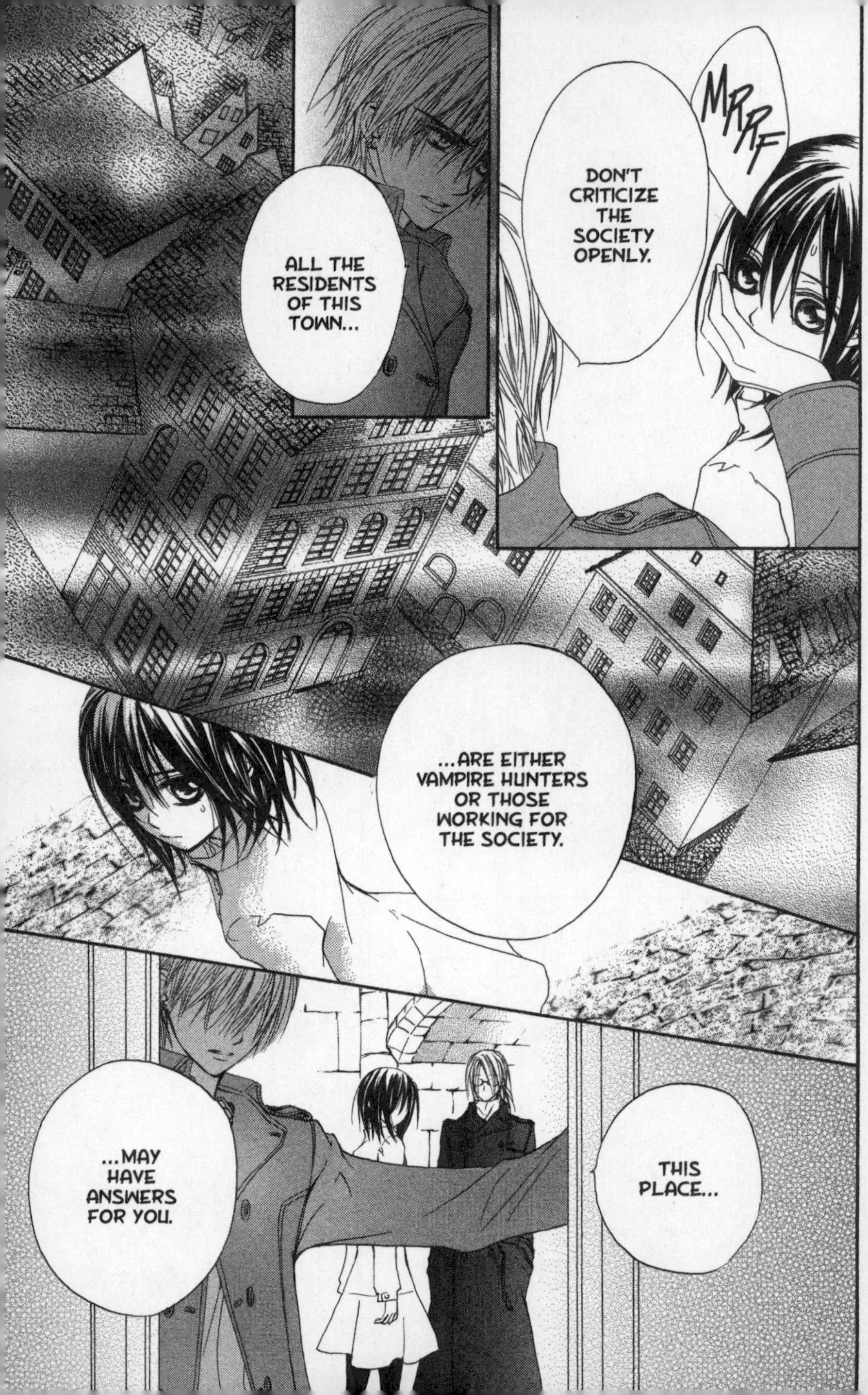
MRRF
DON'T CRITICIZE THE SOCIETY OPENLY.
ALL THE RESIDENTS OF THIS TOWN...
...ARE EITHER VAMPIRE HUNTERS OR THOSE WORKING FOR THE SOCIETY.
THIS PLACE...
...MAY HAVE ANSWERS FOR YOU.

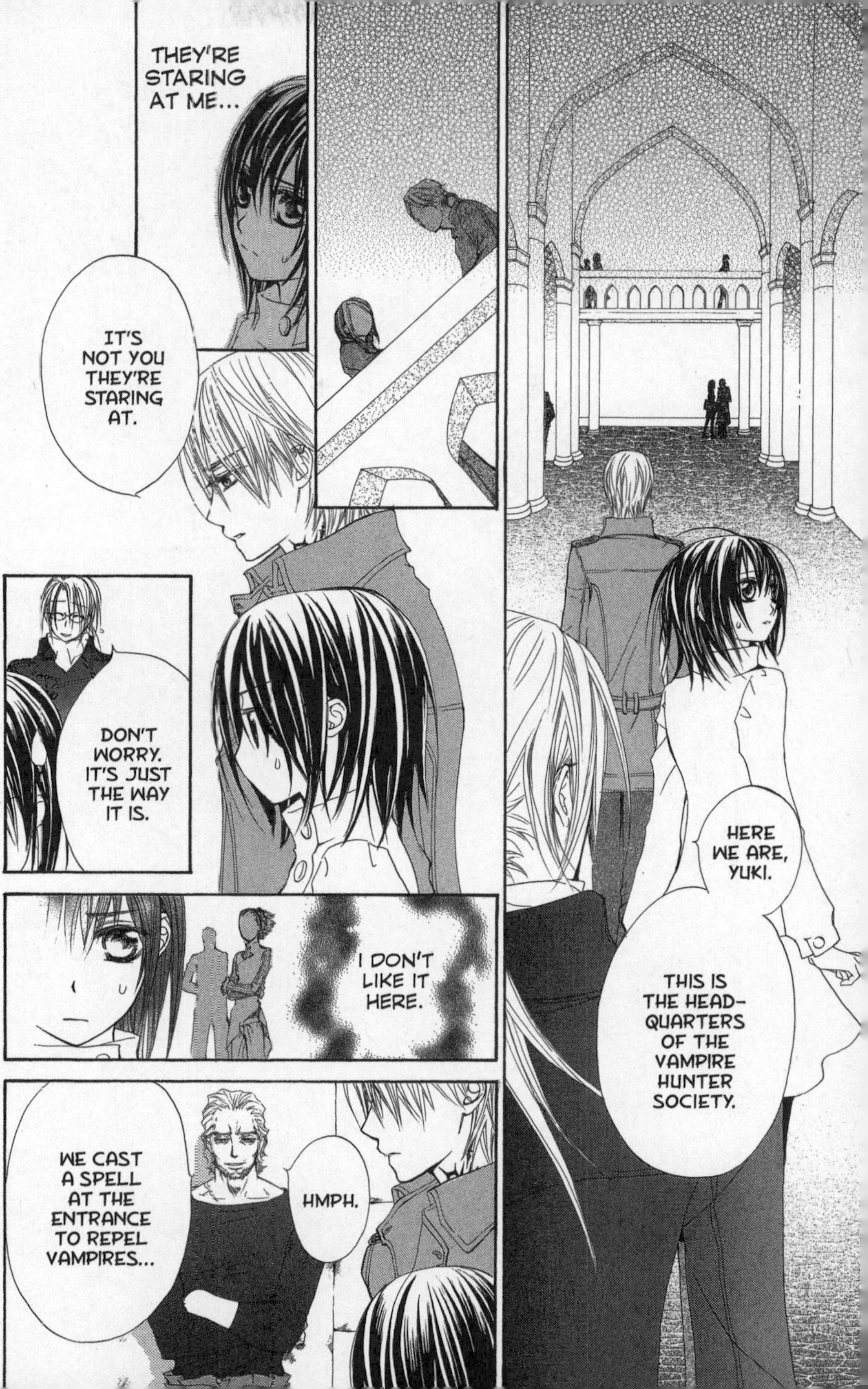
HERE WE ARE, YUKI.
THIS IS THE HEAD-QUARTERS OF THE VAMPIRE HUNTER SOCIETY.
THEY'RE STARING AT ME...
IT'S NOT YOU THEY'RE STARING AT.
DON'T WORRY. IT'S JUST THE WAY IT IS.
I DON'T LIKE IT HERE.
HMPH.
WE CAST A SPELL AT THE ENTRANCE TO REPEL VAMPIRES...

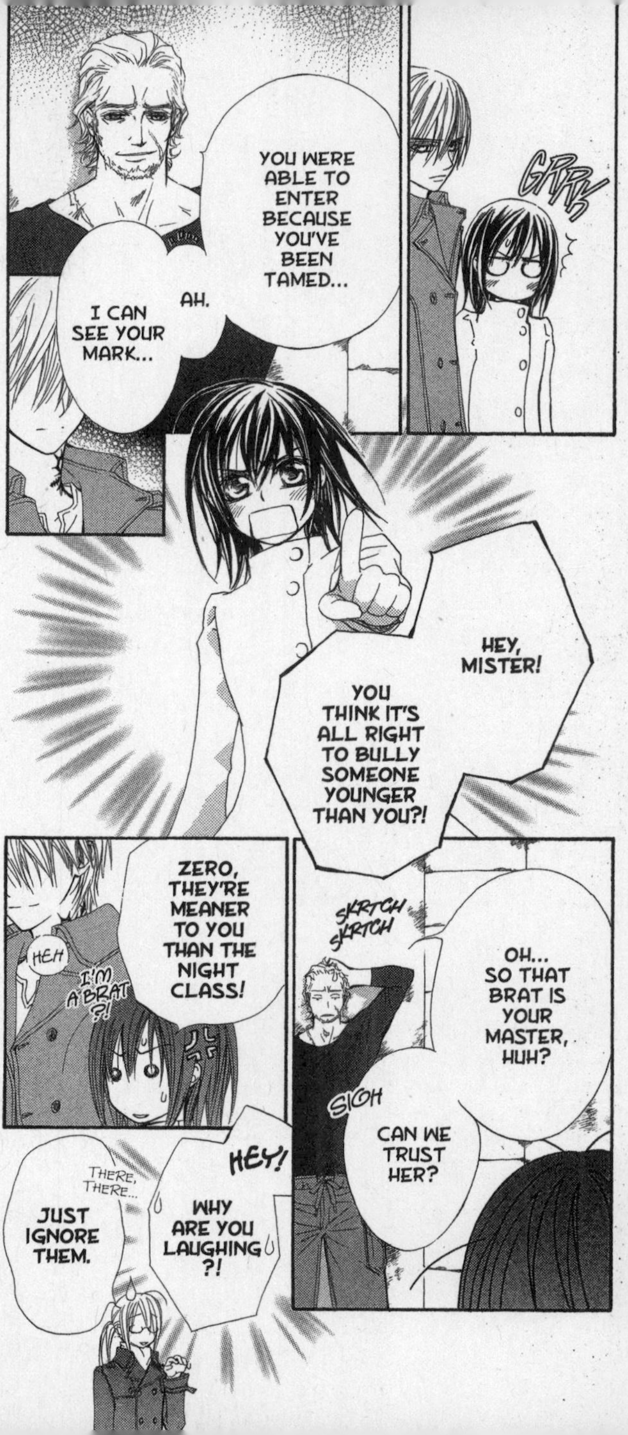
GRRR
YOU WERE ABLE TO ENTER BECAUSE YOU'VE BEEN TAMED...
AH.
I CAN SEE YOUR MARK...
HEY, MISTER!
YOU THINK IT'S ALL RIGHT TO BULLY SOMEONE YOUNGER THAN YOU?!
OH... SO THAT BRAT IS YOUR MASTER, HUH?
SKRTCH SKRTCH
SIGH
CAN WE TRUST HER?
ZERO, THEY'RE MEANER TO YOU THAN THE NIGHT CLASS!
HEH
I'M A BRAT?!
HEY!
WHY ARE YOU LAUGHING?!
THERE, THERE...
JUST IGNORE THEM.

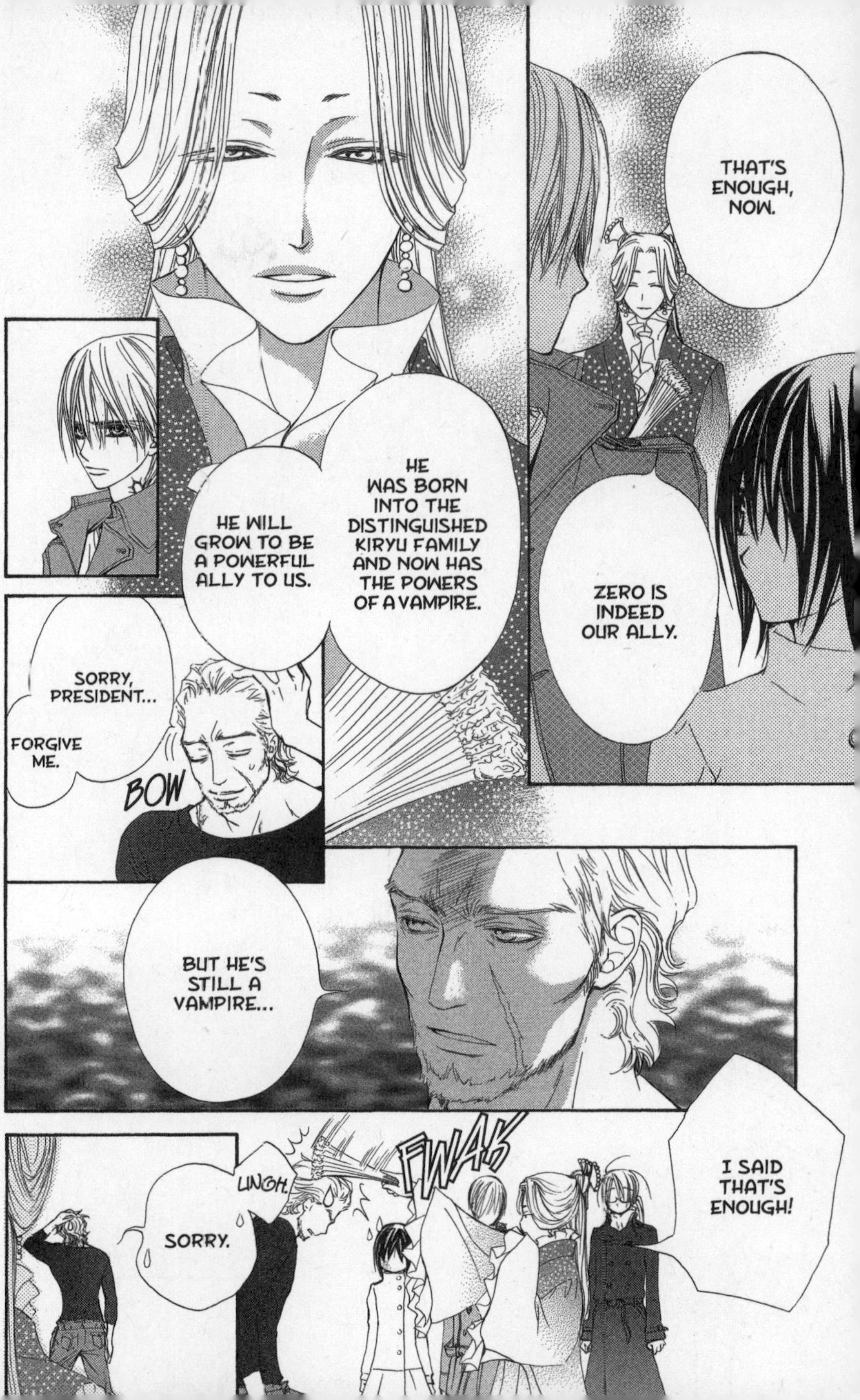
THAT'S ENOUGH, NOW.
ZERO IS INDEED OUR ALLY.
HE WAS BORN INTO THE DISTINGUISHED KIRYU FAMILY AND NOW HAS THE POWERS OF A VAMPIRE.
HE WILL GROW TO BE A POWERFUL ALLY TO US.
SORRY, PRESIDENT...
FORGIVE ME.
BOW
BUT HE'S STILL A VAMPIRE...
I SAID THAT'S ENOUGH!
FWAK
UNGH.
SORRY.

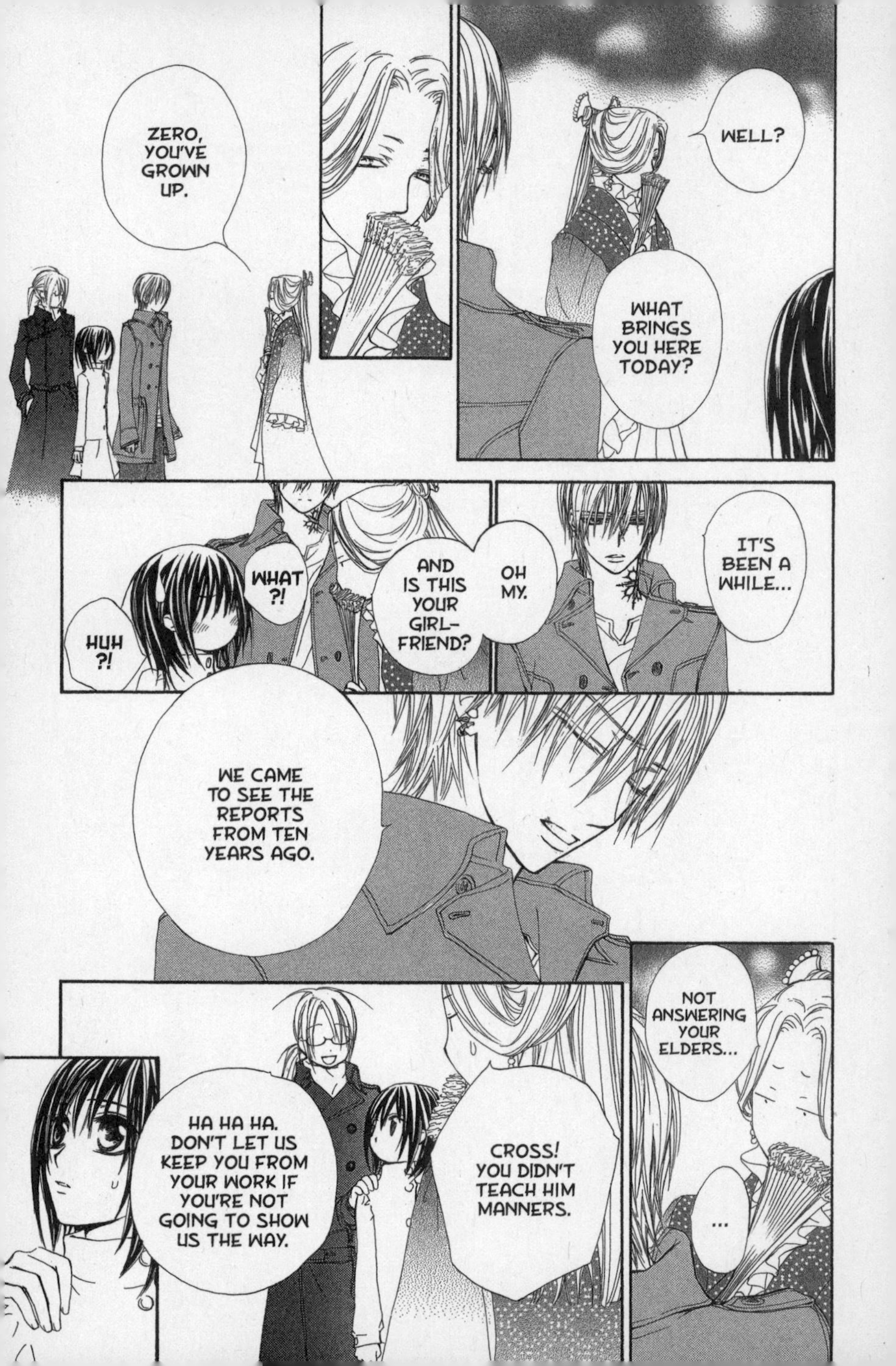
WELL?
WHAT BRINGS YOU HERE TODAY?
ZERO, YOU'VE GROWN UP.
IT'S BEEN A WHILE...
OH MY.
AND IS THIS YOUR GIRL-FRIEND?
WHAT?!
HUH?!
WE CAME TO SEE THE REPORTS FROM TEN YEARS AGO.
NOT ANSWERING YOUR ELDERS...
...
CROSS! YOU DIDN'T TEACH HIM MANNERS.
HA HA HA. DON'T LET US KEEP YOU FROM YOUR WORK IF YOU'RE NOT GOING TO SHOW US THE WAY.

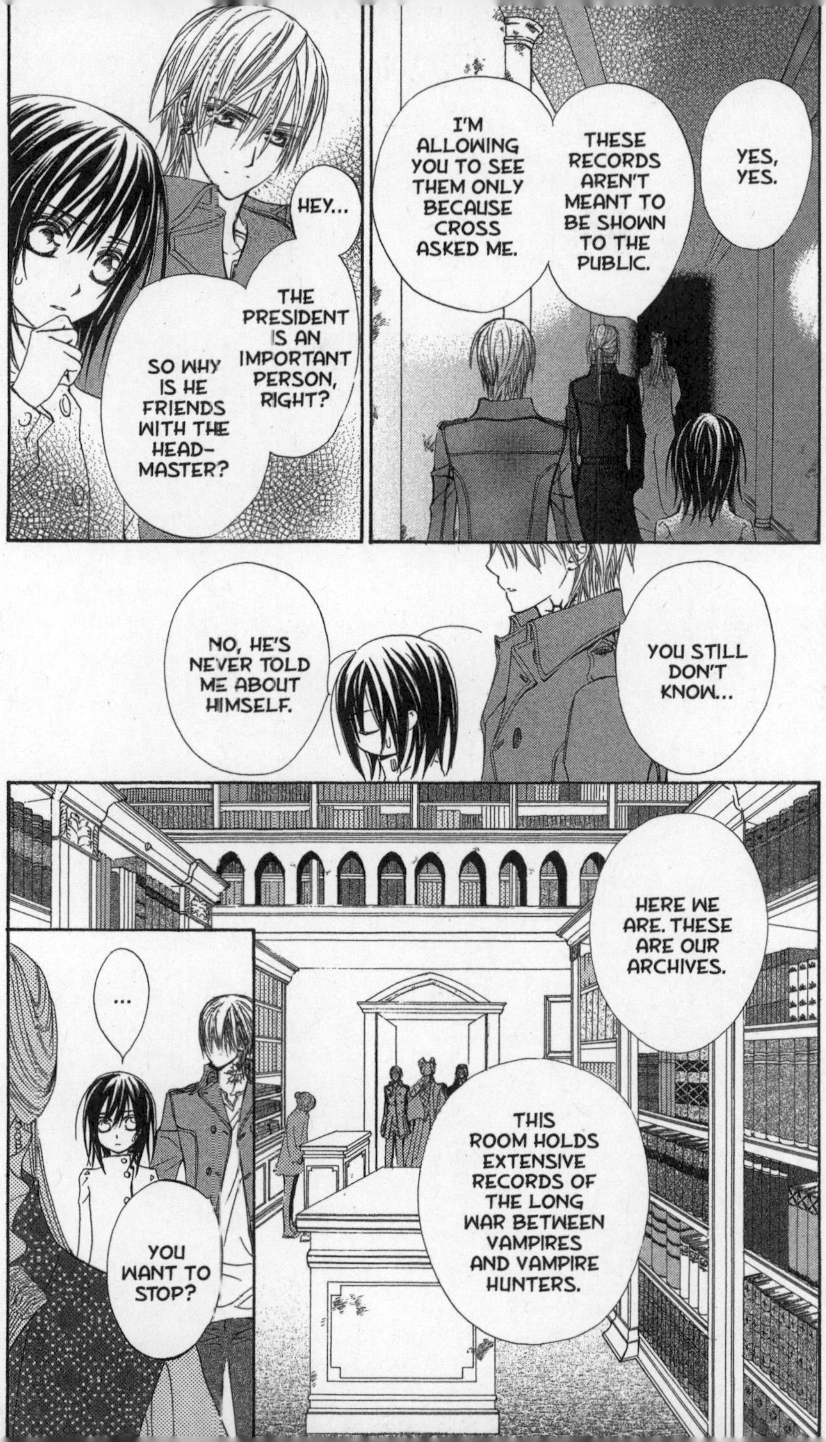

YES, YES.
THESE RECORDS AREN'T MEANT TO BE SHOWN TO THE PUBLIC.
I'M ALLOWING YOU TO SEE THEM ONLY BECAUSE CROSS ASKED ME.
HEY...
THE PRESIDENT IS AN IMPORTANT PERSON, RIGHT?
SO WHY IS HE FRIENDS WITH THE HEAD-MASTER?
YOU STILL DON'T KNOW...
NO, HE'S NEVER TOLD ME ABOUT HIMSELF.
HERE WE ARE. THESE ARE OUR ARCHIVES.
THIS ROOM HOLDS EXTENSIVE RECORDS OF THE LONG WAR BETWEEN VAMPIRES AND VAMPIRE HUNTERS.
...
YOU WANT TO STOP?

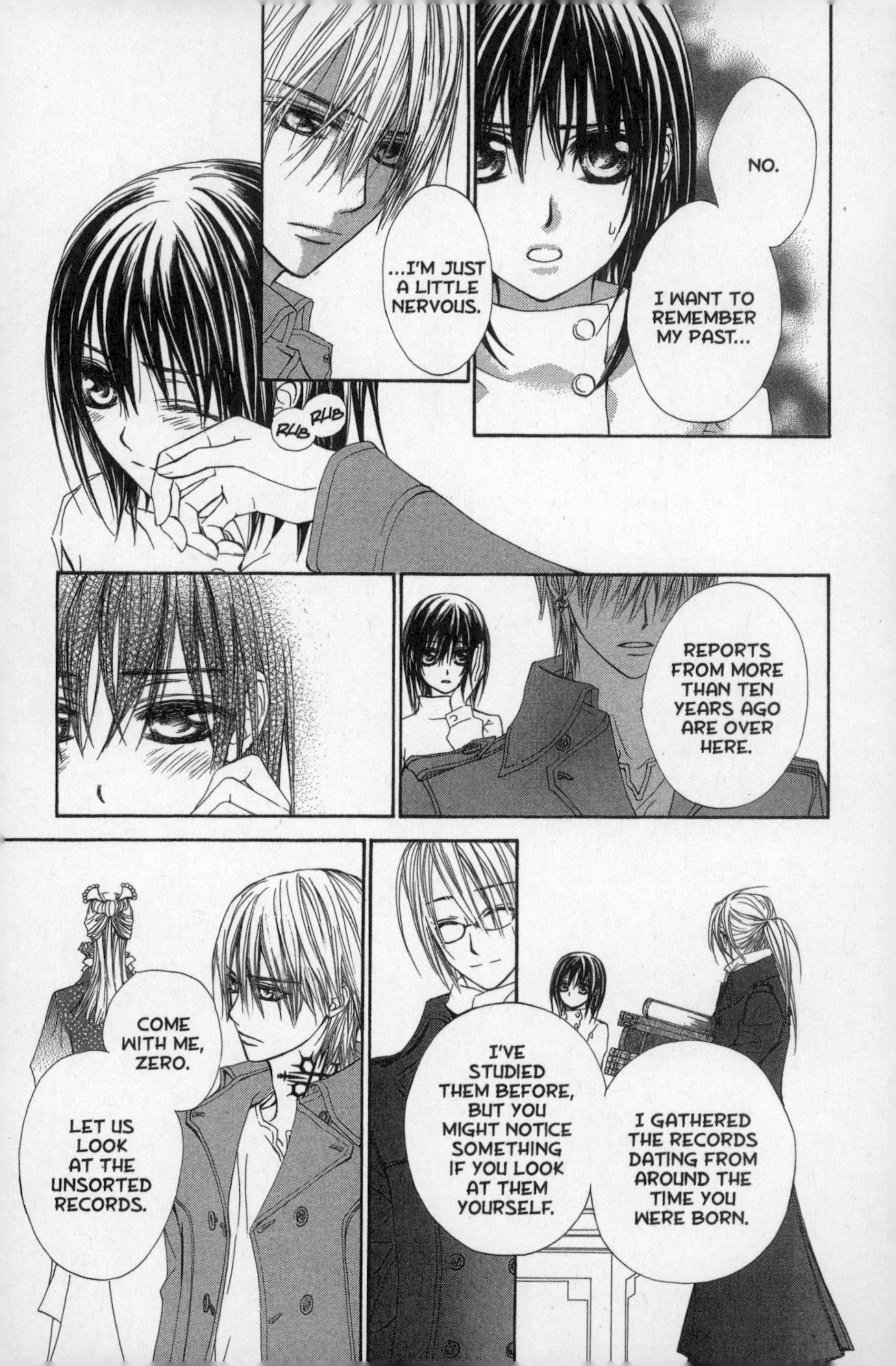
NO.
I WANT TO REMEMBER MY PAST...
...I'M JUST A LITTLE NERVOUS.
RUB RUB
REPORTS FROM MORE THAN TEN YEARS AGO ARE OVER HERE.
I GATHERED THE RECORDS DATING FROM AROUND THE TIME YOU WERE BORN.
I'VE STUDIED THEM BEFORE, BUT YOU MIGHT NOTICE SOMETHING IF YOU LOOK AT THEM YOURSELF.
COME WITH ME, ZERO.
LET US LOOK AT THE UNSORTED RECORDS.

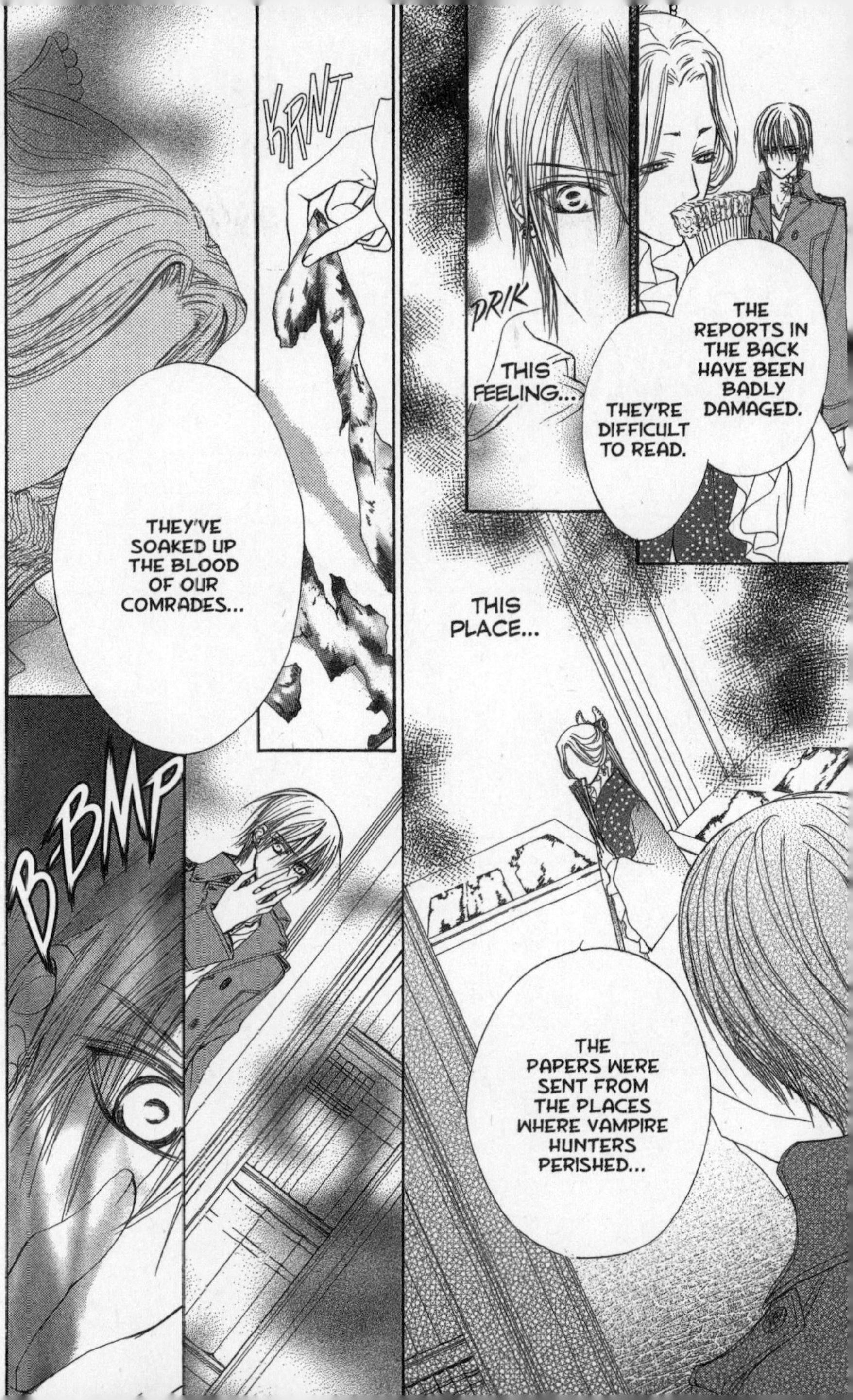
THE REPORTS IN THE BACK HAVE BEEN BADLY DAMAGED.
THEY'RE DIFFICULT TO READ.
DRIK
THIS FEELING...
THIS PLACE...
THE PAPERS WERE SENT FROM THE PLACES WHERE VAMPIRE HUNTERS PERISHED...
KRNT
THEY'VE SOAKED UP THE BLOOD OF OUR COMRADES...
B-BMP

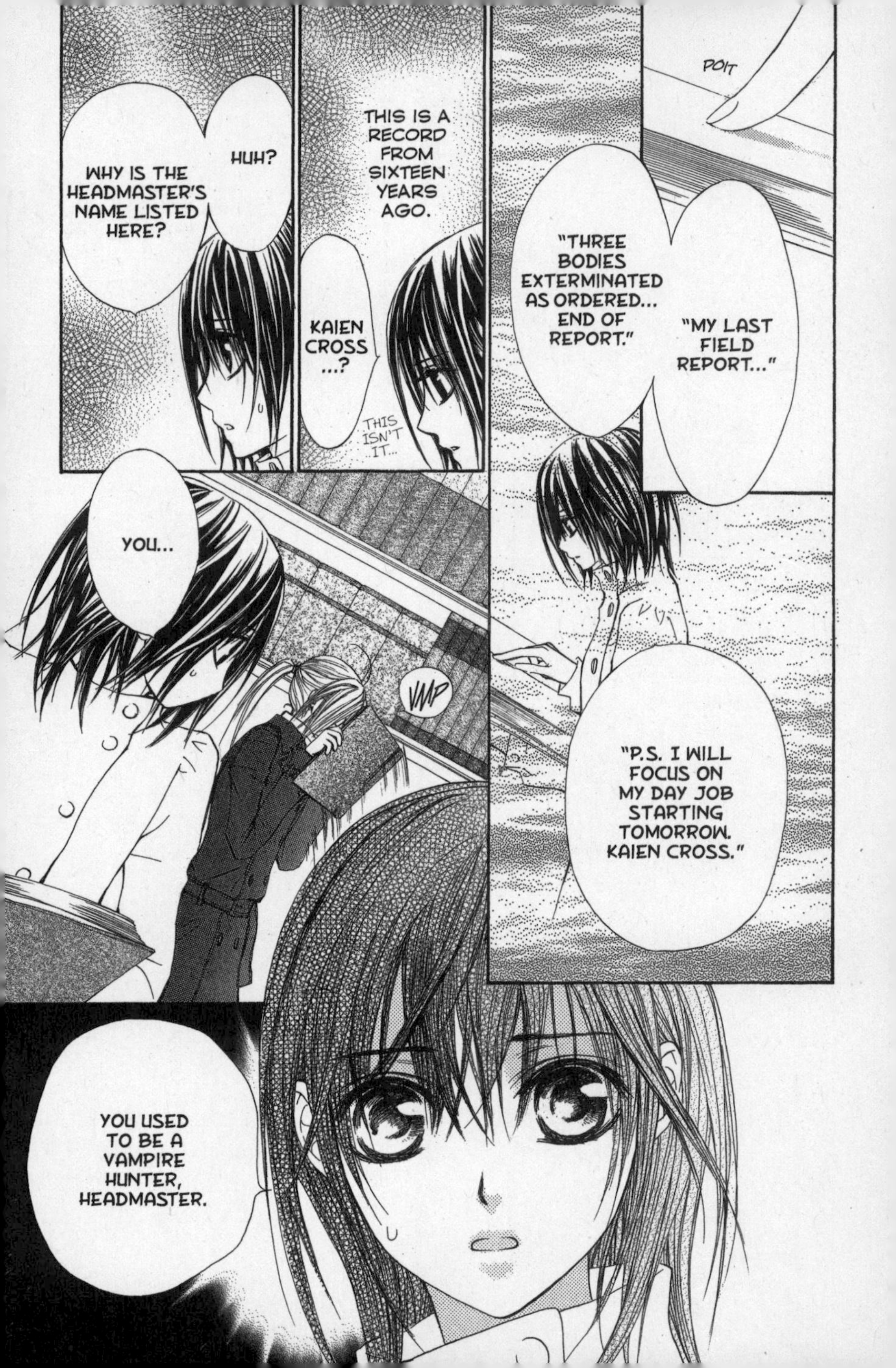
POIT
"MY LAST FIELD REPORT..."
"THREE BODIES EXTERMINATED AS ORDERED... END OF REPORT."
THIS IS A RECORD FROM SIXTEEN YEARS AGO.
KAIEN CROSS ...?
THIS ISN'T IT...
HUH?
WHY IS THE HEADMASTER'S NAME LISTED HERE?
"P.S. I WILL FOCUS ON MY DAY JOB STARTING TOMORROW. KAIEN CROSS."
YOU...
VMP
YOU USED TO BE A VAMPIRE HUNTER, HEADMASTER.

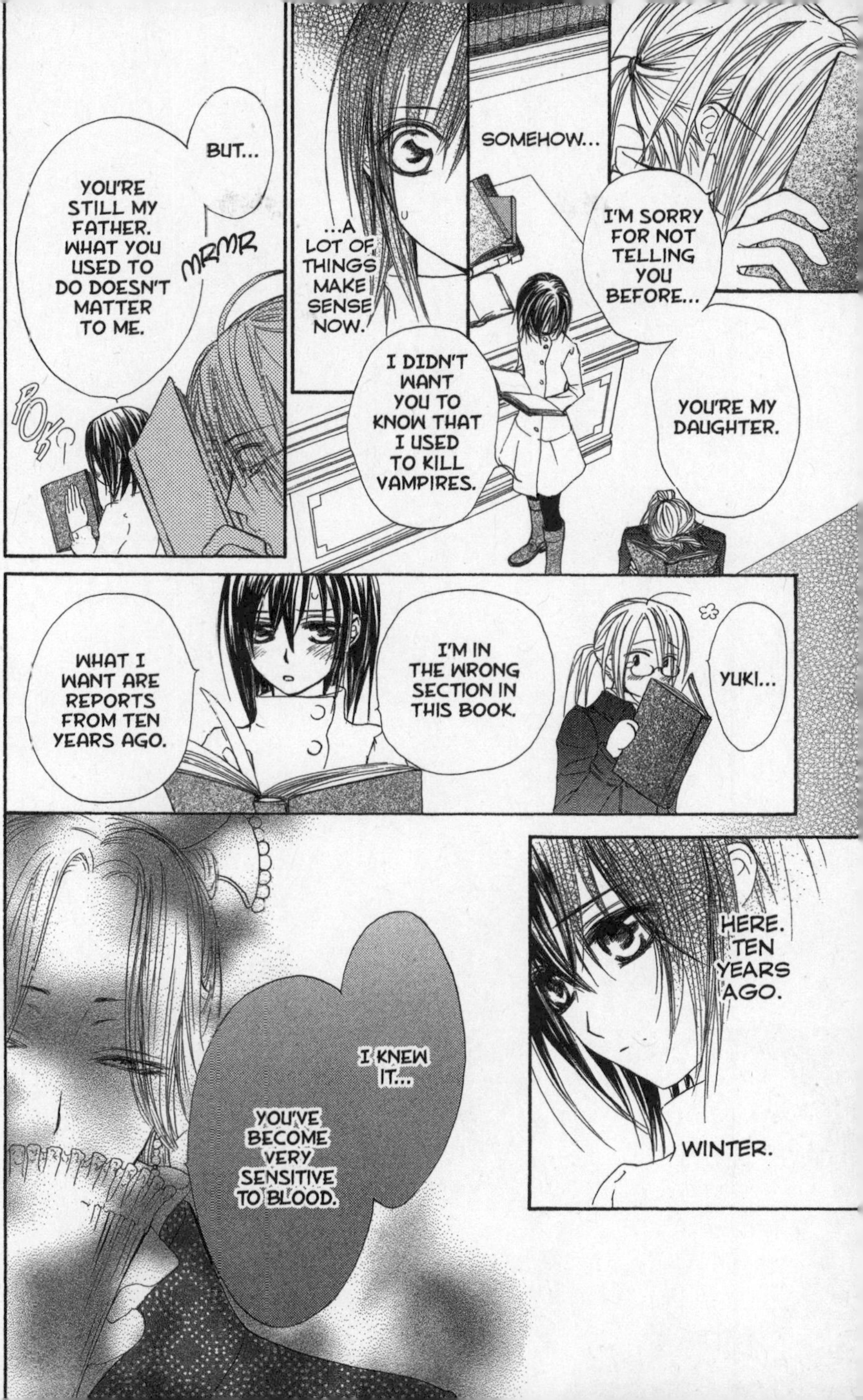
SOMEHOW...
I'M SORRY FOR NOT TELLING YOU BEFORE...
...A LOT OF THINGS MAKE SENSE NOW.
YOU'RE MY DAUGHTER.
I DIDN'T WANT YOU TO KNOW THAT I USED TO KILL VAMPIRES.
BUT...
YOU'RE STILL MY FATHER. WHAT YOU USED TO DO DOESN'T MATTER TO ME.
MRMR
POK
YUKI...
I'M IN THE WRONG SECTION IN THIS BOOK.
WHAT I WANT ARE REPORTS FROM TEN YEARS AGO.
HERE. TEN YEARS AGO.
WINTER.
I KNEW IT...
YOU'VE BECOME VERY SENSITIVE TO BLOOD.

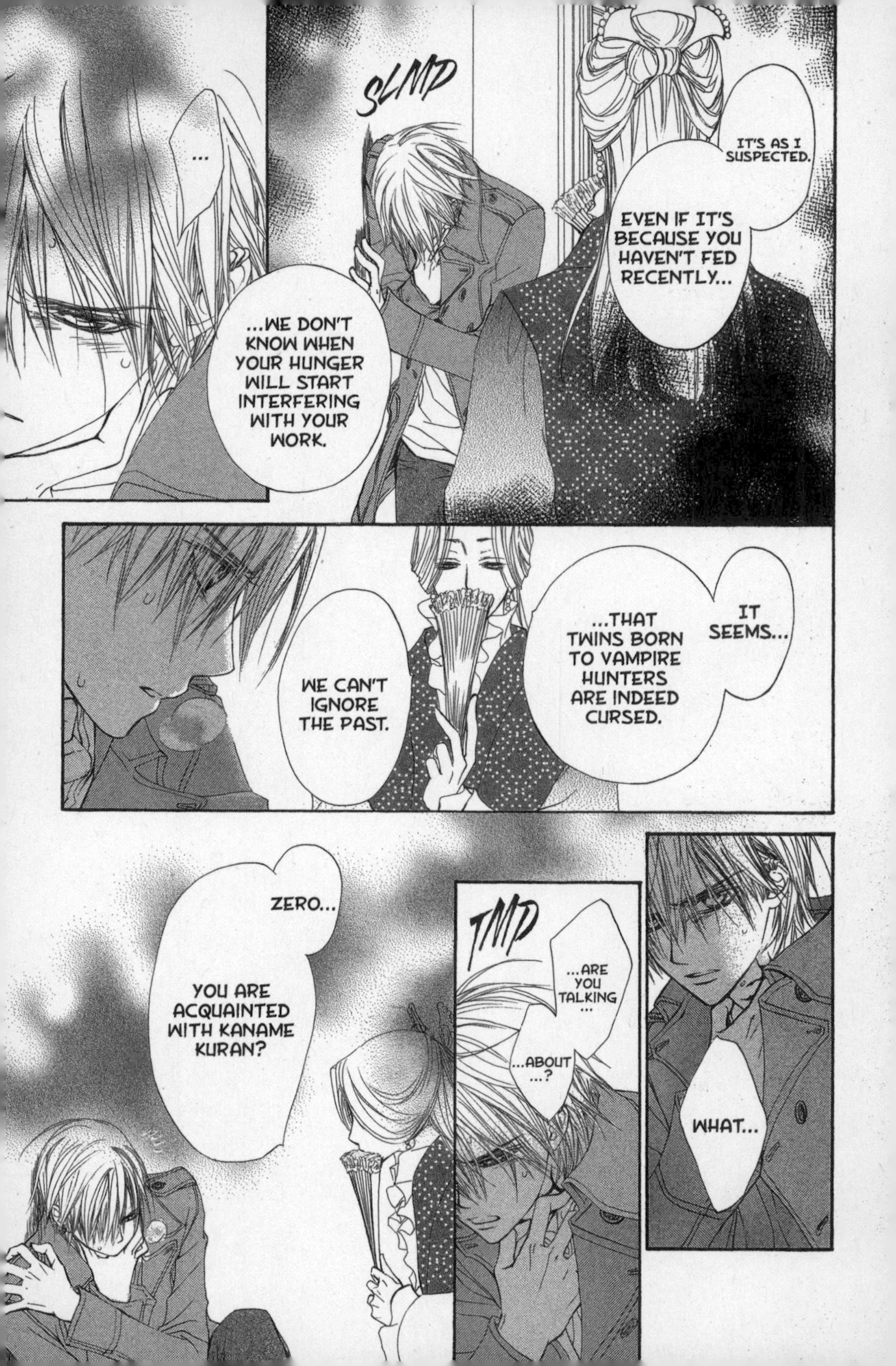
SLMP
IT'S AS I SUSPECTED.
EVEN IF IT'S BECAUSE YOU HAVEN'T FED RECENTLY...
...WE DON'T KNOW WHEN YOUR HUNGER WILL START INTERFERING WITH YOUR WORK.
...
IT SEEMS...
...THAT TWINS BORN TO VAMPIRE HUNTERS ARE INDEED CURSED.
WE CAN'T IGNORE THE PAST.
WHAT...
TMP
...ARE YOU TALKING ...
...ABOUT ...?
ZERO...
YOU ARE ACQUAINTED WITH KANAME KURAN?

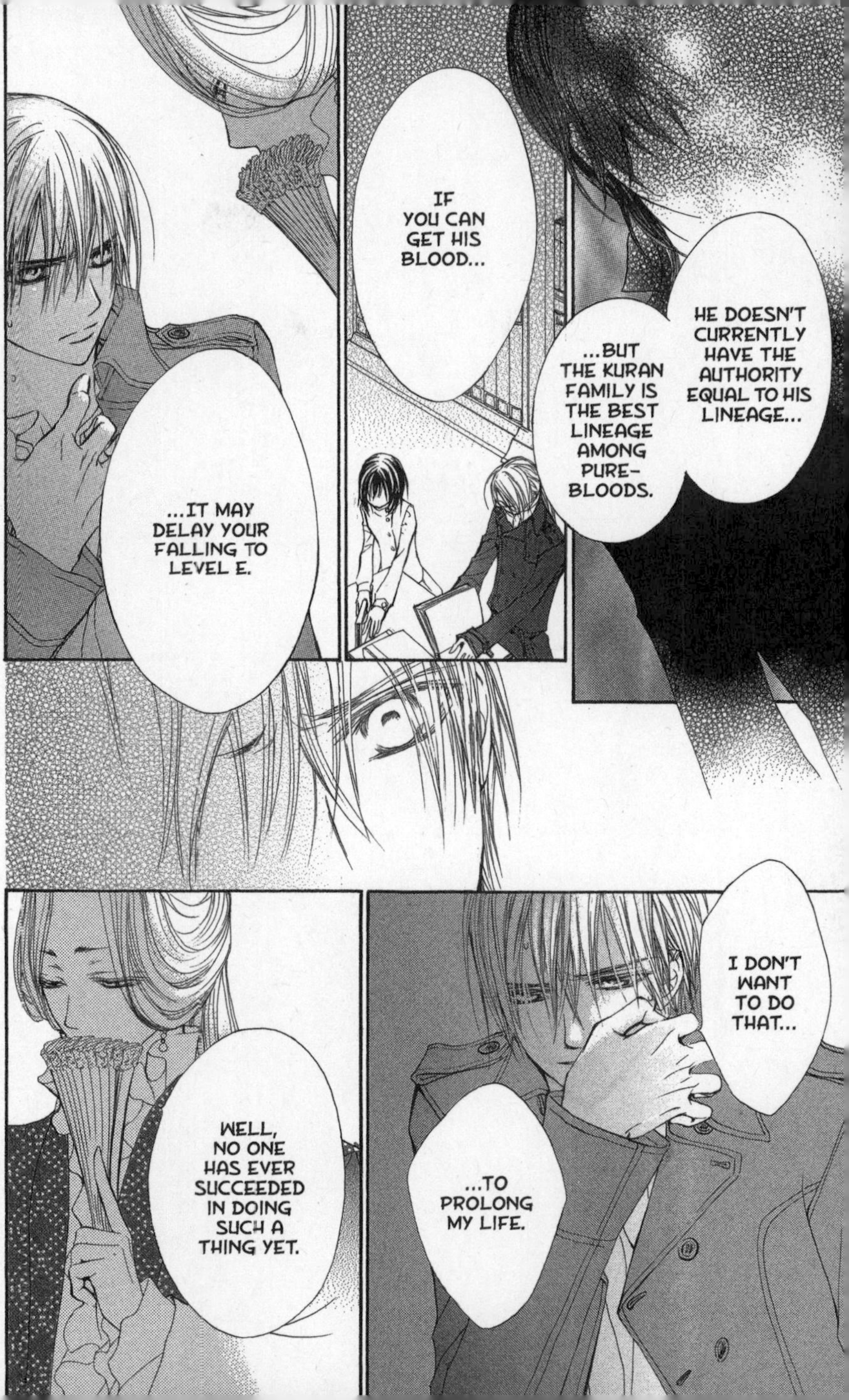
HE DOESN'T CURRENTLY HAVE THE AUTHORITY EQUAL TO HIS LINEAGE...
...BUT THE KURAN FAMILY IS THE BEST LINEAGE AMONG PURE-BLOODS.
IF YOU CAN GET HIS BLOOD...
...IT MAY DELAY YOUR FALLING TO LEVEL E.
I DON'T WANT TO DO THAT...
...TO PROLONG MY LIFE.
WELL, NO ONE HAS EVER SUCCEEDED IN DOING SUCH A THING YET.

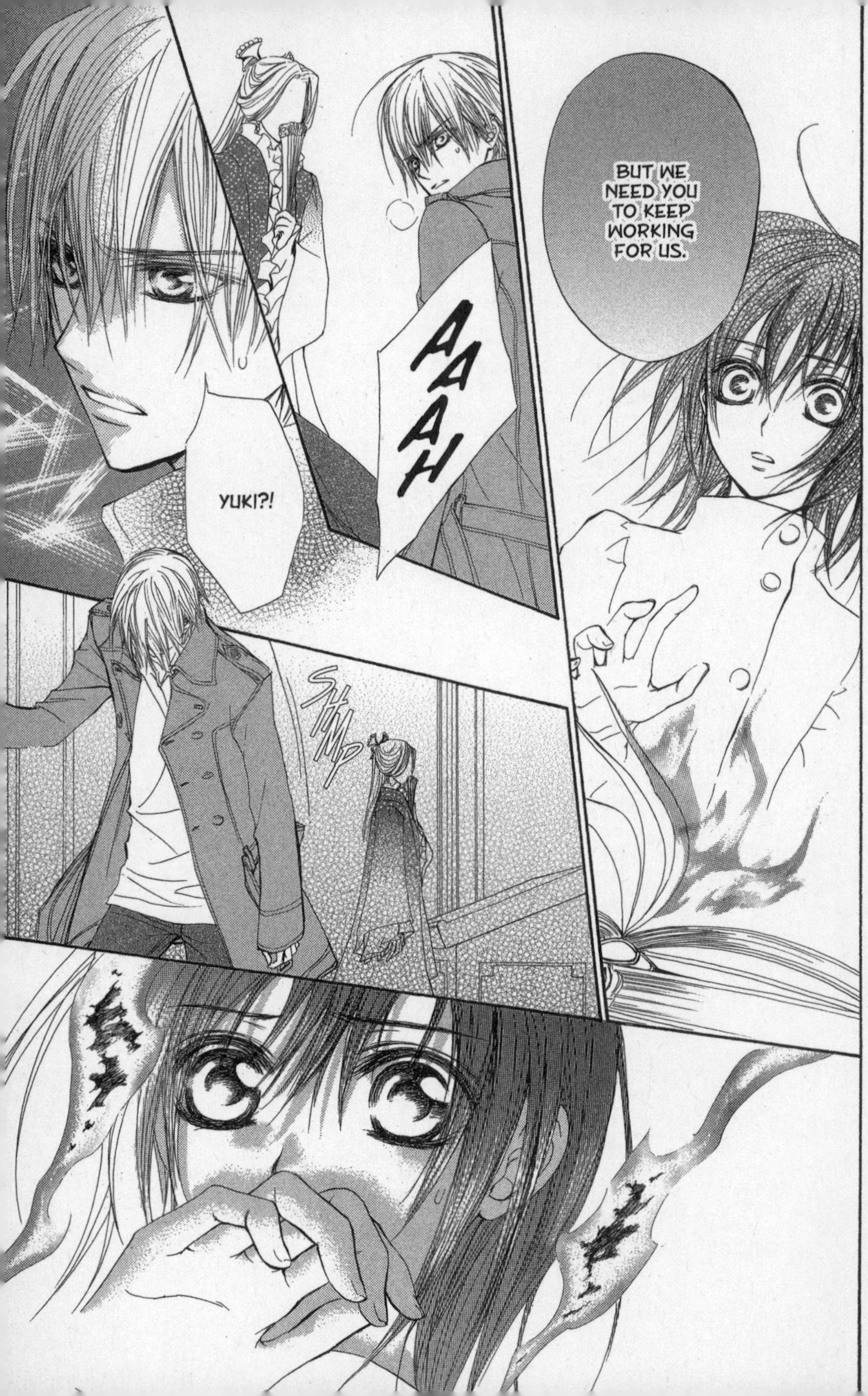
BUT WE NEED YOU TO KEEP WORKING FOR US.
AAAH
YUKI?!
SHMP

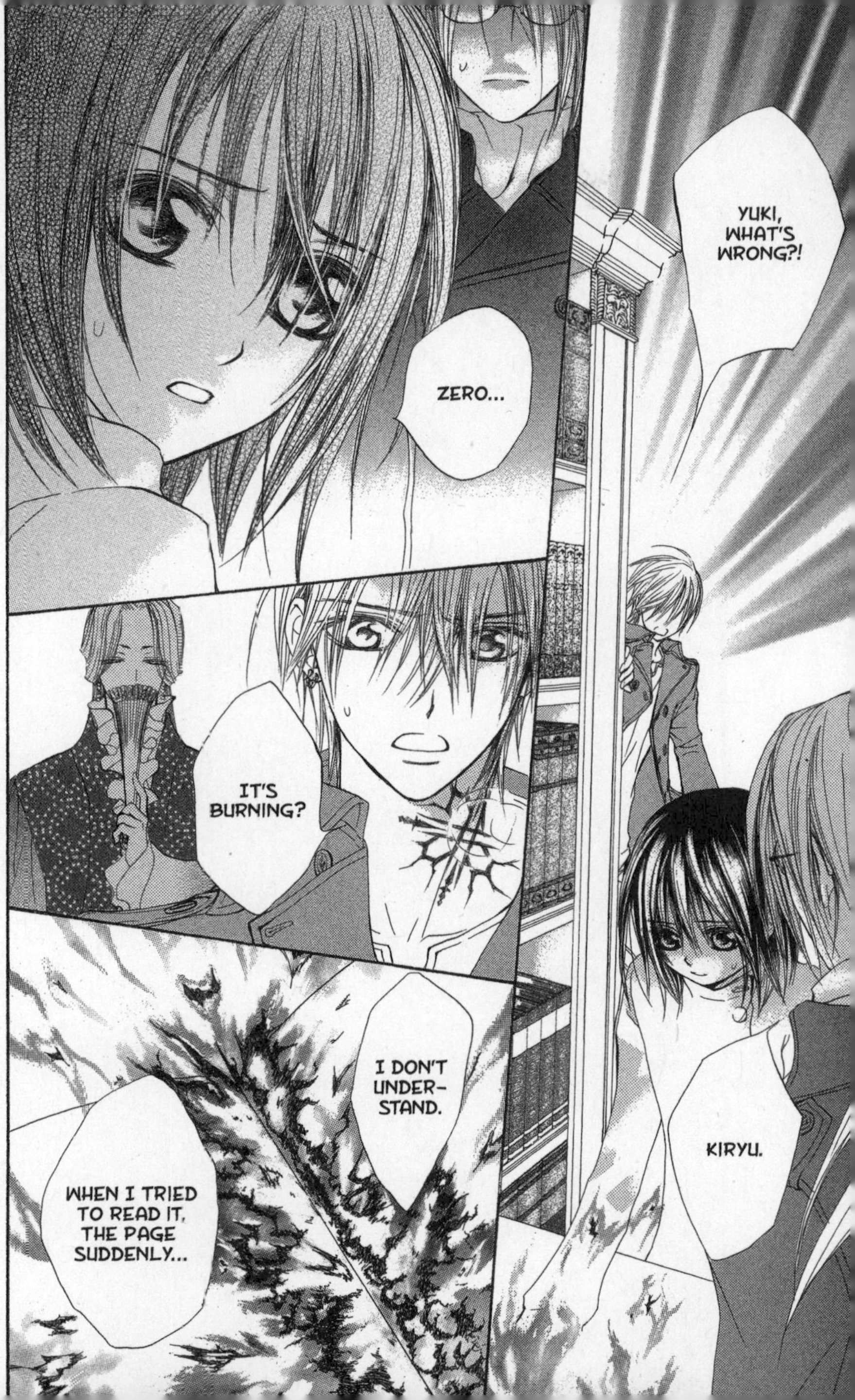
YUKI, WHAT'S WRONG?!
KIRYU.
ZERO...
IT'S BURNING?
I DON'T UNDERSTAND.
WHEN I TRIED TO READ IT, THE PAGE SUDDENLY...

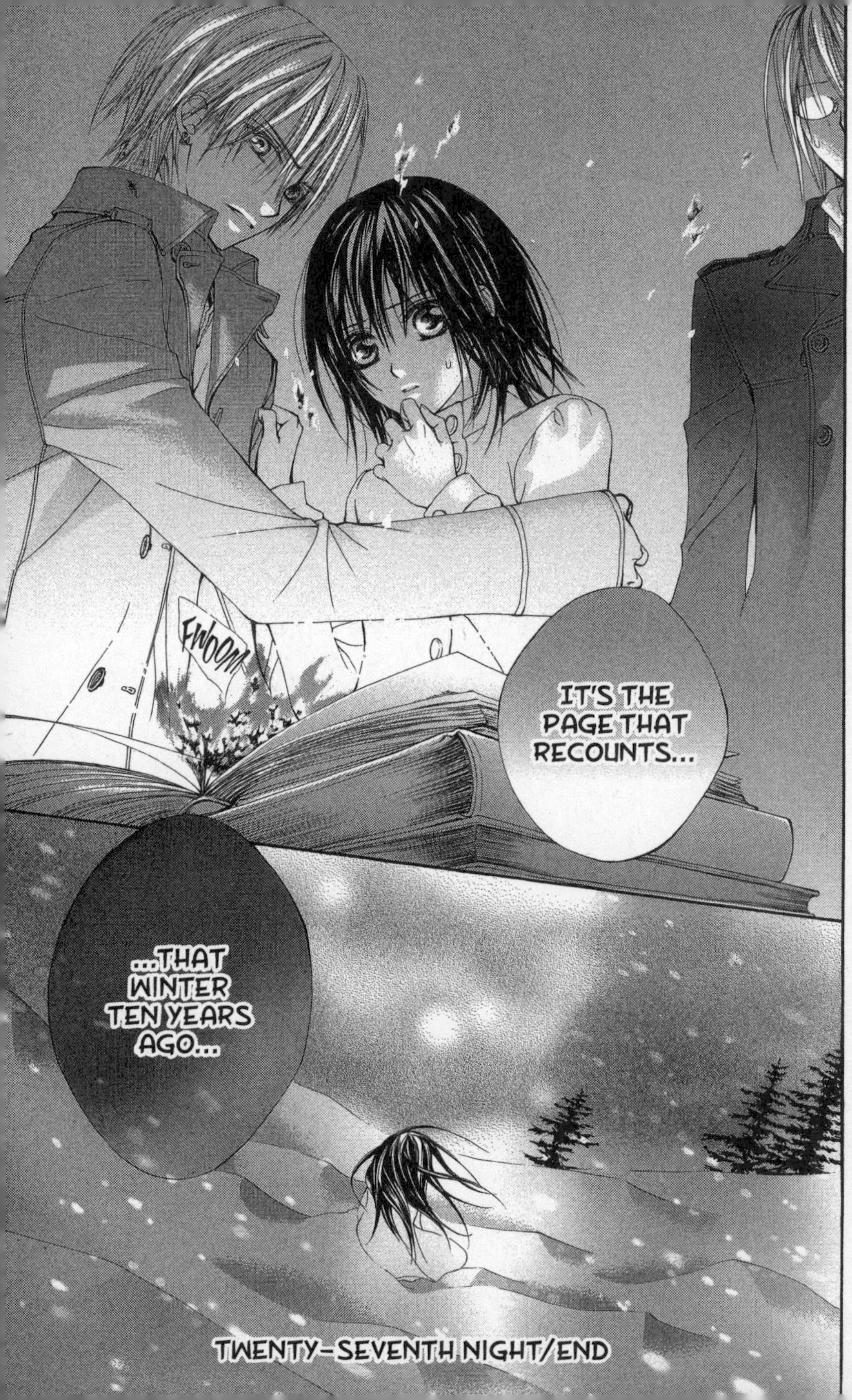
FWOOM
IT'S THE PAGE THAT RECOUNTS...
...THAT WINTER TEN YEARS AGO...
TWENTY-SEVENTH NIGHT/END

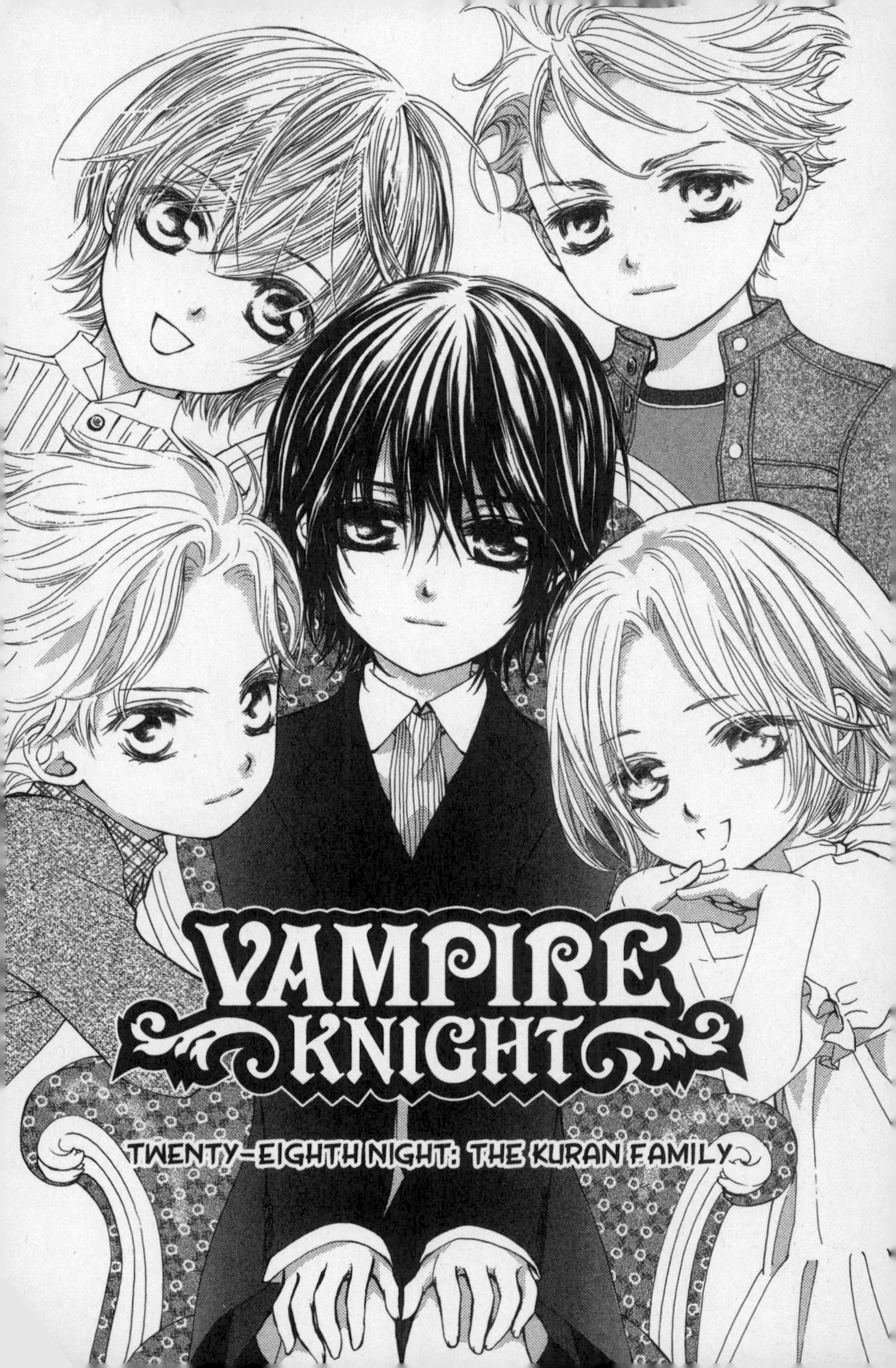
VAMPIRE KNIGHT
TWENTY-EIGHTH NIGHT: THE KURAN FAMILY

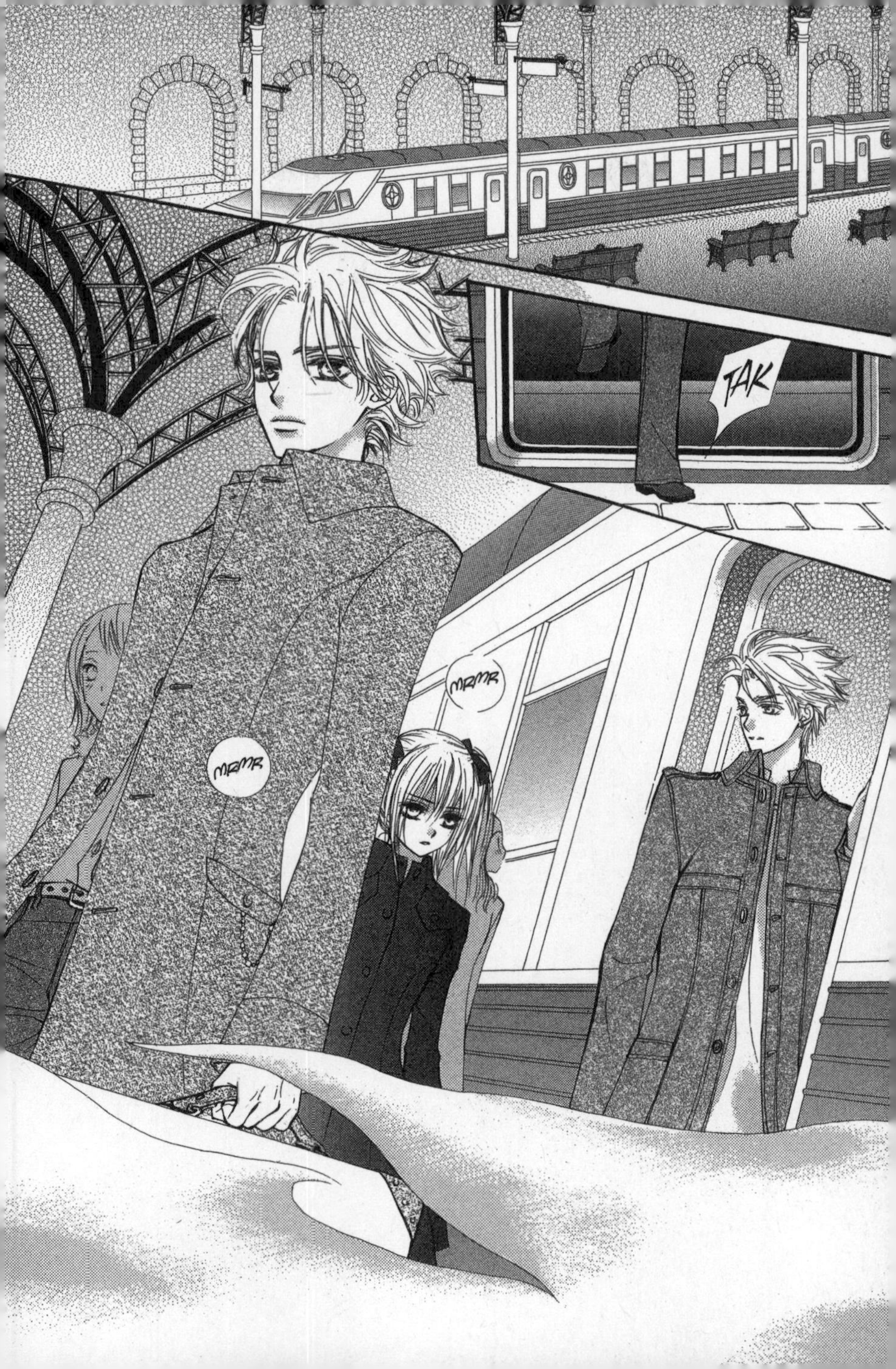
TAK
MRMR
MRMR

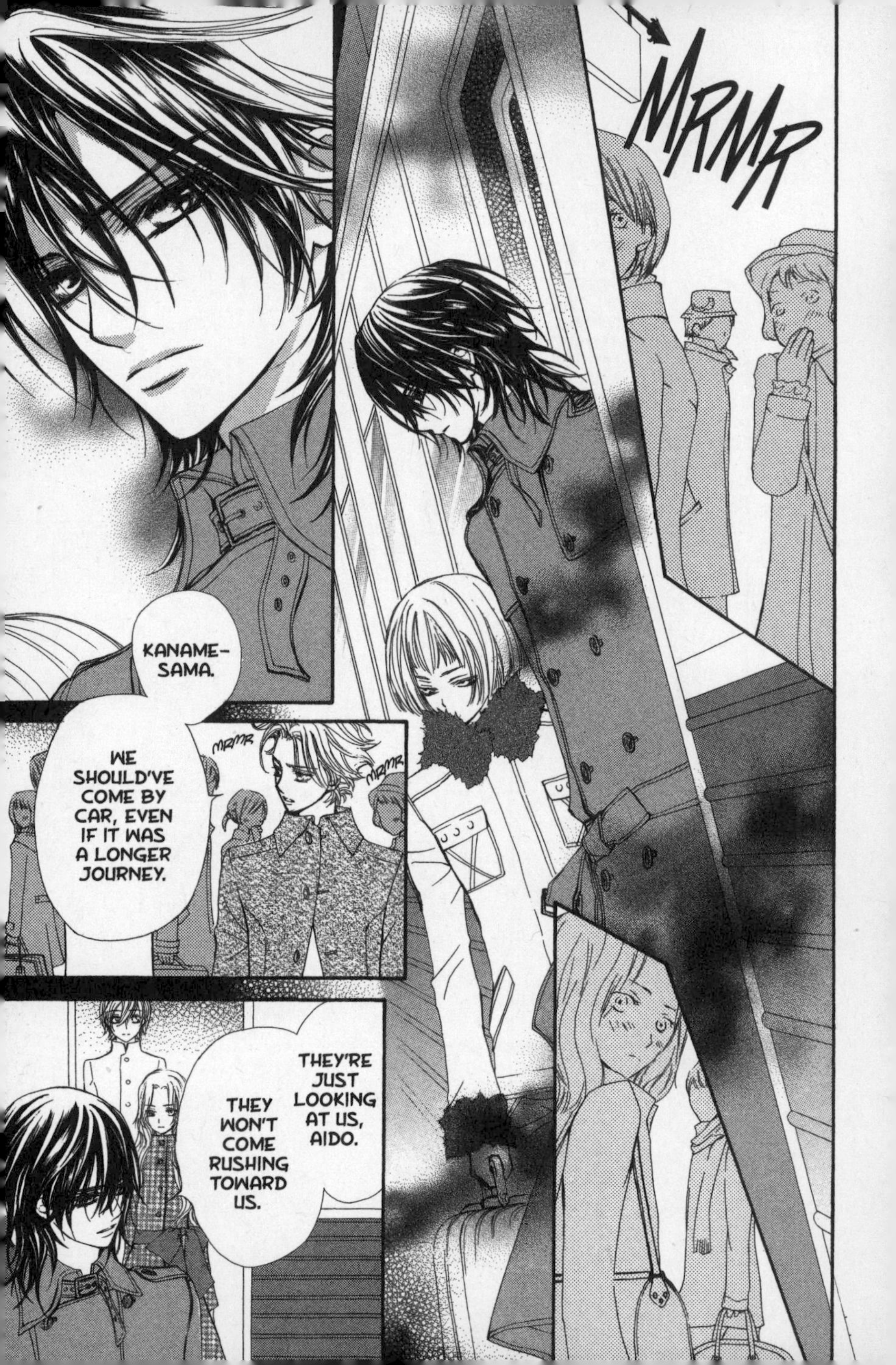
MRMR
KANAME-SAMA.
MRMR
MRMR
WE SHOULD'VE COME BY CAR, EVEN IF IT WAS A LONGER JOURNEY.
THEY'RE JUST LOOKING AT US, AIDO.
THEY WON'T COME RUSHING TOWARD US.

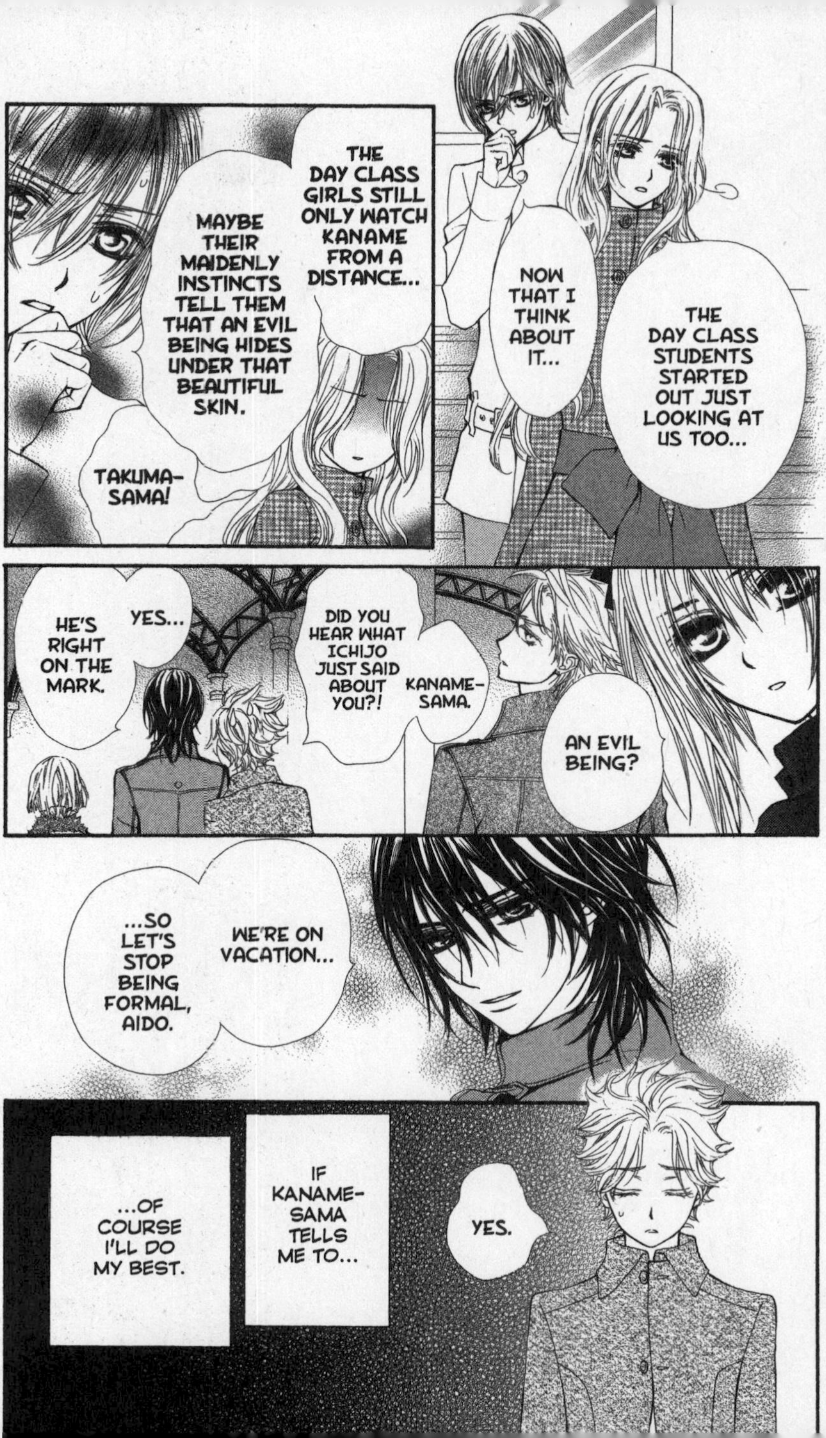
NOW THAT I THINK ABOUT IT...
THE DAY CLASS STUDENTS STARTED OUT JUST LOOKING AT US TOO...
THE DAY CLASS GIRLS STILL ONLY WATCH KANAME FROM A DISTANCE...
MAYBE THEIR MAIDENLY INSTINCTS TELL THEM THAT AN EVIL BEING HIDES UNDER THAT BEAUTIFUL SKIN.
TAKUMA-SAMA!
AN EVIL BEING?
KANAME-SAMA.
DID YOU HEAR WHAT ICHIJO JUST SAID ABOUT YOU?!
YES...
HE'S RIGHT ON THE MARK.
WE'RE ON VACATION...
...SO LET'S STOP BEING FORMAL, AIDO.
YES.
IF KANAME-SAMA TELLS ME TO...
...OF COURSE I'LL DO MY BEST.

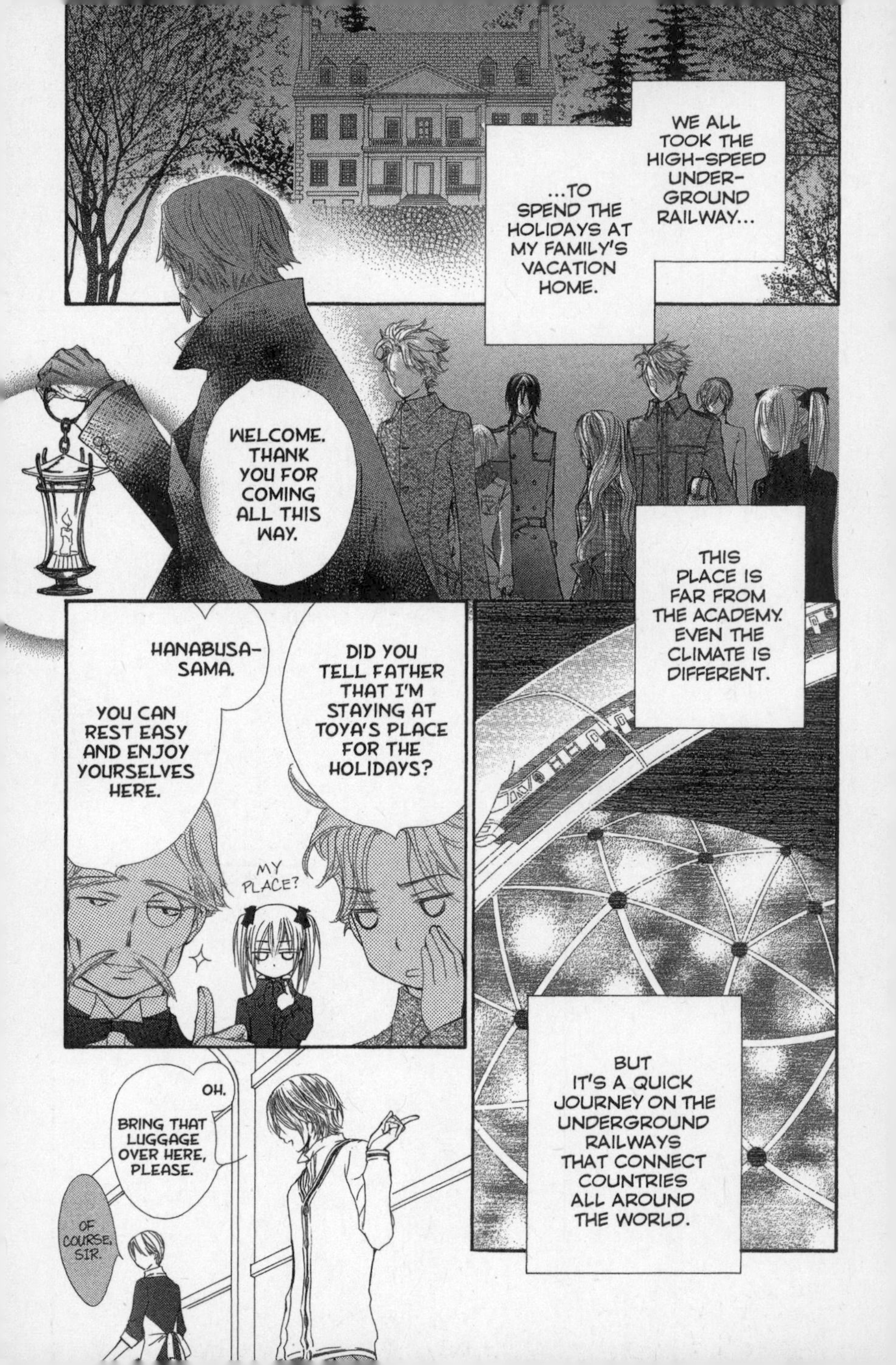
WE ALL TOOK THE HIGH-SPEED UNDER-GROUND RAILWAY...
...TO SPEND THE HOLIDAYS AT MY FAMILY'S VACATION HOME.
WELCOME. THANK YOU FOR COMING ALL THIS WAY.
THIS PLACE IS FAR FROM THE ACADEMY. EVEN THE CLIMATE IS DIFFERENT.
BUT IT'S A QUICK JOURNEY ON THE UNDERGROUND RAILWAYS THAT CONNECT COUNTRIES ALL AROUND THE WORLD.
DID YOU TELL FATHER THAT I'M STAYING AT TOYA'S PLACE FOR THE HOLIDAYS?
HANABUSA-SAMA.
YOU CAN REST EASY AND ENJOY YOURSELVES HERE.
MY PLACE?
OH.
BRING THAT LUGGAGE OVER HERE, PLEASE.
OF COURSE, SIR.

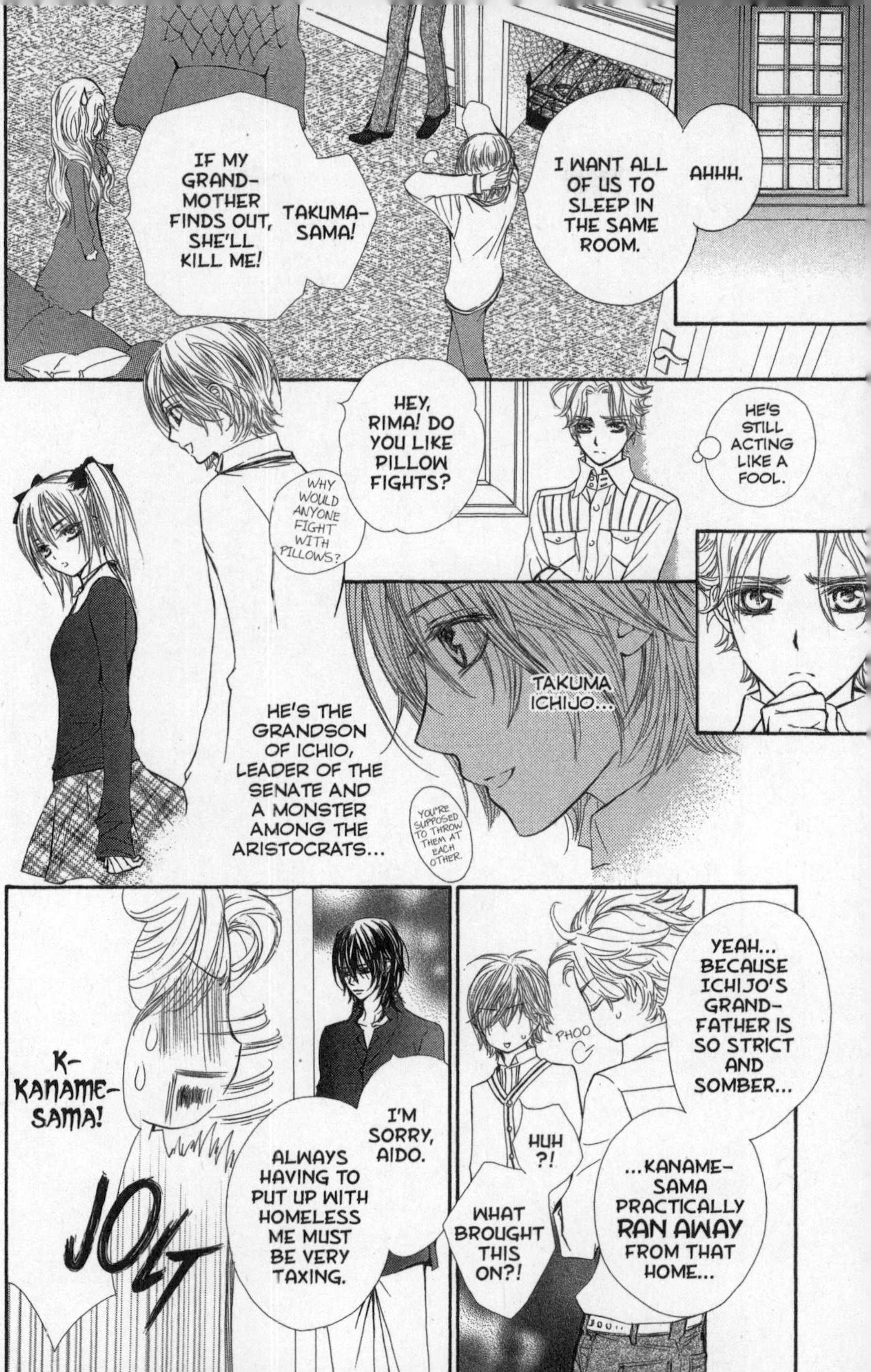
AHHH.
I WANT ALL OF US TO SLEEP IN THE SAME ROOM.
TAKUMA-SAMA!
IF MY GRANDMOTHER FINDS OUT, SHE'LL KILL ME!
HE'S STILL ACTING LIKE A FOOL.
TAKUMA ICHIJO...
HE'S THE GRANDSON OF ICHIO, LEADER OF THE SENATE AND A MONSTER AMONG THE ARISTOCRATS...
HEY, RIMA! DO YOU LIKE PILLOW FIGHTS?
WHY WOULD ANYONE FIGHT WITH PILLOWS?
YOU'RE SUPPOSED TO THROW THEM AT EACH OTHER.
YEAH... BECAUSE ICHIJO'S GRANDFATHER IS SO STRICT AND SOMBER...
PHOO
HUH?!
...KANAME-SAMA PRACTICALLY RAN AWAY FROM THAT HOME...
WHAT BROUGHT THIS ON?!
I'M SORRY, AIDO.
ALWAYS HAVING TO PUT UP WITH HOMELESS ME MUST BE VERY TAXING.
K-KANAME-SAMA!
JOLT

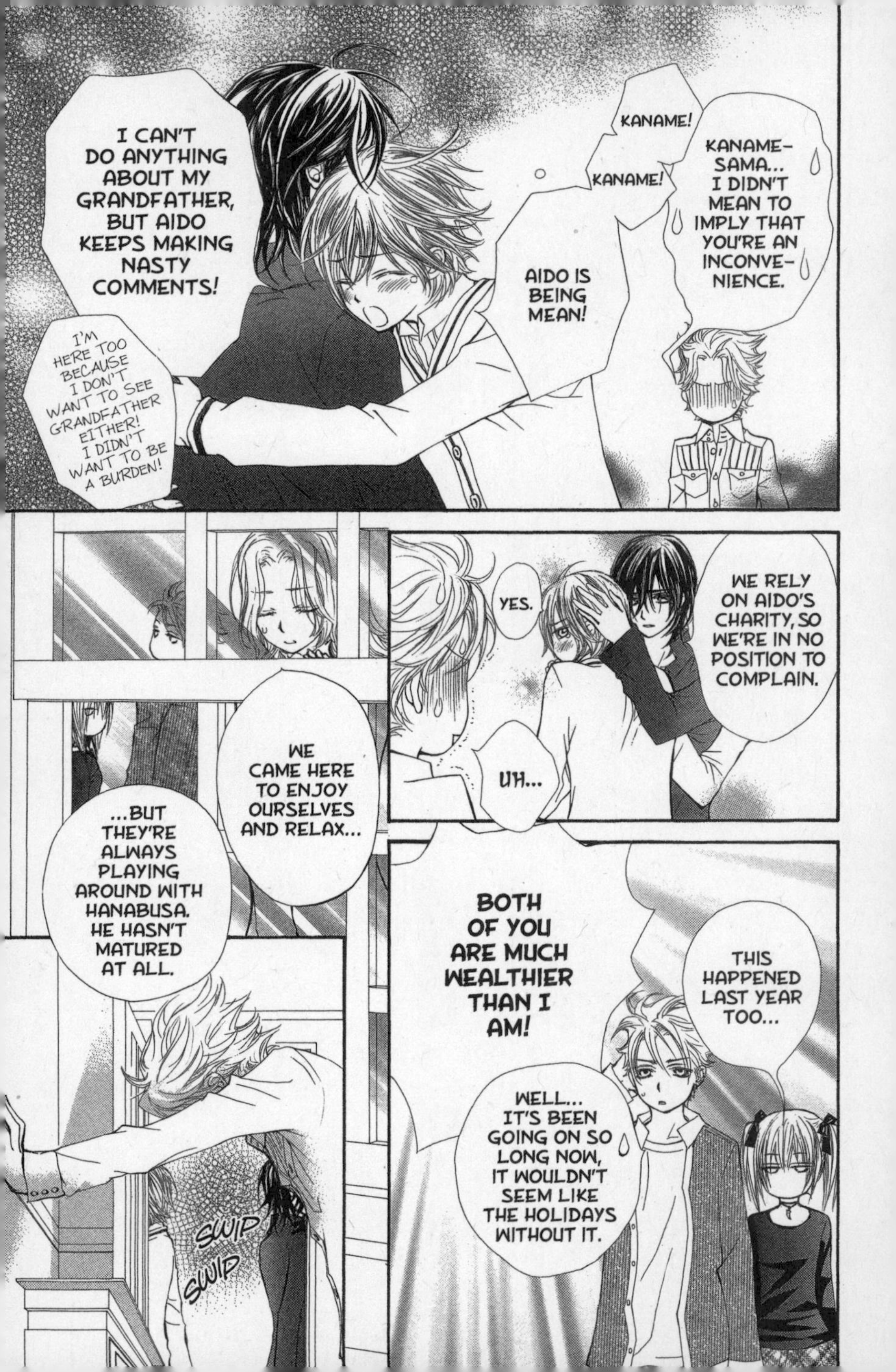
KANAME-SAMA... I DIDN'T MEAN TO IMPLY THAT YOU'RE AN INCONVENIENCE.
KANAME!
KANAME!
AIDO IS BEING MEAN!
I CAN'T DO ANYTHING ABOUT MY GRANDFATHER, BUT AIDO KEEPS MAKING NASTY COMMENTS!
I'M HERE TOO BECAUSE I DON'T WANT TO SEE GRANDFATHER EITHER! I DIDN'T WANT TO BE A BURDEN!
WE RELY ON AIDO'S CHARITY, SO WE'RE IN NO POSITION TO COMPLAIN.
YES.
UH...
WE CAME HERE TO ENJOY OURSELVES AND RELAX...
...BUT THEY'RE ALWAYS PLAYING AROUND WITH HANABUSA. HE HASN'T MATURED AT ALL.
THIS HAPPENED LAST YEAR TOO...
BOTH OF YOU ARE MUCH WEALTHIER THAN I AM!
WELL... IT'S BEEN GOING ON SO LONG NOW, IT WOULDN'T SEEM LIKE THE HOLIDAYS WITHOUT IT.
SWIP
SWIP

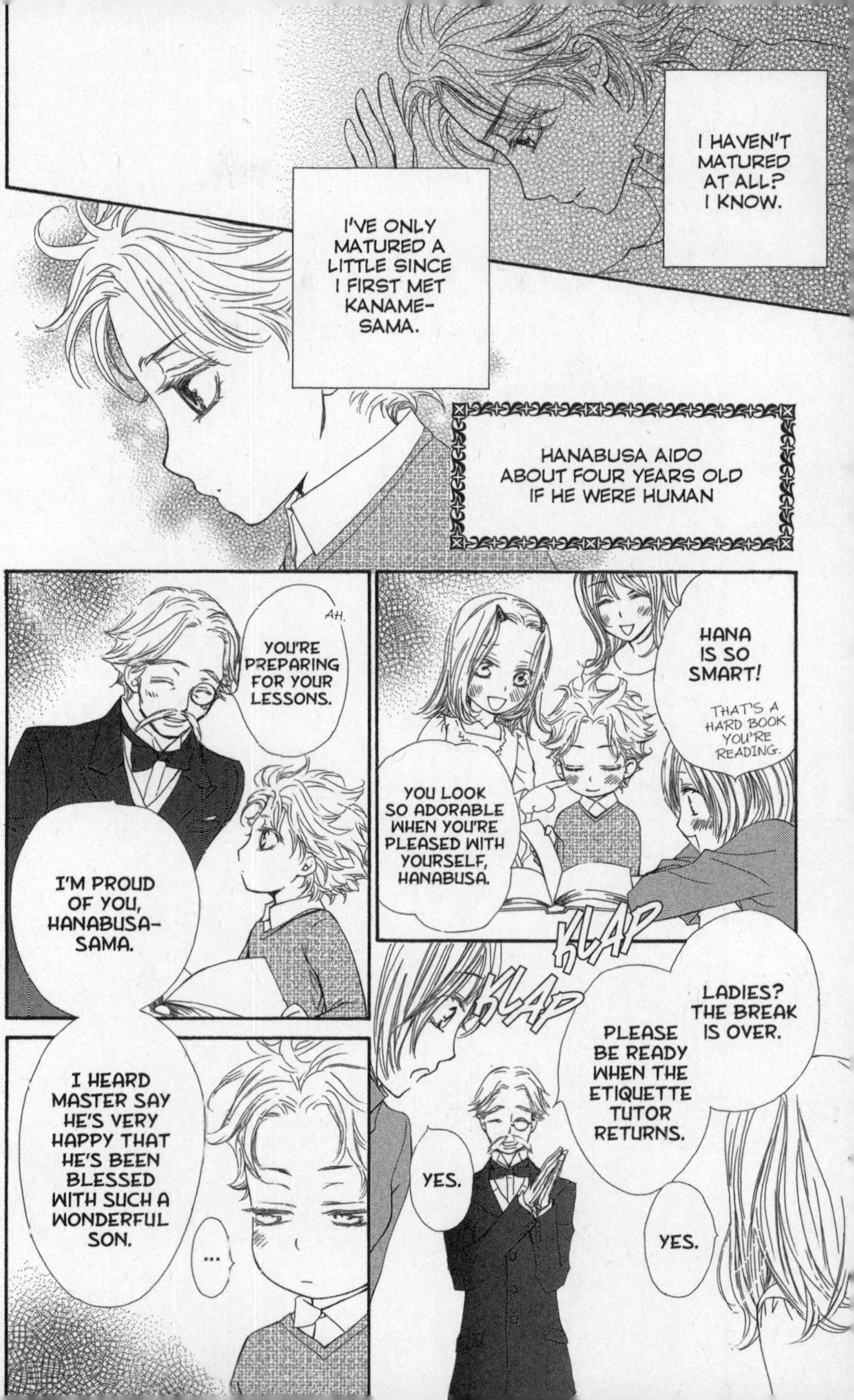
I HAVEN'T MATURED AT ALL? I KNOW.
I'VE ONLY MATURED A LITTLE SINCE I FIRST MET KANAME-SAMA.
HANABUSA AIDO ABOUT FOUR YEARS OLD IF HE WERE HUMAN
HANA IS SO SMART!
THAT'S A HARD BOOK YOU'RE READING.
YOU LOOK SO ADORABLE WHEN YOU'RE PLEASED WITH YOURSELF, HANABUSA.
AH.
YOU'RE PREPARING FOR YOUR LESSONS.
I'M PROUD OF YOU, HANABUSA-SAMA.
KLAP
KLAP
LADIES? THE BREAK IS OVER.
PLEASE BE READY WHEN THE ETIQUETTE TUTOR RETURNS.
YES.
YES.
I HEARD MASTER SAY HE'S VERY HAPPY THAT HE'S BEEN BLESSED WITH SUCH A WONDERFUL SON.
...

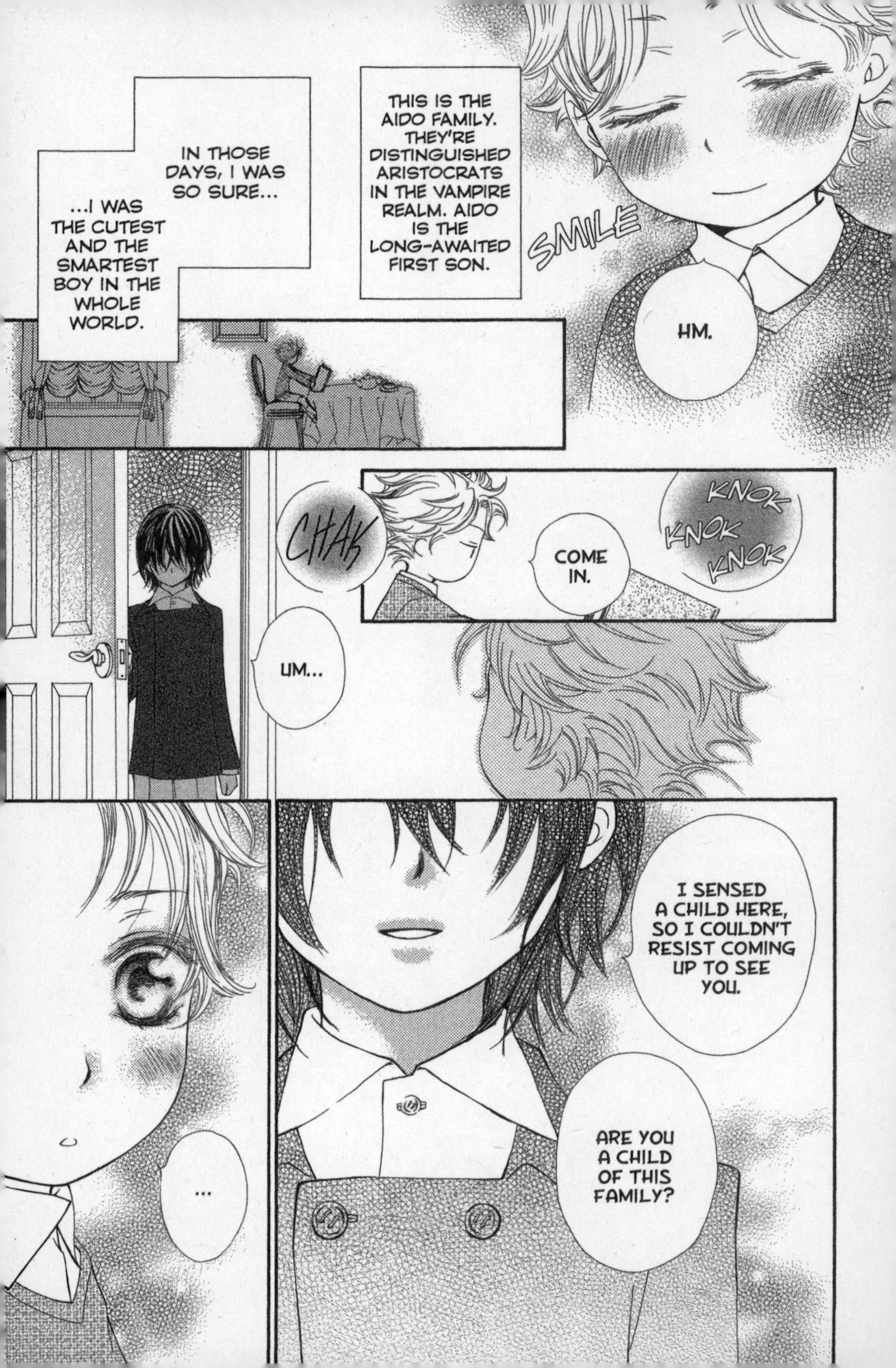
THIS IS THE AIDO FAMILY. THEY'RE DISTINGUISHED ARISTOCRATS IN THE VAMPIRE REALM. AIDO IS THE LONG-AWAITED FIRST SON.
IN THOSE DAYS, I WAS SO SURE...
...I WAS THE CUTEST AND THE SMARTEST BOY IN THE WHOLE WORLD.
SMILE
HM.
KNOK KNOK KNOK
COME IN.
CHAK
UM...
I SENSED A CHILD HERE, SO I COULDN'T RESIST COMING UP TO SEE YOU.
ARE YOU A CHILD OF THIS FAMILY?
...

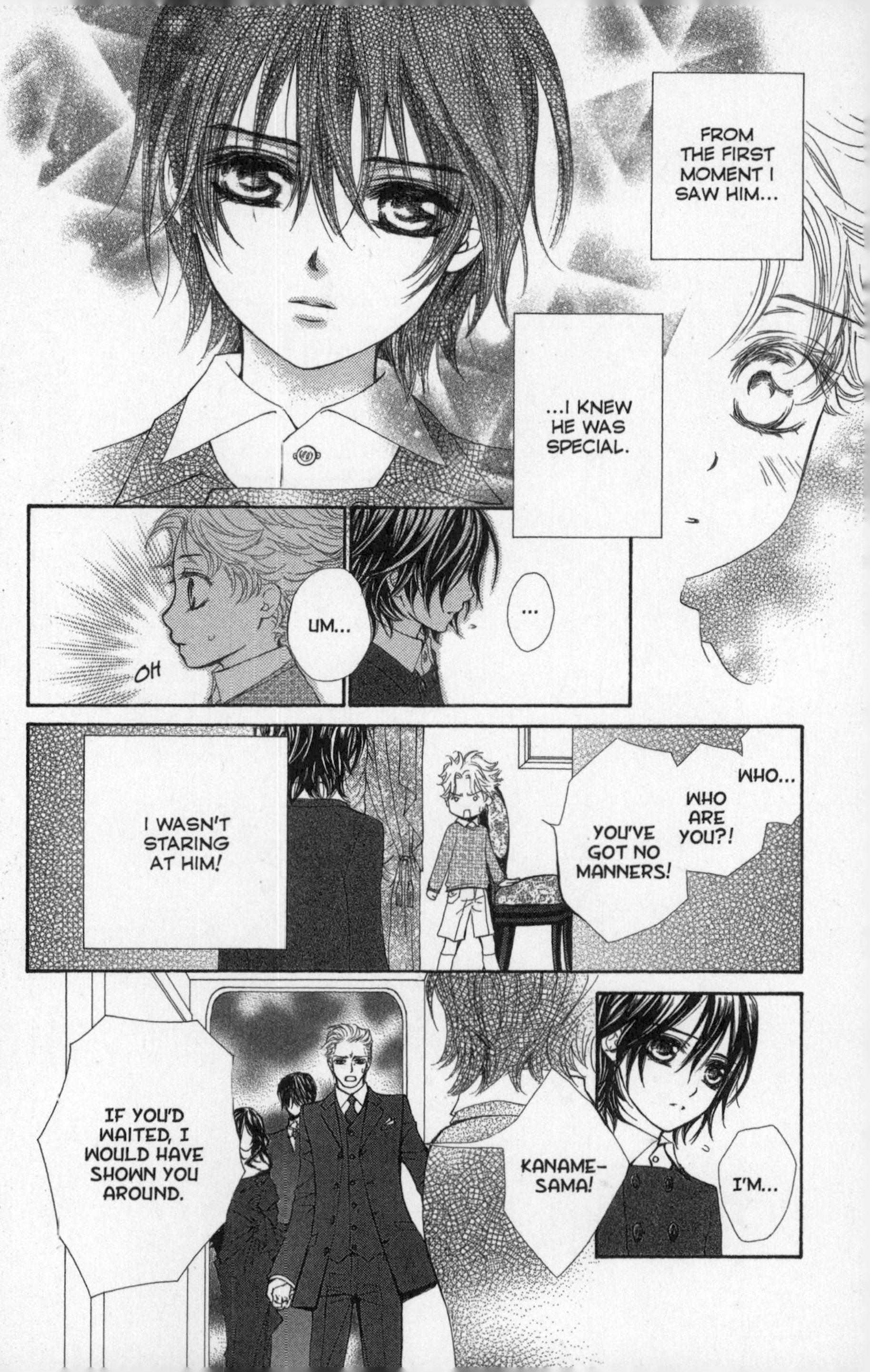
FROM THE FIRST MOMENT I SAW HIM...
...I KNEW HE WAS SPECIAL.
...
UM...
OH
WHO...
WHO ARE YOU?!
YOU'VE GOT NO MANNERS!
I WASN'T STARING AT HIM!
I'M...
KANAME-SAMA!
IF YOU'D WAITED, I WOULD HAVE SHOWN YOU AROUND.

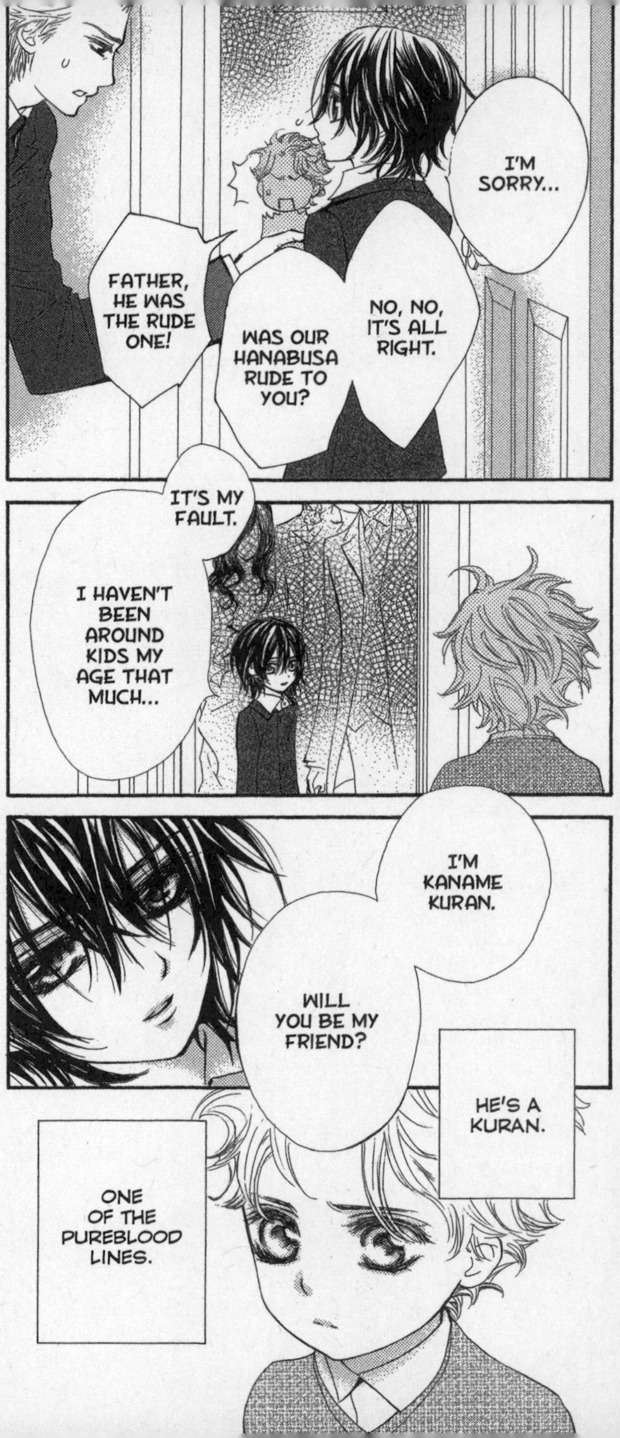
I'M SORRY...
NO, NO, IT'S ALL RIGHT.
WAS OUR HANABUSA RUDE TO YOU?
FATHER, HE WAS THE RUDE ONE!
IT'S MY FAULT.
I HAVEN'T BEEN AROUND KIDS MY AGE THAT MUCH...
I'M KANAME KURAN.
WILL YOU BE MY FRIEND?
HE'S A KURAN.
ONE OF THE PUREBLOOD LINES.

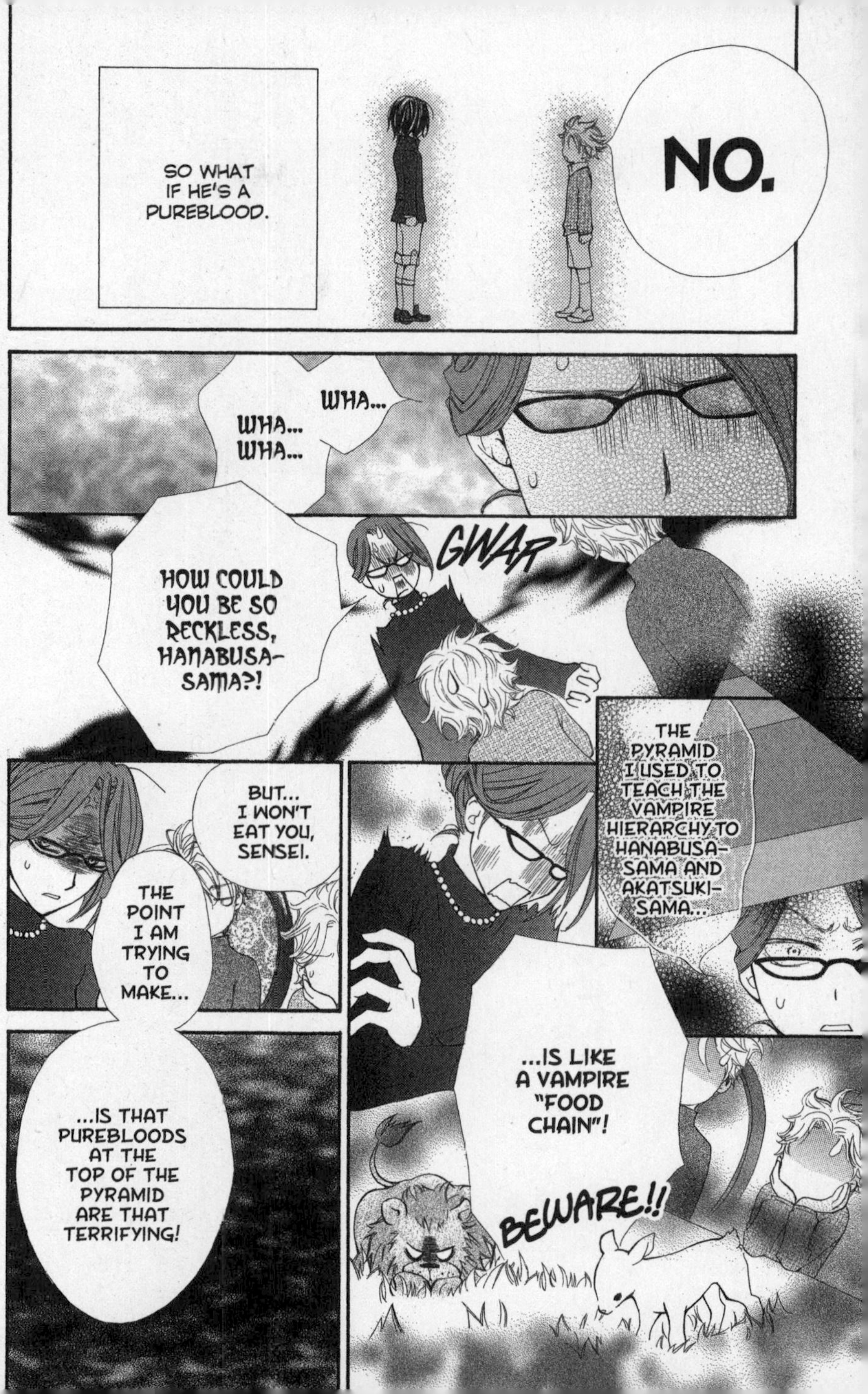
NO.
SO WHAT IF HE'S A PUREBLOOD.
WHA...
WHA... WHA...
GWAR
HOW COULD YOU BE SO RECKLESS, HANABUSA-SAMA?!
THE PYRAMID I USED TO TEACH THE VAMPIRE HIERARCHY TO HANABUSA-SAMA AND AKATSUKI-SAMA...
BUT... I WON'T EAT YOU, SENSEI.
THE POINT I AM TRYING TO MAKE...
...IS LIKE A VAMPIRE "FOOD CHAIN"!
BEWARE!!
...IS THAT PUREBLOODS AT THE TOP OF THE PYRAMID ARE THAT TERRIFYING!

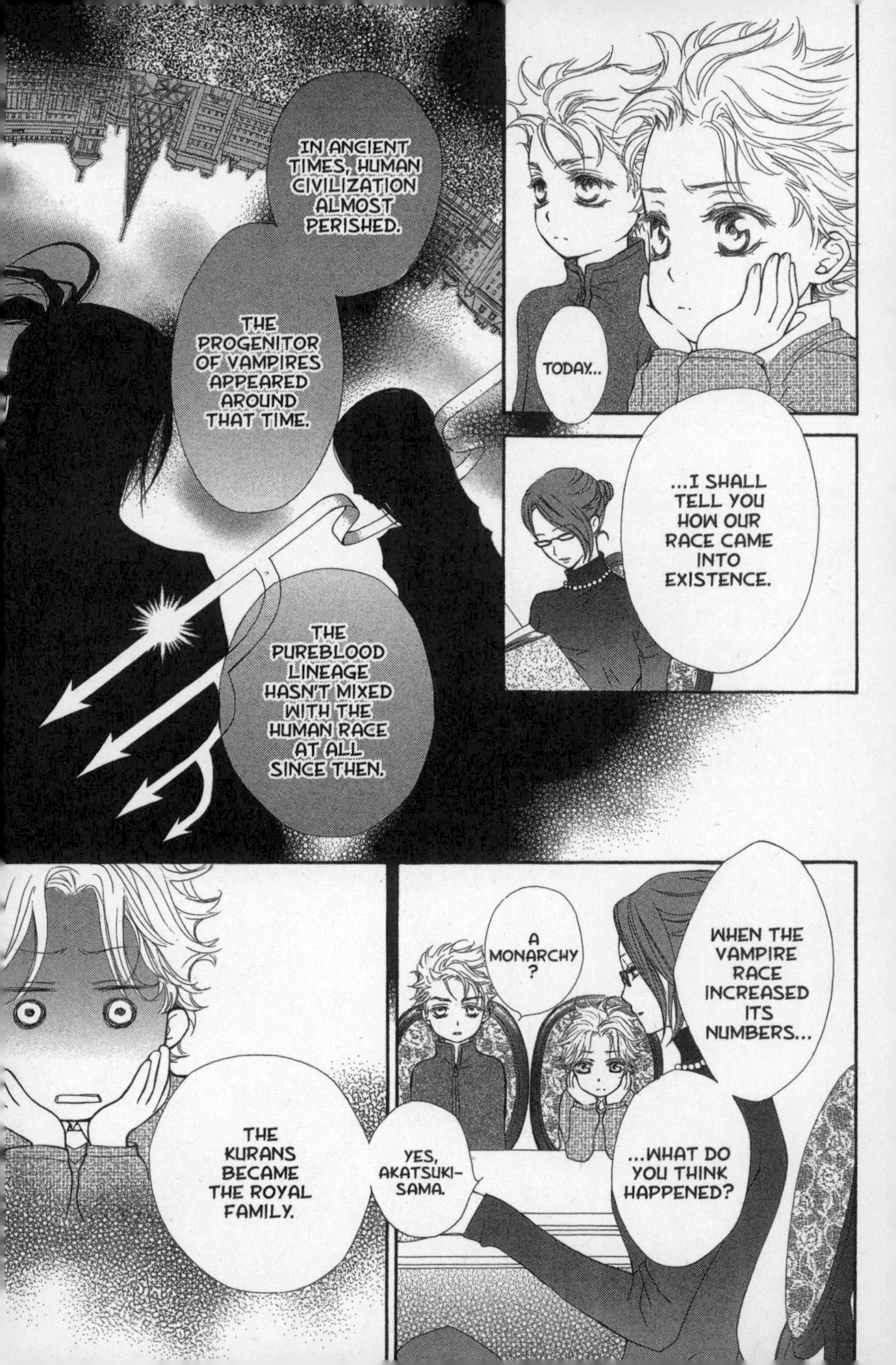
TODAY...
...I SHALL TELL YOU HOW OUR RACE CAME INTO EXISTENCE.
IN ANCIENT TIMES, HUMAN CIVILIZATION ALMOST PERISHED.
THE PROGENITOR OF VAMPIRES APPEARED AROUND THAT TIME.
THE PUREBLOOD LINEAGE HASN'T MIXED WITH THE HUMAN RACE AT ALL SINCE THEN.
WHEN THE VAMPIRE RACE INCREASED ITS NUMBERS...
...WHAT DO YOU THINK HAPPENED?
A MONARCHY?
YES, AKATSUKI-SAMA.
THE KURANS BECAME THE ROYAL FAMILY.

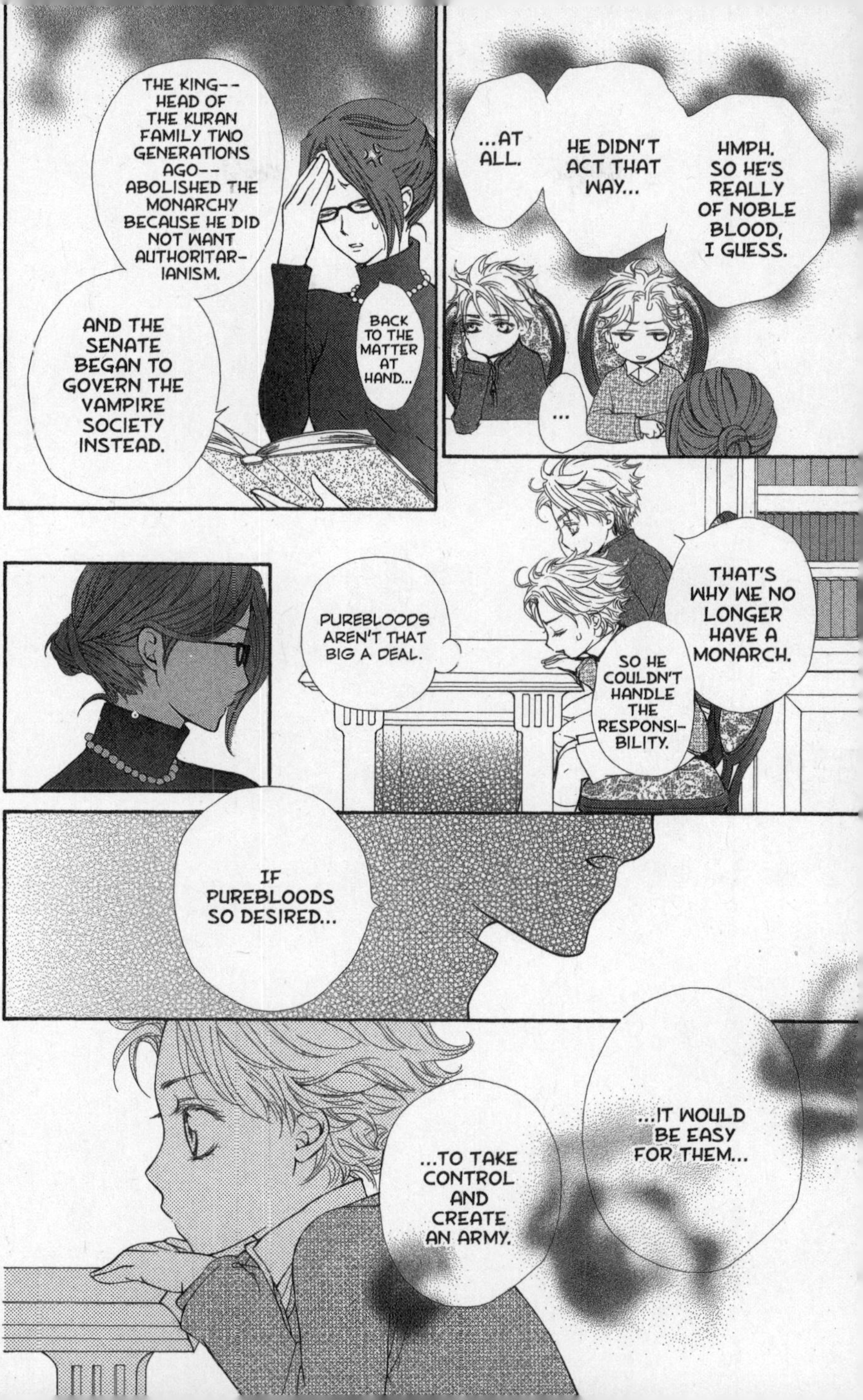
HMPH. SO HE'S REALLY OF NOBLE BLOOD, I GUESS.
HE DIDN'T ACT THAT WAY...
...AT ALL.
...
THE KING--HEAD OF THE KURAN FAMILY TWO GENERATIONS AGO--ABOLISHED THE MONARCHY BECAUSE HE DID NOT WANT AUTHORITARIANISM.
AND THE SENATE BEGAN TO GOVERN THE VAMPIRE SOCIETY INSTEAD.
BACK TO THE MATTER AT HAND...
THAT'S WHY WE NO LONGER HAVE A MONARCH.
SO HE COULDN'T HANDLE THE RESPONSIBILITY.
PUREBLOODS AREN'T THAT BIG A DEAL.
IF PUREBLOODS SO DESIRED...
...IT WOULD BE EASY FOR THEM...
...TO TAKE CONTROL AND CREATE AN ARMY.

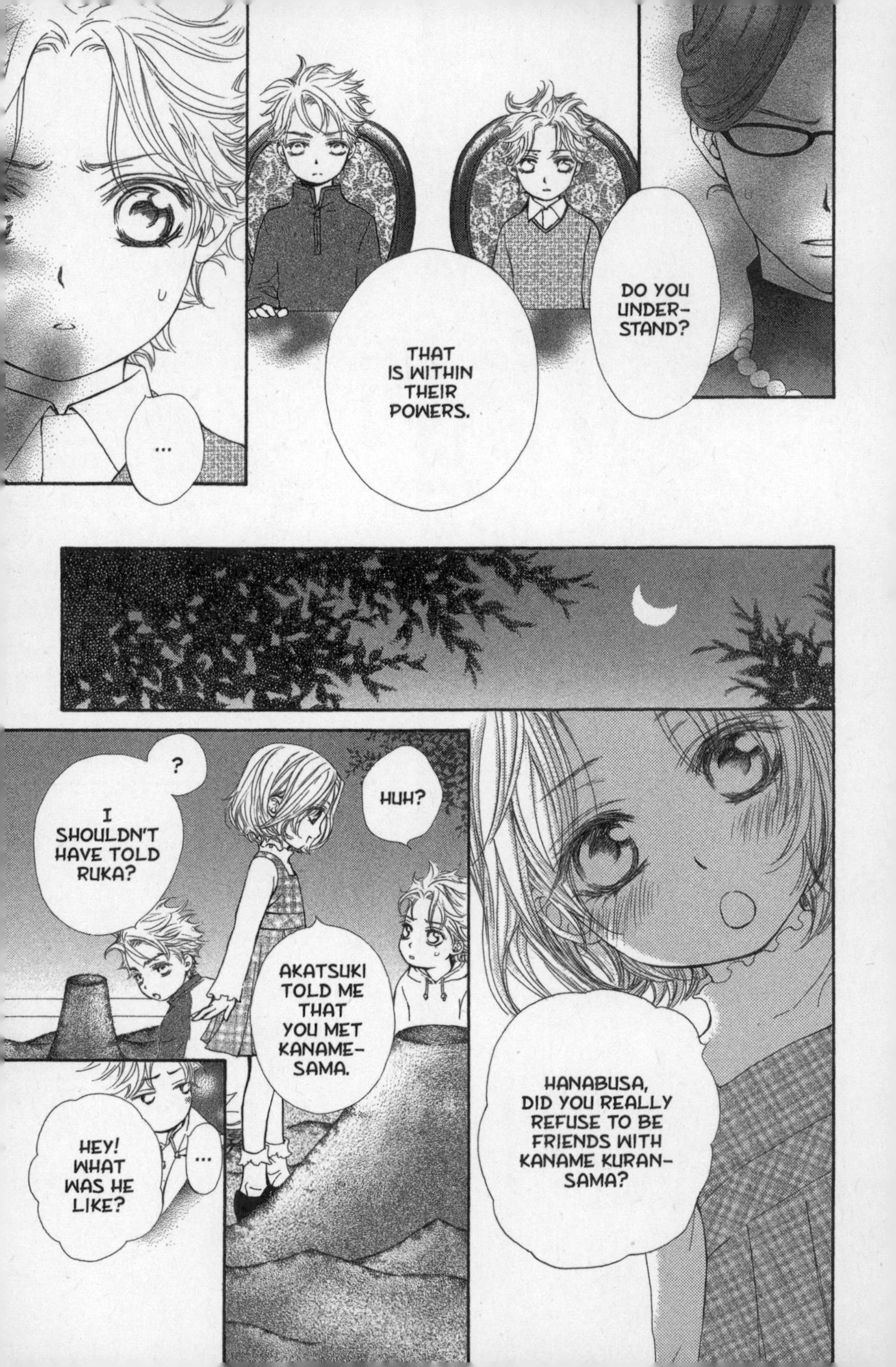
DO YOU UNDER-STAND?
THAT IS WITHIN THEIR POWERS.
...
HANABUSA, DID YOU REALLY REFUSE TO BE FRIENDS WITH KANAME KURAN-SAMA?
HUH?
AKATSUKI TOLD ME THAT YOU MET KANAME-SAMA.
?
I SHOULDN'T HAVE TOLD RUKA?
...
HEY! WHAT WAS HE LIKE?

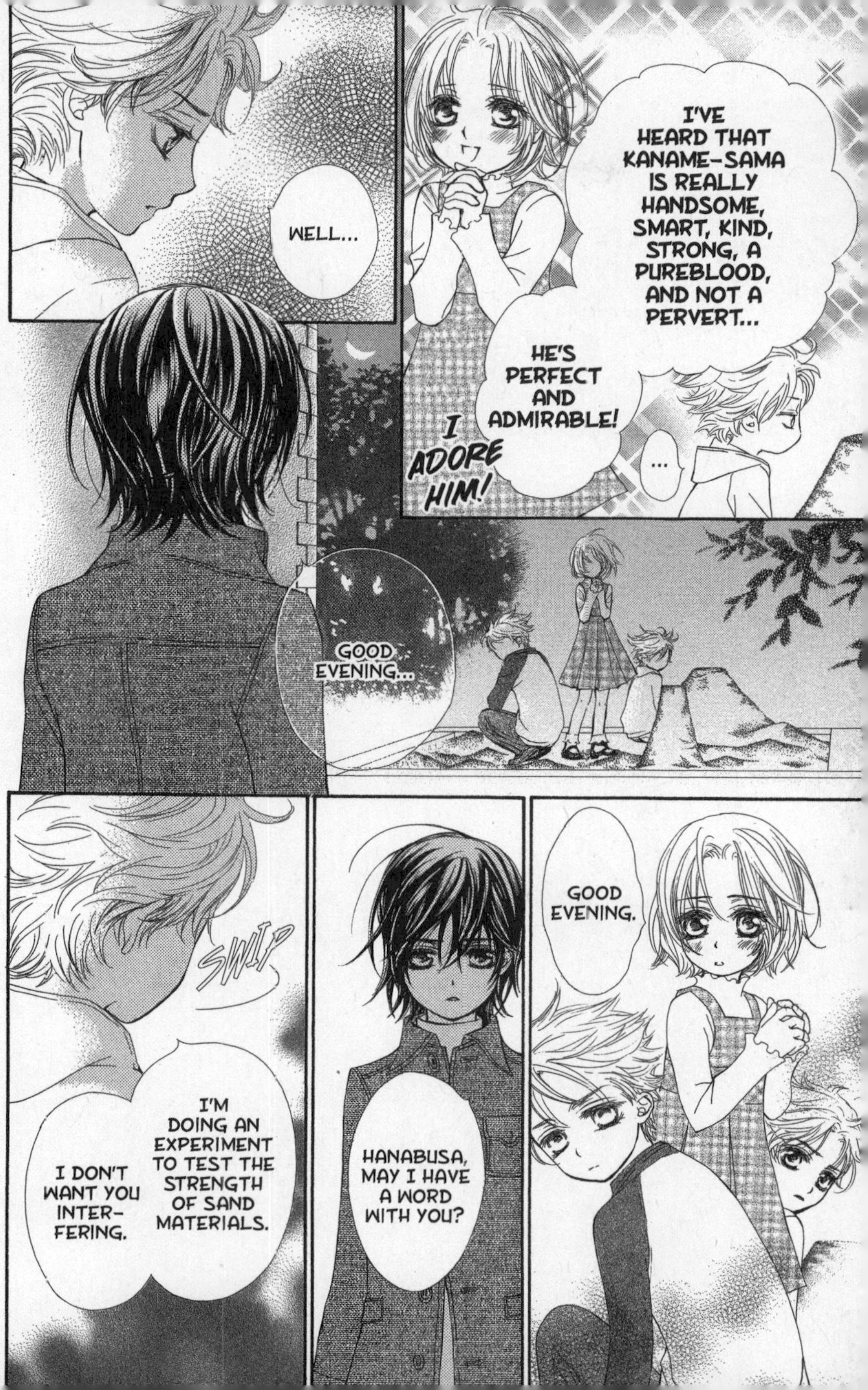
I'VE HEARD THAT KANAME-SAMA IS REALLY HANDSOME, SMART, KIND, STRONG, A PUREBLOOD, AND NOT A PERVERT...
HE'S PERFECT AND ADMIRABLE!
I ADORE HIM!
...
WELL...
GOOD EVENING...
GOOD EVENING.
HANABUSA, MAY I HAVE A WORD WITH YOU?
SWIP
I'M DOING AN EXPERIMENT TO TEST THE STRENGTH OF SAND MATERIALS.
I DON'T WANT YOU INTER-FERING.

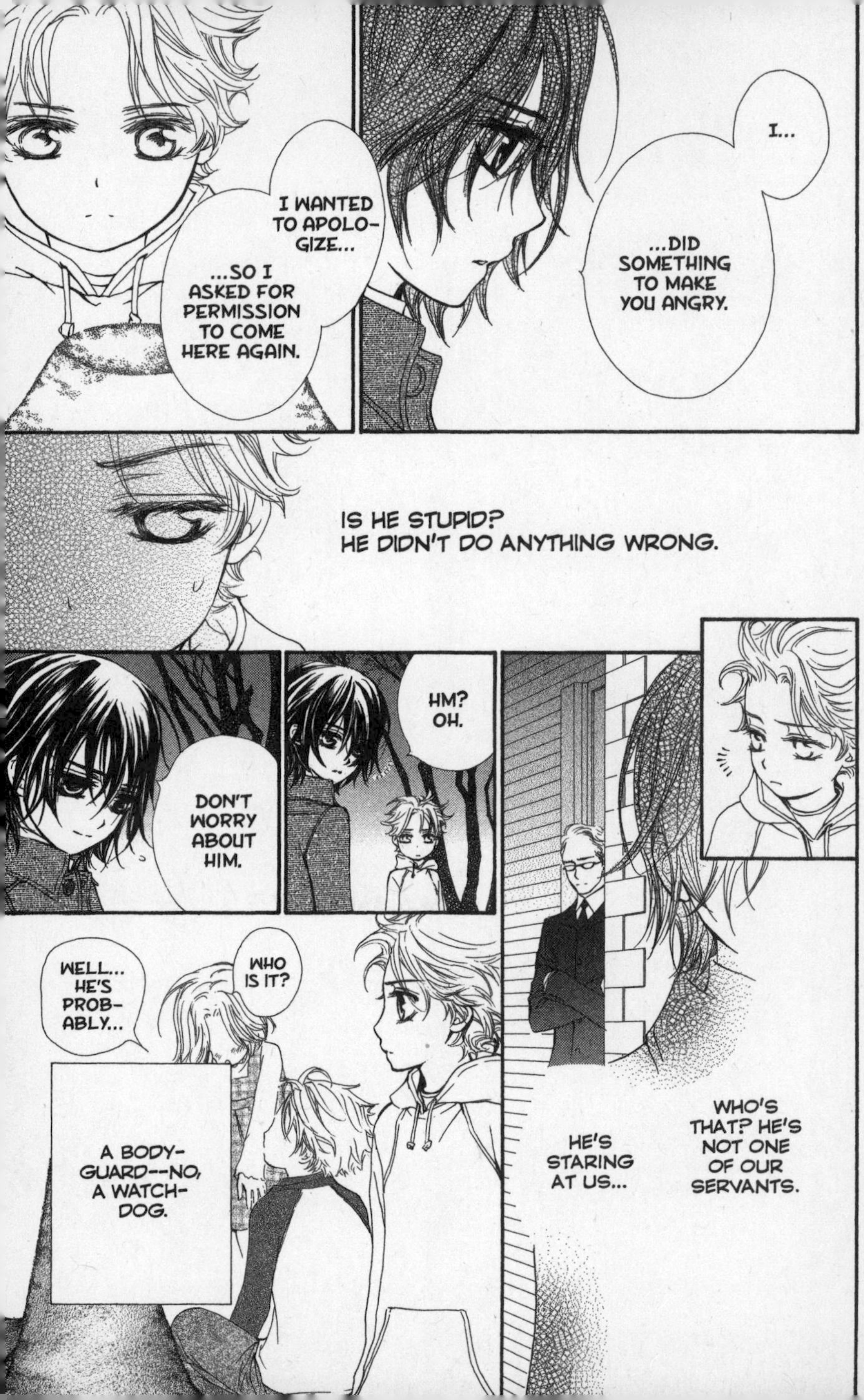

I...
...DID SOMETHING TO MAKE YOU ANGRY.
I WANTED TO APOLOGIZE...
...SO I ASKED FOR PERMISSION TO COME HERE AGAIN.
IS HE STUPID? HE DIDN'T DO ANYTHING WRONG.
WHO'S THAT? HE'S NOT ONE OF OUR SERVANTS.
HE'S STARING AT US...
HM? OH.
DON'T WORRY ABOUT HIM.
WHO IS IT?
WELL... HE'S PROBABLY...
A BODYGUARD--NO, A WATCHDOG.

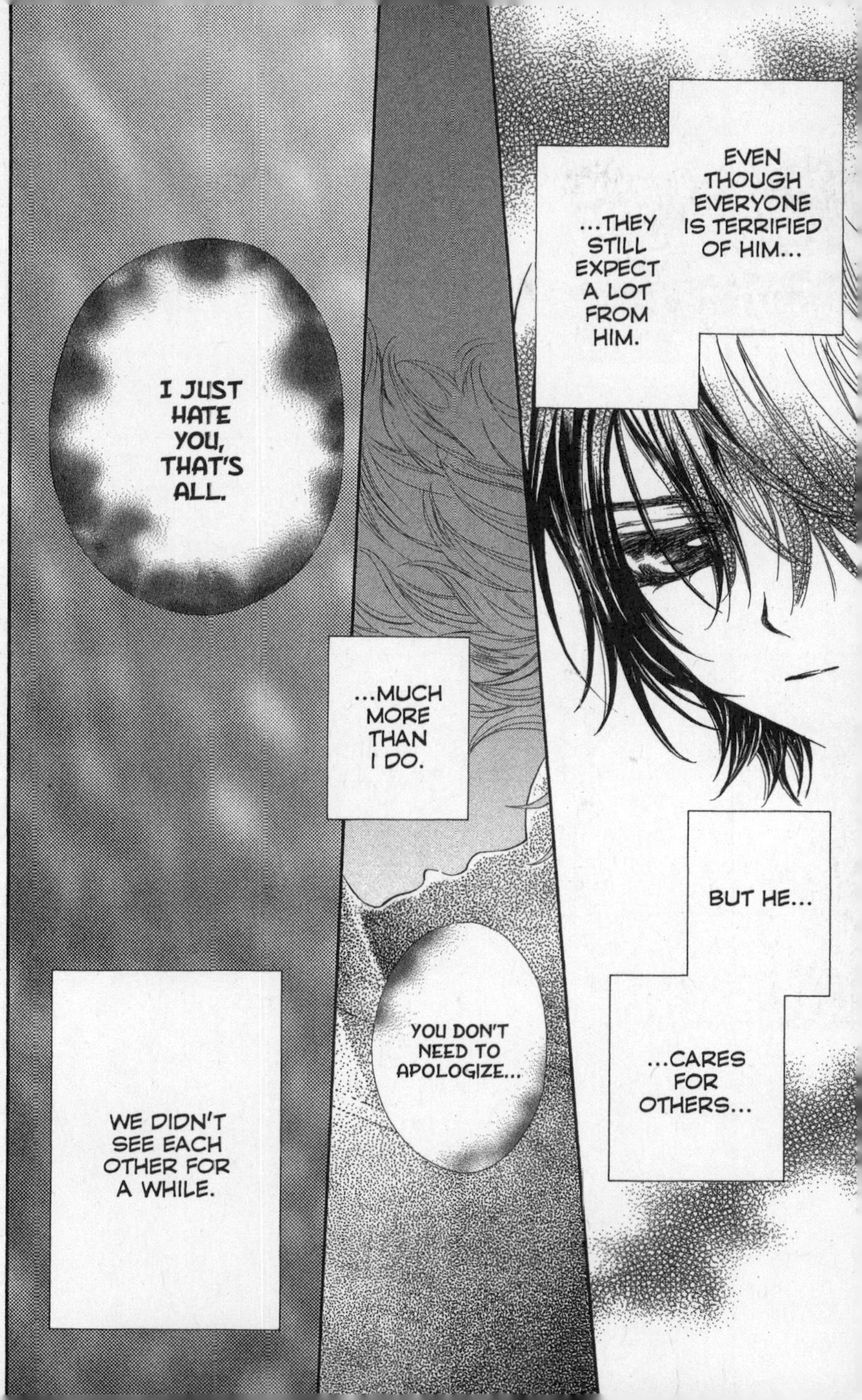
EVEN THOUGH EVERYONE IS TERRIFIED OF HIM...
...THEY STILL EXPECT A LOT FROM HIM.
BUT HE...
...CARES FOR OTHERS...
...MUCH MORE THAN I DO.
YOU DON'T NEED TO APOLOGIZE...
I JUST HATE YOU, THAT'S ALL.
WE DIDN'T SEE EACH OTHER FOR A WHILE.

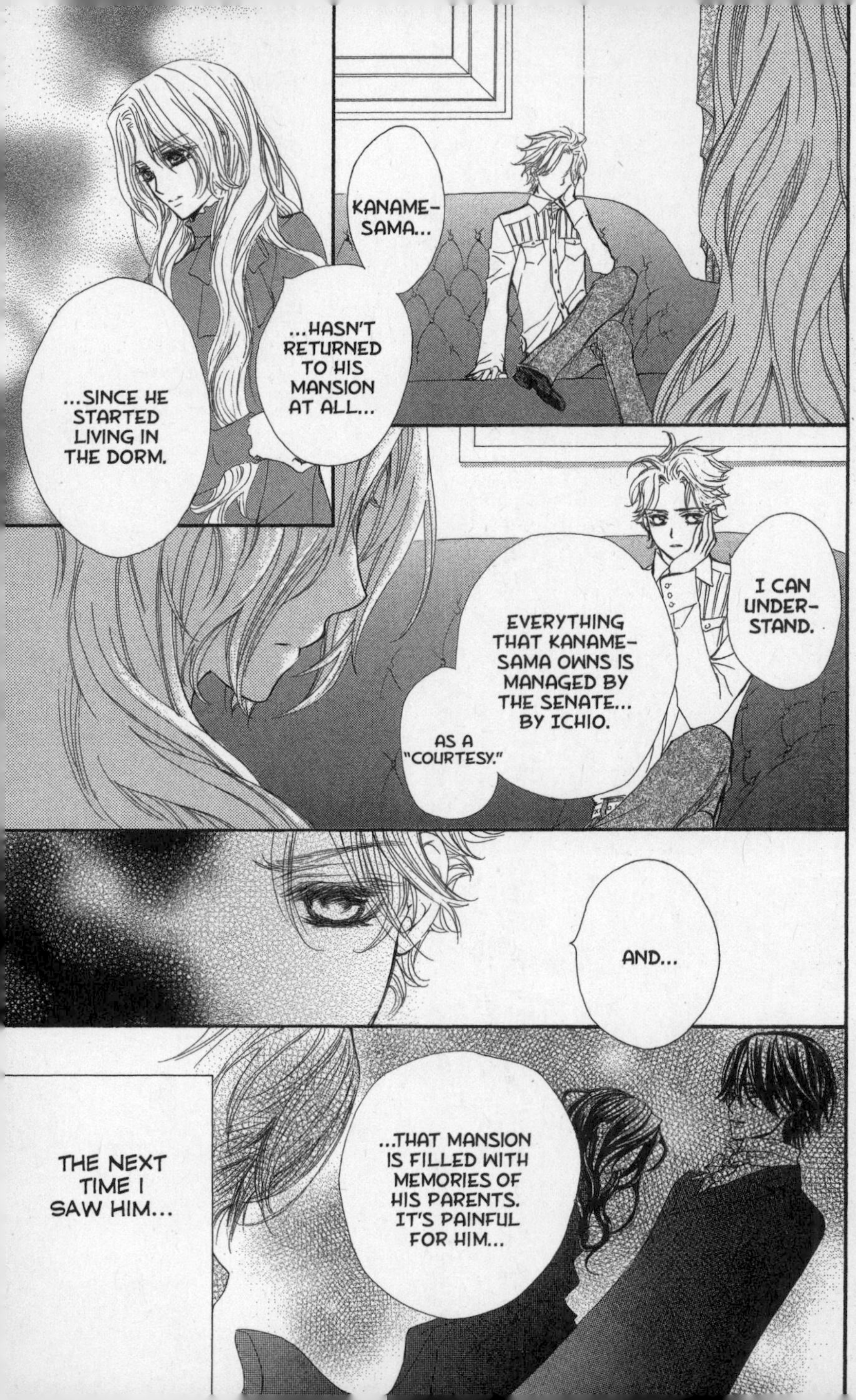
KANAME-SAMA...
...HASN'T RETURNED TO HIS MANSION AT ALL...
...SINCE HE STARTED LIVING IN THE DORM.
I CAN UNDERSTAND.
EVERYTHING THAT KANAME-SAMA OWNS IS MANAGED BY THE SENATE... BY ICHIO.
AS A "COURTESY."
AND...
...THAT MANSION IS FILLED WITH MEMORIES OF HIS PARENTS. IT'S PAINFUL FOR HIM...
THE NEXT TIME I SAW HIM...

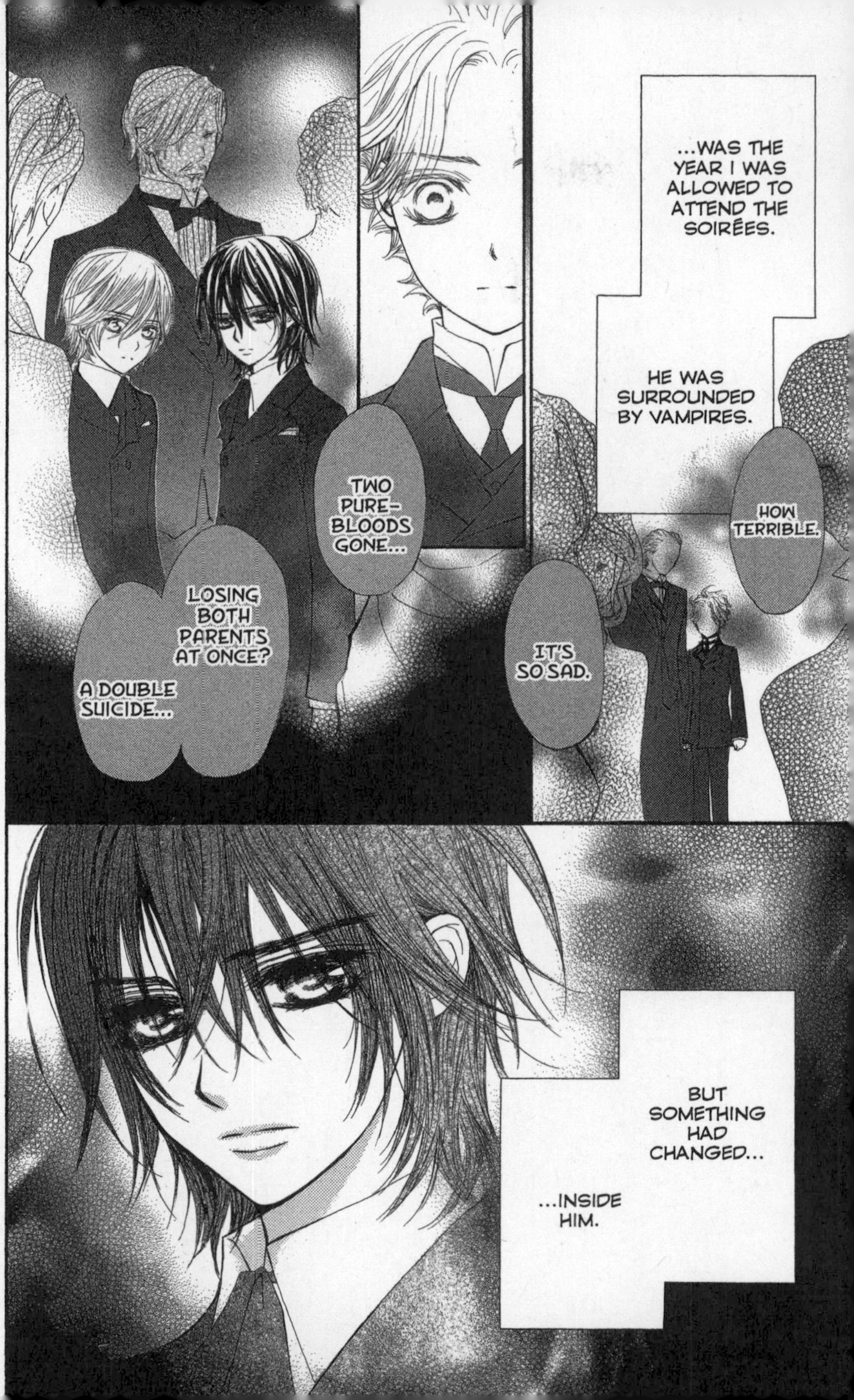
...WAS THE YEAR I WAS ALLOWED TO ATTEND THE SOIRÉES.
HE WAS SURROUNDED BY VAMPIRES.
HOW TERRIBLE.
IT'S SO SAD.
TWO PURE-BLOODS GONE...
LOSING BOTH PARENTS AT ONCE?
A DOUBLE SUICIDE...
BUT SOMETHING HAD CHANGED...
...INSIDE HIM.

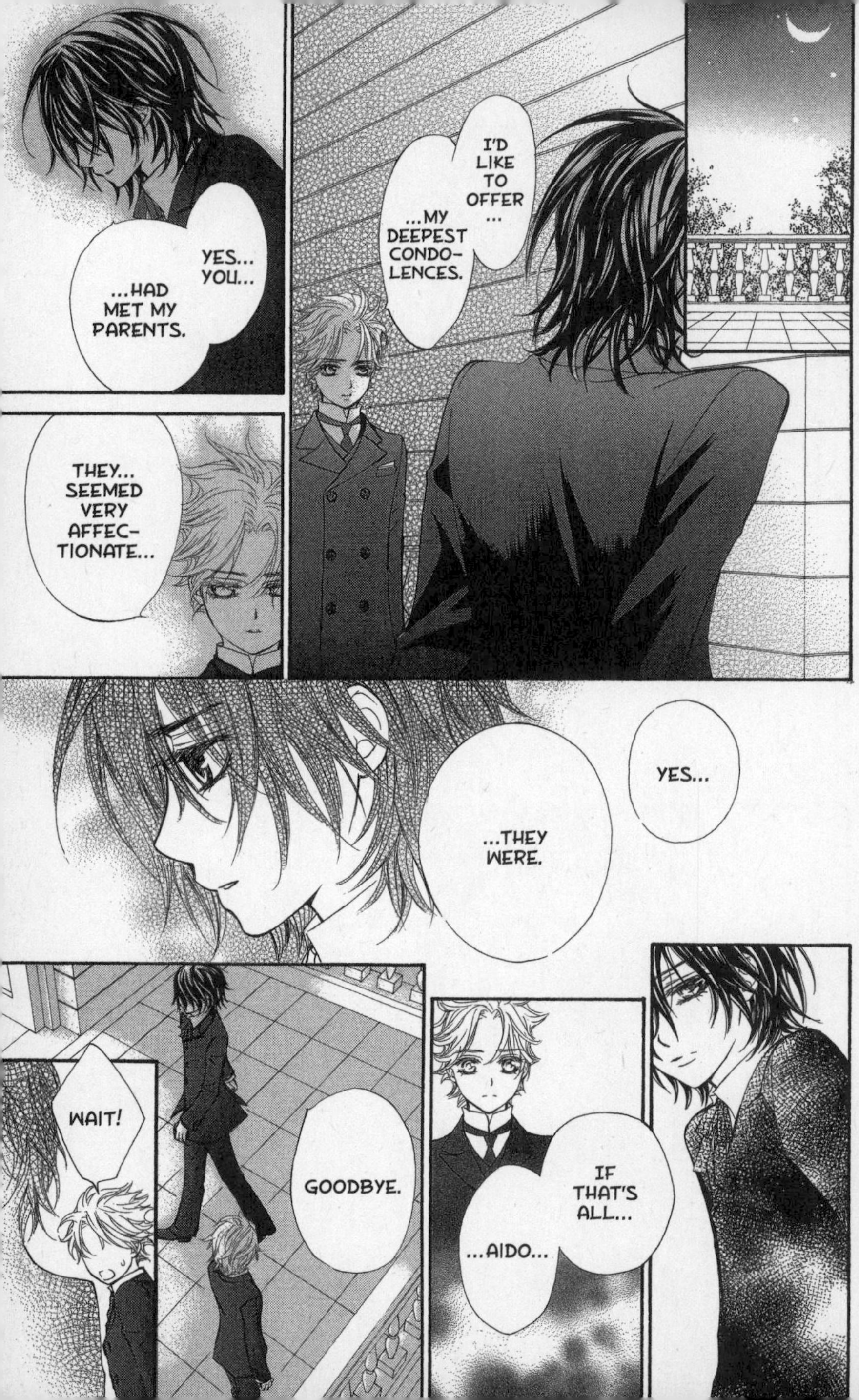
I'D LIKE TO OFFER...
...MY DEEPEST CONDOLENCES.
YES... YOU...
...HAD MET MY PARENTS.
THEY... SEEMED VERY AFFECTIONATE...
YES...
...THEY WERE.
IF THAT'S ALL...
...AIDO...
GOODBYE.
WAIT!

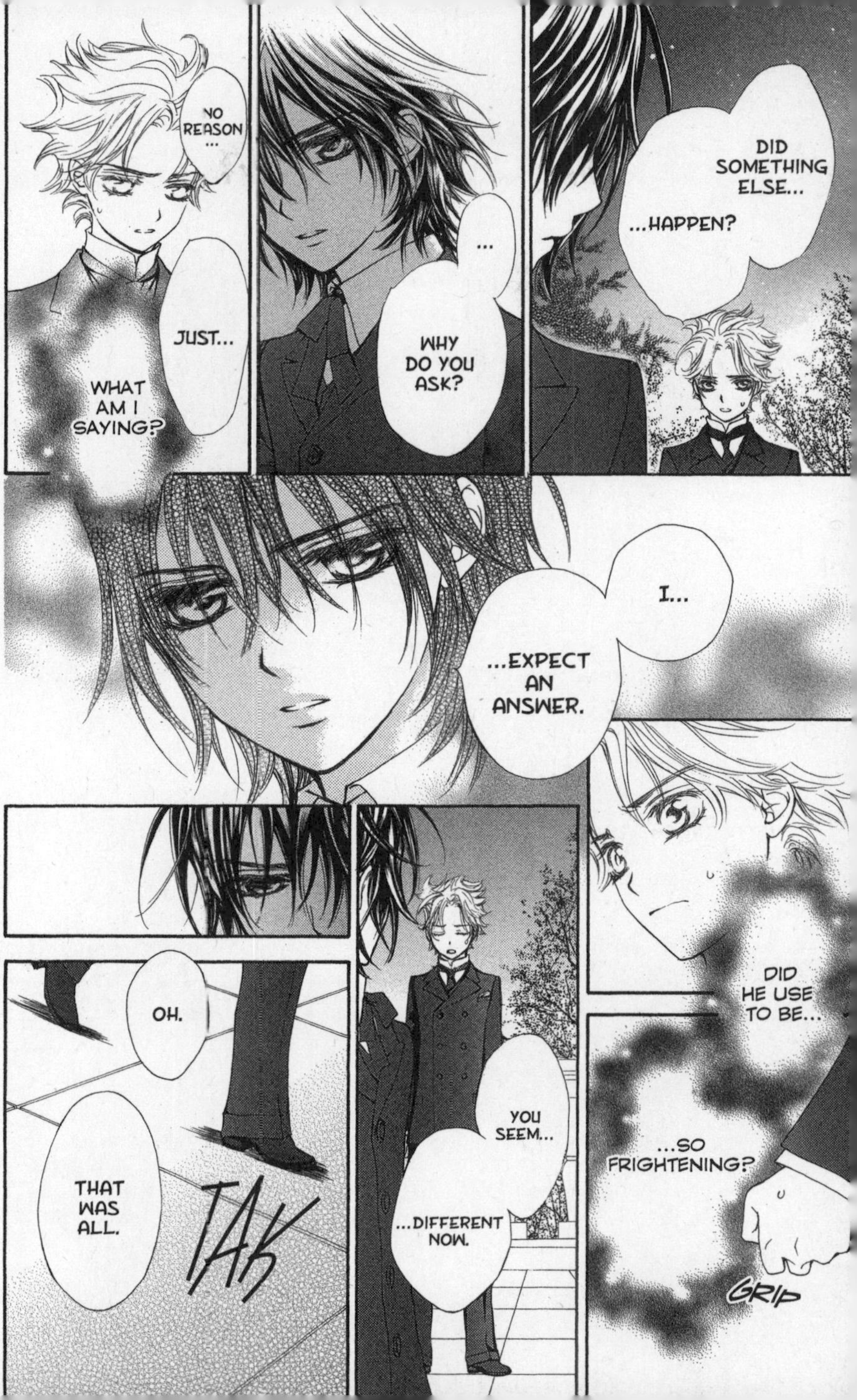
DID SOMETHING ELSE...
...HAPPEN?
...
WHY DO YOU ASK?
NO REASON...
JUST...
WHAT AM I SAYING?
I...
...EXPECT AN ANSWER.
DID HE USE TO BE...
...SO FRIGHTENING?
GRIP
YOU SEEM...
...DIFFERENT NOW.
OH.
THAT WAS ALL.
TAK

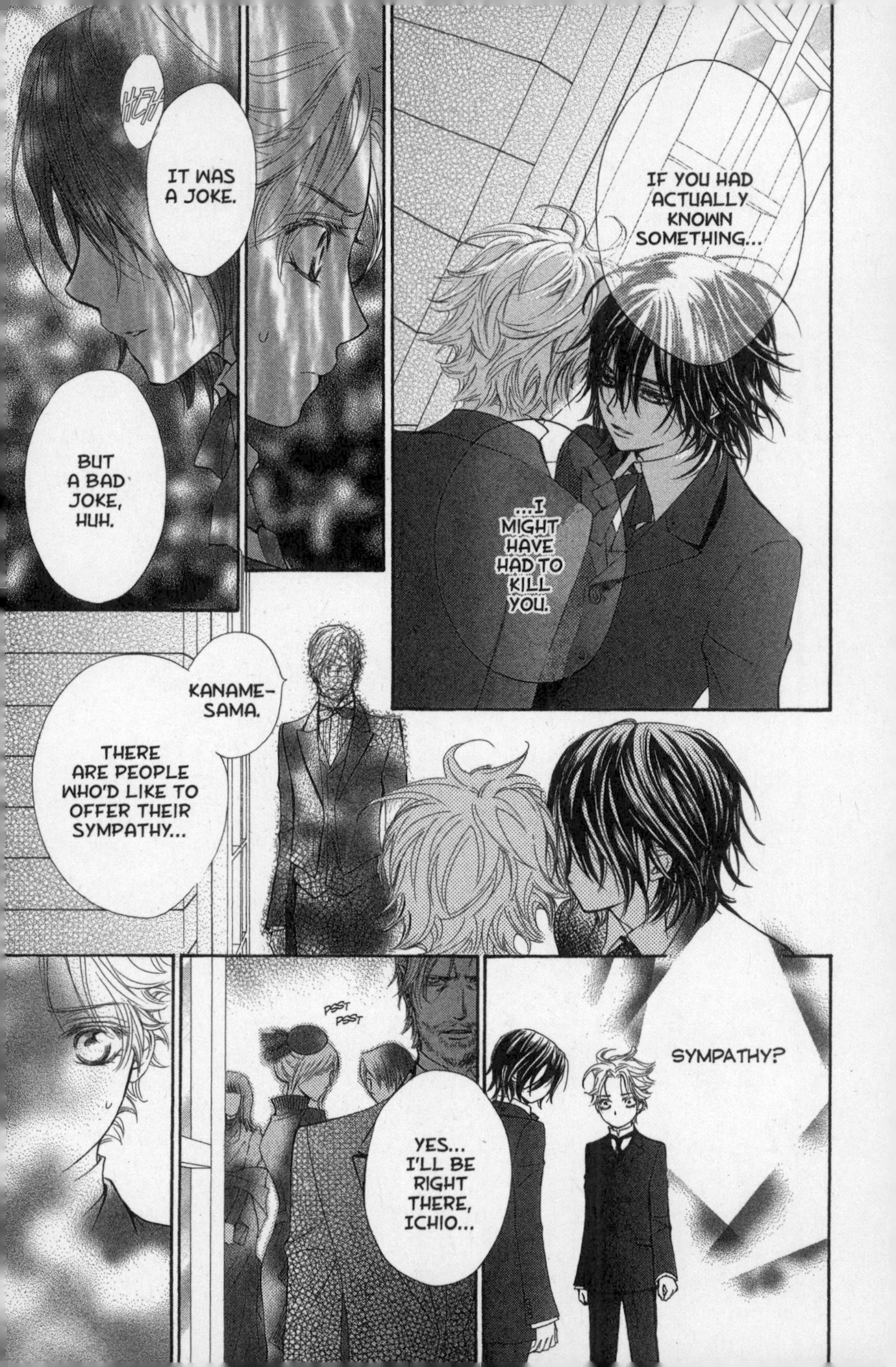

IF YOU HAD ACTUALLY KNOWN SOMETHING...
...I MIGHT HAVE HAD TO KILL YOU.
KEH
IT WAS A JOKE.
BUT A BAD JOKE, HUH.
KANAME-SAMA.
THERE ARE PEOPLE WHO'D LIKE TO OFFER THEIR SYMPATHY...
SYMPATHY?
PSST PSST
YES... I'LL BE RIGHT THERE, ICHIO...

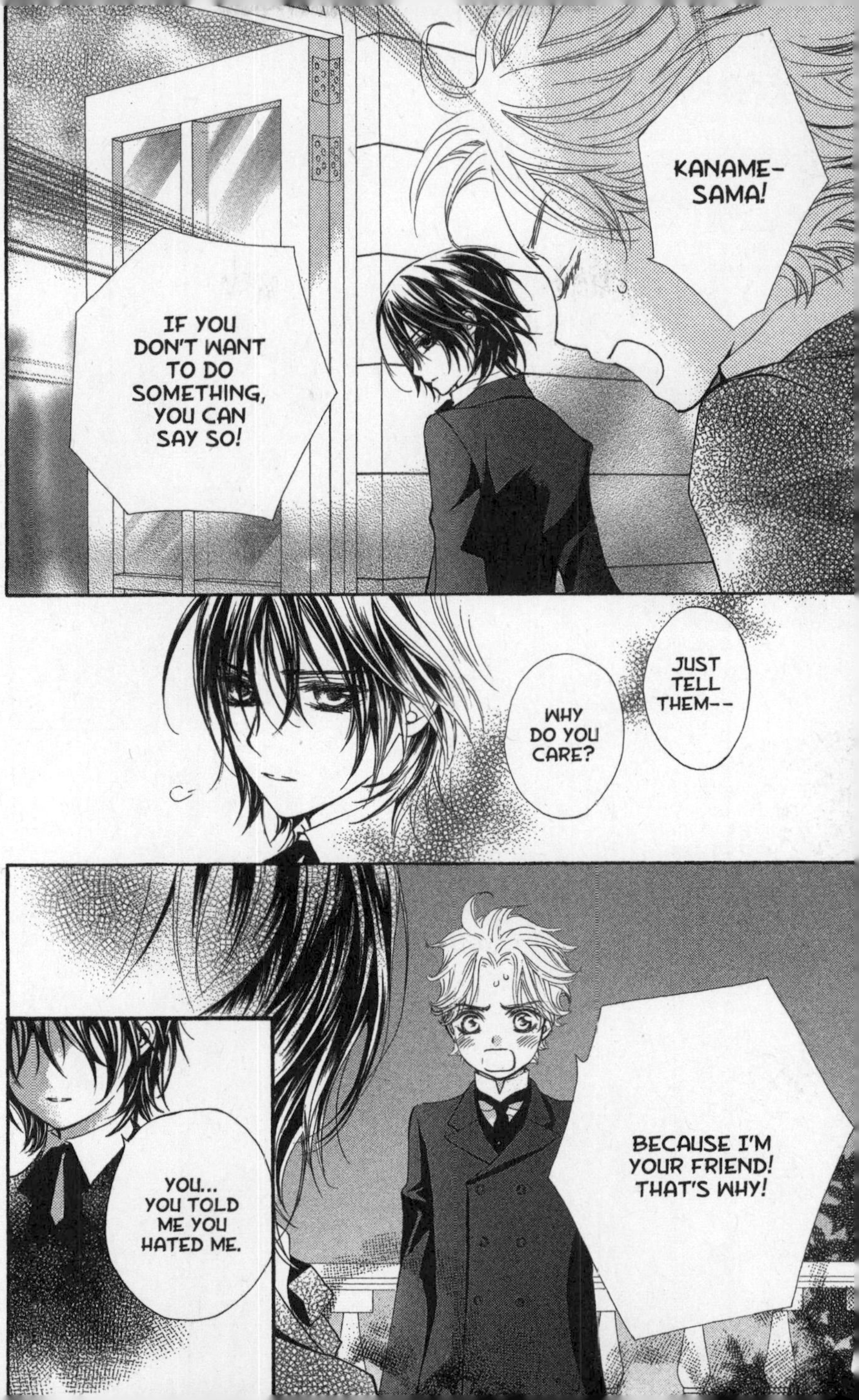
KANAME-SAMA!
IF YOU DON'T WANT TO DO SOMETHING, YOU CAN SAY SO!
JUST TELL THEM--
WHY DO YOU CARE?
BECAUSE I'M YOUR FRIEND! THAT'S WHY!
YOU... YOU TOLD ME YOU HATED ME.

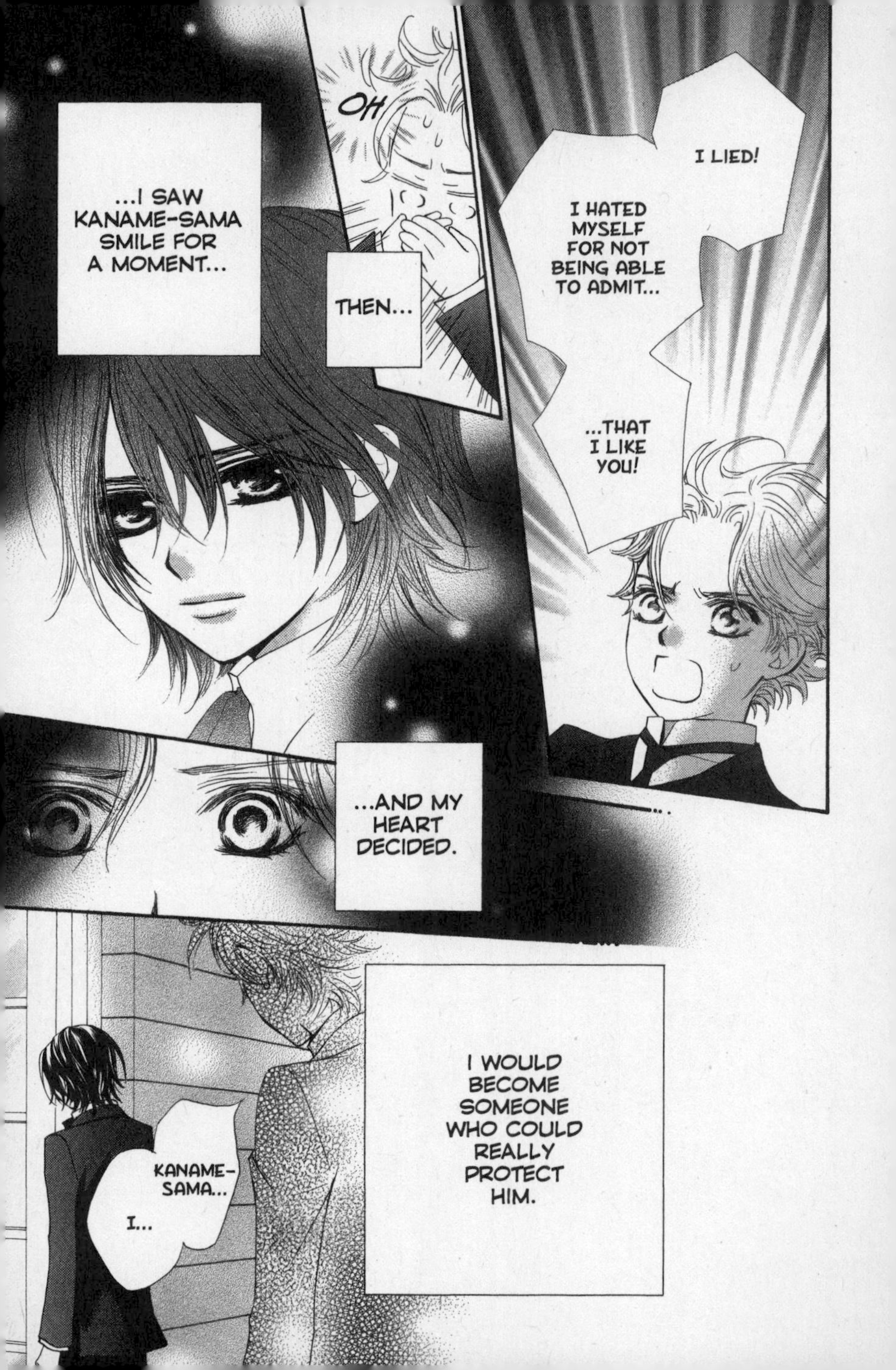
I LIED!
I HATED MYSELF FOR NOT BEING ABLE TO ADMIT...
...THAT I LIKE YOU!
OH
THEN...
...I SAW KANAME-SAMA SMILE FOR A MOMENT...
...AND MY HEART DECIDED.
I WOULD BECOME SOMEONE WHO COULD REALLY PROTECT HIM.
KANAME-SAMA...
I...

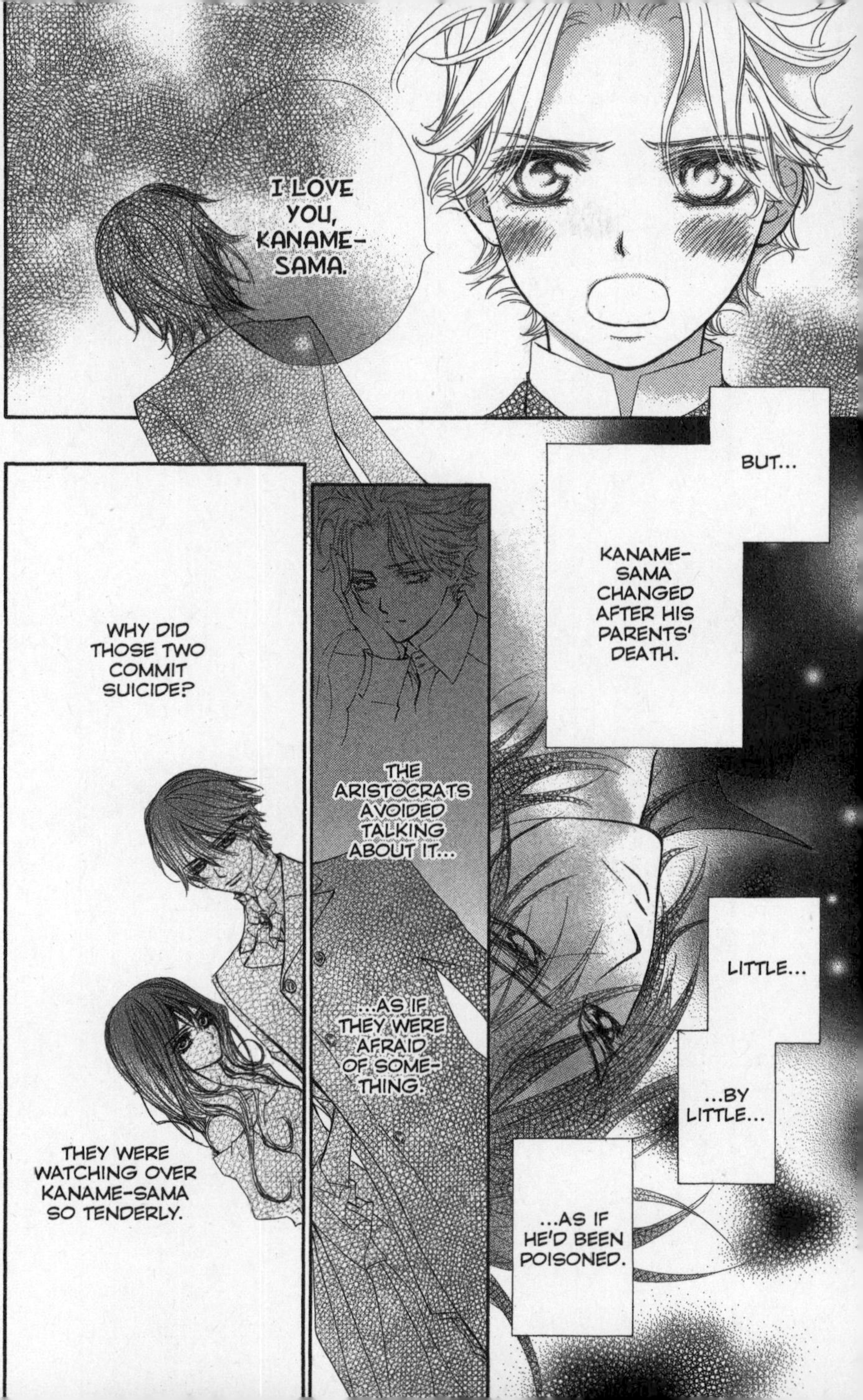
I LOVE YOU, KANAME-SAMA.
BUT...
KANAME-SAMA CHANGED AFTER HIS PARENTS' DEATH.
LITTLE...
...BY LITTLE...
...AS IF HE'D BEEN POISONED.
THE ARISTOCRATS AVOIDED TALKING ABOUT IT...
...AS IF THEY WERE AFRAID OF SOME-THING.
WHY DID THOSE TWO COMMIT SUICIDE?
THEY WERE WATCHING OVER KANAME-SAMA SO TENDERLY.

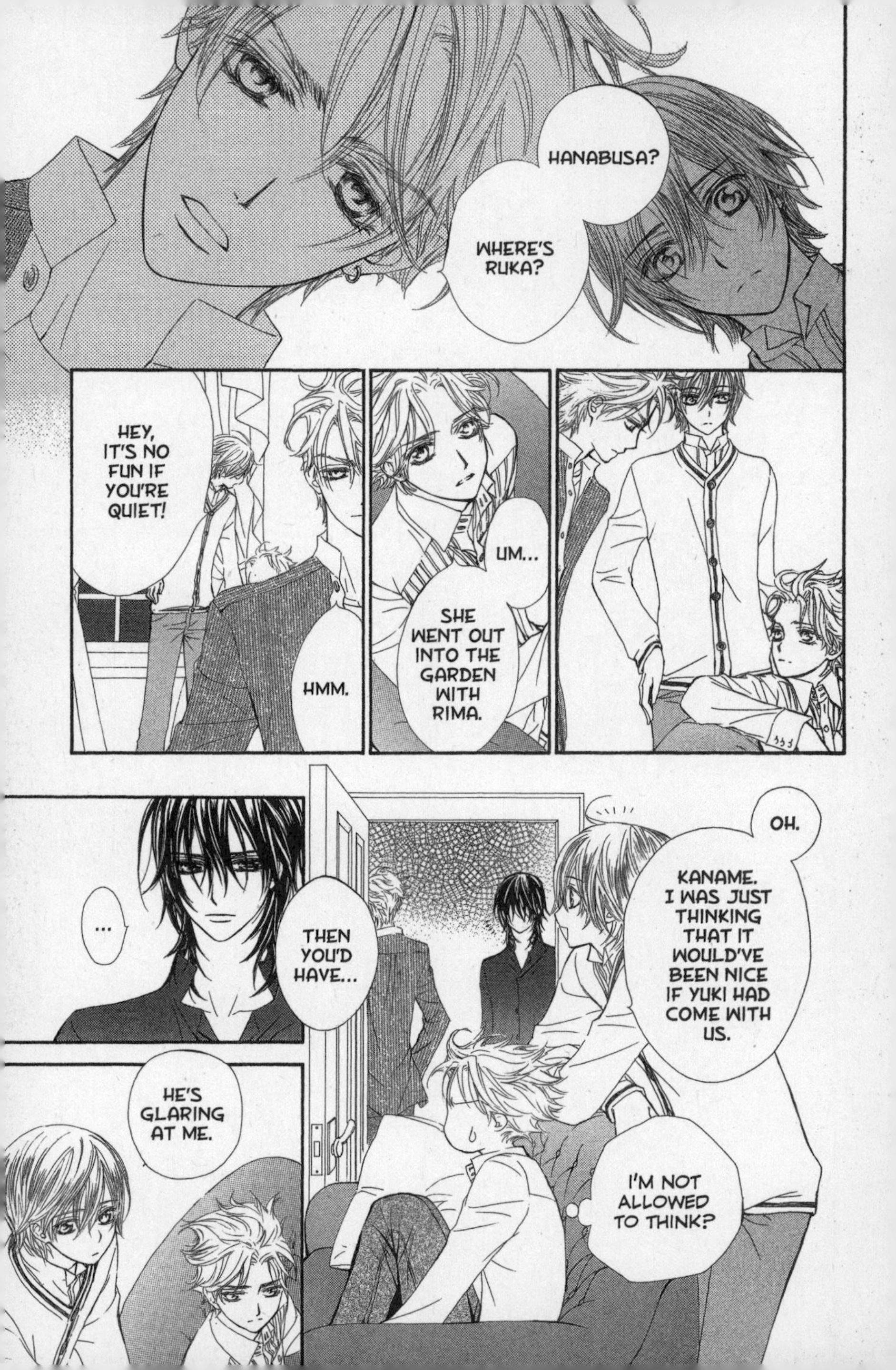
HANABUSA?
WHERE'S RUKA?
UM...
SHE WENT OUT INTO THE GARDEN WITH RIMA.
HMM.
HEY, IT'S NO FUN IF YOU'RE QUIET!
OH.
KANAME. I WAS JUST THINKING THAT IT WOULD'VE BEEN NICE IF YUKI HAD COME WITH US.
THEN YOU'D HAVE...
...
I'M NOT ALLOWED TO THINK?
HE'S GLARING AT ME.

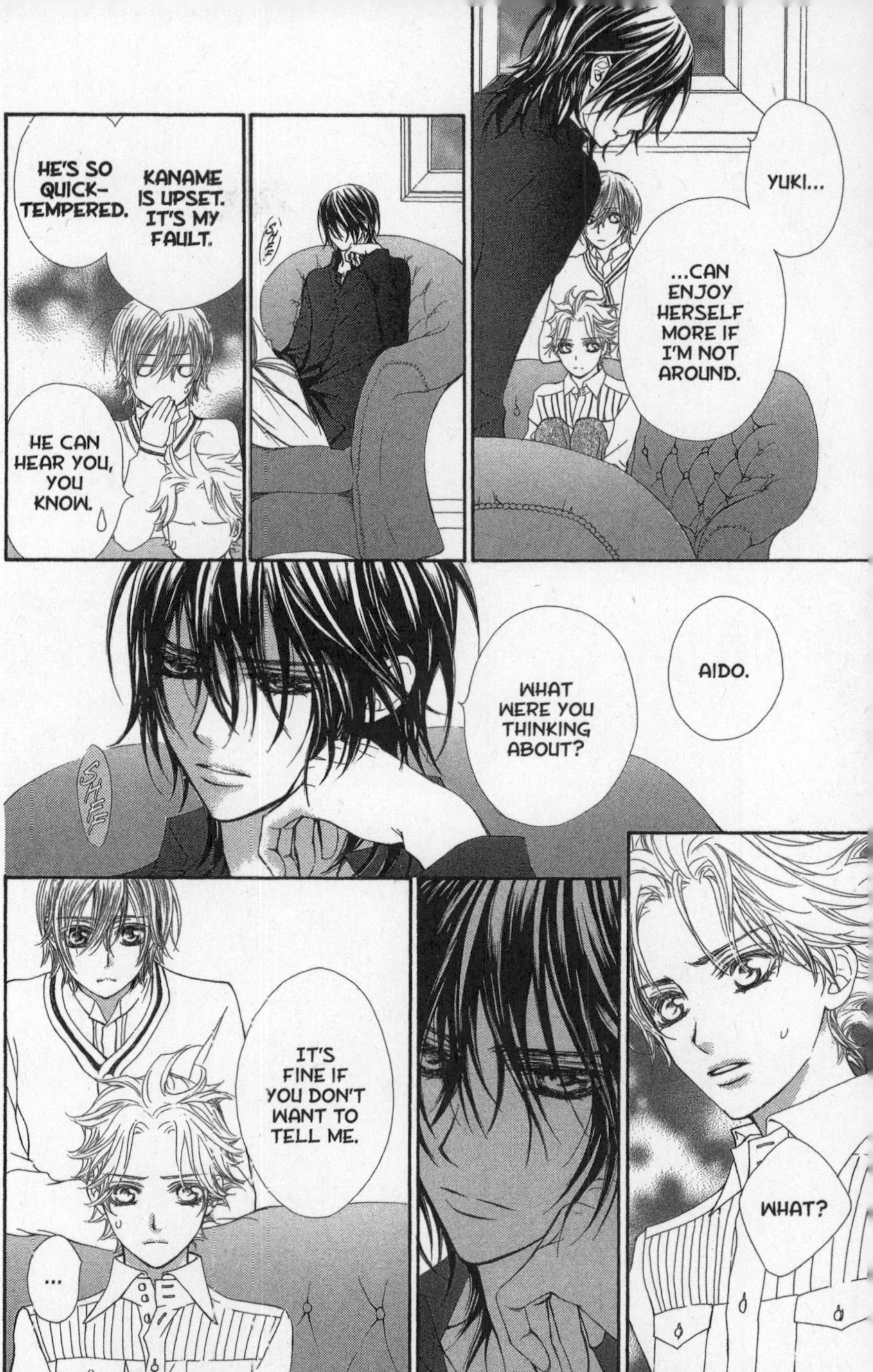
YUKI...
...CAN ENJOY HERSELF MORE IF I'M NOT AROUND.
KANAME IS UPSET. IT'S MY FAULT.
HE'S SO QUICK-TEMPERED.
HE CAN HEAR YOU, YOU KNOW.
AIDO.
WHAT WERE YOU THINKING ABOUT?
WHAT?
IT'S FINE IF YOU DON'T WANT TO TELL ME.
...

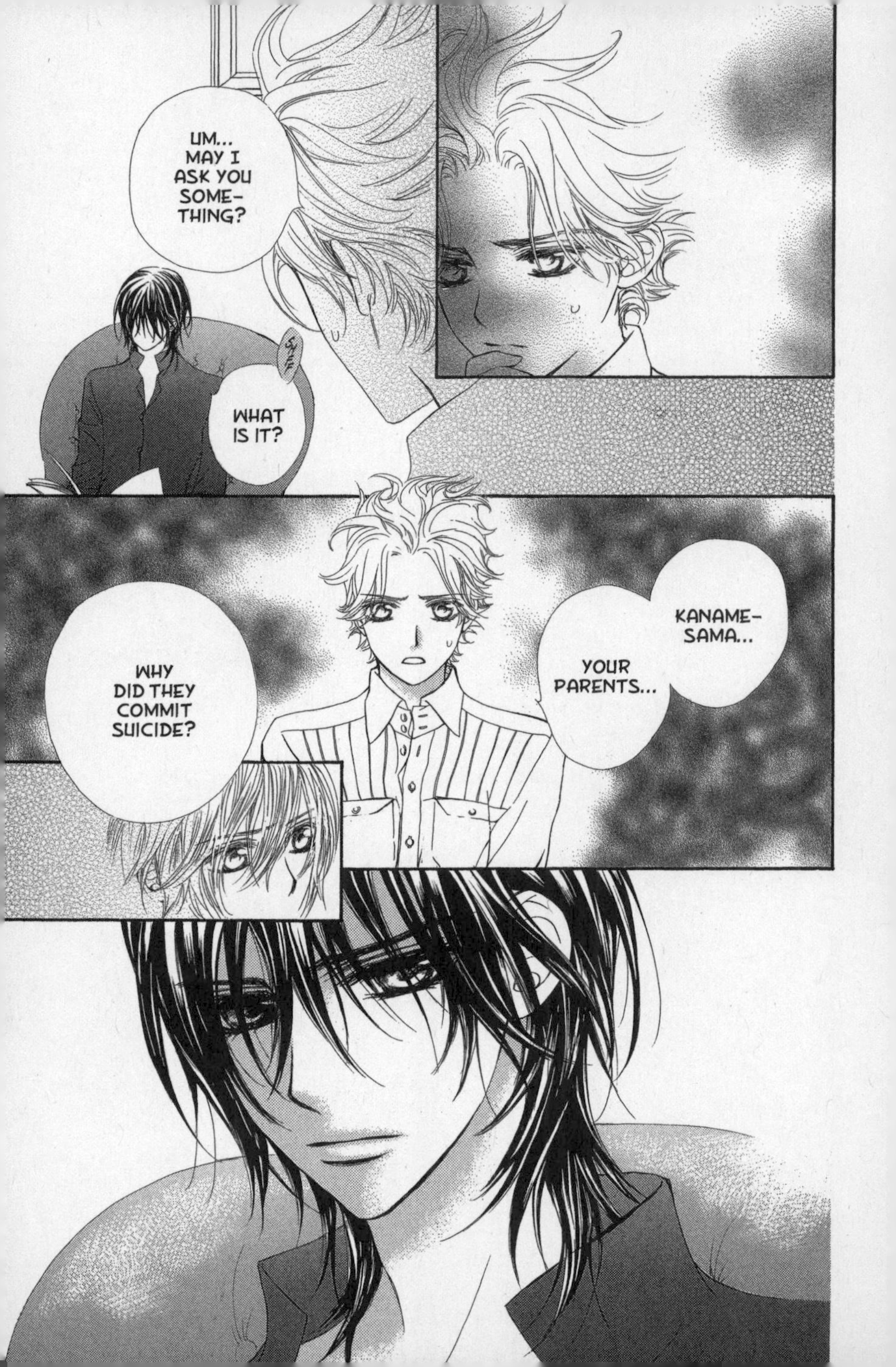
UM... MAY I ASK YOU SOME-THING?
WHAT IS IT?
KANAME-SAMA...
YOUR PARENTS...
WHY DID THEY COMMIT SUICIDE?

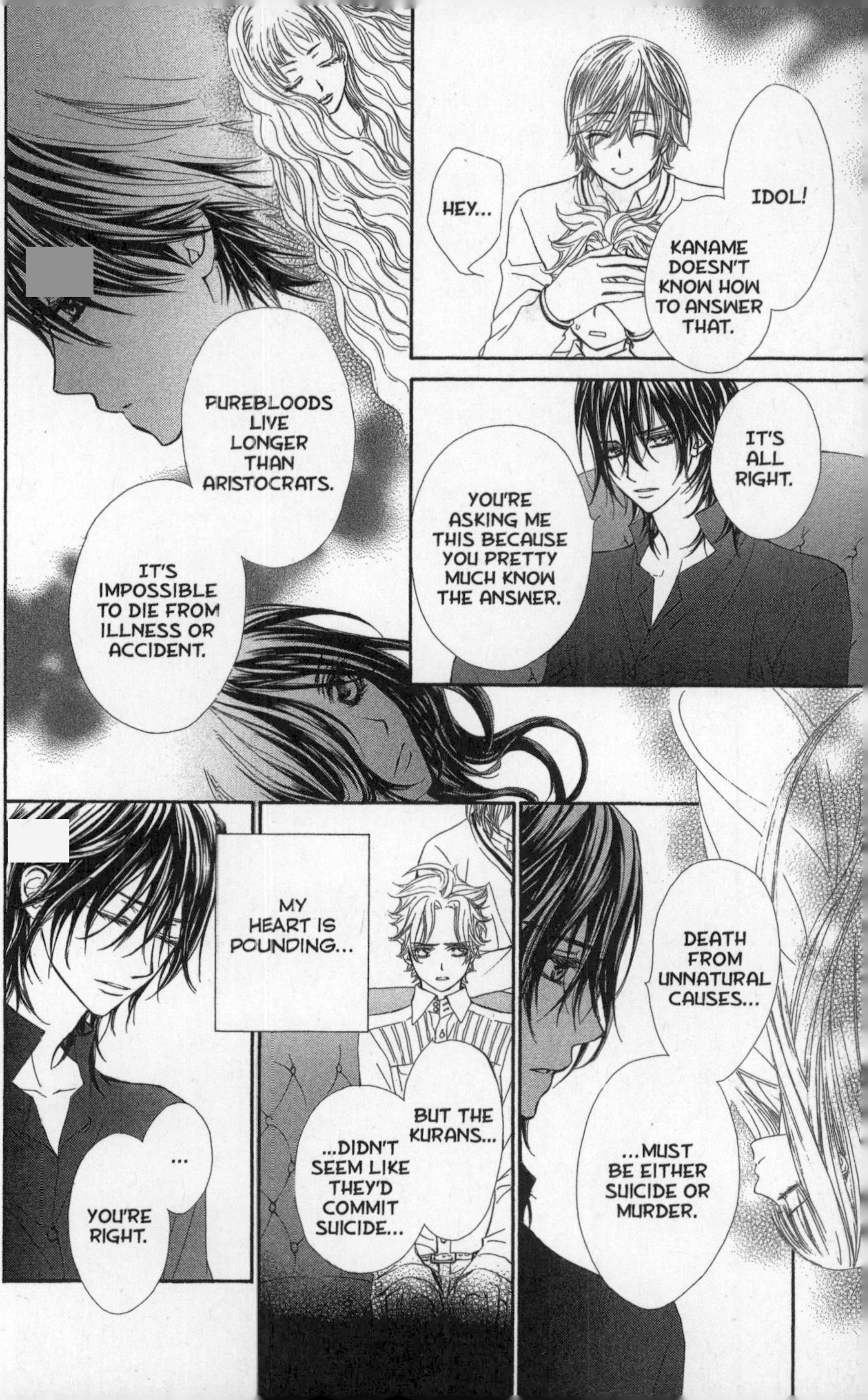
IDOL!
KANAME DOESN'T KNOW HOW TO ANSWER THAT.
HEY...
IT'S ALL RIGHT.
YOU'RE ASKING ME THIS BECAUSE YOU PRETTY MUCH KNOW THE ANSWER.
PUREBLOODS LIVE LONGER THAN ARISTOCRATS.
IT'S IMPOSSIBLE TO DIE FROM ILLNESS OR ACCIDENT.
DEATH FROM UNNATURAL CAUSES...
...MUST BE EITHER SUICIDE OR MURDER.
MY HEART IS POUNDING...
BUT THE KURANS...
...DIDN'T SEEM LIKE THEY'D COMMIT SUICIDE...
...
YOU'RE RIGHT.

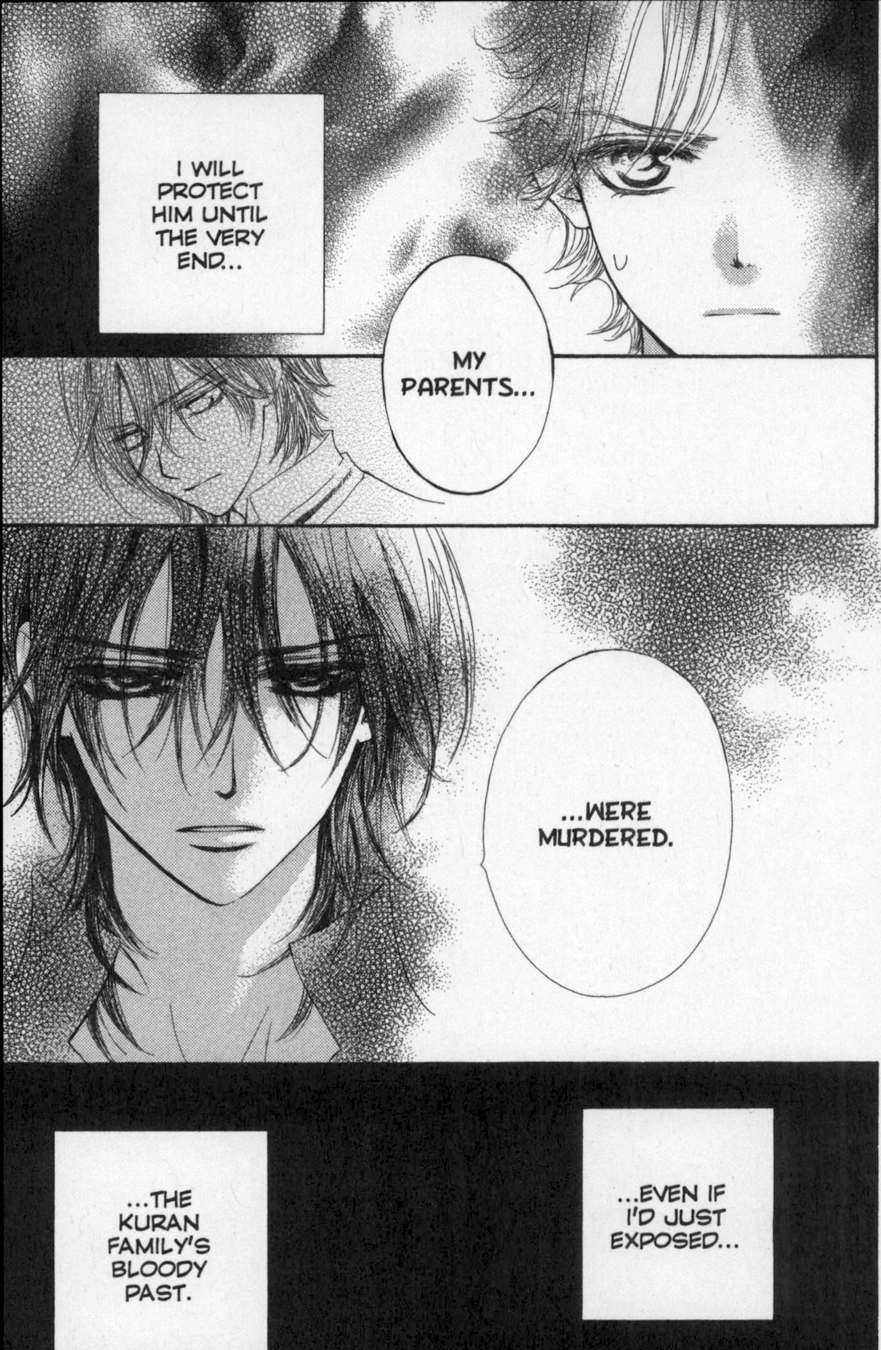
I WILL PROTECT HIM UNTIL THE VERY END...
MY PARENTS...
...WERE MURDERED.
...EVEN IF I'D JUST EXPOSED...
...THE KURAN FAMILY'S BLOODY PAST.

TWENTY-EIGHTH NIGHT/END

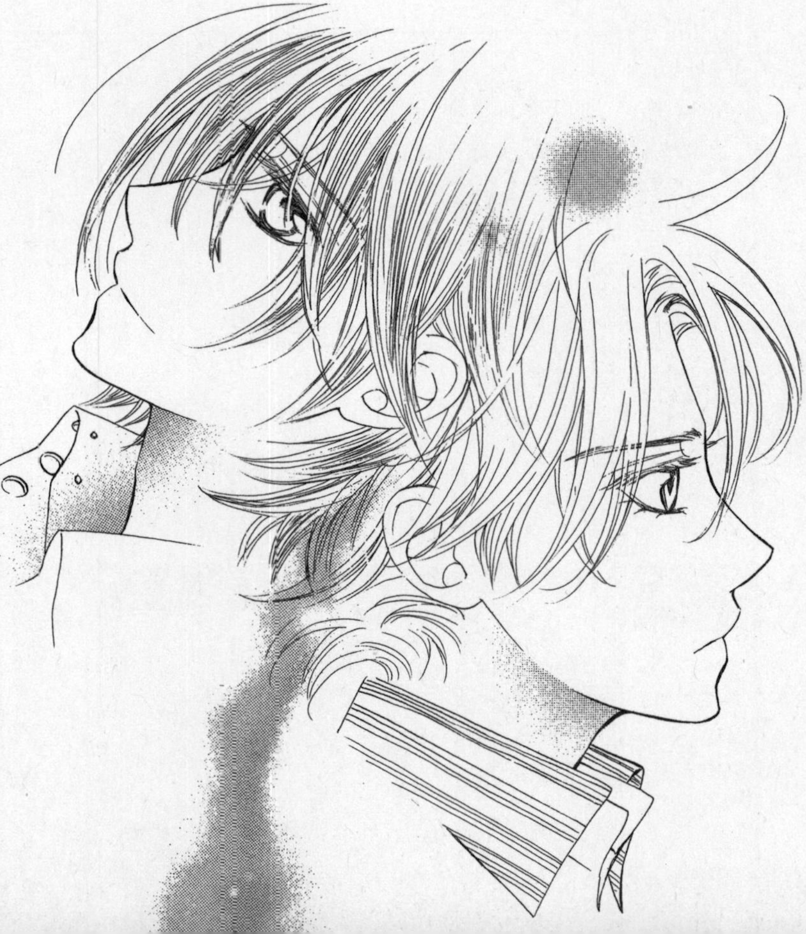

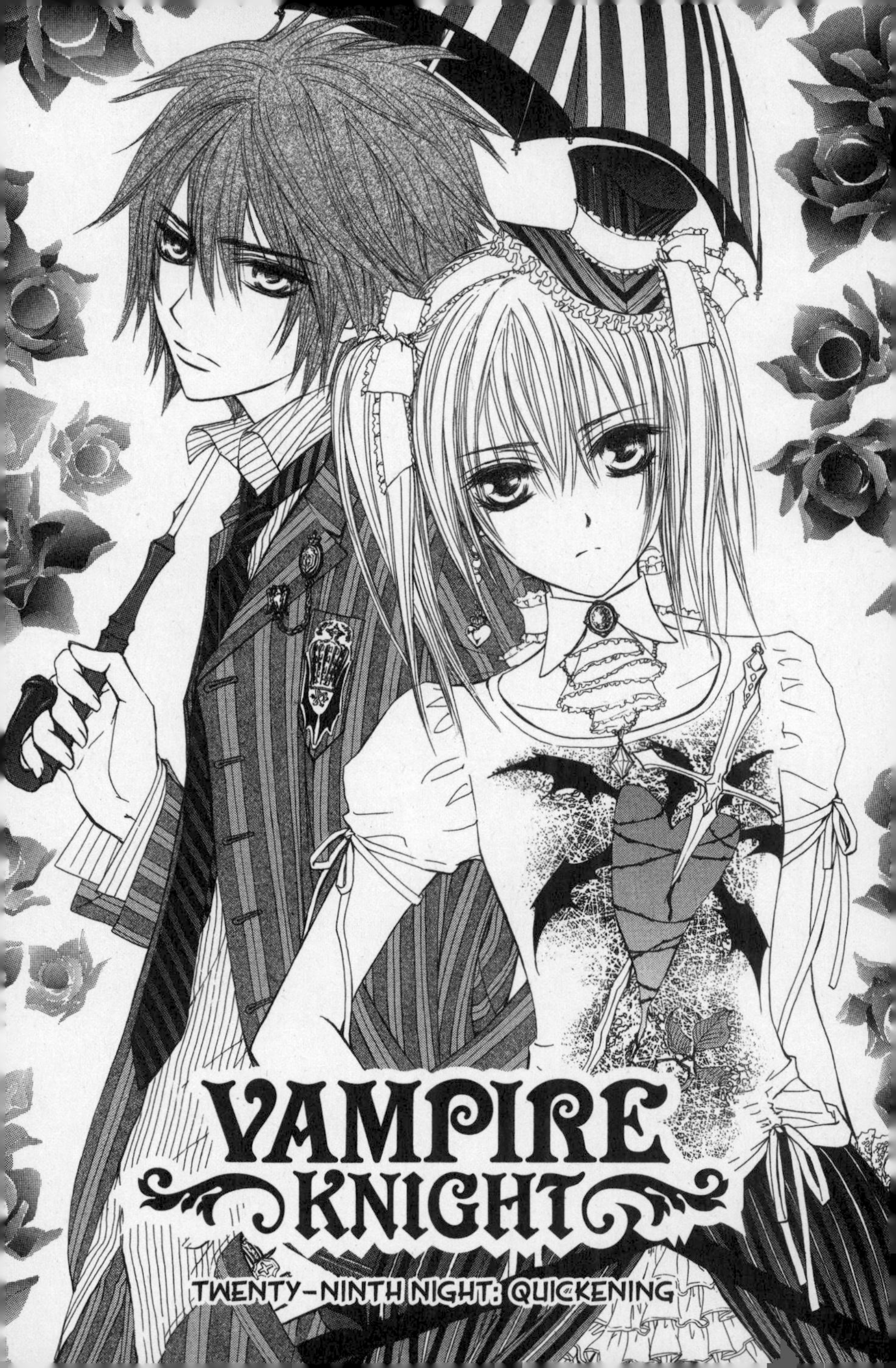
VAMPIRE
KNIGHT
TWENTY-NINTH NIGHT: QUICKENING

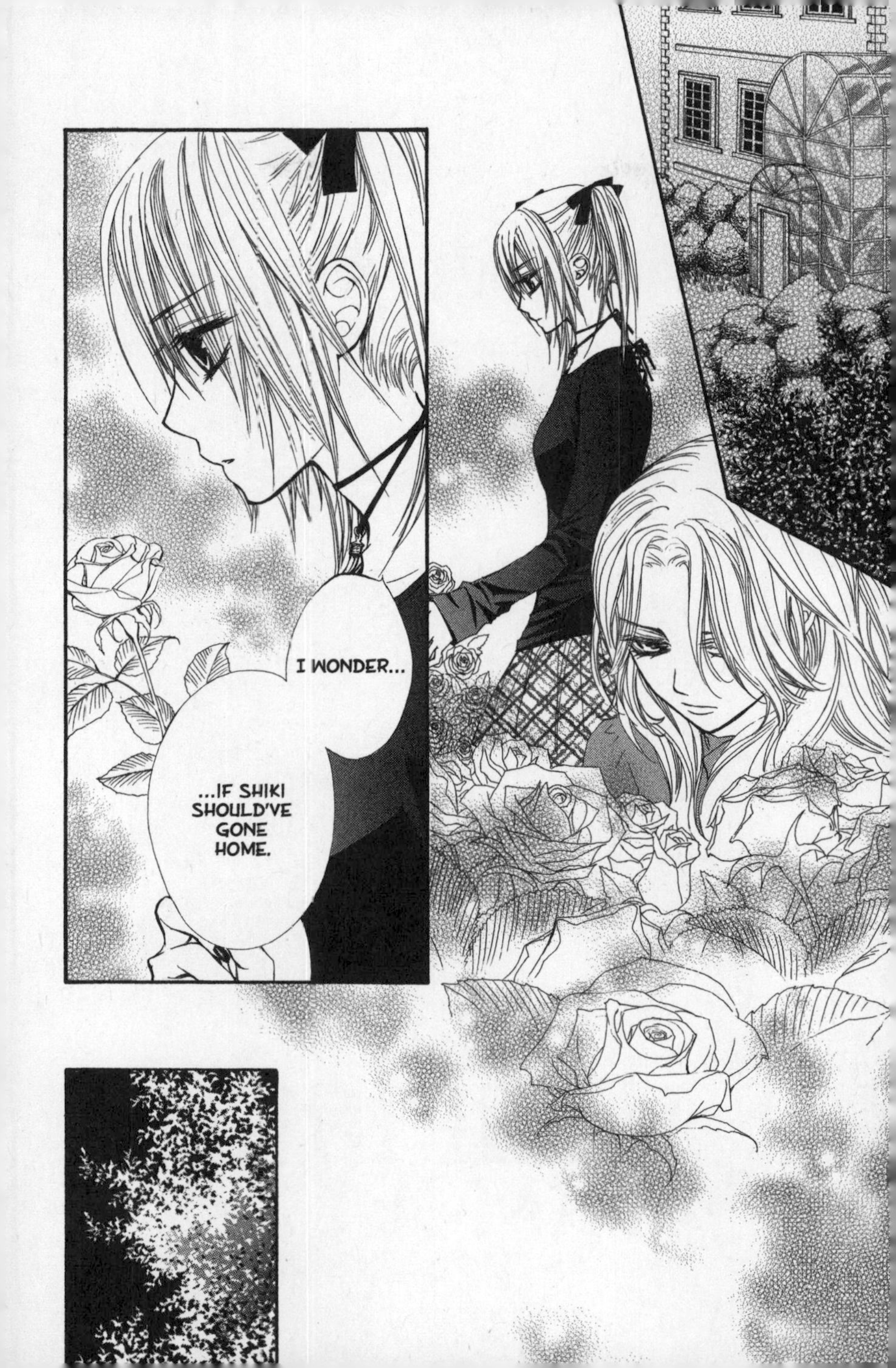
I WONDER...
...IF SHIKI SHOULD'VE GONE HOME.

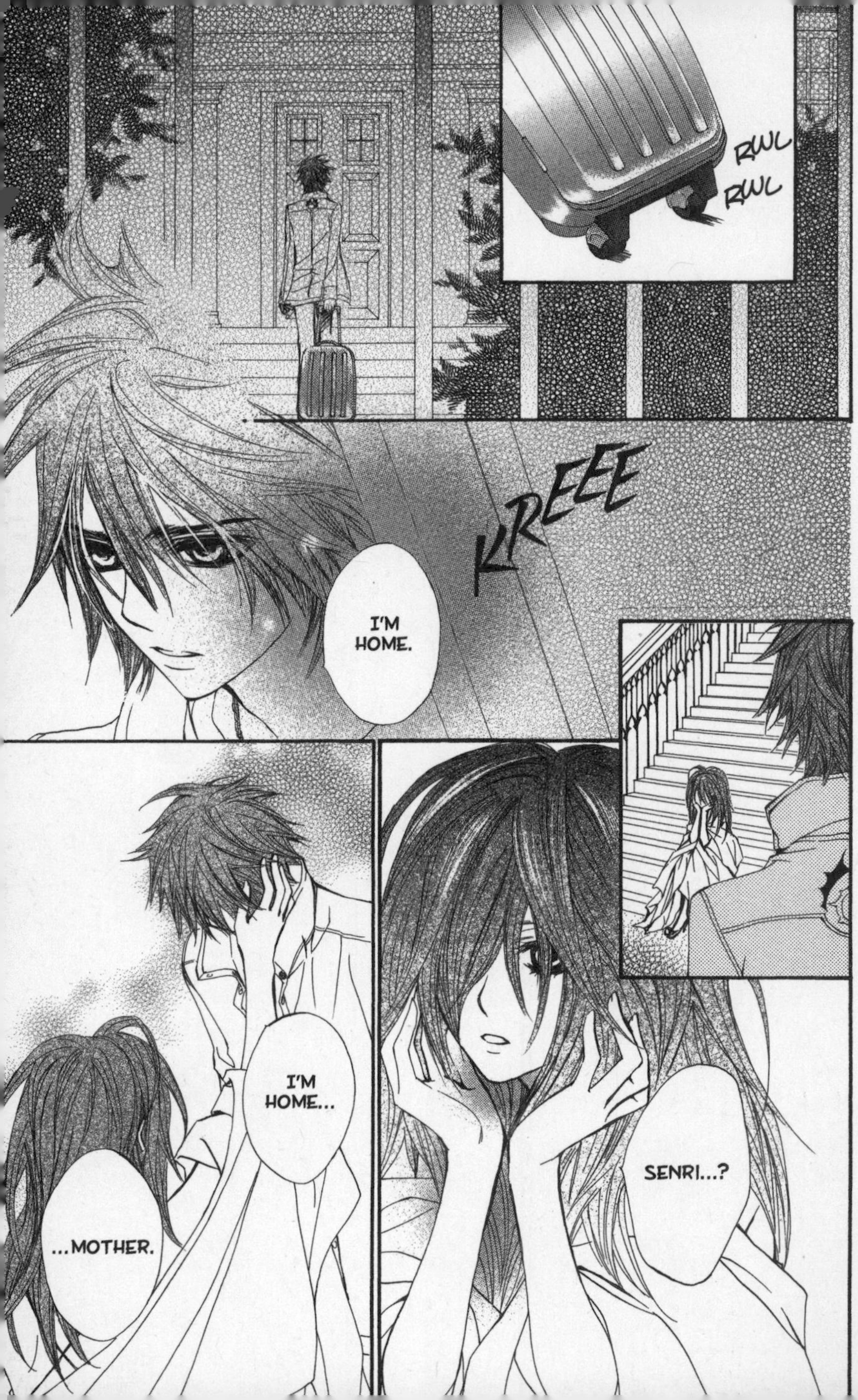
RWL
RWL
KREEE
I'M HOME.
SENRI...?
I'M HOME...
...MOTHER.

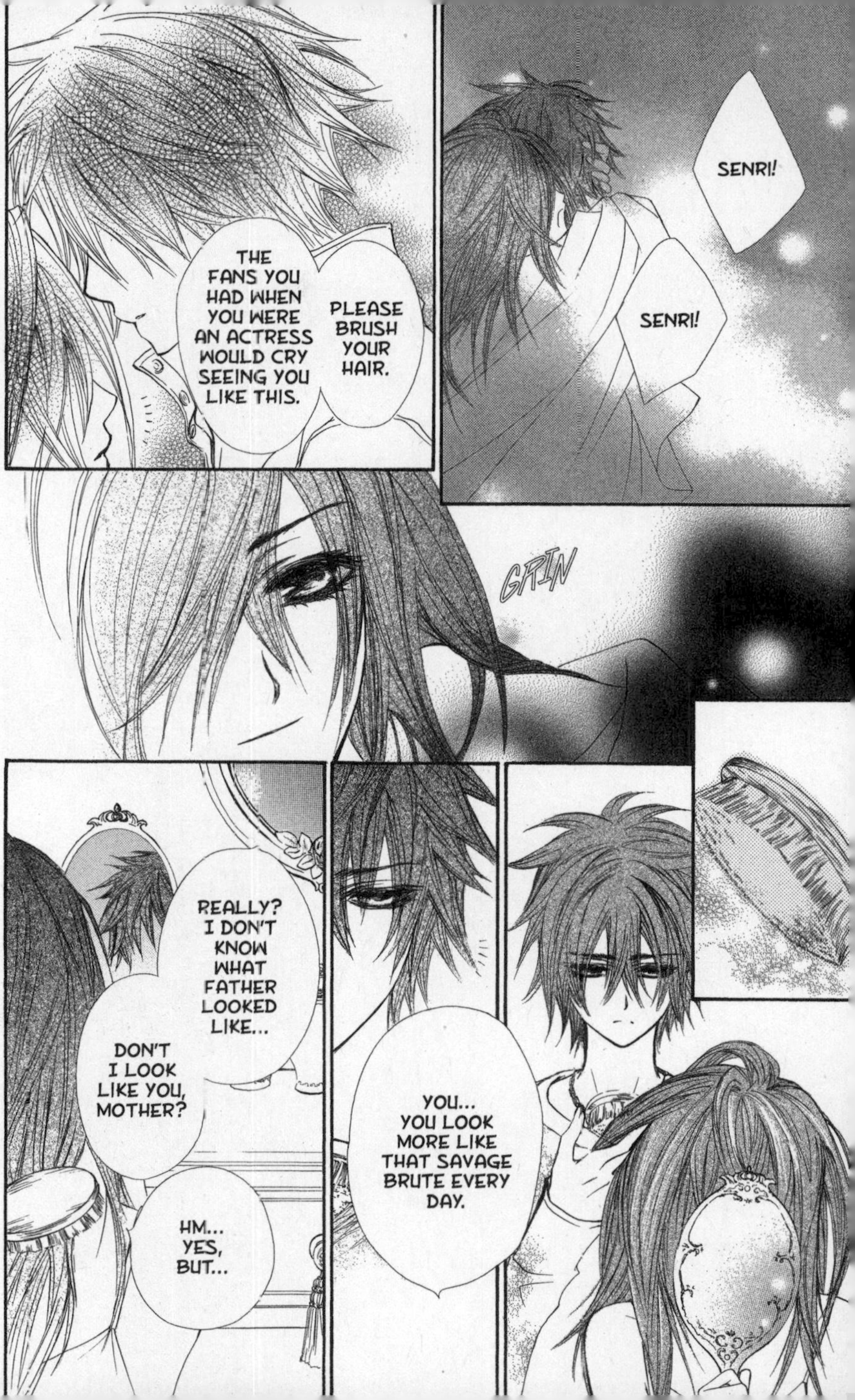
SENRI!
SENRI!
PLEASE BRUSH YOUR HAIR.
THE FANS YOU HAD WHEN YOU WERE AN ACTRESS WOULD CRY SEEING YOU LIKE THIS.
GRIN
YOU... YOU LOOK MORE LIKE THAT SAVAGE BRUTE EVERY DAY.
REALLY? I DON'T KNOW WHAT FATHER LOOKED LIKE...
DON'T I LOOK LIKE YOU, MOTHER?
HM... YES, BUT...

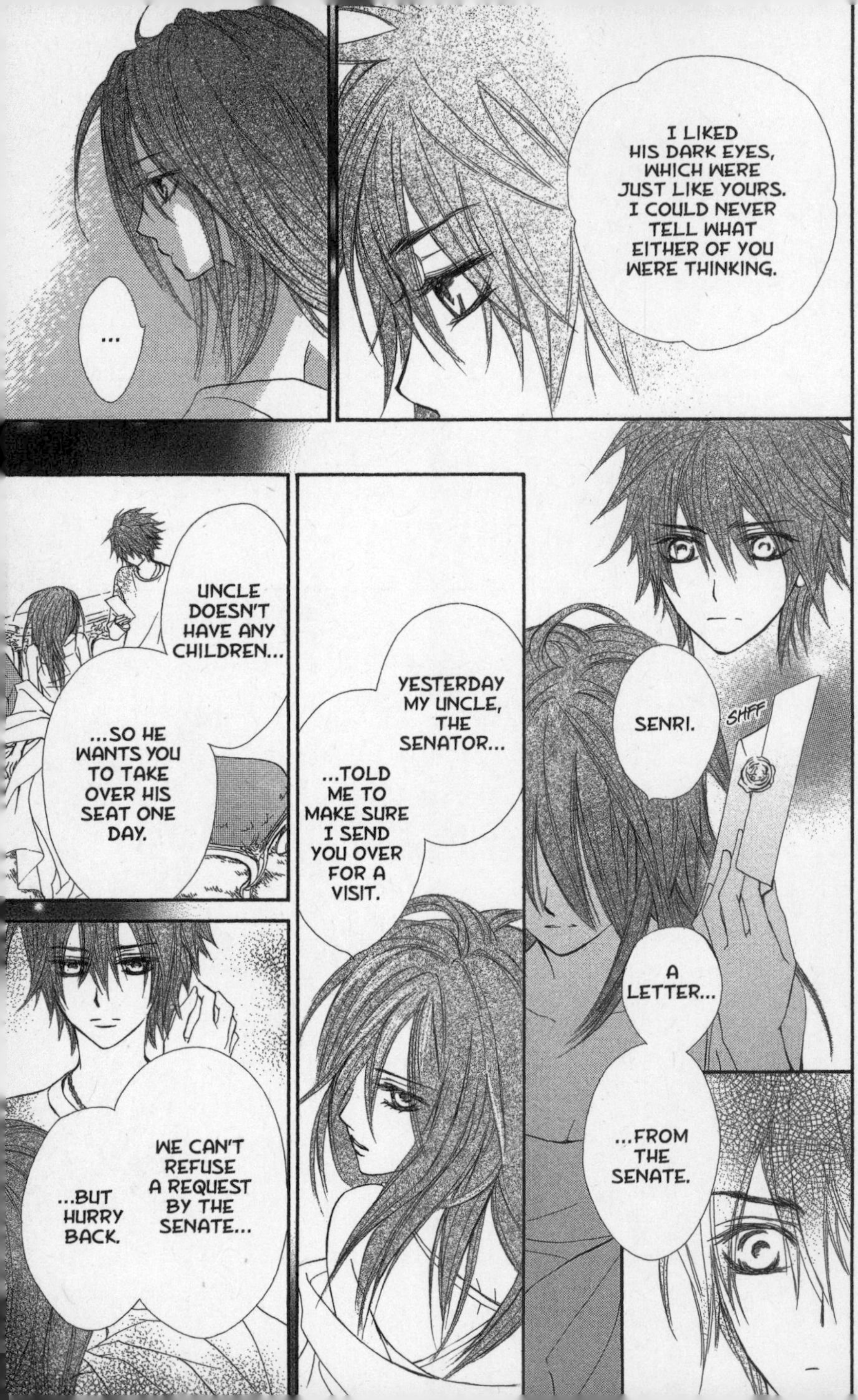
I LIKED HIS DARK EYES, WHICH WERE JUST LIKE YOURS. I COULD NEVER TELL WHAT EITHER OF YOU WERE THINKING.
...
SENRI.
SHFF
A LETTER...
...FROM THE SENATE.
YESTERDAY MY UNCLE, THE SENATOR...
...TOLD ME TO MAKE SURE I SEND YOU OVER FOR A VISIT.
UNCLE DOESN'T HAVE ANY CHILDREN...
...SO HE WANTS YOU TO TAKE OVER HIS SEAT ONE DAY.
WE CAN'T REFUSE A REQUEST BY THE SENATE...
...BUT HURRY BACK.

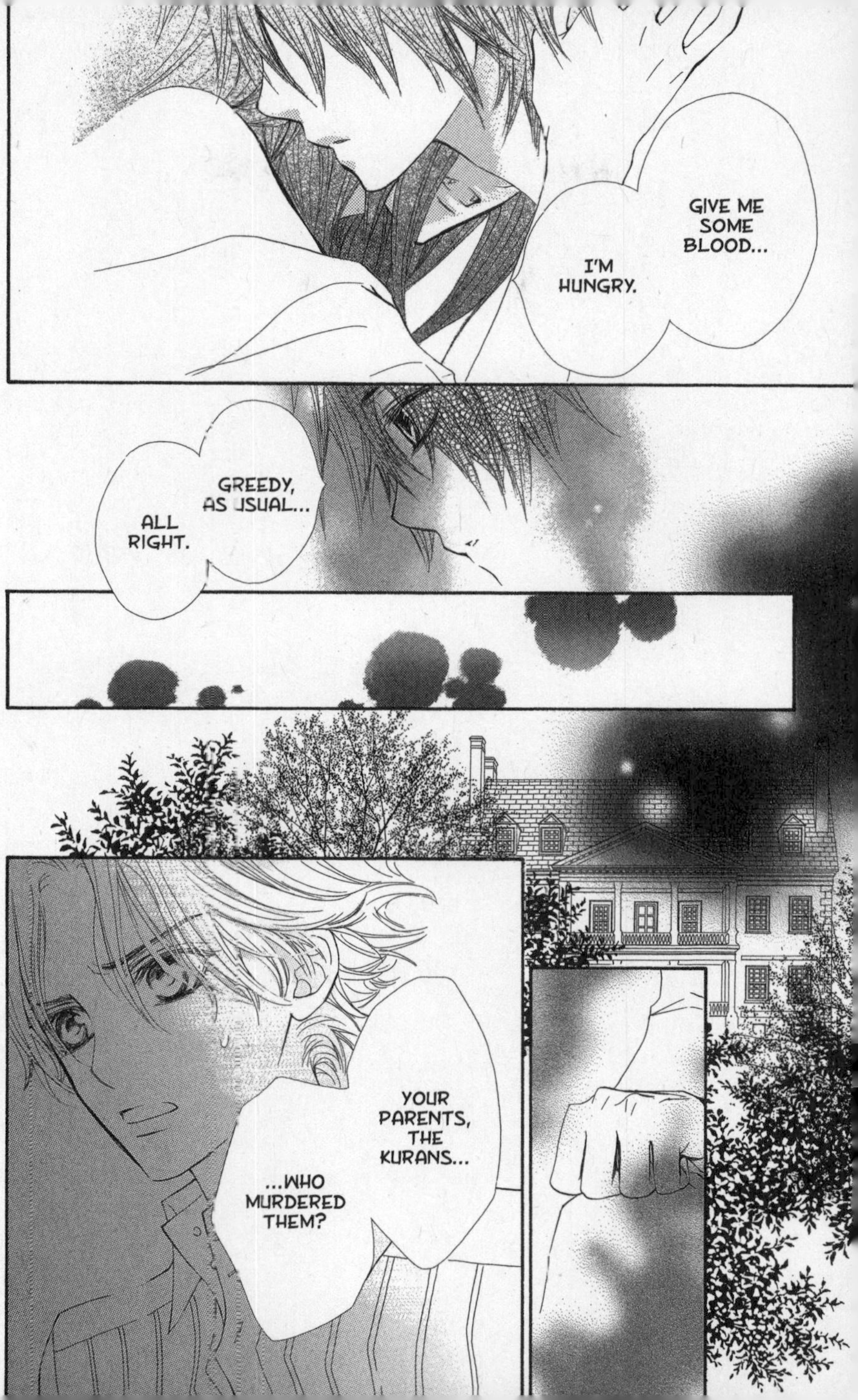
GIVE ME SOME BLOOD...
I'M HUNGRY.
GREEDY, AS USUAL...
ALL RIGHT.
YOUR PARENTS, THE KURANS...
...WHO MURDERED THEM?

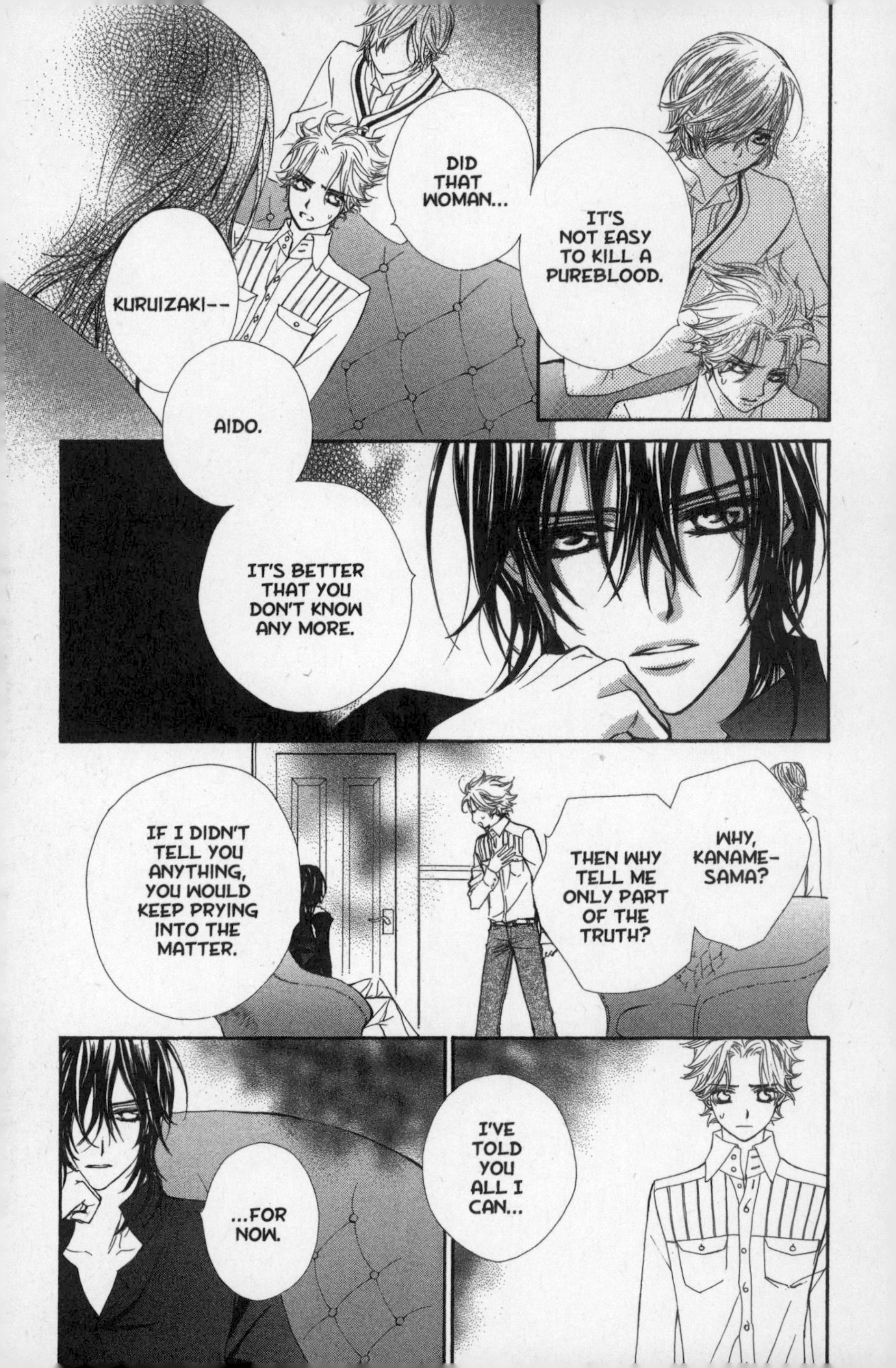
IT'S NOT EASY TO KILL A PUREBLOOD.
DID THAT WOMAN...
KURUIZAKI--
AIDO.
IT'S BETTER THAT YOU DON'T KNOW ANY MORE.
WHY, KANAME-SAMA?
THEN WHY TELL ME ONLY PART OF THE TRUTH?
IF I DIDN'T TELL YOU ANYTHING, YOU WOULD KEEP PRYING INTO THE MATTER.
I'VE TOLD YOU ALL I CAN...
...FOR NOW.

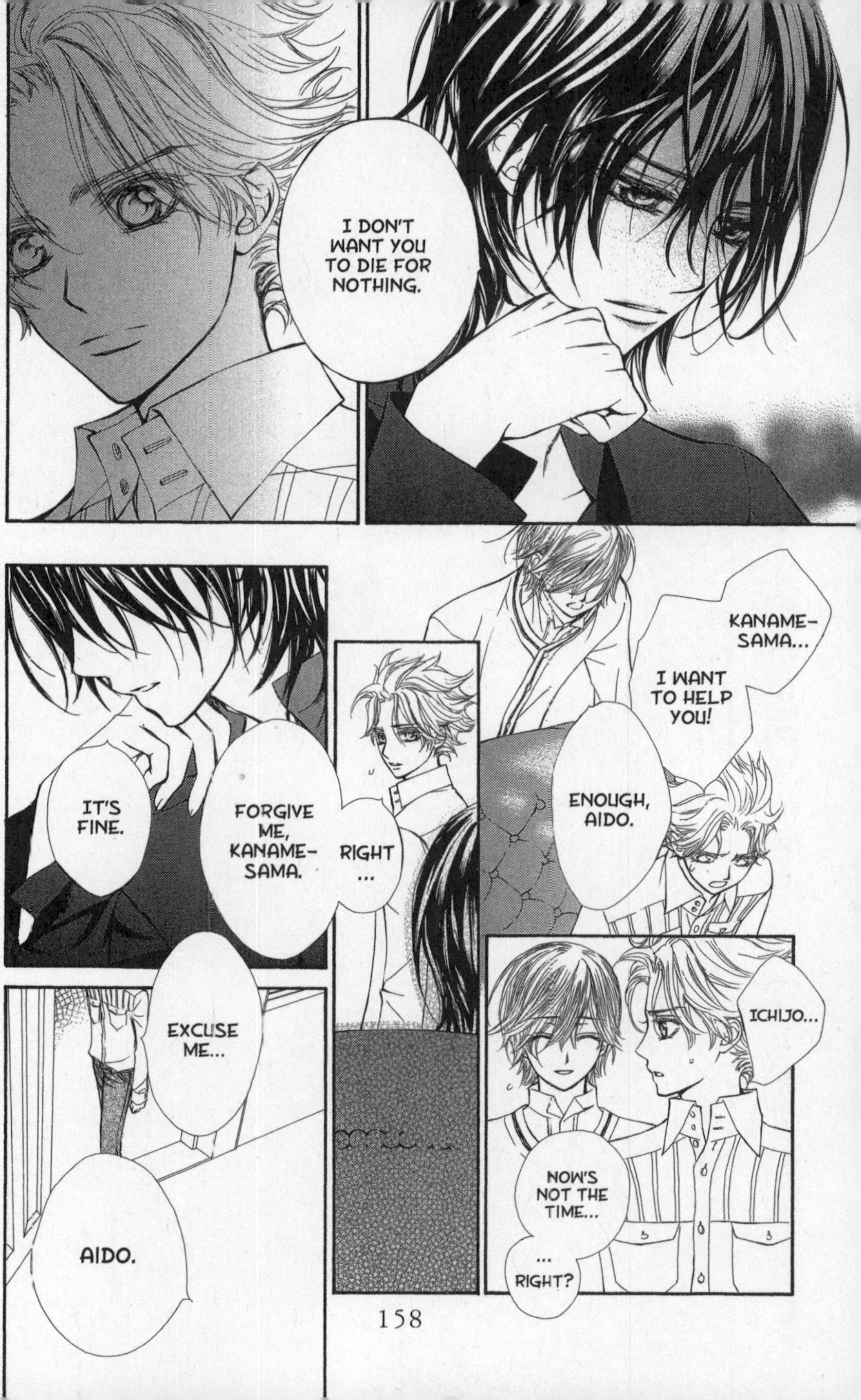
I DON'T WANT YOU TO DIE FOR NOTHING.
KANAME-SAMA...
I WANT TO HELP YOU!
ENOUGH, AIDO.
RIGHT ...
FORGIVE ME, KANAME-SAMA.
IT'S FINE.
ICHIJO...
NOW'S NOT THE TIME...
... RIGHT?
EXCUSE ME...
AIDO.

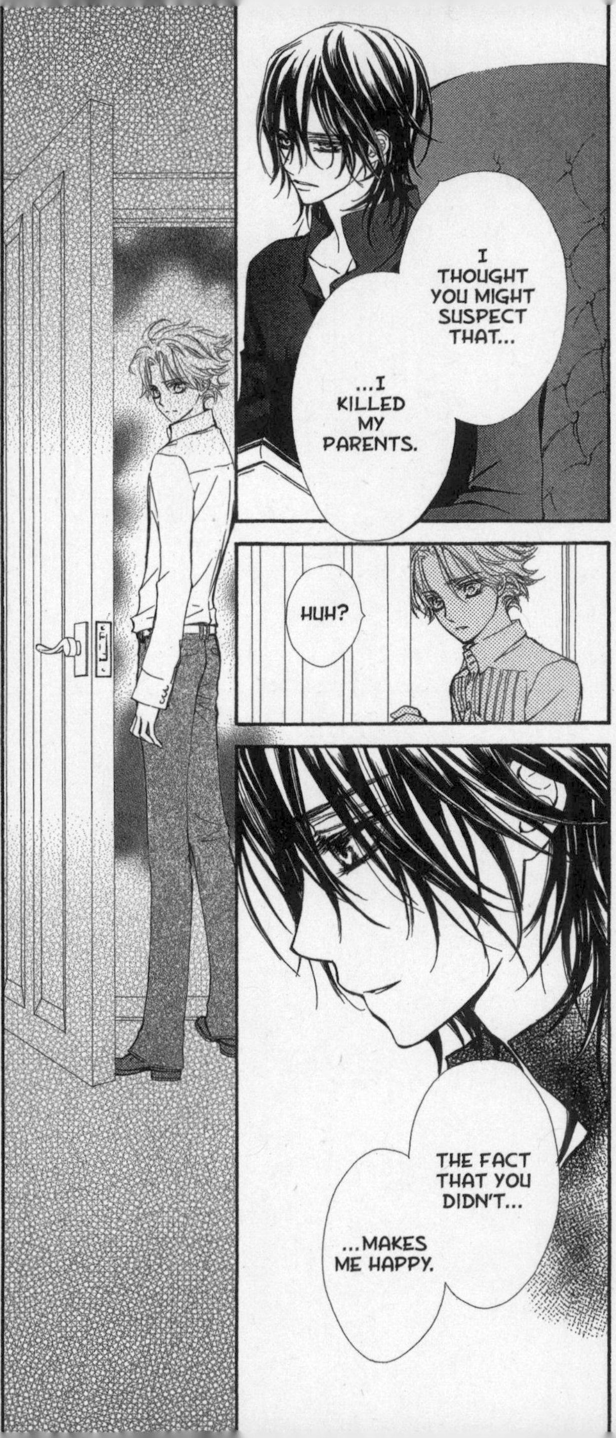
I THOUGHT YOU MIGHT SUSPECT THAT...
...I KILLED MY PARENTS.
HUH?
THE FACT THAT YOU DIDN'T...
...MAKES ME HAPPY.

Thank You

Thank you to my editor, the LaLa department, and everyone involved in this work. (I apologize for inconveniencing all of you...)

Thank you O. Mio-sama, K. Midori-sama, M. Kaoru-sama, my family and friends. You always really help me out.

I.A.-sama, please continue helping me!

Thanks also to Y.Y.-sama and H.W.-sama, whom I suddenly asked for help. They assisted me after finishing their own manuscripts--I'm sure they were tired!! Thanks to you, I was able to avoid the worst. Thank you!

And to all my readers, thank you for reading...! You might have noticed, but the focus of the story is gradually shifting from Zero to Yuki. You might find things slow, but I'd be happy if you read volume 7 too.

Bye...!

樋野まつり
Matsuri Hino

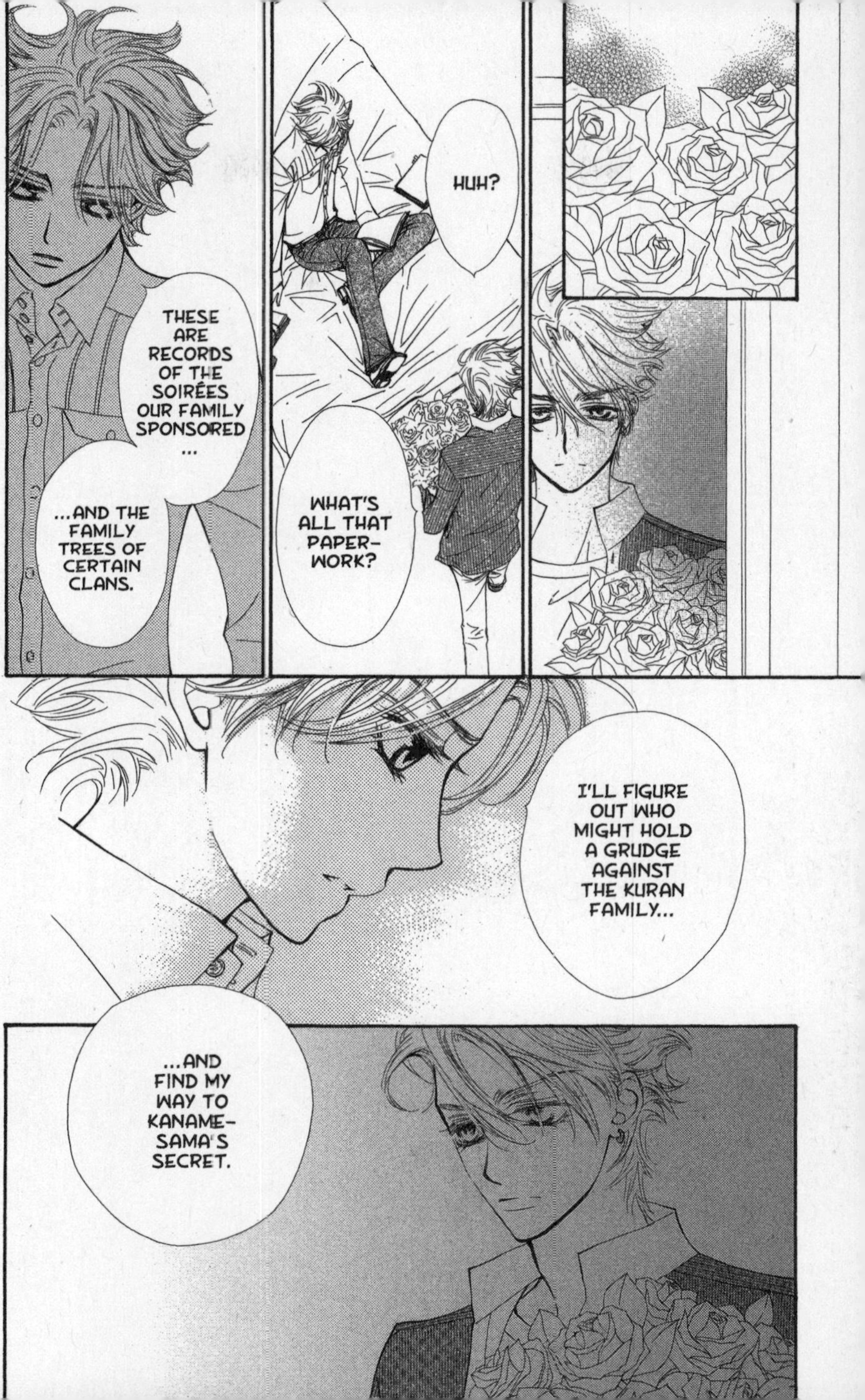
HUH?
WHAT'S ALL THAT PAPER-WORK?
THESE ARE RECORDS OF THE SOIRÉES OUR FAMILY SPONSORED ...
...AND THE FAMILY TREES OF CERTAIN CLANS.
I'LL FIGURE OUT WHO MIGHT HOLD A GRUDGE AGAINST THE KURAN FAMILY...
...AND FIND MY WAY TO KANAME-SAMA'S SECRET.

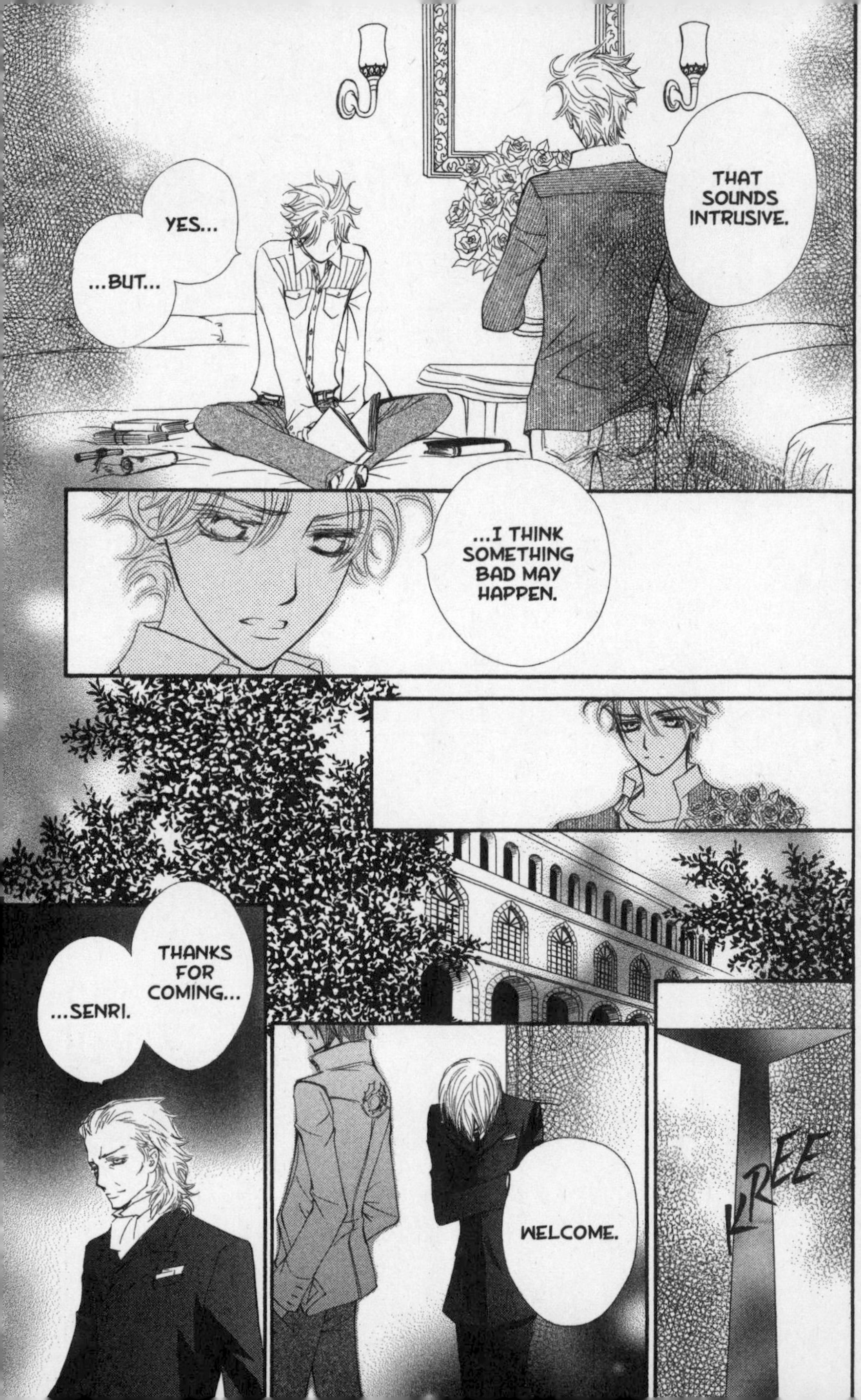
THAT SOUNDS INTRUSIVE.
YES...
...BUT...
...I THINK SOMETHING BAD MAY HAPPEN.
KREE
WELCOME.
THANKS FOR COMING...
...SENRI.

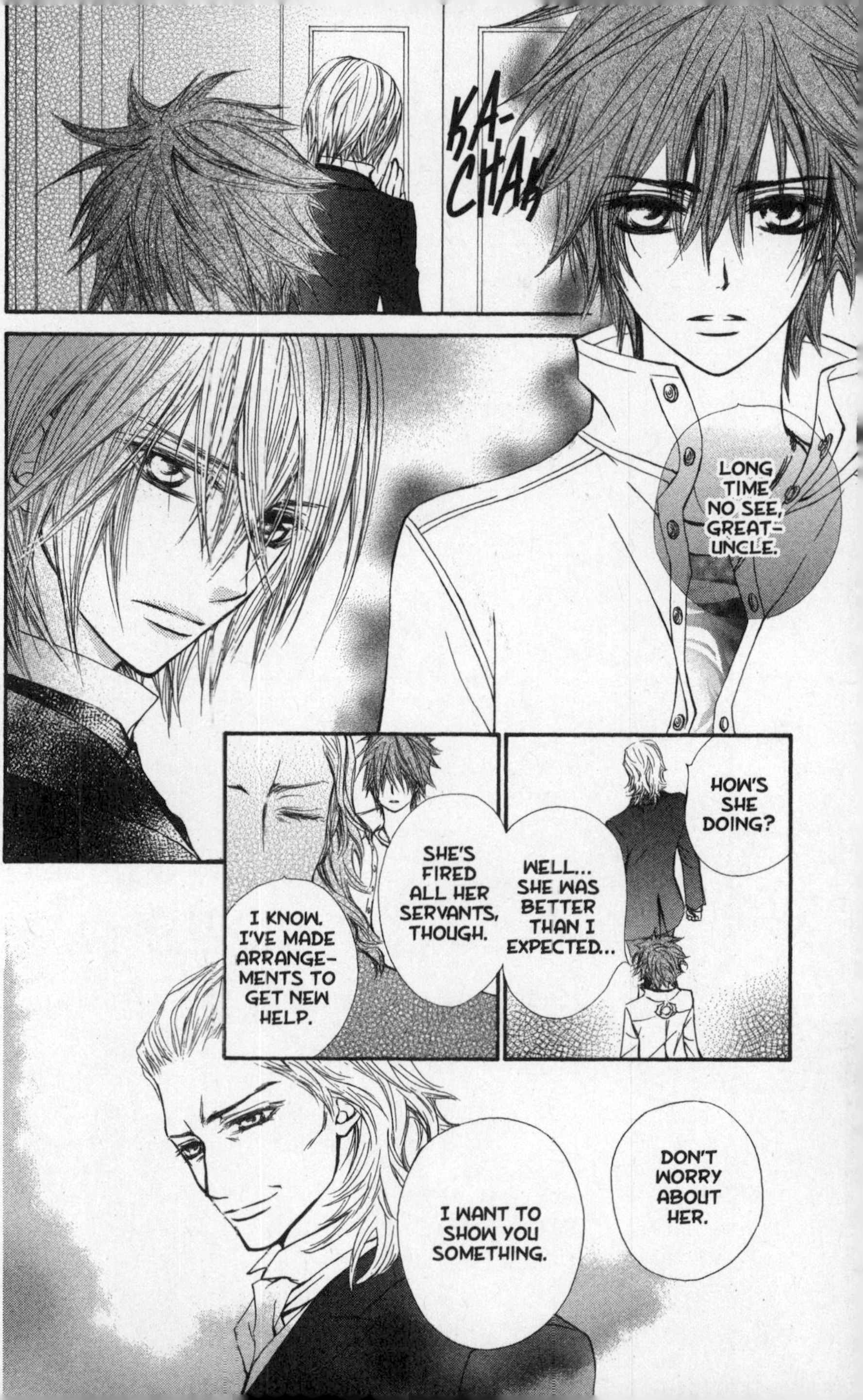
KA-CHAK
LONG TIME NO SEE, GREAT-UNCLE.
HOW'S SHE DOING?
WELL... SHE WAS BETTER THAN I EXPECTED...
SHE'S FIRED ALL HER SERVANTS, THOUGH.
I KNOW. I'VE MADE ARRANGE-MENTS TO GET NEW HELP.
DON'T WORRY ABOUT HER.
I WANT TO SHOW YOU SOMETHING.

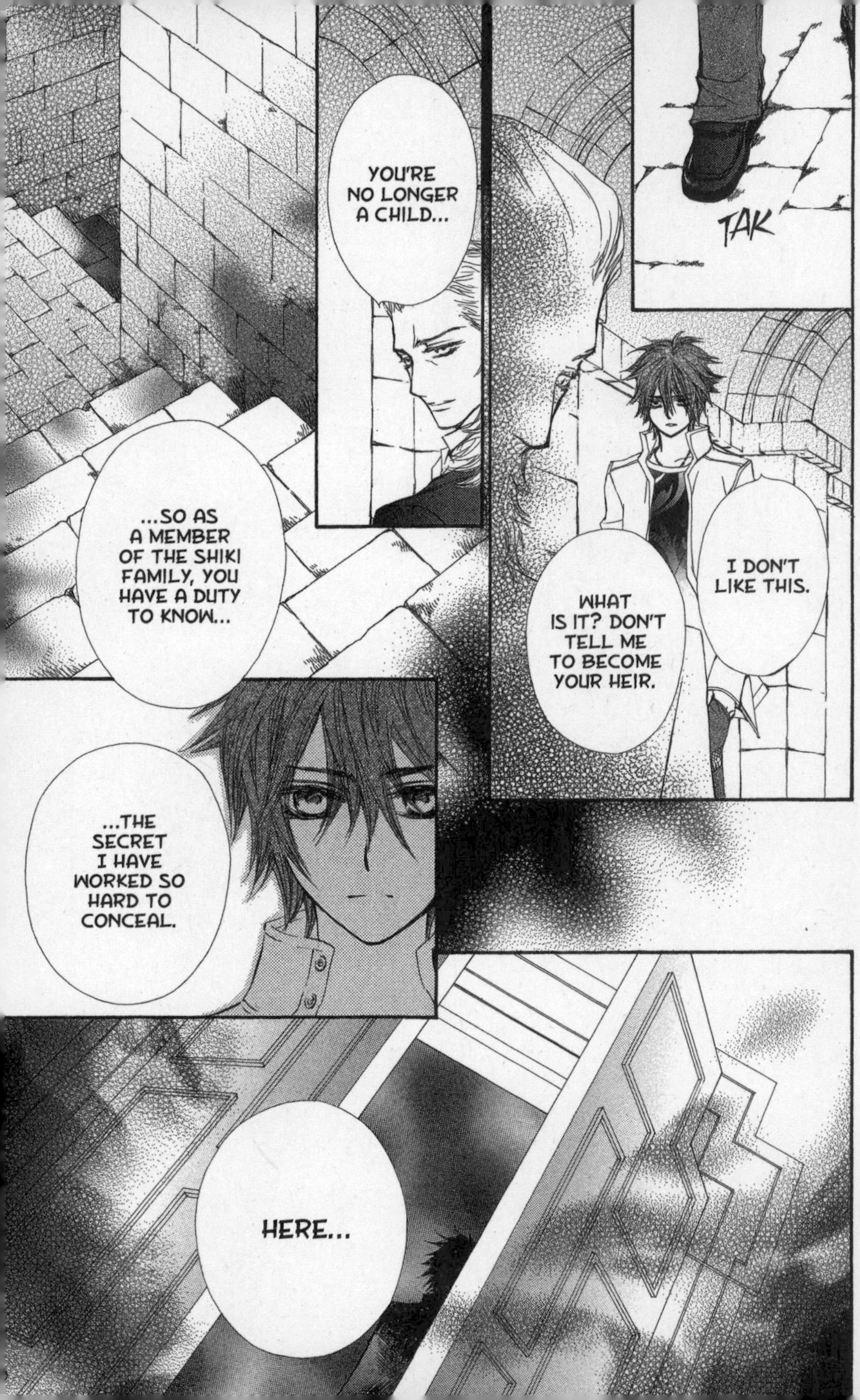
TAK
I DON'T LIKE THIS.
WHAT IS IT? DON'T TELL ME TO BECOME YOUR HEIR.
YOU'RE NO LONGER A CHILD...
...SO AS A MEMBER OF THE SHIKI FAMILY, YOU HAVE A DUTY TO KNOW...
...THE SECRET I HAVE WORKED SO HARD TO CONCEAL.
HERE...

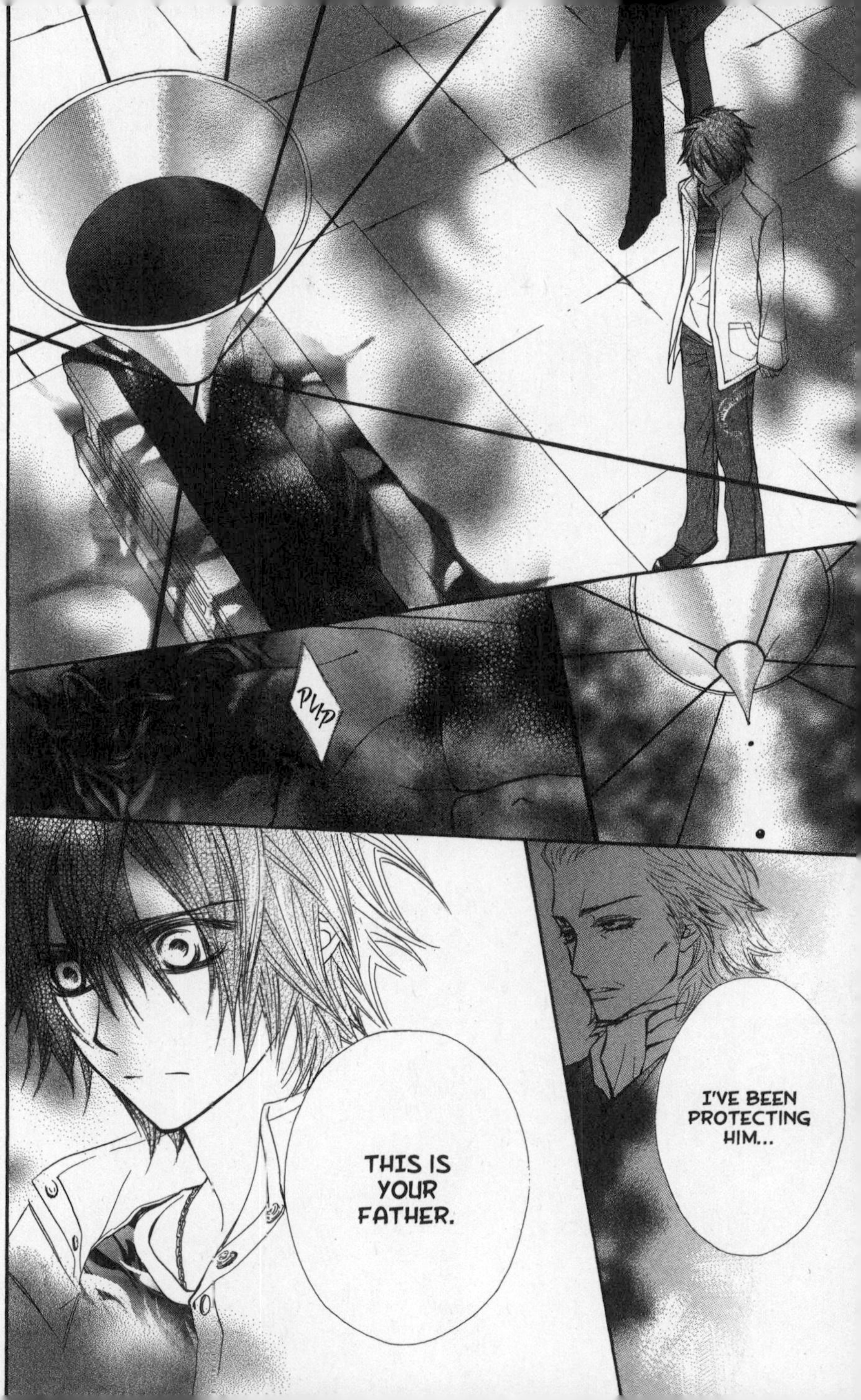
PLIP
I'VE BEEN PROTECTING HIM...
THIS IS YOUR FATHER.

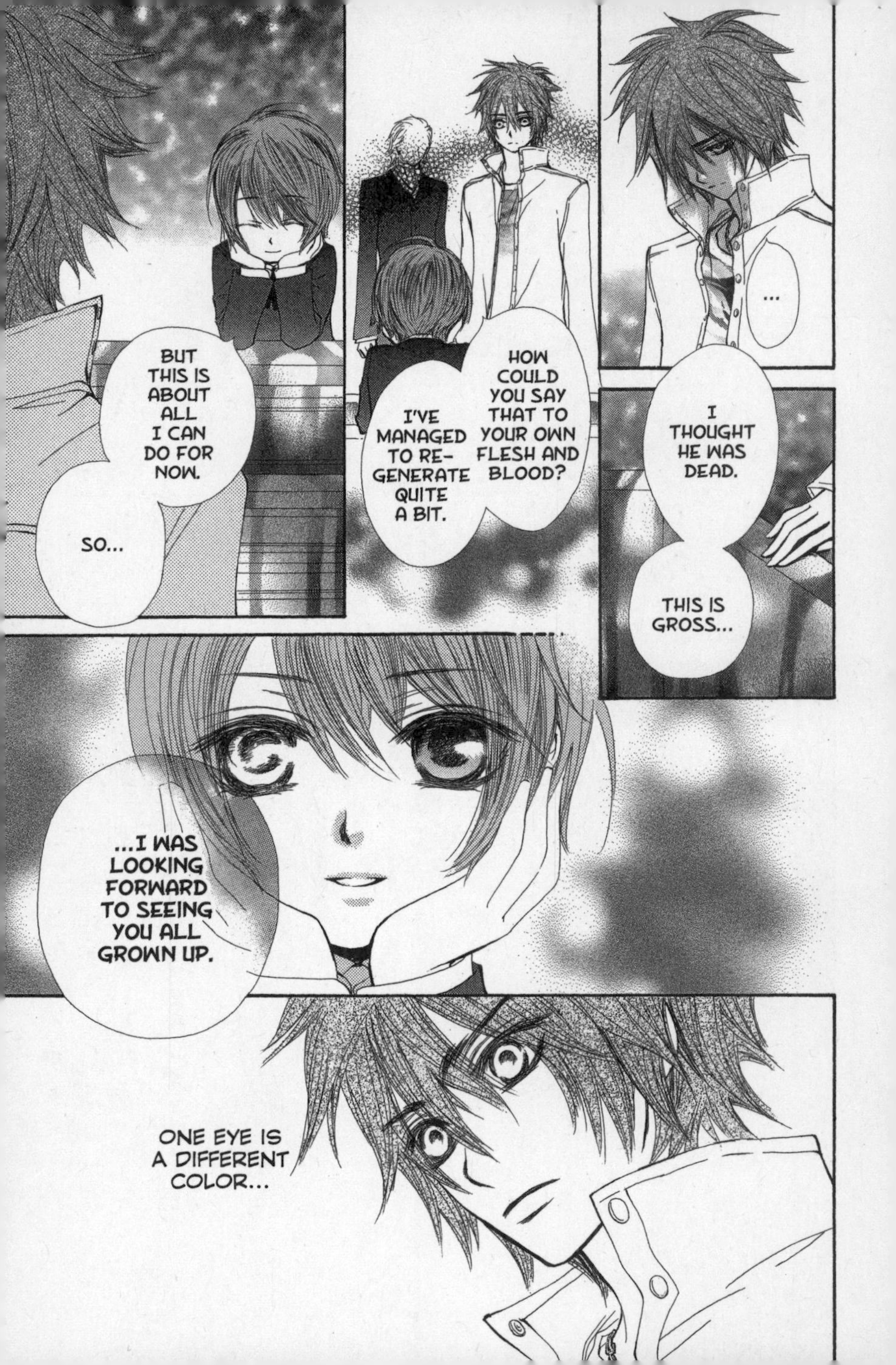
...
I THOUGHT HE WAS DEAD.
THIS IS GROSS...
HOW COULD YOU SAY THAT TO YOUR OWN FLESH AND BLOOD?
I'VE MANAGED TO RE-GENERATE QUITE A BIT.
BUT THIS IS ABOUT ALL I CAN DO FOR NOW.
SO...
...I WAS LOOKING FORWARD TO SEEING YOU ALL GROWN UP.
ONE EYE IS A DIFFERENT COLOR...

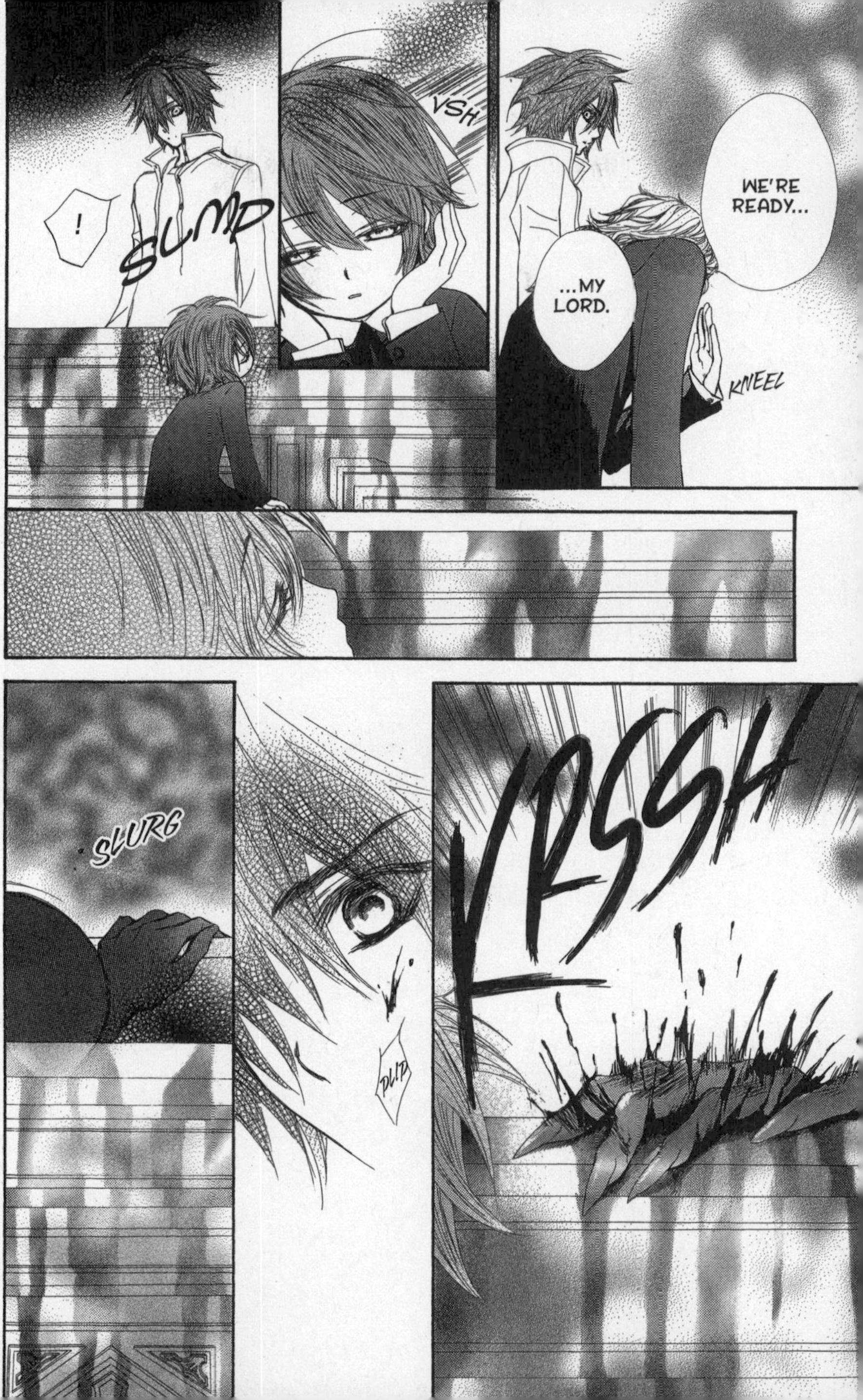
WE'RE READY...
...MY LORD.
KNEEL
VSH
!
SLUMP
KRSSH
PLIP
SLURG

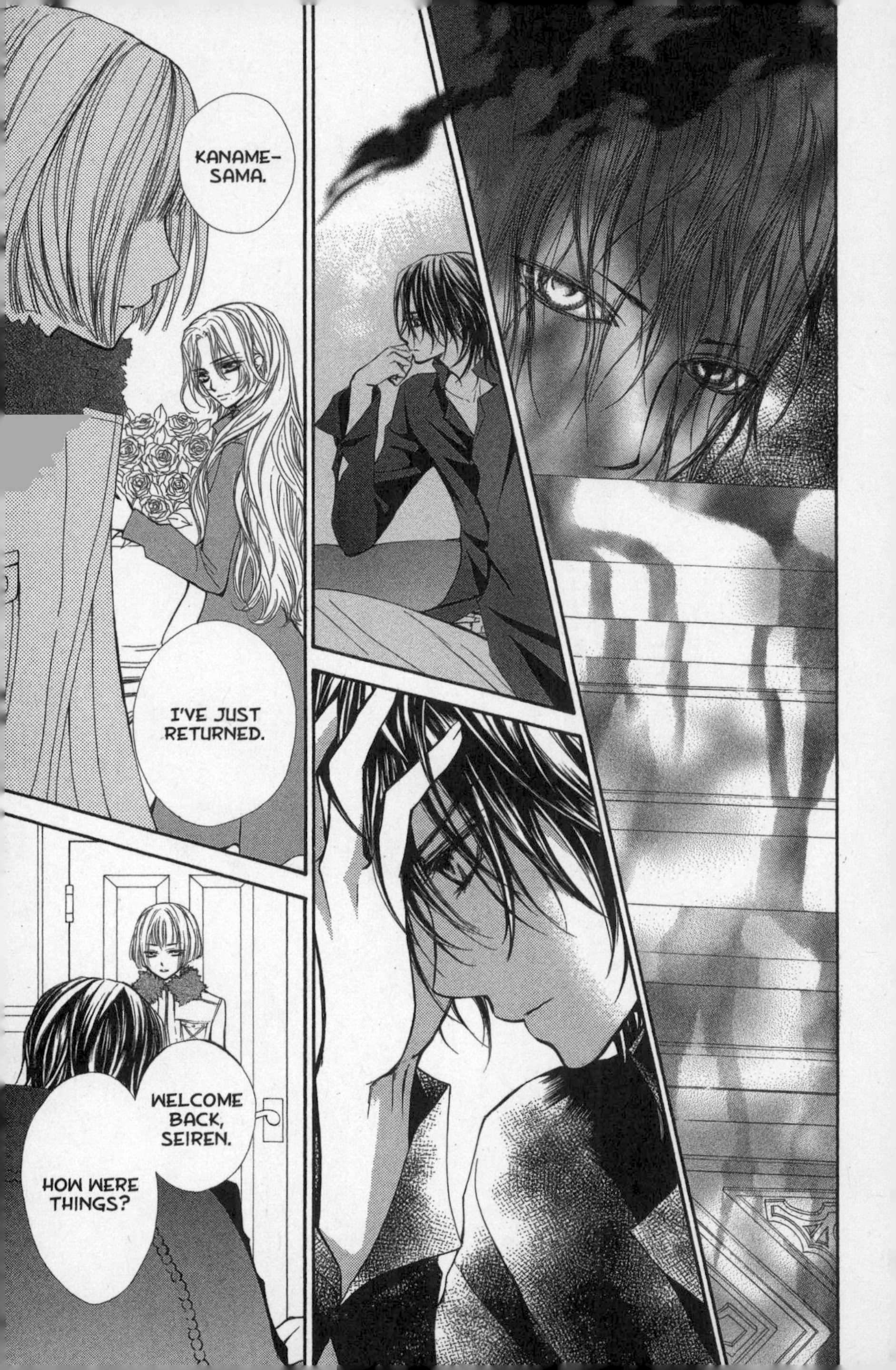
KANAME-SAMA.
I'VE JUST RETURNED.
WELCOME BACK, SEIREN.
HOW WERE THINGS?

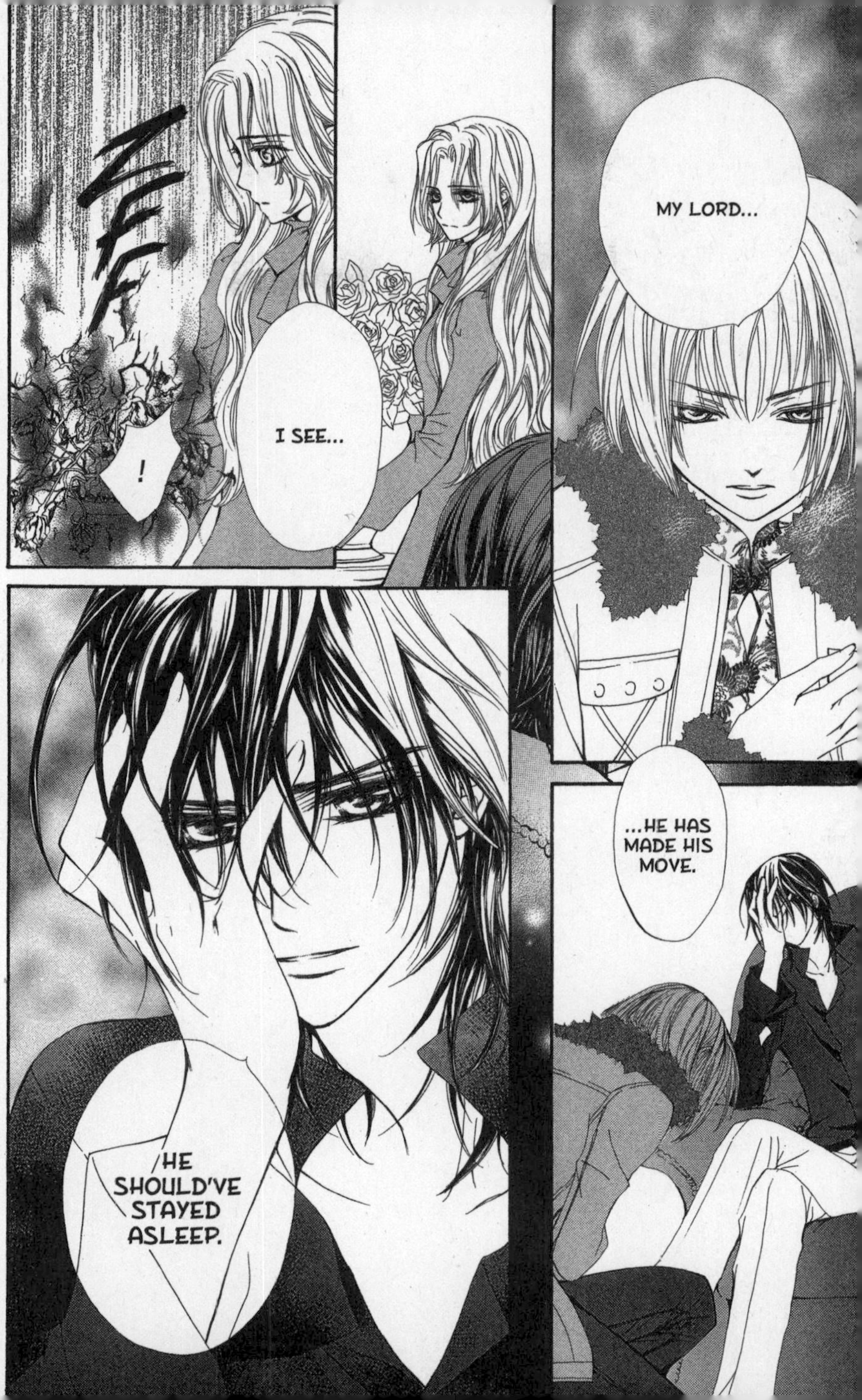
MY LORD...
I SEE...
!
...HE HAS MADE HIS MOVE.
HE SHOULD'VE STAYED ASLEEP.

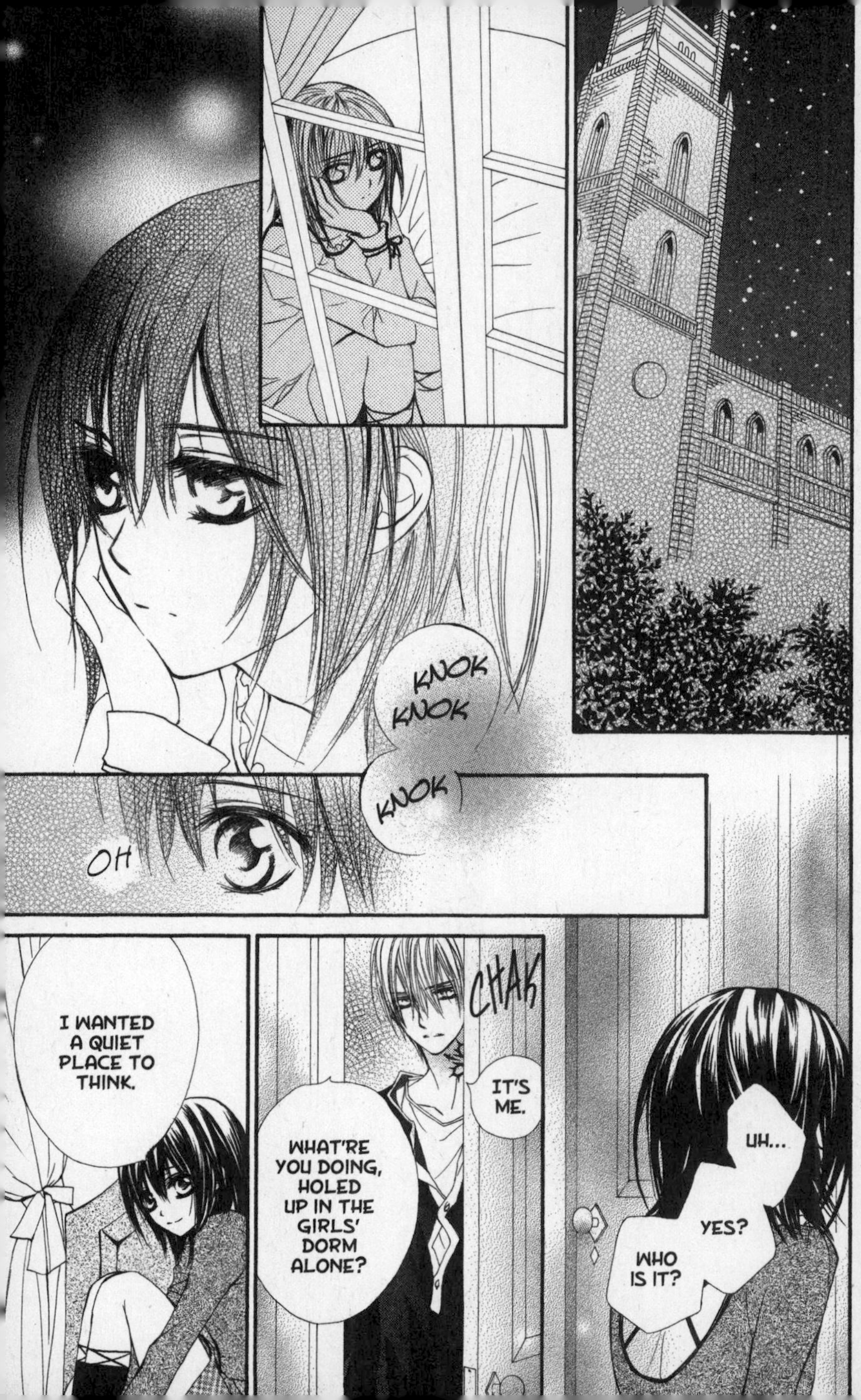
KNOK KNOK
KNOK
OH
UH...
YES?
WHO IS IT?
CHAK
IT'S ME.
WHAT'RE YOU DOING, HOLED UP IN THE GIRLS' DORM ALONE?
I WANTED A QUIET PLACE TO THINK.

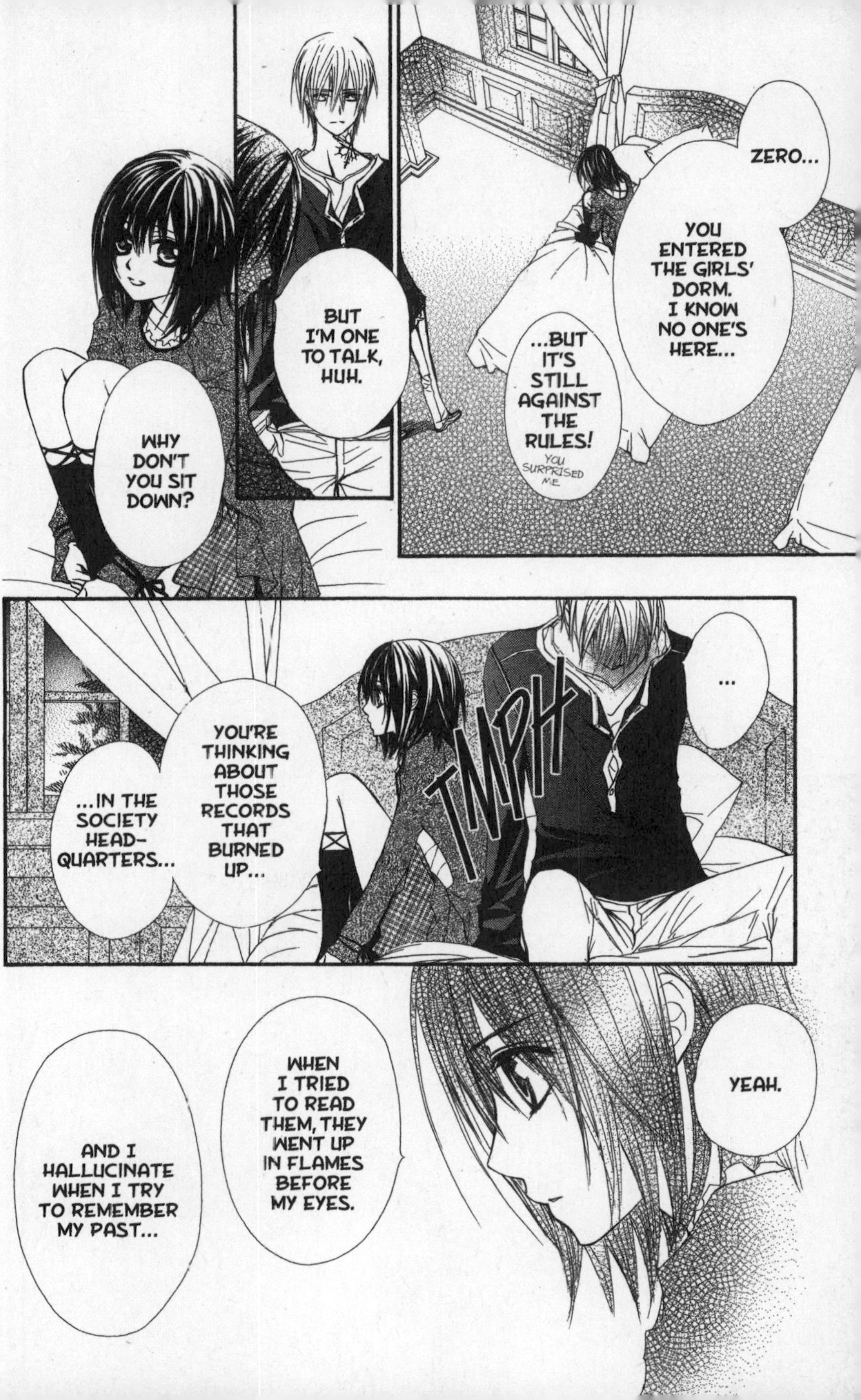
ZERO...
YOU ENTERED THE GIRLS' DORM. I KNOW NO ONE'S HERE...
...BUT IT'S STILL AGAINST THE RULES!
YOU SURPRISED ME
BUT I'M ONE TO TALK, HUH.
WHY DON'T YOU SIT DOWN?
...
TMPH
YOU'RE THINKING ABOUT THOSE RECORDS THAT BURNED UP...
...IN THE SOCIETY HEAD-QUARTERS...
YEAH.
WHEN I TRIED TO READ THEM, THEY WENT UP IN FLAMES BEFORE MY EYES.
AND I HALLUCINATE WHEN I TRY TO REMEMBER MY PAST...

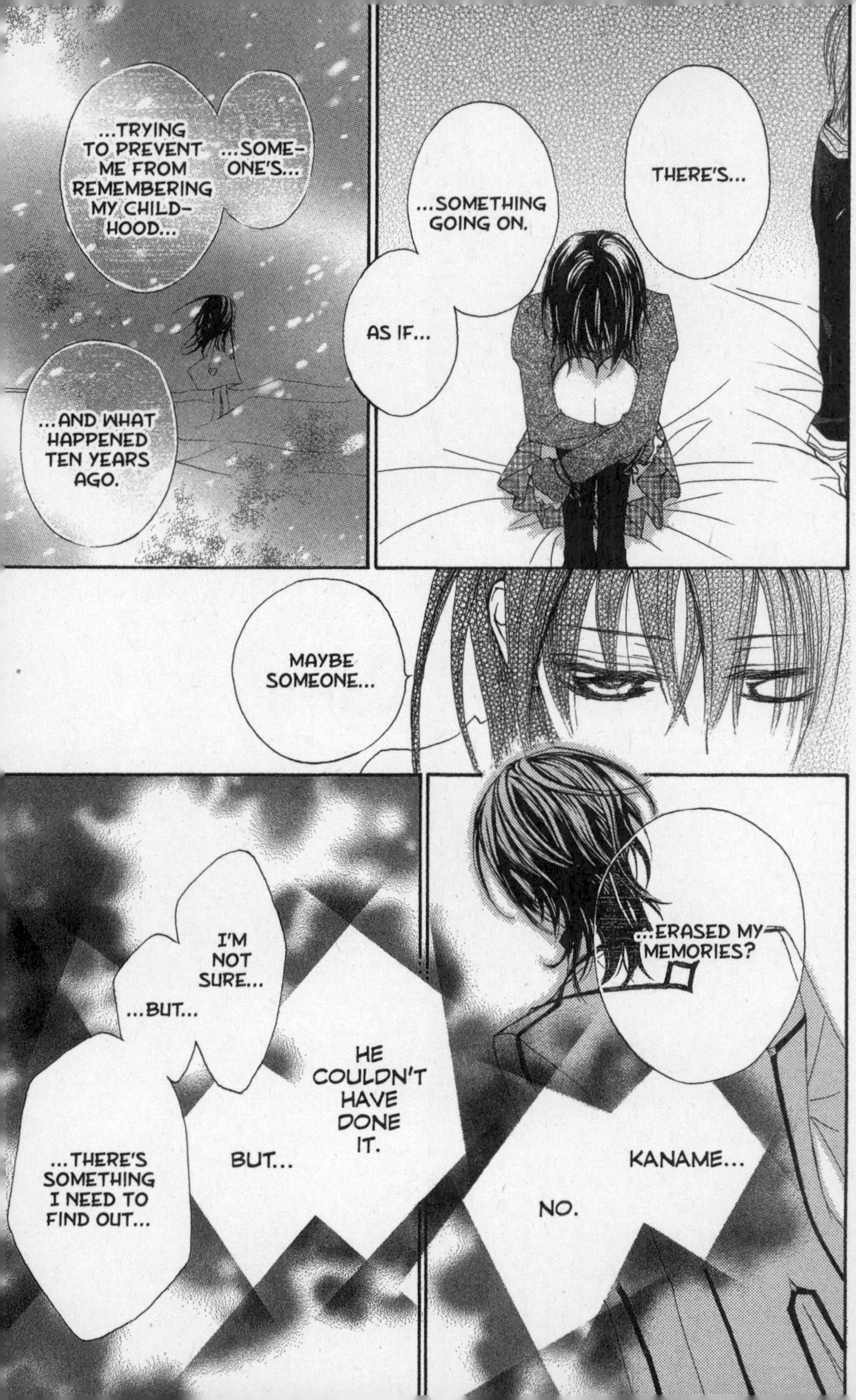
THERE'S...
...SOMETHING GOING ON.
AS IF...
...SOME-ONE'S...
...TRYING TO PREVENT ME FROM REMEMBERING MY CHILD-HOOD...
...AND WHAT HAPPENED TEN YEARS AGO.
MAYBE SOMEONE...
...ERASED MY MEMORIES?
KANAME...
NO.
HE COULDN'T HAVE DONE IT.
BUT...
I'M NOT SURE...
...BUT...
...THERE'S SOMETHING I NEED TO FIND OUT...

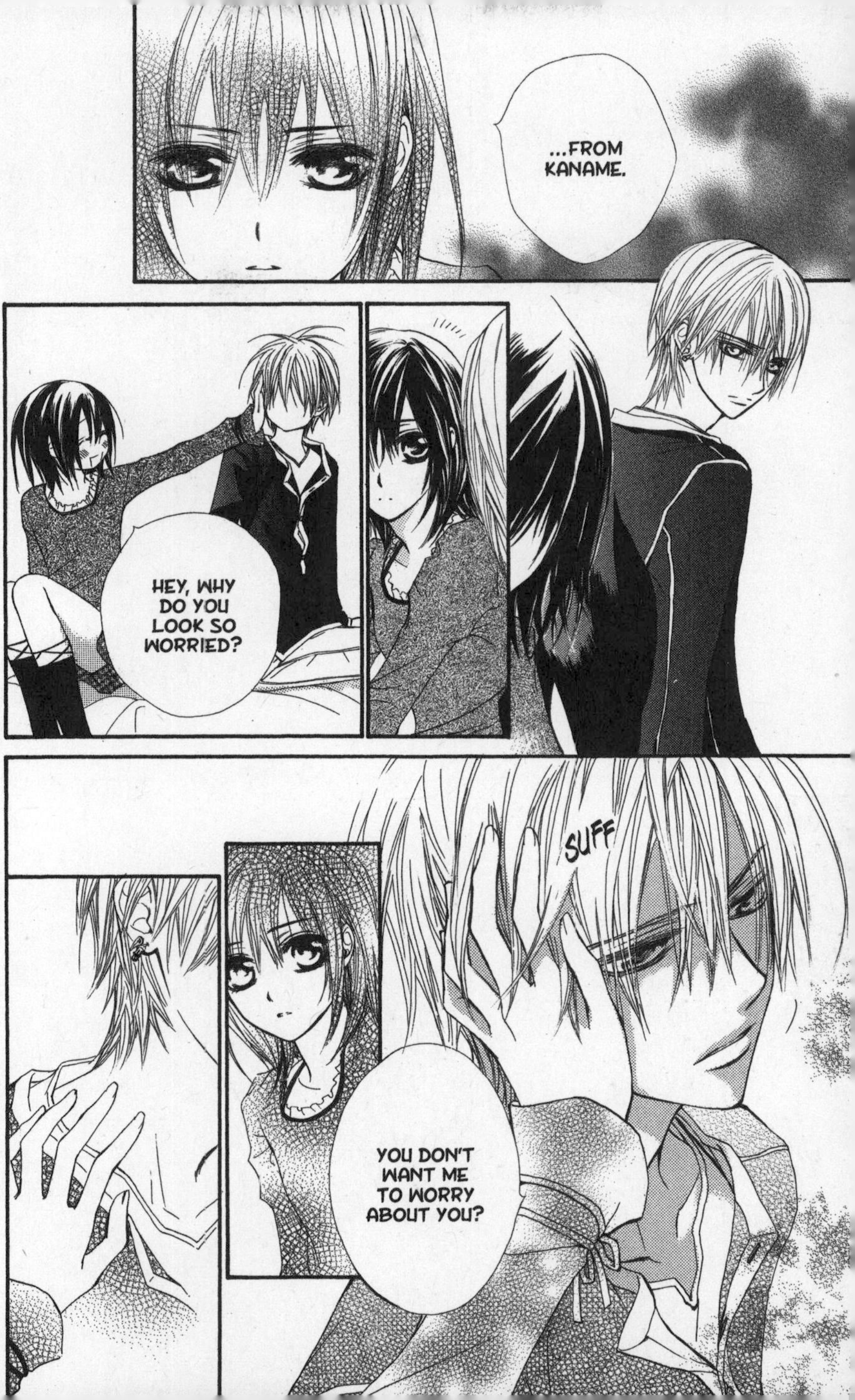
...FROM KANAME.
HEY, WHY DO YOU LOOK SO WORRIED?
SUFF
YOU DON'T WANT ME TO WORRY ABOUT YOU?

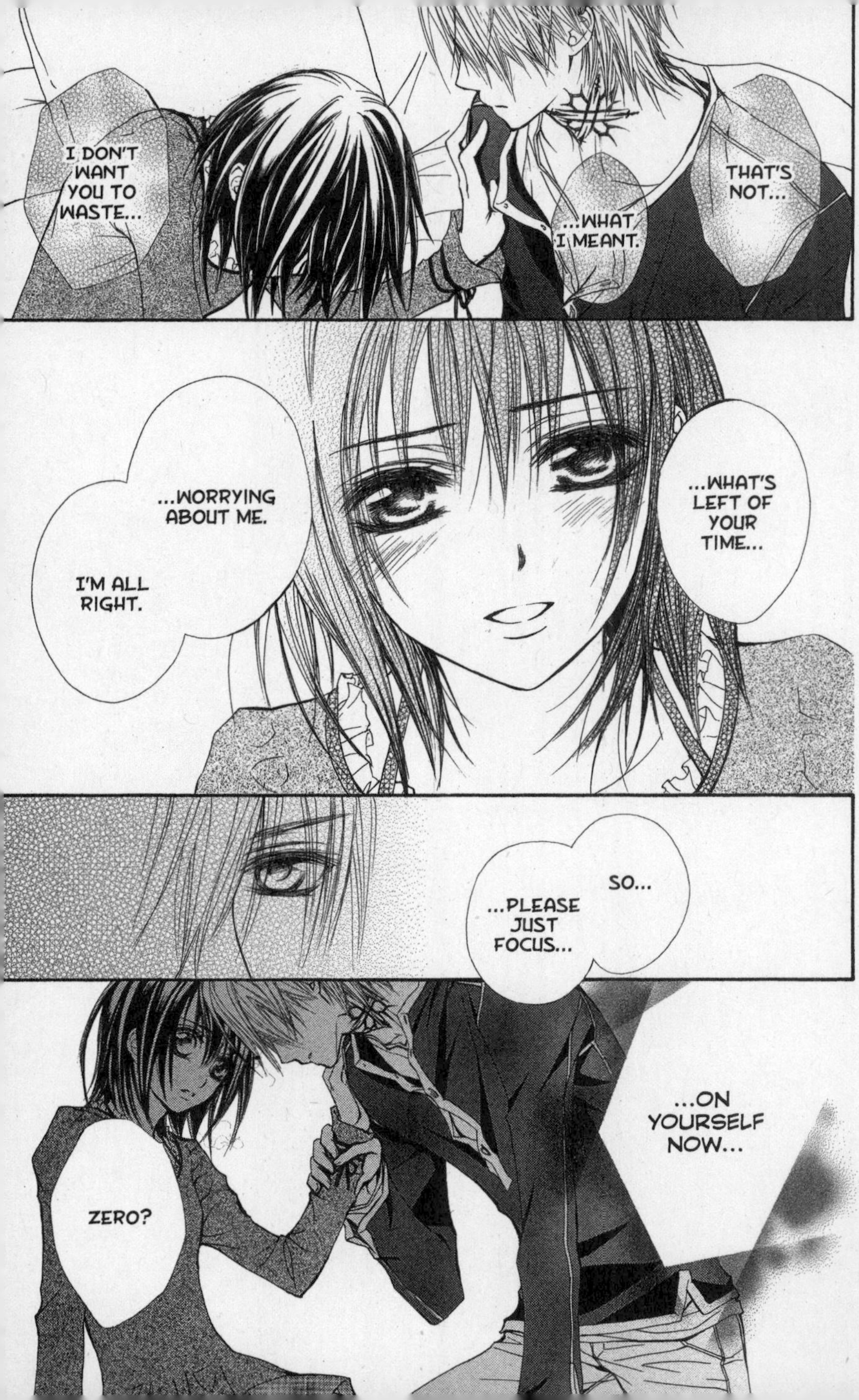
THAT'S NOT...
...WHAT I MEANT.
I DON'T WANT YOU TO WASTE...
...WHAT'S LEFT OF YOUR TIME...
...WORRYING ABOUT ME.
I'M ALL RIGHT.
SO...
...PLEASE JUST FOCUS...
...ON YOURSELF NOW...
ZERO?

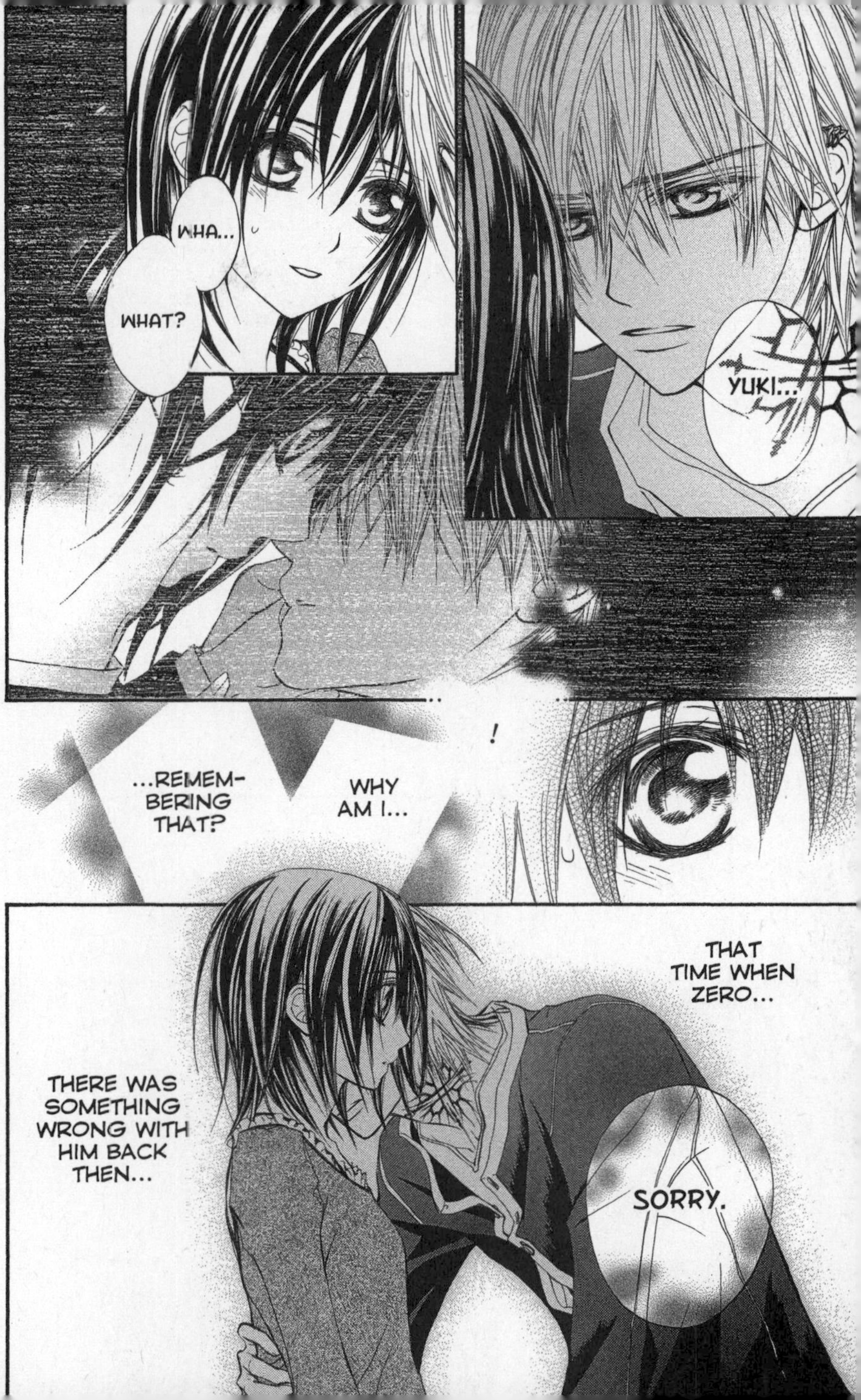
YUKI...
WHA...
WHAT?
!
WHY AM I...
...REMEMBERING THAT?
THAT TIME WHEN ZERO...
THERE WAS SOMETHING WRONG WITH HIM BACK THEN...
SORRY.

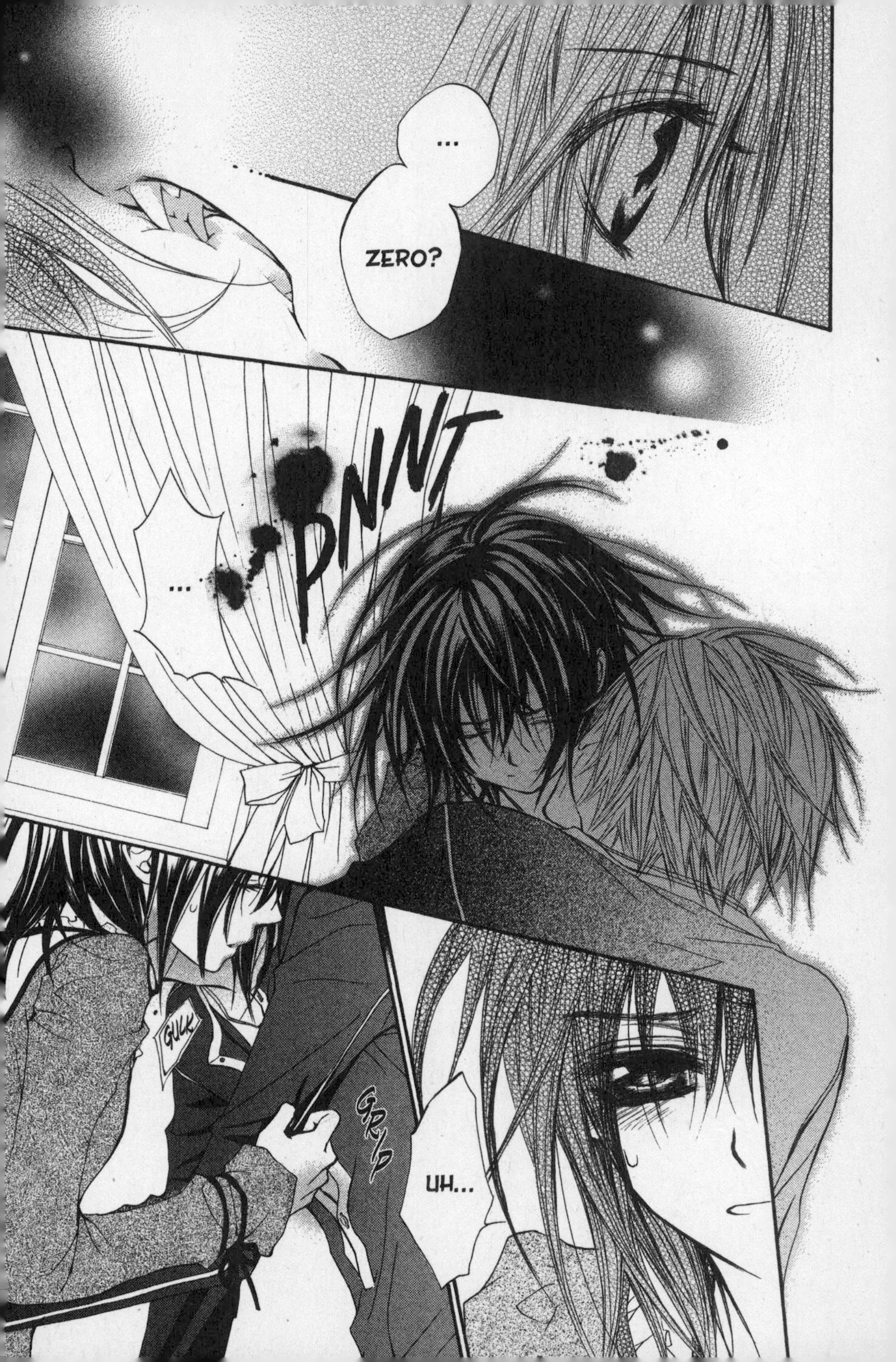
...
ZERO?
PNNT
...
UH...
GRYP
GULK

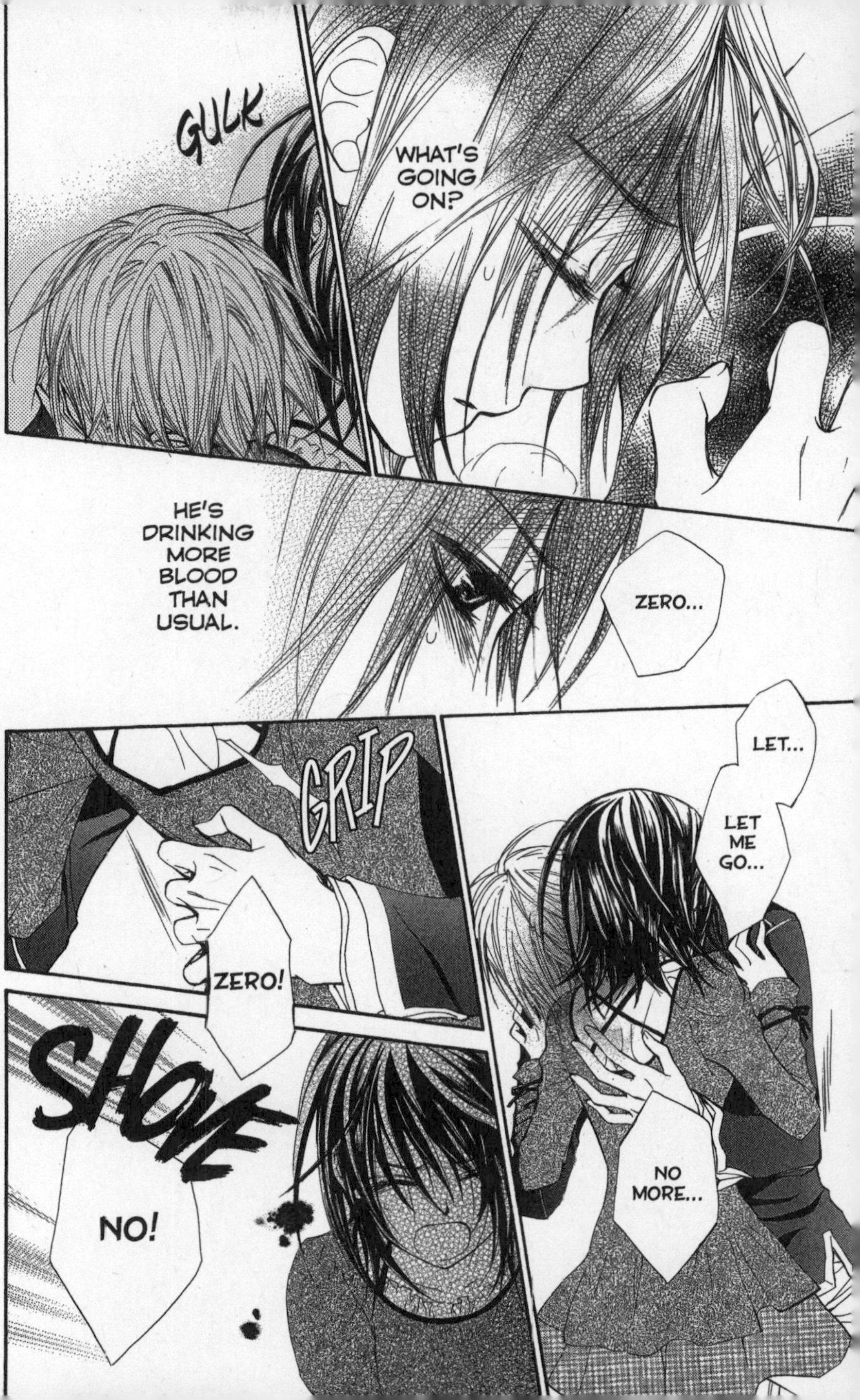
WHAT'S GOING ON?
GULK
ZERO...
HE'S DRINKING MORE BLOOD THAN USUAL.
LET...
LET ME GO...
NO MORE...
GRIP
ZERO!
SHOVE
NO!

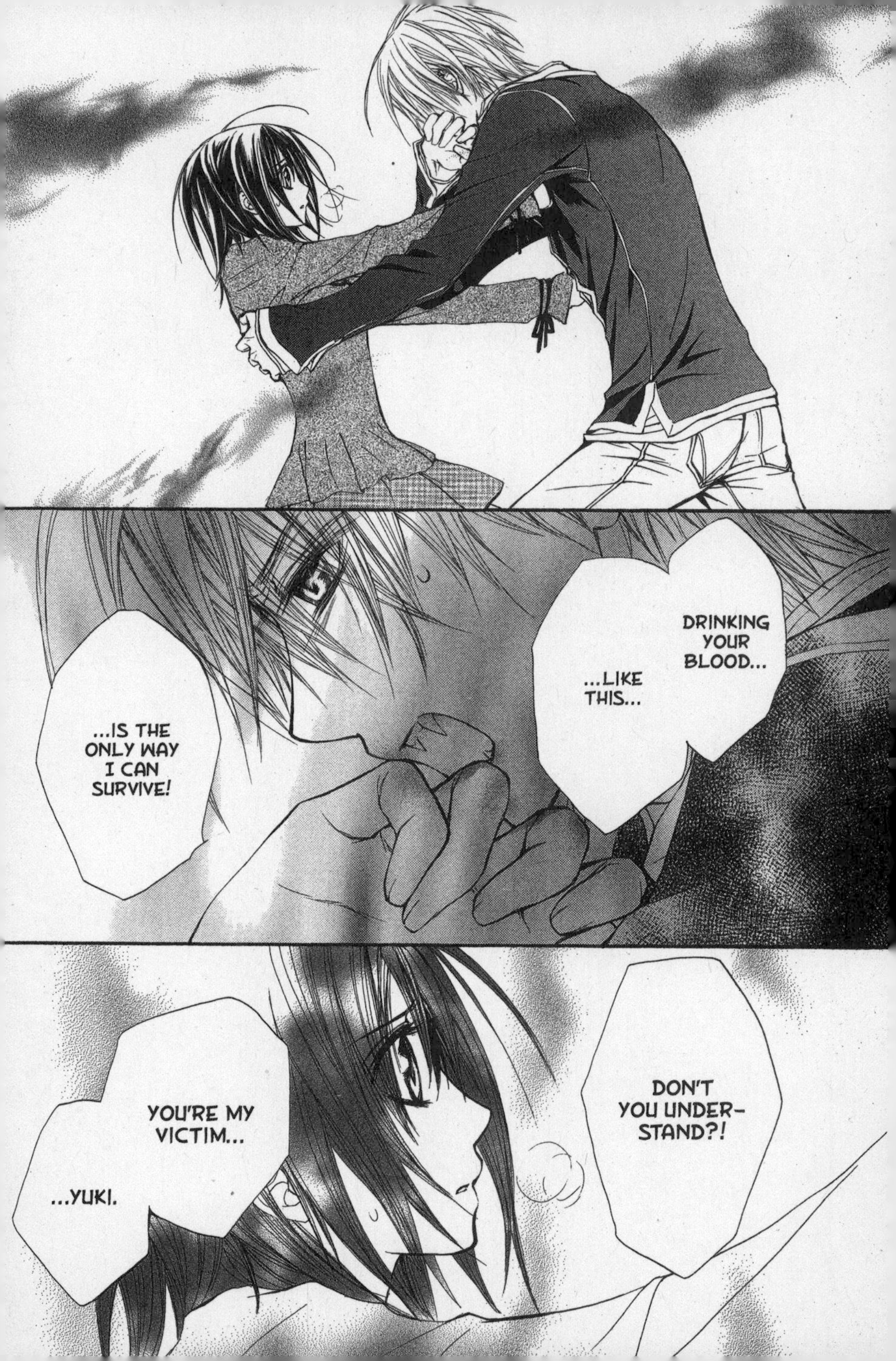
DRINKING YOUR BLOOD...
...LIKE THIS...
...IS THE ONLY WAY I CAN SURVIVE!
DON'T YOU UNDER-STAND?!
YOU'RE MY VICTIM...
...YUKI.

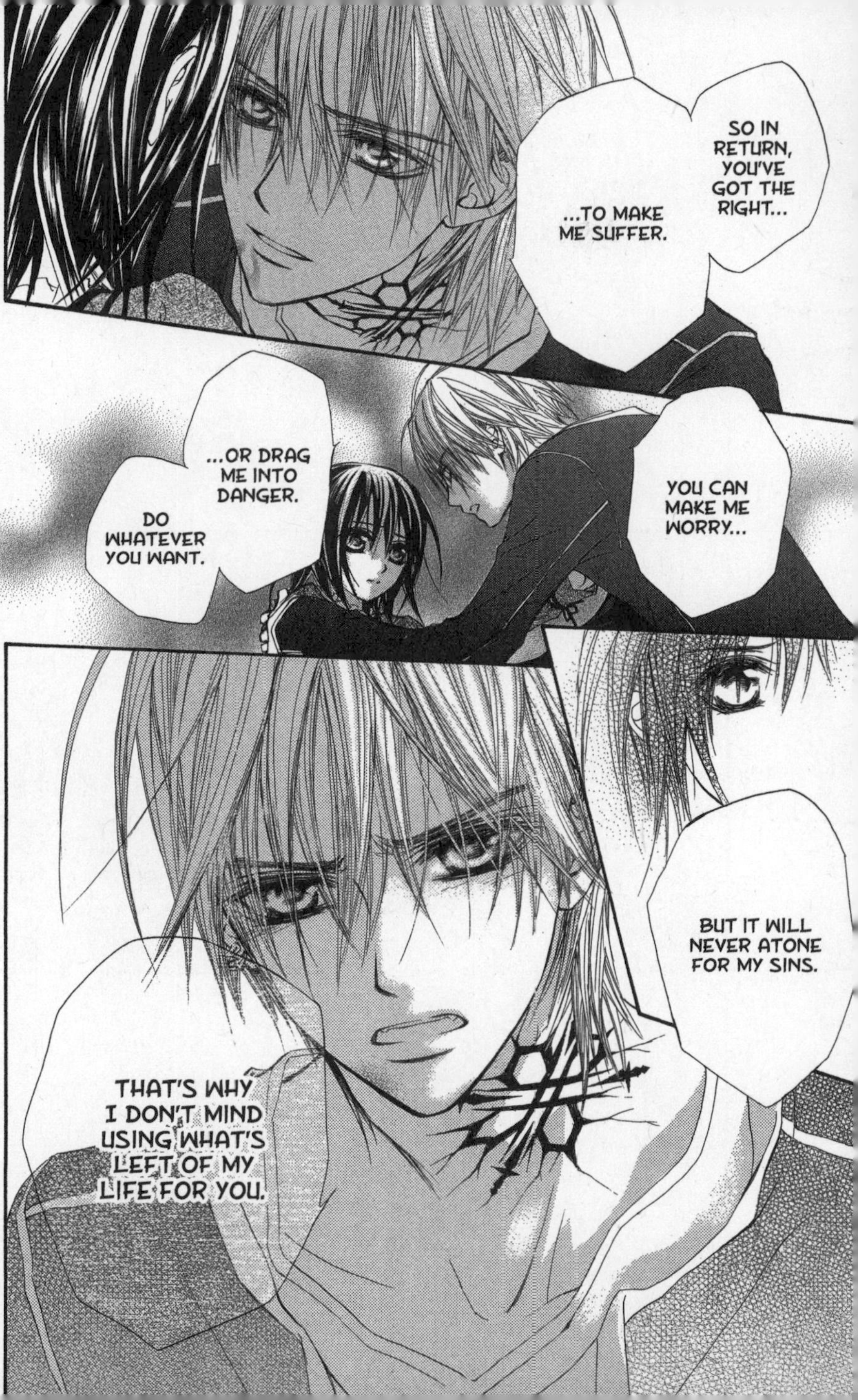
SO IN RETURN, YOU'VE GOT THE RIGHT...
...TO MAKE ME SUFFER.
YOU CAN MAKE ME WORRY...
...OR DRAG ME INTO DANGER.
DO WHATEVER YOU WANT.
BUT IT WILL NEVER ATONE FOR MY SINS.
THAT'S WHY I DON'T MIND USING WHAT'S LEFT OF MY LIFE FOR YOU.

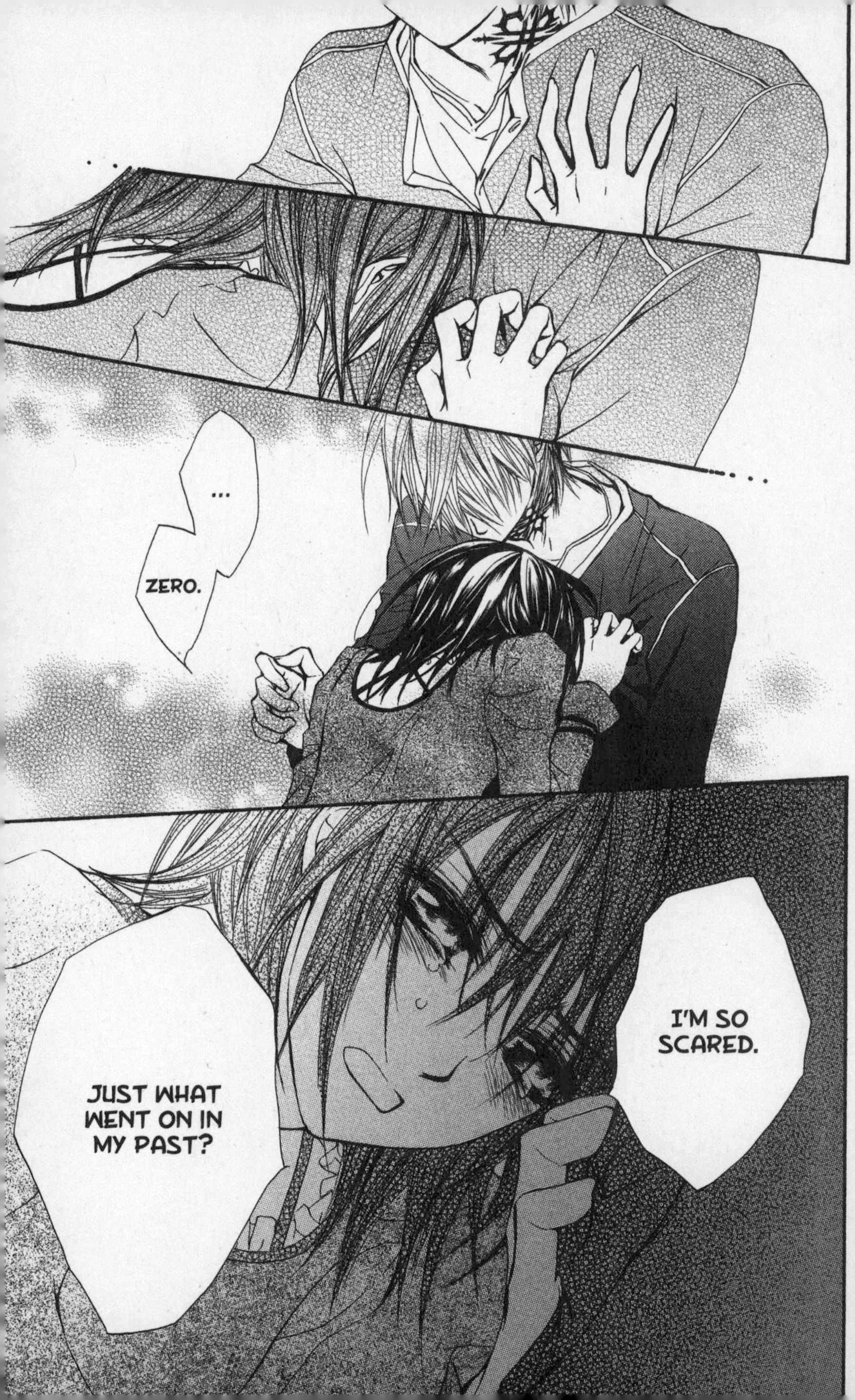
...
ZERO.
I'M SO SCARED.
JUST WHAT WENT ON IN MY PAST?

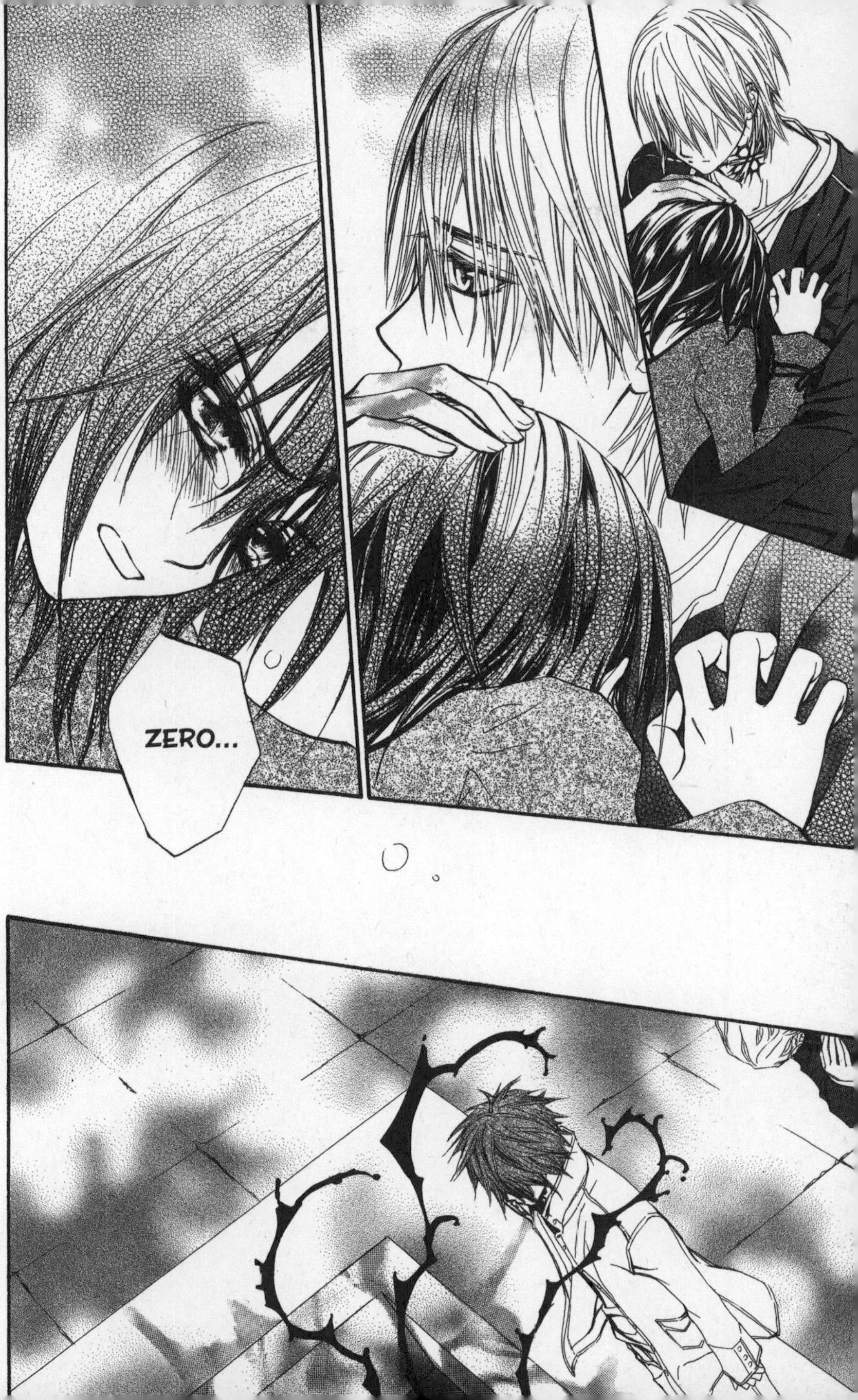
ZERO...

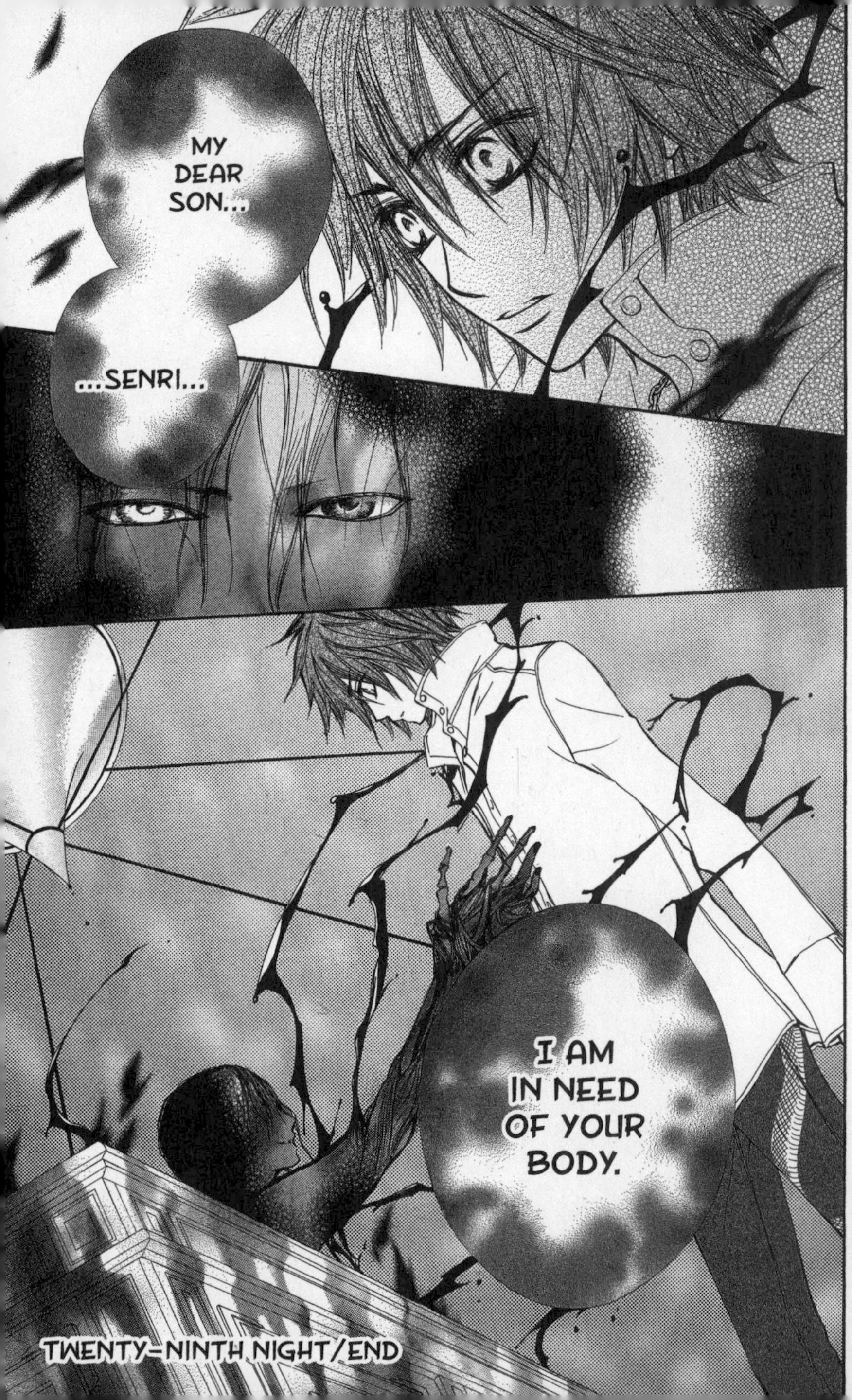
MY DEAR SON...
...SENRI...
I AM IN NEED OF YOUR BODY.
TWENTY-NINTH NIGHT/END

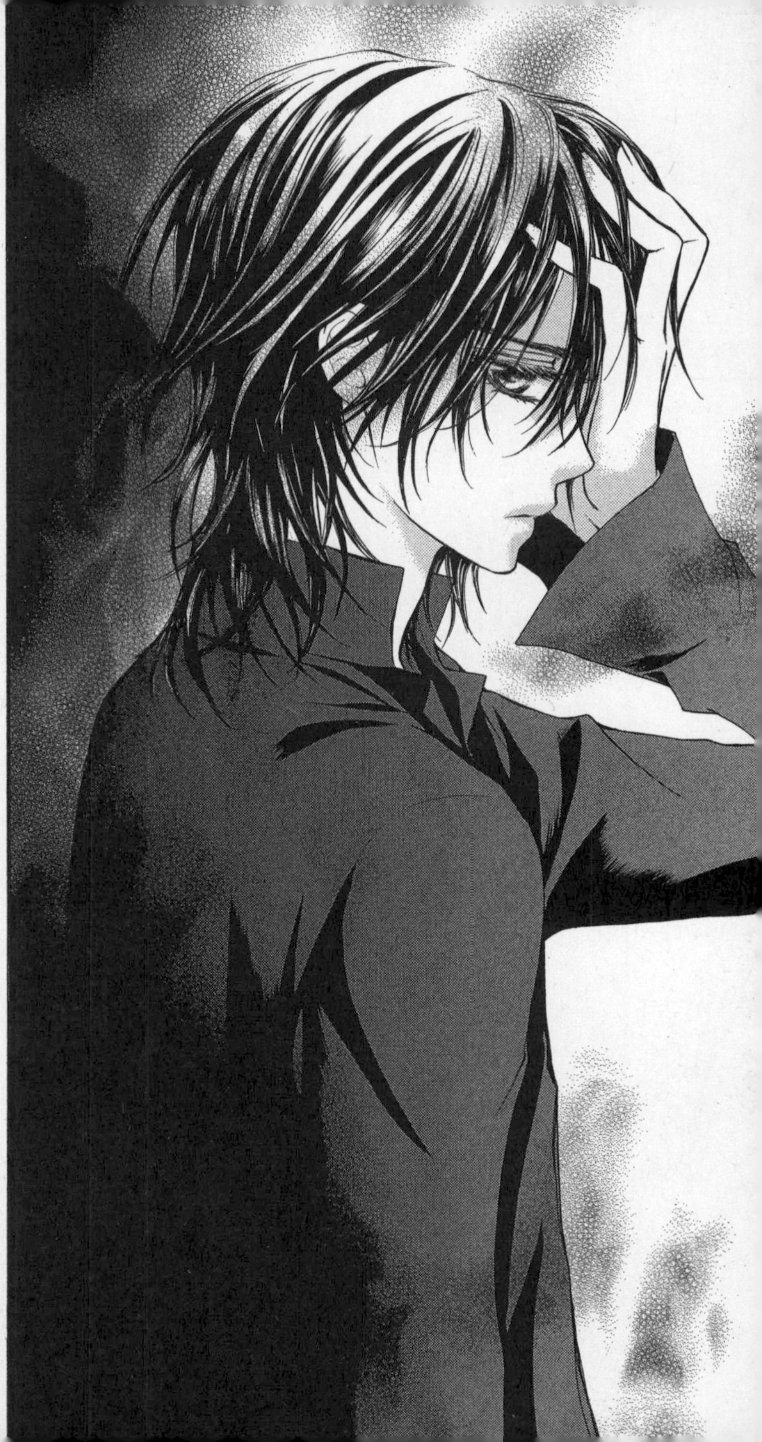

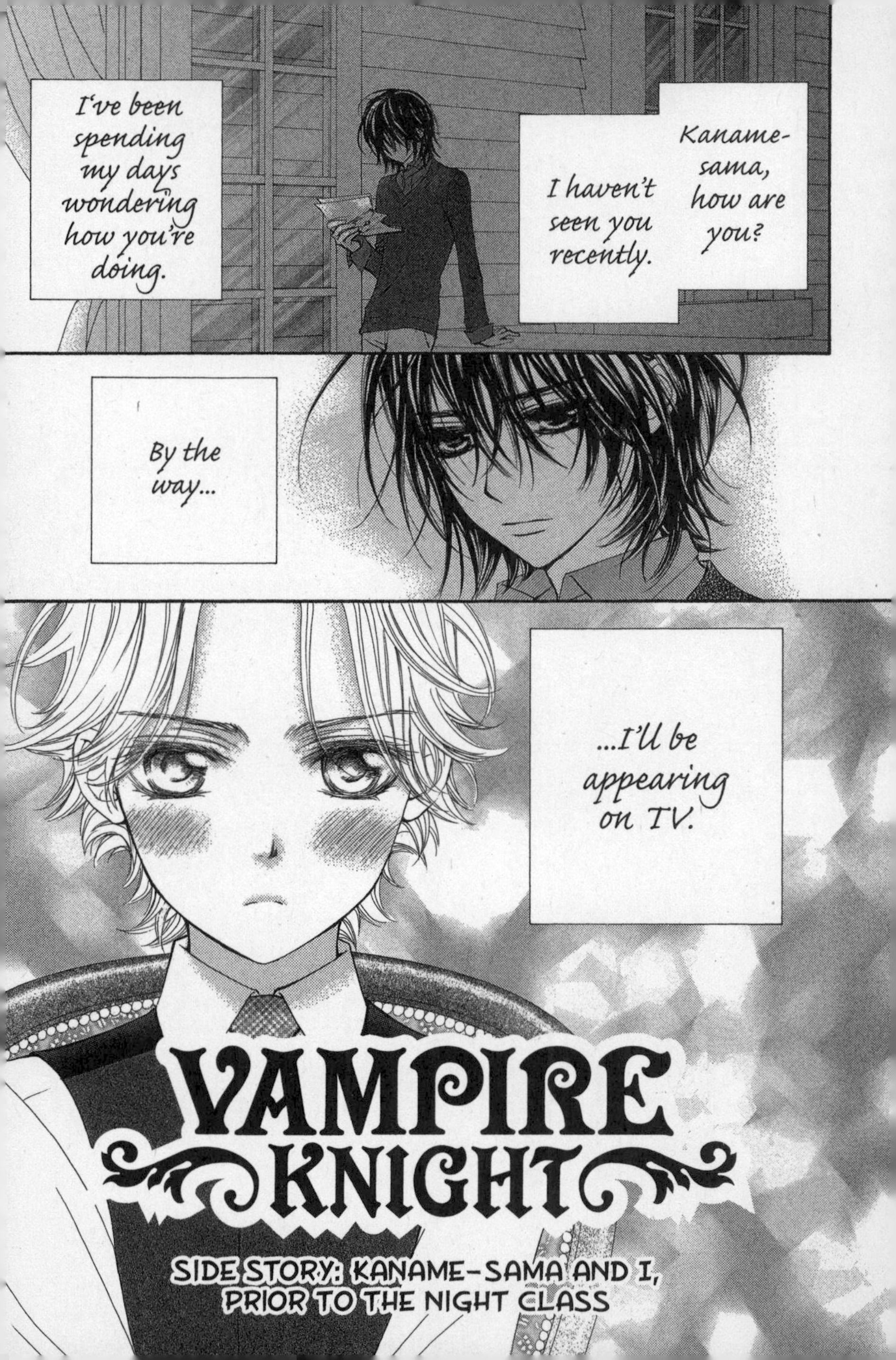
Kaname-sama, how are you?
I haven't seen you recently.
I've been spending my days wondering how you're doing.
By the way...
...I'll be appearing on TV.
VAMPIRE KNIGHT
SIDE STORY: KANAME-SAMA AND I, PRIOR TO THE NIGHT CLASS

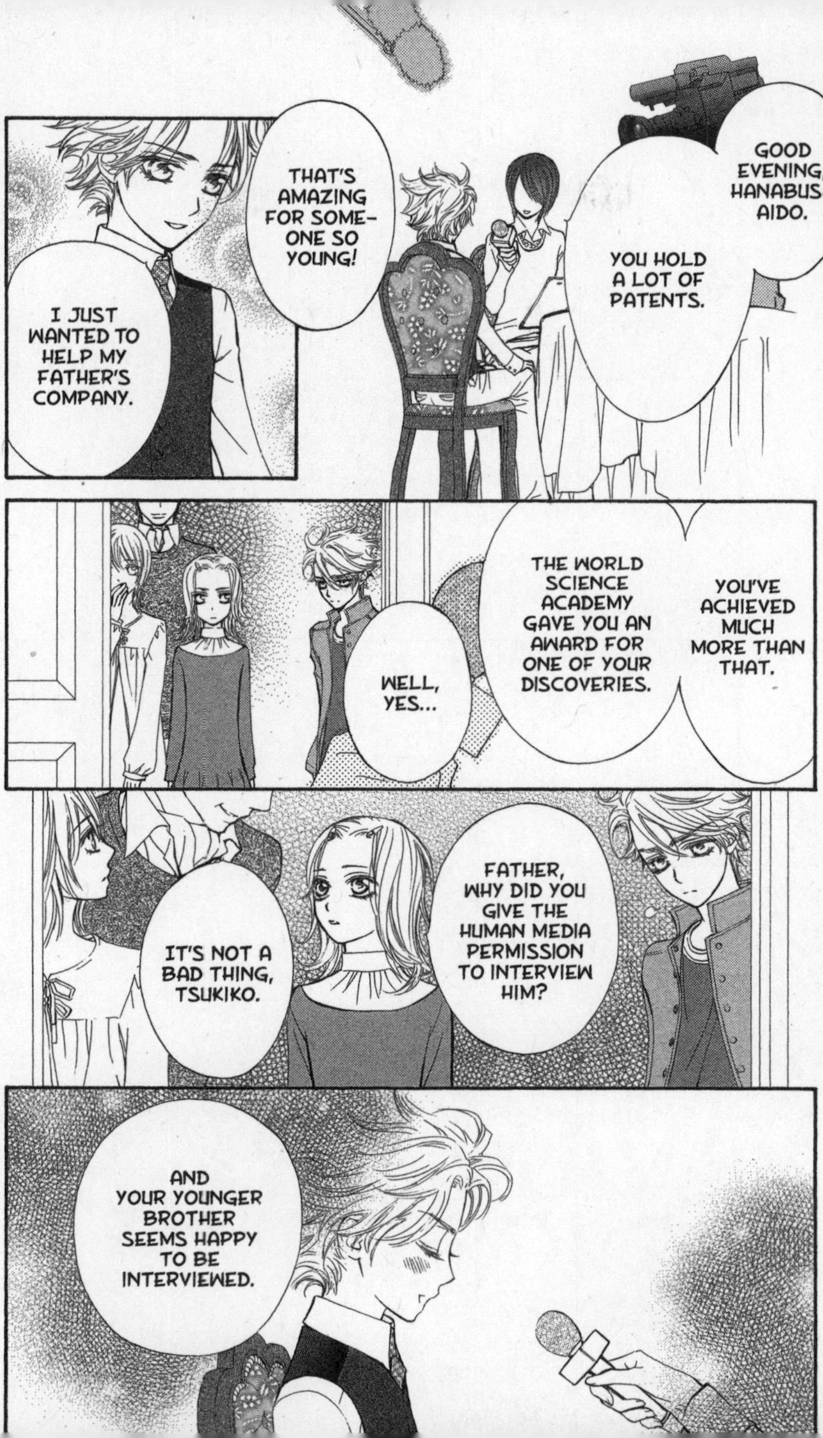
GOOD EVENING, HANABUSA AIDO.
YOU HOLD A LOT OF PATENTS.
THAT'S AMAZING FOR SOME-ONE SO YOUNG!
I JUST WANTED TO HELP MY FATHER'S COMPANY.
YOU'VE ACHIEVED MUCH MORE THAN THAT.
THE WORLD SCIENCE ACADEMY GAVE YOU AN AWARD FOR ONE OF YOUR DISCOVERIES.
WELL, YES...
FATHER, WHY DID YOU GIVE THE HUMAN MEDIA PERMISSION TO INTERVIEW HIM?
IT'S NOT A BAD THING, TSUKIKO.
AND YOUR YOUNGER BROTHER SEEMS HAPPY TO BE INTERVIEWED.

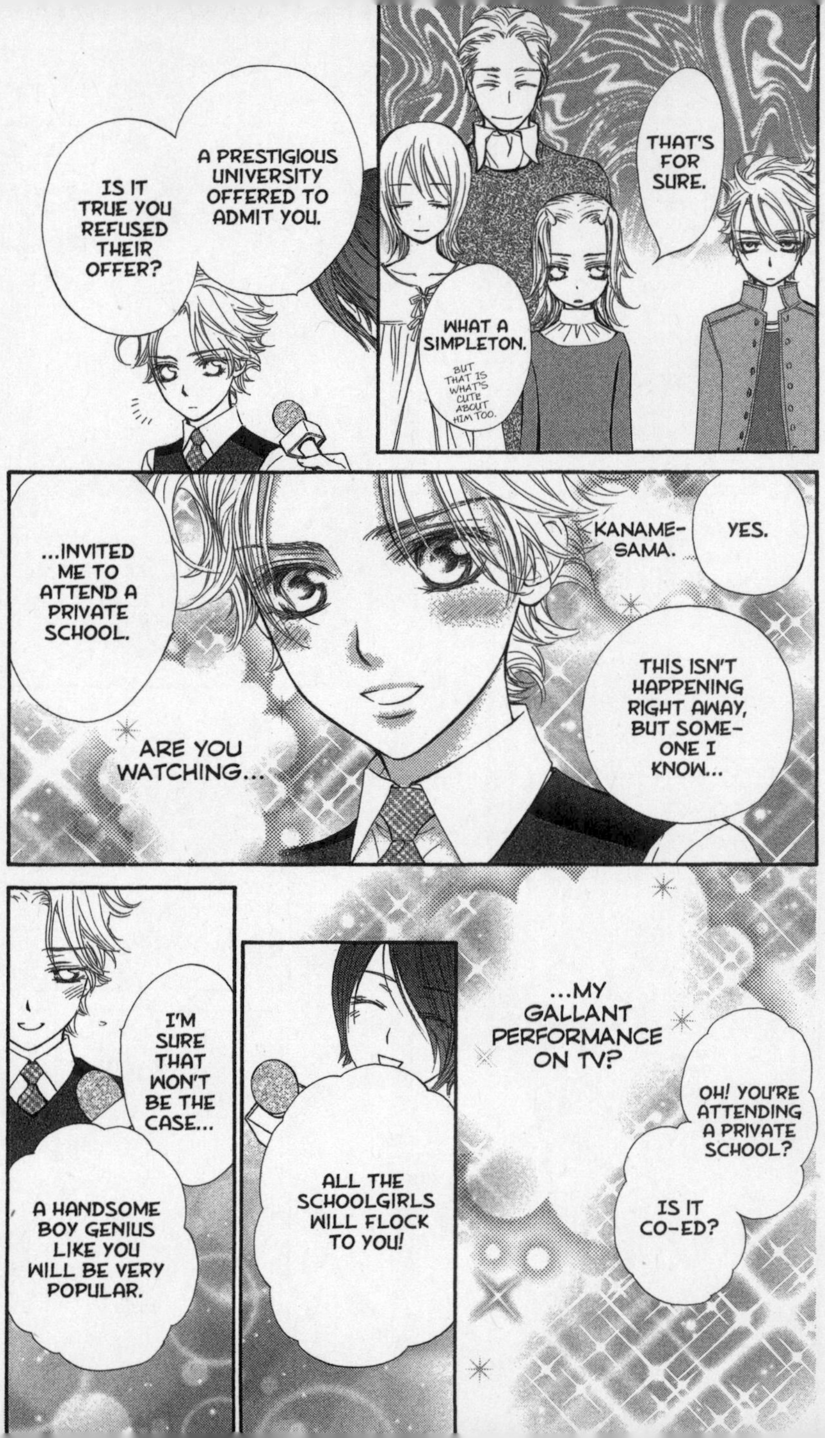
THAT'S FOR SURE.
WHAT A SIMPLETON.
BUT THAT IS WHAT'S CUTE ABOUT HIM TOO.
A PRESTIGIOUS UNIVERSITY OFFERED TO ADMIT YOU.
IS IT TRUE YOU REFUSED THEIR OFFER?
YES.
KANAME-SAMA.
THIS ISN'T HAPPENING RIGHT AWAY, BUT SOME-ONE I KNOW...
...INVITED ME TO ATTEND A PRIVATE SCHOOL.
ARE YOU WATCHING...
...MY GALLANT PERFORMANCE ON TV?
OH! YOU'RE ATTENDING A PRIVATE SCHOOL?
IS IT CO-ED?
ALL THE SCHOOLGIRLS WILL FLOCK TO YOU!
I'M SURE THAT WON'T BE THE CASE...
A HANDSOME BOY GENIUS LIKE YOU WILL BE VERY POPULAR.

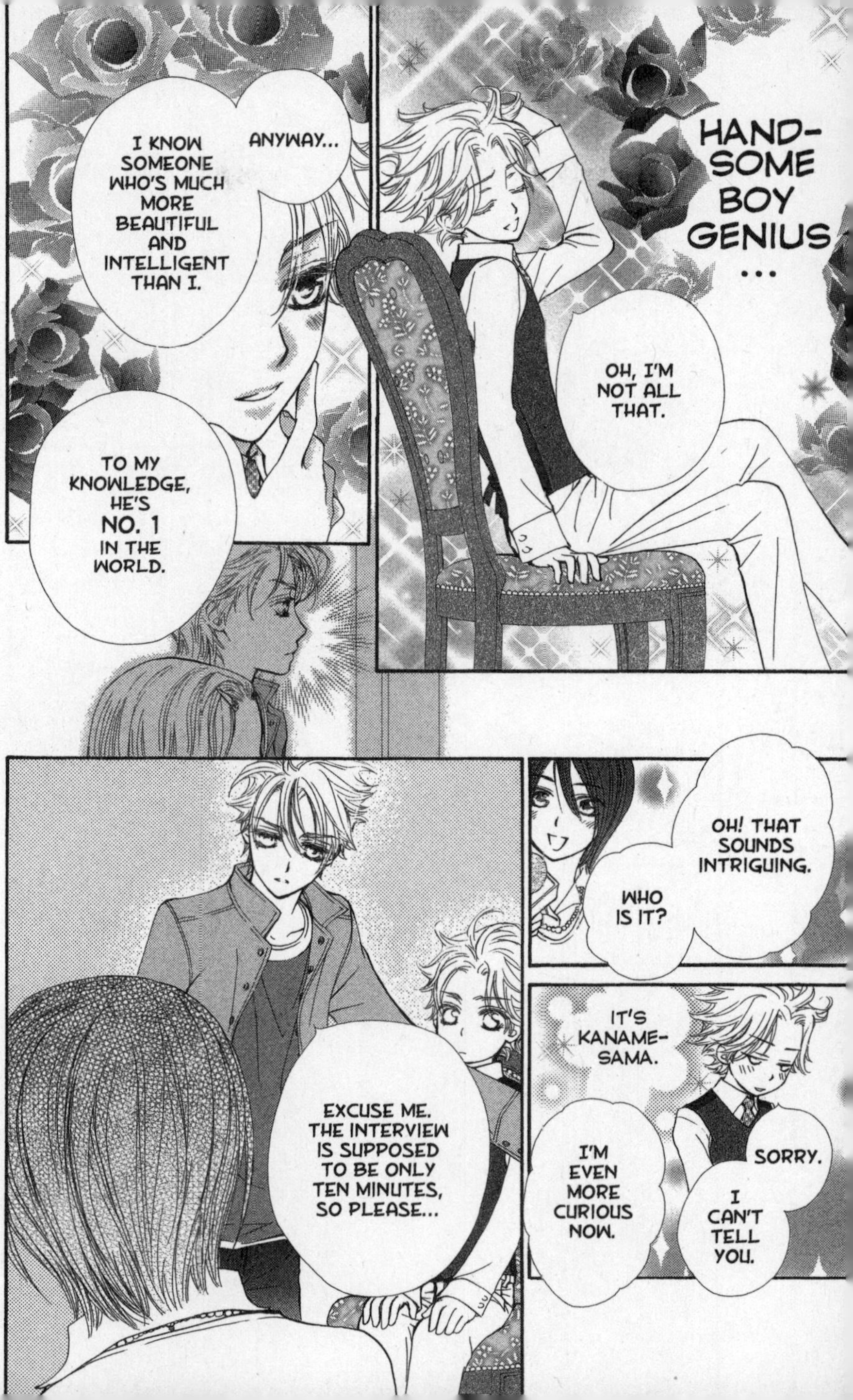
HAND-SOME BOY GENIUS...
OH, I'M NOT ALL THAT.
ANYWAY...
I KNOW SOMEONE WHO'S MUCH MORE BEAUTIFUL AND INTELLIGENT THAN I.
TO MY KNOWLEDGE, HE'S NO. 1 IN THE WORLD.
OH! THAT SOUNDS INTRIGUING.
WHO IS IT?
IT'S KANAME-SAMA.
SORRY.
I CAN'T TELL YOU.
I'M EVEN MORE CURIOUS NOW.
EXCUSE ME. THE INTERVIEW IS SUPPOSED TO BE ONLY TEN MINUTES, SO PLEASE...

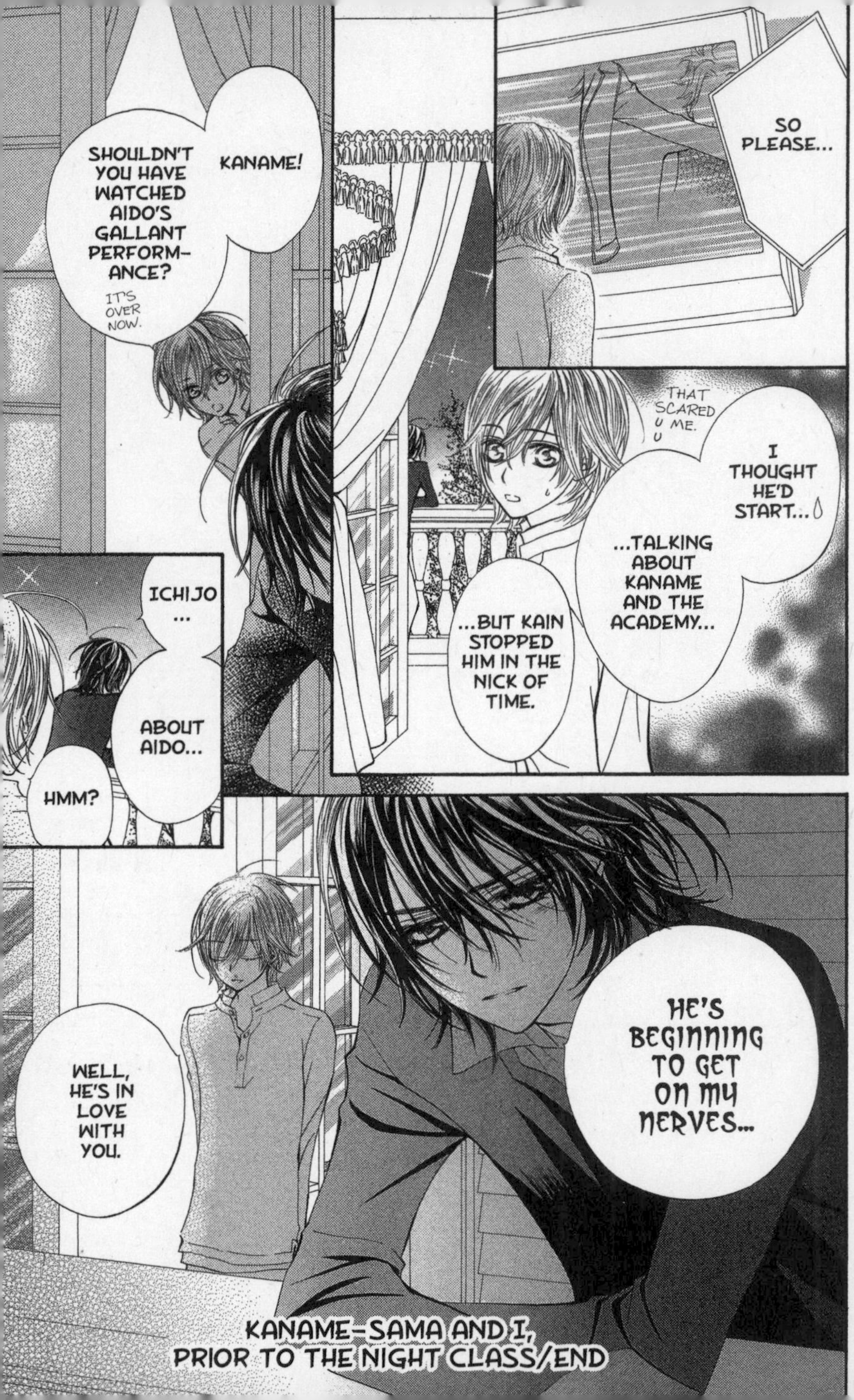
SO PLEASE...
THAT SCARED ME.
I THOUGHT HE'D START...
...TALKING ABOUT KANAME AND THE ACADEMY...
...BUT KAIN STOPPED HIM IN THE NICK OF TIME.
KANAME!
SHOULDN'T YOU HAVE WATCHED AIDO'S GALLANT PERFORMANCE?
IT'S OVER NOW.
ICHIJO...
ABOUT AIDO...
HMM?
HE'S BEGINNING TO GET ON MY NERVES...
WELL, HE'S IN LOVE WITH YOU.
KANAME-SAMA AND I, PRIOR TO THE NIGHT CLASS/END

STATIONARY CAMERA (YUKI AND ZERO)

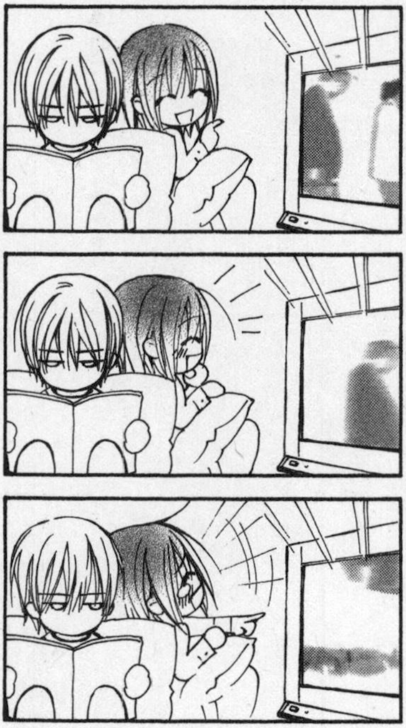

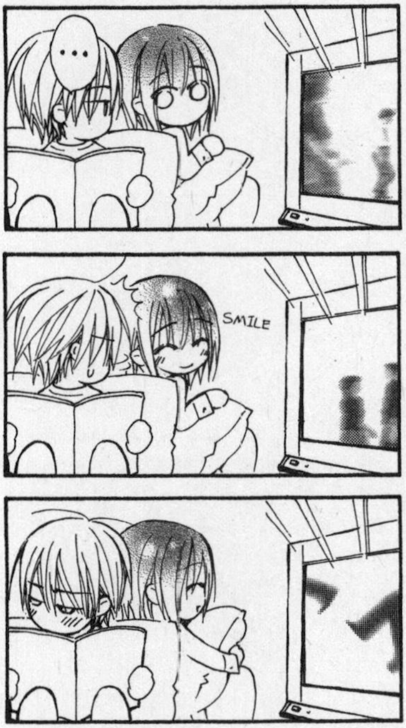
...
SMILE

EDITOR'S NOTES

Characters

Matsuri Hino puts careful thought into the names of her characters in *Vampire Knight*. Below is the collection of characters through volume 6. Each character's name is presented family name first, per the kanji reading.

黒主優姫

Cross Yuki
Yuki's last name, *Kurosu*, is the Japanese pronunciation of the English word "cross." However, the kanji has a different meaning—*kuro* means "black" and *su* means "master." Her first name is a combination of *yuu*, meaning "tender" or "kind," and *ki*, meaning "princess."

錐生零

Kiryu Zero
Zero's first name is the kanji for *rei*, meaning "zero." In his last name, *Kiryu*, the *ki* means "auger" or "drill," and the *ryu* means "life."

玖蘭枢

Kuran Kaname

Kaname means "hinge" or "door." The kanji for his last name is a combination of the old-fashioned way of writing *ku*, meaning "nine," and *ran*, meaning "orchid": "nine orchids."

藍堂英

Aido Hanabusa

Hanabusa means "petals of a flower." *Aido* means "indigo temple." In Japanese, the pronunciation of *Aido* is very close to the pronunciation of the English word *idol*.

架院暁

Kain Akatsuki

Akatsuki means "dawn," or "day-break." In *Kain, ka* is a base or support, while *in* denotes a building that has high fences around it, such as a temple or school.

早園瑠佳

Souen Ruka

In *Ruka*, the *ru* means "lapis lazuli" while the *ka* means "good-looking," or "beautiful." The *sou* in Ruka's surname, *Souen*, means "early," but this kanji also has an obscure meaning of "strong fragrance." The *en* means "garden."

一条拓麻

Ichijo Takuma

Ichijo can mean a "ray" or "streak." The kanji for *Takuma* is a combination of *taku*, meaning "to cultivate" and *ma*, which is the kanji for *asa*, meaning "hemp" or "flax," a plant with blue flowers.

支葵千里

Shiki Senri

Shiki's last name is a combination of *shi*, meaning "to support" and *ki*, meaning "mallow"—a flowering plant with pink or white blossoms. The *ri* in *Senri* is a traditional Japanese unit of measure for distance, and one *ri* is about 2.44 miles. *Senri* means "1,000 *ri*."

夜刈十牙

Yagari Toga

Yagari is a combination of *ya*, meaning "night," and *gari*, meaning "to harvest." *Toga* means "ten fangs."

一条麻遠, 一翁

Ichijo Asato, aka "Ichio"

Ichijo can mean a "ray" or "streak." Asato's first name is comprised of *asa*, meaning "hemp" or "flax," and *tou*, meaning "far off." His nickname is *ichi*, or "one," combined with *ou*, which can be used as an honorific when referring to an older man.

若葉沙頼

Wakaba Sayori

Yori's full name is Sayori Wakaba. *Wakaba* means "young leaves." Her given name, *Sayori*, is a combination of *sa*, meaning "sand," and *yori*, meaning "trust."

星煉
Seiren
Sei means "star" and *ren* means "to smelt" or "refine." *Ren* is also the same kanji used in *rengoku*, or "purgatory."

遠矢莉磨
Toya Rima
Toya means a "far-reaching arrow." Rima's given name is a combination of *ri*, or "jasmine," and *ma*, which signifies enhancement by wearing away, such as by polishing or scouring.

紅まり亜
Kurenai Maria
Kurenai means "crimson." The kanji for the last *a* in Maria's given name is the same that is used in "Asia."

錐生壱縷
Kiryu Ichiru

Ichi is the old-fashioned way of writing "one," and *ru* means "thread." He shares the same surname as his twin, Zero.

緋桜閑, 狂咲姫
Hio Shizuka, Kuruizaki-hime

Shizuka means "calm and quiet." In Shizuka's family name, *hi* is "scarlet," and *ou* is "cherry blossoms." Shizuka Hio is also referred to as the "Kuruizaki-hime." *Kuruizaki* means "flowers blooming out of season," and *hime* means "princess."

藍堂月子
Aido Tsukiko

Aido means "indigo temple." *Tsukiko* means "moon child."

白蔽更

Shirabuki Sara

Shira is "white," and *buki* is
"butterbur," a plant with white
flowers. *Sara* means "renew."

黒主灰闇

Cross Kaien

Cross, or *Kurosu*, means "black master."
Kaien is a combination of *kai*, meaning
"ashes," and *en*, meaning "village gate."
The kanji for *en* is also used for Enma,
the ruler of the Underworld in Buddhist
mythology.

Terms

-sama: The suffix *sama* is used in formal address for someone who
ranks higher in the social hierarchy. The vampires call their leader
"Kaname-sama" only when they are among their own kind.

Matsuri Hino burst onto the manga scene with her series *Kono Yume ga Sametara* (When This Dream Is Over), which was published in *LaLa DX* magazine. Hino was a manga artist a mere nine months after she decided to become one.

With the success of her popular series *Captive Hearts* and *MeruPuri*, Hino has established herself as a major player in the world of shojo manga. *Vampire Knight* is currently serialized in *LaLa* magazine.

Hino enjoys creative activities and has commented that she would have been either an architect or an apprentice to traditional Japanese craft masters if she had not become a manga artist.